PAPER
BEFORE
PRINT

PAPER
BEFORE
PRINT

The HISTORY
AND IMPACT
OF PAPER
in the ISLAMIC
WORLD

Jonathan M. Bloom

Yale University Press

New Haven and London

Designed by Diane Gottardi
Set in Mrs. Eaves and Trajan type by Amy Storm
Maps by Anandaroop Roy
Printed in Singapore by CS Graphics

Library of Congress Cataloging-in-Publication Data

Bloom, Jonathan (Jonathan M.)
Paper before print: the history and impact of paper in the Islamic world/Jonathan
M. Bloom
    p.   cm.
Includes bibliographical references and index.
ISBN 0–300–08955–4
1. Paper—Middle East—History. I. Title.
TS1091 .B56 2001
676'.0917'671—dc21
                                                                        2001001526

A catalogue record for this book is available from the British Library.

10 9 8 7 6 5 4 3 2 1

For Sheila

·CONTENTS·

In the Middle Ages, paper—a material now so common that it is taken for granted—transformed the ways that people living in West Asia and North Africa thought and worked. It became the prime medium of memory. I have spent my professional life studying and writing about the history of art and architecture in the Islamic lands, but I was suddenly confronted with the complex relation between memory and the written record about ten years ago, when my two-year-old daughter came downstairs one morning and asked why various objects, such as the sugar bowl and the pepper mill, were in different places on the kitchen shelf than they had been the night before. I realized that she noticed exactly where things were because she believed it an important thing to know and that she had no other way of recording this information: she was a preliterate child. Adults know that the position of the sugar bowl is normally irrelevant; and were it relevant, they know, if they are literate, they can record the information. Illiterate adults often have prodigious memories, but learning to read and write seems to destroy the inclination or capacity to remember. It seemed to me then—and still seems to me—that much in the history of Islamic civilization in the Middle Ages, between 600 and 1500, can be seen in terms of the conflicting claims of memory and the written record; the triumph of notation—whether written or drawn—came with paper. Although I subsequently discovered that these concepts have interested several historians of European civilization, only a few scholars have begun to apply them to Islamic civilization.

This book deals with Islamic history and visual culture in the premodern period, but the more general questions with which it is concerned are central to the development of modern Western culture—namely, the media by which ideas are transferred and the transition from memory to notation. Western historians like M. T. Clanchy and Lucien Febvre and Henri-Jean Martin have explored the transition from memory to notation in medieval and postmedieval Europe, examining, for example, how traditional methods of mental recordkeeping were replaced by account books, deeds, and charters, or

how the printing press spurred a typographical revolution, exposing a swath of
society to the written word for the first time. In the Islamic lands, the great
time lapse between the introduction of paper and the introduction of printing reveals for the first time how important the medium of paper itself was in
this giant step in human history. Many of the ideas discussed in the following
pages have long been known to specialists, but they have never been brought
together before. Many of my predecessors have seen the trees, but few, apart
from the prescient Alfred von Kremer, whose words open this book, have seen
the forest.

In this book I bridge several disciplines. Because the histories of paper in
China and Europe are relatively accessible to the general reader, I have concentrated on revealing the exciting story of paper before print in the Islamic
lands. To do so requires stringing together miscellaneous facts into a coherent
narrative. Marshall G. S. Hodgson, the great American historian of Islamic
civilization, noted that medieval Muslim historians focused their attention not
on cultural developments but on the responsible acts of individuals. Consequently
the sources ignore many of the very questions that interest the contemporary cultural historian, such as the introduction and diffusion of technology. The historian must connect the dots established by the occasional remark in a medieval
text or the evidence in the often incomplete archaeological and artistic records.
Only infrequently does the available evidence lead to a story as straightforward
or clear as the researcher might like. Paper is no longer made in many of the
regions discussed in this book, and the only evidence for how a particular sheet
of paper was made is the usually ambiguous testimony of the paper itself.

In the interests of telling the tale, I may have tweaked circumstantial evidence in my favor. As a historian, I believe that my explanation of the invention, diffusion, and development of paper best serves the evidence I have
found, but I also admit that other explanations are possible, if less probable.
At the very least, I hope my explanation challenges others to come forth with
other evidence and answers. I also trust that historians of paper, Islam and
Islamic art will excuse my sometimes sweeping generalizations for the sake of
making this arcane but important subject accessible to a wide audience.

In writing this book for a general audience, I have tried to avoid many of
the conventions that scholars normally use when writing for each other about
the history of the Islamic lands of West Asia and North Africa. For example, I
have used a simplified system to transcribe words taken from Arabic, Persian,
and Turkish, giving common English equivalents wherever possible and avoid-
ing special characters, except in the list of works cited at the end of the book.
Those who know these languages will appreciate what I have done to avoid

frightening those who don't, and those who don't, won't care. For simplicity's sake I have referred to the regions of West Asia and North Africa—such as Iran, Egypt, Morocco—by their modern names, although virtually all are creations of the twentieth century, and their current borders are more restrictive than their borders in the past.

I have also given all dates according to the Common Era (B.C.E. and C.E., instead of B.C. and A.D.). Muslims used a lunar calendar that does not correspond exactly to the solar calendar used elsewhere; hence, some brief events dated on the basis of their calendar may appear to straddle two Western-calendar years. When I have occasionally been unable to precisely date some historical process, I have used the convention of dynastic dating by referring to the Umayyad (661–750) and Abbasid (749–1258) periods.

I have lightly edited some quotations and translations to improve the sense without, I trust, any substantive change of meaning. To help the reader enjoy the flow of my argument, I have also replaced potential footnotes and endnotes with a bibliographical essay and complete list of works cited, to be found at the end of the book. Discussion of specialized topics, such as the physics and chemistry of paper or the operation of the Hollander beater, will be found in a series of sidebars placed appropriately throughout the chapters.

I can trace my interest in paper and papermaking to my childhood in the 1950s, when I watched a science television program for children called *Watch Mr. Wizard*. Mr. Wizard explained how paper was made and showed how you could make paper by dissolving toilet paper in a basin of water and collecting the pulp on a small piece of wire screening. Growing up in a cramped New York City apartment, I had to make do. After dissolving half a roll of toilet paper in the bathroom sink and catching most of the sludgy mess on a window screen, I placed the screen precariously on a radiator to dry, where it promptly fell into the dust between the radiator and the wall. The drain of the bathroom sink was clogged, and I had to explain my scientific experiment first to displeased parents and then to an unsympathetic building superintendent. Not until years later did I rediscover the missing window screen and the moldy remains of my papermaking experiment. Nor did I even remember this youthful experiment until I began to learn exactly how paper was made.

Even after spending several years researching and writing this book, my interest in the history of paper has not waned. I have been gratified to discover that other scholars are working on similar and related problems, and I trust that this book will not be my last word on the subject as our knowledge of the history of paper deepens and grows.

Many institutions and individuals have helped bring this book to fruition.

An initial travel grant from the American Council of Learned Societies allowed me to present my work at a conference in Edinburgh. An Andrew W. Mellon Senior Research Fellowship from the Metropolitan Museum of Art in New York gave me the luxury of working with medieval papers for six months, as well as talking and working alongside conservators and curators. Among the staff at the Metropolitan Museum, Sarah Bertalan, Stefano Carboni, Marjorie Shelley, and Daniel Walker deserve special thanks for taking the time to shepherd a novice through the marvels of their treasurehouse. Karen Sack's boundless hospitality made it possible to explore the delights of the Big Apple. In Washington, D.C., Massumeh Farhad and Martha Smith of the Freer Gallery of Art and Sackler Museum, Smithsonian Institution, were generous with their time and expertise, as were Alan and Lois Fern with their hospitality. David Wise of the National Endowment for the Humanities, a federal agency, encouraged me to persist with my project, and the generous NEH fellowship for Independent Research allowed me to spend an entire year finishing the text. Geoffrey Verney, Jr., graciously escorted me through Monadnock Paper Mills and lent me several specialist books from his collection. Stefan Reif of the Taylor-Schechter Research Unit at the Cambridge University Library let me lay my hands (ever so gingerly) on Geniza documents in his care. The Center for Middle Eastern Studies at Harvard University generously made the incomparable riches of the Harvard University Library available to an independent scholar. Publication of this book was helped by a generous grant from the Norma Jean Calderwood University Professorship support fund at Boston College.

Some of the material in the Introduction first appeared in my article "Revolution by the Ream: A History of Paper," *Aramco World Magazine* 50, no. 3 (June 1999): 26–39; it is used with permission. Likewise, some of the material in Chapter 5 first appeared in my articles "On the Transmission of Designs in Early Islamic Architecture," *Muqarnas* 10 (1993): 21–28, and "The Introduction of Paper to the Islamic Lands and the Development of the Illustrated Manuscript," *Muqarnas* 17 (2000): 17–23.

Other friends and colleagues have helped in innumerable ways to make this book what it is. They include Rick Asher, Vlad Atanasiu, Marianne Barrucand, Craigen Bowen, Jerry Carbone, Anthony Cutler, David Dempsey, Helen Evans, Annette Fern, William Graham, Prudence O. Harper, Carole Hillenbrand, Candace Howes, Robert Irwin, Marilyn Jenkins-Madina and Maan Z. Madina, Linda Komaroff, Michael G. LaFosse, Helen Loveday, Richard Parkinson, David Powers, Neeta Premchand, Geoffrey Roper, D. Fairchild Ruggles, A. I. Sabra, George Scanlan, Nancy Shatzman-Steinhardt, Nicholas Sims-Williams, P. Octor Skjervø, Joseph Taylor, Richard Verdery,

William Voelkle, Anne Wardwell, Oliver Watson, the late Estelle Whelan, M. Lesley Wilkins, Owen Wright, and Claus von Zastrow. At Yale University Press, John Nicoll and Judy Metro encouraged me to refine and improve my project. Patricia Fidler graciously and ably stepped into the project midstream. Mary Pasti's sharp eyes and sensitive editorial cursor saved me from many infelicities and mistakes. That this book reads so well is largely due to her. John Long, the photo editor, heroically procured art and permissions, and Mary Mayer and Diane Gottardi transformed it all into the handsome book you now hold in your hands.

Two people deserve special mention for their special efforts. Robert Hillenbrand nobly and selflessly gave up a well-deserved holiday to read through a late draft of the manuscript; the book is much better for his discerning eye and trenchant comments. Throughout this long project, my colleague and wife, Sheila Blair, has been a constant source of encouragement, a sounding board for wacky ideas, a fount of knowledge on specialized topics, and a patient reader. I thank them both.

The Spread of Paper and Papermaking

0° 30°E

60°N

Kazan

area of detail, over

Mainz
Nuremberg

TRANSYLVANIA

Azov
Moshchevaya Balka
CRIMEA
CAUCASUS

Cluny
ALPS
Venice
Avignon Genoa
Fabriano
Bilbao
Santiago de
Compostela
Barcelona
Rome
Amalfi

Caspian Sea

Constantinople/Istanbul
Bursa Iznik
Amasya
Pergamon/Bergama

40°N
Toledo Valencia
MAJORCA
Játiva
Córdoba
Seville Granada

Ushak
Konya
Ardabil
Tabriz
Aleppo Manbij Sinjar
Mosul

Trapani Palermo
SICILY Catania
Tunis
Kairouan Sousse
Mahdiya

SYRIA MESOPOTAMIA
Damascus
Baghdad
Isfaha
Yazd
Tigris
Euphrates
Basra
Shi

Ceuta Tlemcen
Fez Taza
Rabat

Sijilmasa

Alexandria
Fustat/Cairo
Arsinoë/Fayyum

Jerusalem

Ashmunayn
Akhmim
Isna

Medina

SAHARA DESERT

Nile

Mecca

20°N

Awdagusht

Aden

0°

°E   90°E   120°E

                                                                                         60°N

                                    SIBERIA

                        • Pazyryk

ZM   40°N
                        • Talas   Turfan •
            Syr Darya
                    • Tashkent   • Karakhoto
    Zrafshan   Loulan •   Lop Nor
ukhara •   • Samarqand   • Dunhuang
            ▲ Mount Mug   • Kashgar
    Amu Darya   • Wuwei   SHANXI   KOREA
shed   • Balkh   Khotan • Dandan Uiluq   SHAANXI
AN   KASHMIR   • Xian
  • Herat   • Kabul
                                                                          • Suzhou
            • Multan   ZHEJIANG
        Indus   • Delhi   • Mawangdui
                        Ganges

            • Ahmadabad   20°N
        GUJARAT

            • Dawlatabad
        DECCAN
                                                       VIETNAM

    MALABAR
    COAST

                                                                                         0°

Detail of West Asia

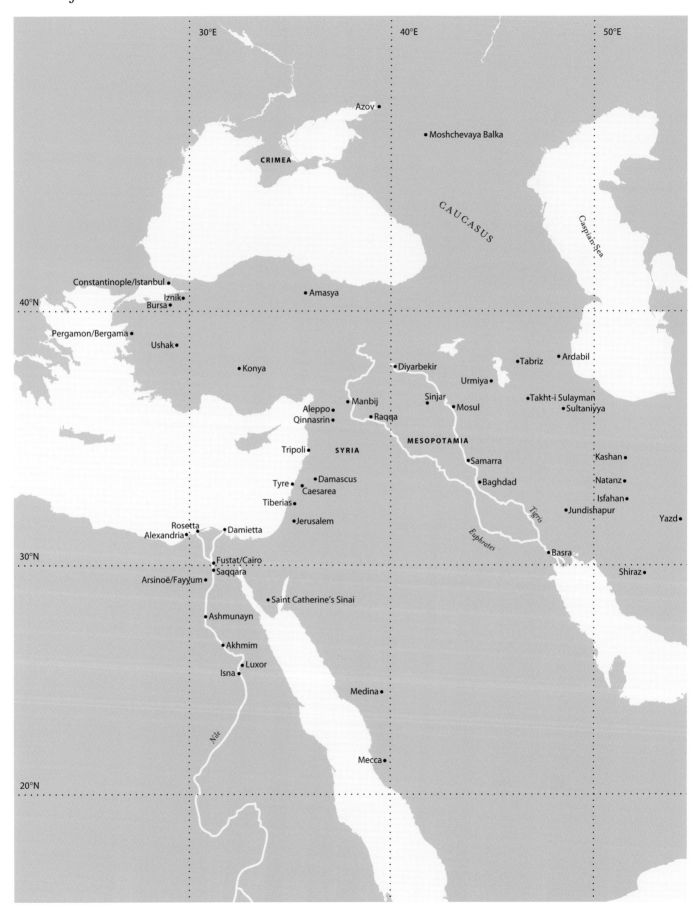

- Azov
- Moshchevaya Balka
- CRIMEA
- CAUCASUS
- Caspian Sea
- Constantinople/Istanbul
- Iznik
- Bursa
- Amasya
- Pergamon/Bergama
- Ushak
- Konya
- Diyarbekir
- Tabriz
- Ardabil
- Urmiya
- Manbij
- Sinjar
- Takht-i Sulayman
- Aleppo
- Raqqa
- Mosul
- Sultaniyya
- Qinnasrin
- MESOPOTAMIA
- Tripoli
- SYRIA
- Kashan
- Samarra
- Tyre
- Damascus
- Natanz
- Caesarea
- Baghdad
- Isfahan
- Tiberias
- Tigris
- Jundishapur
- Yazd
- Jerusalem
- Rosetta
- Euphrates
- Alexandria
- Damietta
- Basra
- Fustat/Cairo
- Shiraz
- Saqqara
- Arsinoë/Fayyum
- Saint Catherine's Sinai
- Ashmunayn
- Akhmim
- Luxor
- Isna
- Medina
- Nile
- Mecca

30°E   40°E   50°E

40°N
30°N
20°N

From a cultural and historical point of view the reduction in the cost of writing material, which went hand in hand with the production of paper, was of great importance. Books on parchment or papyrus were so expensive that they were available to very few. By the production of a cheap writing material, and its supply to markets both east and west, the Arabs made learning accessible to all. It ceased to be the privilege of only one class, initiating that blossoming of mental activity that burst the chains of fanaticism, superstition and despotism. So started a new era of civilisation. The one we live in now.
—ALFRED VON KREMER, *Culturgeschichte des Orients*

Paper, one of the most ubiquitous materials in modern life, was invented in China a century or two before the Common, or Christian, Era. Nearly a millennium passed, however, before Europeans first used the stuff, and they did not make it themselves until the eleventh and twelfth centuries. European Christians learned about making paper from the Muslims ("Moors") who then ruled Spain and who established the first papermills in Europe. The papermakers transformed linen rags and other waste fibers into a strong and supple writing material by first beating the fibers with water-powered trip-hammers. The resultant pulp was mixed with water, gathered on screens by hand, and dried. Monks continued to copy their manuscripts on expensive parchment, made from the skins of sheep, goats, and calves, but the emerging middle class of notaries and merchants in southern Europe found paper to be a perfect medium for registers, deeds, and commercial documents, which they were producing in increasing numbers. In the late fourteenth century the German entrepreneur Ulman Stromer, who had seen papermills in Italy—themselves modeled on West Asian prototypes—established the first papermill north of the Alps, at Nuremberg (fig. 1).

European papermaking took off when Johann Gutenberg began printing books in fifteenth-century Mainz. Although Gutenberg is thought to have printed thirty-five copies of his great Bible on parchment, the remainder of the edition—perhaps two hundred copies in all—were printed on sheets of handmade paper. The subsequent print revolution was dependent on the prior existence of papermills like Stromer's, for economics demanded that printers amortize the high costs of making the type and running the press by printing in large editions. Reams and reams of laboriously handmade paper were now needed to make the burgeoning numbers of printed books that sixteenth-century Europeans read, and to make all that paper, linen rags had to be collected, sorted, and prepared. To be a ragman was an important job. Demand for paper only increased in the following centuries as Europeans

FIG. 1. *View of Nuremberg showing Ulman Stromer's papermill in the lower right. From Hartmann Schedel,* Liber chronicarum *(1493)*

PAPER

Suspending cellulose fibers in water and then depositing them on a screen to remove the excess water yields, after drying, a fiber mat: paper. Cellulose fibers, found in the cell walls of plants, may be extracted either directly from the bast or woody parts or indirectly from rags or textile waste, such as cotton lint, left over from some other process. Paper owes its distinctive qualities of strength and flexibility to the chemical and physical qualities of cellulose ($C_6H_7O_2[OH]_3$), which plants make from glucose ($C_6H_{12}O_6$), a simple sugar produced during photosynthesis. The plant links glucose molecules, which are shaped like branched rings, with oxygen atoms into an alternating pattern. Because every other ring is inverted, the cellulose molecule has weak alternating positive and negative charges along each face, and these charges allow the molecules to pack together to form microfibrils and fibers. The close physical contact between the cellulose molecules leads to hydrogen bonding, the attraction between negatively charged oxygen atoms and positively charged hydrogen atoms that gives the fibers structure and strength.

The molecular structure of cellulose

. . . continued

developed new and varied uses for this versatile material—from teabags to wall-paper—and discovered new sources, particularly woodpulp, for the fiber from which paper could be made.

Even today, despite the promise of computers, we use more paper than ever before. In 1996, for example, the computer manufacturer Hewlett-Packard estimated that copiers, fax machines, and computer printers spewed out 860 *billion* pages in the United States alone. Laid side by side, these single sheets from countless reports, interoffice memos, and newsletters would cover approximately 200,000 square miles, or 18 percent of the surface of the United States. Were we to achieve the improbable goal of the paperless, computerized office, paper manufacturers would still have outlets for their product, for paper is now used for a myriad of other purposes, including packaging, filtering, and construction. The 1996 edition of the standard guide to the U.S. paper industry, *Lockwood-Post's Directory of Products of Pulp, Paper Mills, Converters and Merchants,* lists over four hundred distinct uses for paper, ranging from abrasive backings (sandpaper) to paper yarns.

Because the introduction of paper in northern Europe in the fourteenth century was followed closely by the introduction of printing with movable type in the fifteenth, historians have tended to subsume the history of paper within the larger story of printing and the printed book. Henri-Jean Martin, in his magisterial *History and Power of Writing* (1994), gives the history of paper relatively short shrift, although he acknowledges its importance in his larger story. Even in China, where paper (and printing) was invented, the history of paper and the history of printing are usually considered together, as in Tsien Tsuen-Hsuin's masterpiece, *Paper and Printing* (1985).

Nevertheless, paper has its own story, although comparatively few historians have studied it. Of those who have, most have been specialists writing for specialist audiences. One of the first Europeans to study the history of paper was the French astronomer royal, Jérôme de Lalande, who in 1762 published a complete manual on the history and technique of papermaking, *L'art de faire le papier.* A few years later, many of de Lalande's engraved plates showing the process of papermaking resurfaced in Diderot and d'Alembert's *Encyclopédie,* the ambitious compendium of eighteenth-century European knowledge and technology (fig. 2). For the modern reader, the most accessible history of paper remains the classic by an American, Dard Hunter: *Papermaking: The History and Technique of an Ancient Craft* (1943; rev. 1947), which, though dated, remains in print. More recently the French author Lucien Polastron has given a comprehensive overview to the history of papermaking from its Asian origins to modern European industrial processes in his *Le Papier: 2000 ans d'histoire et de savoir-faire* (1999).

Eighteenth-century descriptions and engravings of papermaking indicate that papermaking, like most industrial processes in Europe before the Industrial Revolution, had changed little over the last thousand years, apart from the introduction of the Hollander beater (the Dutch invention that mechanized and sped up the transformation of rags into pulp) in the late seventeenth century. From the middle of the eighteenth century, however, papermaking, like such other basic industrial processes as spinning and weaving, was transformed by several discoveries and inventions.

First, the identification of the element chlorine and its bleaching properties expanded the range of cloth (and ultimately other fibers) that could be made into white paper suitable for printing. The color of a sheet of paper was primarily dependent on the color of the fibers from which it was made. Clean white fibers made white paper, while dirty dark fibers made dull dark paper. The Swedish chemist Karl Wilhelm Scheele first prepared chlorine gas in 1774, and its bleaching properties were first demonstrated a decade later by the French chemist Claude Berthollet. The English brothers Clement and George Taylor were granted a patent covering a bleaching agent in 1792, and seven years later the Scottish chemist Charles Tennant introduced bleaching powder, a solid combination of chlorine and slaked lime, which had the same effect as the poisonous chlorine gas and could be handled and shipped easily. The powder was used extensively to bleach cloth and rags for papermaking, as well as to bleach printed and written paper for recycling. By 1829, however, reports had appeared indicating that bleaching caused paper to degrade.

Second, the invention of a practical papermaking machine meant that large quantities of paper could be made relatively easily and quickly by fewer people. After working in François Didot's papermill at Essonnes, in France,

Cellulose, the most abundant of all naturally occurring organic compounds, makes up about 33 percent of all plant material (about 90 percent of cotton and about 50 percent of wood). The plant material may be treated by moisture, heat, or beating, or a combination, to release the cellulose fibers. The stalks of flax plants are soaked in water and fermented (retted), dried, and beaten to release the fiber, which may be spun into linen thread or further processed into paper. The inner bark of kozo, which is used by Japanese papermakers, is steamed, dried, soaked, softened, scraped, washed, and cooked. These processes are skipped when materials such as rags, old ropes, or old fishing nets are used; these materials are sorted, cleaned, soaked, and left to ferment to begin breaking down the fibers.

After fermenting, the fibers, whatever their origin, are beaten in water to further break them down and make them swell and join together. During fibrillation, as this process is called, the outer layers of the fibers partially detach as microfibrils, causing water molecules (which have either a positive or a negative charge) to attach themselves to the exposed hydrogen atoms along the edges of the cellulose molecules of the microfibrils. The pulp, or "stuff," is then said to be "hydrated," and a mat of it is collected on a screen

. . . continued

3

and drained. On the intertwined fibers the microfibrils form physical and chemical links. As the mat dries, the water that was attached to the outer layers of the cellulose fibers evaporates, drawing the fibers closer together and allowing the microfibrils to form the same type of hydrogen bonds with neighboring fibers that exist within individual fibers. This combination of physical and chemical bonding of the cellulose fibers gives paper its strength and flexibility.

Cotton fibers, seen under a scanning electron microscope

After the sheet is formed and dried, the cellulose in paper can continue to absorb water. Wet paper is weaker than dry paper, as anyone who has used paper towels or tried to read a wet newspaper knows. Liquids will also spread in the sheet, as in blotting paper, unless it has been coated or impregnated ("sized") with some substance, such as wax, starch, or glue, to retard penetration. Differences in fibers, processing, and finishing result in papers of

. . . continued

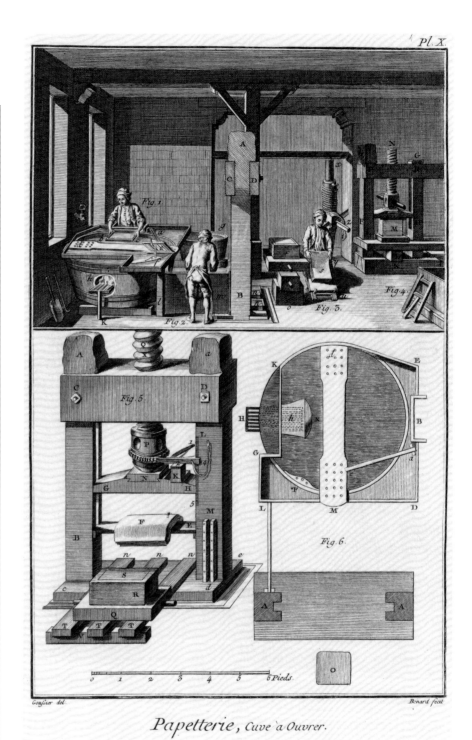

Papetterie, Cuve à Ouvrer.

FIG. 2. *Papermakers forming the sheets in molds (top left), couching, or layering, the sheets (top center), and pressing the stack (top right). The press and vat are detailed below. From Denis Diderot and Jean d'Alembert,* Encyclopédie *(1765)*

the former soldier Nicholas-Louis Robert tried inventing a machine to speed up the process of making paper. His first attempts failed, but in 1798 he was ready to apply for a patent on a machine that made an endless strip of paper rather than individual sheets. Although the French government recognized the importance of Robert's invention, he was forced to sell his patent to Didot, who approached John Gamble, his English brother-in-law, about building Robert's machine in England. Gamble in turn approached the London stationers Henry and Sealy Fourdrinier, who then hired Bryan Donkin, a talented mechanic, to build a machine patterned after Robert's, and the Fourdrinier brothers secured several English patents. Although they spent about sixty thousand pounds developing and patenting their machine, there was a flaw in the patent, and the only recognition they received was that papermaking machines are known to this day as Fourdrinier machines.

different quality, strength, appearance, flexibility, and feel. Thin papers can be extremely strong; thick papers can tear easily. The surface can be rough or as smooth as glass.

Finally, the chemical and physical analysis of paper and the discovery of cellulose led inventors to find several processes to release cellulose fibers from wood, a virtually limitless source of fiber. In 1800 and 1801 the British patent office granted the papermaker Matthias Koops a patent for the manufacture of paper "fit for printing and other useful purposes" from "straw, hay, thistles, waste and refuse of hemp and flax and different kinds of wood and bark," but Koops's process is now unknown, and his company soon went bankrupt. By the middle of the nineteenth century the French chemist Anselme Payen had isolated cellulose among the chemical components of wood, and in 1840, Friedrich Gottlob Keller, a German weaver, was granted a patent for a machine to grind wood to use in making paper. Although Keller's pulp had to have an almost equal quantity of rag fiber added to give it sufficient strength to make paper, six years later, Heinrich Voelter, who ran a papermill in Saxony, bought the Keller patent and devised a method for quantity production. Simultaneously, Charles Fenerty, in Nova Scotia, began experiments to make paper from ground wood; he produced his first sheet in Halifax in 1841. The process did not come into extensive use until about 1870.

Meanwhile, in 1851 the Englishmen Hugh Burgess and Charles Watt developed a technique for pulping softwood with caustic soda (sodium hydroxide, $NaOH$) at high temperatures; sodawood pulp was used from 1856, but the pulp was of relatively low strength and had to be mixed with stronger fibers to make a paper suitable for printing. As early as 1857, B. C. Tilghman, an American chemist, experimented with using sulfurous acid (H_2SO_3) to soften and defiber wood, but his sulfite process (patented in the United States in 1867) was not commercially used until the 1870s, when further experiments in Europe led to its widespread adoption there and in North America.

By the second half of the nineteenth century papermakers were able to make great quantities of cheap paper, and a veritable explosion of books, magazines, and newspapers ensued. Many other uses for paper were found as well. By 1908 the handbook of the paper industry in the United States, *Lockwood's Directory of the Paper and Stationery Trades,* listed nearly two hundred uses for paper-mill products, ranging from "album board" and "anti-tarnish paper" to "writing paper" and "yellow way-bill copying paper."

During the same years the history of paper in Europe was placed on a more secure scientific basis when Charles-Moïse Bricquet began to collect and organize thousands of ancient watermarks—faint designs often of animals and figures introduced into the paper during the manufacturing process—which he found on specimens of old paper. Italian papermakers in the late thirteenth century had been the first to add watermarks to their products, probably to serve as trademarks and guarantees of quality, and Bricquet was able to arrange and date them on the basis of the dated documents that were written on watermarked papers. His massive catalogues of European watermarks outlined the general history of the craft and remain essential reference tools to this day, nearly a hundred years later.

Europeans long debated the origins of paper. Until relatively recently, most Westerners thought that Europeans or Arabs had invented papermaking from the ancient Egyptian technique of transforming papyrus reeds into sheets of writing material. In the *Encyclopédie,* for example, Diderot differentiated European or rag paper from "Egyptian paper" (papyrus), as well as from "cotton" paper (which he believed the Byzantines had invented) and from Chinese and Japanese paper. He believed rag paper to be a European invention and examined possible sources: Germans, Italians, or Greek refugees in Basle. He dismissed the possibility that it came from the "Orient" or the "Saracens" of Spain. There was some justification for Diderot's confusion: the word *paper,* which is attested in English since the fourteenth century, derives via Old French and Spanish from the Latin word *papyrus,* as does the French or German *papier* and the Spanish *papel.* The Italians, on the other hand, call paper *carta,* a word derived from *khartes,* the Greek term for papyrus. Many common English words associated with paper and writing, such as *card, cardboard, cartography, carton, cartoon, cartouche, cartridge, cartulary, chart,* and *charter,* also derive from this Greek root.

For centuries Europeans had no clue that the Chinese had invented paper long before the Arabs and that all papermaking could be traced back to China. Consequently, when Europeans came into direct contact with the Japanese and Chinese in the seventeenth century, they were amazed to discover paper very much like—but, to their minds, inferior to—their own. They chauvinistically imagined that Asians must have learned papermaking from Europeans some time in the past; they could not imagine that the truth lay quite the other way round. One Englishman, reporting to the East India Company from Patani in 1614, requested paper from Europe, even though local paper was available: "For want of paper all our books are kept in China paper, having not so much other as to write a letter to your worships; I therefore entreat your worships to remember us with books, paper and ink of which we have great need, the cockroaches eating the China paper."

In spite of growing European demand for paper, European merchants active in Asia rarely sent local paper back home, although they themselves used it for on-the-spot recordkeeping. One reason was that the local paper had a soft finish, unsuitable for the goose-quill pens that Europeans normally used. As Adam Olearius, ambassador from the Duke of Holstein to Persia in the seventeenth century, explained, "The best [ink] comes from the Indies, which though it be not all equally good and fine, is yet very fit for their pens, which are not made of Goose-quills, as ours in Europe are, in regard they would be too hard for their Paper, which being of Silk or Cotton, is very tender, but they make them of Canes or Reeds, and a little bigger than our Pens."

In addition, Japan, which made wonderful paper, was largely closed to Europeans, apart from the Dutch, who alone among European powers had access to Japanese harbors for the two centuries between 1639 and 1854. The Dutch East India Company is recorded to have shipped Japanese paper only twice, however, in 1643 and 1644. It is probable that one of these lots reached Holland and was the source of the Japanese paper on which Rembrandt, the Dutch painter and printer, who was something of a fanatic about paper, printed several etchings. Otherwise, European artists did not discover the beauty and strength of Japanese paper until the nineteenth century.

Expensive handpainted Chinese wallpaper first appeared in Europe in the late seventeenth century, but other Asian paper remained a relative rarity there until the mid-eighteenth century, when the first "India paper," made from bamboo and rice straw, was imported into Europe. In a pamphlet that appeared in London in 1797, "an ingenious Literary Gentleman, long resident in India," proposed making paper from paut (*Crotalaria juncea*) or jute (*Corchorus capsularis*), undoubtedly because he had seen papermakers use it in India. Had Europeans been more receptive to learning from Asian papermakers, who used a wide variety of fibers extracted from grasses and the barks of several perennial shrubs, Europe's long search for new sources of fiber from which to make paper might have met with success earlier.

The French naturalist and physicist René-Antoine Ferchault de Réamur had observed that certain American wasps made paperlike nests from wood filaments. In a treatise presented to the Académie Royale on 15 November 1719, he noted that rags were becoming increasingly scarce and concluded that paper could be made directly from plant fibers and even from certain woods, although he did not go on to any practical experiments. In the following decades other Europeans attempted to increase the amount of paper produced, either by making paper out of materials other than rags or by bulking up the available rag fibers with fillers such as clay. Perhaps the most dogged was the German clergyman and amateur naturalist Jacob Christian Schäffer, who published the first volume of a treatise on papermaking in 1765. In each of the five volumes he included samples of paper he had himself made from such materials as hemp, bark, straw, asbestos, cabbage stalks, wasps' nests, cattails, burdock, thistles, turf, mallow, St. John's wort, corn husks, genista, pinecones, potatoes, old shingles, reeds, yellowwood, brazilwood, and leaves of bean plants and horse chestnut, walnut, tulip, and linden trees, all with the admixture of about one-fifth cotton rags. But none was commercially viable.

The Chinese had initially used rags and other waste fibers to make paper, but they soon used only bast or woody fibers, obtained from the phloem layer of such plants as hemp, jute, bamboo, and ramie. Soon after the invention of paper, merchants and Buddhist missionaries took paper and papermaking techniques from China to neighboring lands, including Japan, Korea, and Central Asia. Specimens of very old paper have been discovered at various sites in western China, where the extreme dryness of the climate helped preserve them. In 1900 a Chinese Buddhist monk accidentally discovered a huge cache of more than thirty thousand paper rolls in a cave in Dunhuang, used between the fourth and the tenth centuries. The rolls included Buddhist, Taoist, and Confucian texts, government documents, business contracts, calendars, and miscellaneous exercises written in a variety of languages. They made up the monastery library, stored for safekeeping at a time when the government was persecuting Buddhists. A few years later, in 1907, the Hungarian-British explorer Sir Marc Aurel Stein discovered a small group of paper documents in a ruined watchtower between Dunhuang and Loulan. Written in Soghdian and dating between the fourth century and the sixth, the five almost-complete letters and several fragments probably represent the contents of a lost or abandoned mailbag. One of the letters, enclosed in a coarse cloth envelope addressed to Samarqand, about two thousand miles west of the site, shows that Silk Road merchants throughout the oasis cities of Central Asia used paper well before the coming of Islam, several centuries later.

Muslims first encountered paper when Muslim Arab armies conquered Central Asia in the eighth century. According to the eleventh-century Arab historian Thaalibi, in his *Book of Curious and Entertaining Information,* Chinese prisoners captured by the Arab commander Ziyad ibn Salih introduced paper-making to Samarqand after the battle of Talas in 751. After that, Thaalibi wrote, "paper was manufactured on a wide scale and passed into general use, until it became an important export commodity for the people of Samarqand. Its value was universally recognized and people everywhere used it." As entertaining as this story is—and it has been repeated in virtually every history of paper—it is unlikely to be factual. Paper had been known and used for too long in Central Asia to require Chinese prisoner papermakers to be on the scene.

Nor could Muslim papermakers make paper from the same materials as the Chinese did. Although the earliest specimens of Chinese paper have been found in the arid regions of western China, paper was apparently first made in the warm and moist semitropical regions of southern China. The semitropical plants used by the Chinese did not grow in the arid lands of Central or West Asia, so paper-makers there turned to other sources of fiber—specifically, rags from linen and cotton cloth. Although the Chinese occasionally extended the supply of bast fibers with textile waste, old cloth was always a minor component in the pulp. Central Asian papermakers were the first to perfect the manufacture of paper entirely from rags, probably after the coming of Islam. Muslims then carried this new way of making paper to Iraq, Syria, Egypt, North Africa, Sicily, and finally Spain, developing and improving the techniques of manufacture as they went.

One important vestige of the pivotal role of Islamic civilization in the transfer of papermaking to Europe survives in the way we still count paper in quantities called reams. Originally the term referred to twenty quires (booklets of twenty-four pages), or 480 sheets; a ream has 500 sheets today. The English word "ream" comes via the Old French *rayme* from the Spanish *resma*, which itself comes from the Arabic *rizma,* meaning "bale or bundle." Because the first European papermills were established when Arabic was the common language in much of Spain, the derivation of the word should come as no surprise.

Still, apart from reams, the Islamic contribution to the story of paper has not been generally recognized. Diderot is not the only one who missed the connection. This neglect has several explanations. First, soon after Italians began making paper in the thirteenth century, they added it to their exports to North Africa and West Asia. Because the Italians had access to more water-power and were eager to develop their technology, they developed a stronger and cheaper product than was locally available. Papermakers in the Islamic lands were unable to compete. By the sixteenth century paper manufacturing had disappeared almost everywhere in the Islamic world, except in Turkey, Iran, and India. By the nineteenth century most Europeans would have had no idea that papermaking had once been an important industry in all the Islamic lands.

A second reason that people have bypassed the history of paper in the

Islamic lands is that it is extremely difficult to study. In contrast to European papers, whose history is established by the identification of watermarks and the dated documents or books on watermarked paper, the study of "Islamic" or "Arab" paper is obscured by the total absence of watermarks. Islamic papers were never watermarked, and they can be dated only by reference to the texts written on them and to the scripts in which the texts were written. Although many Arabic and Persian texts were dated, many more were not, and many dates—usually given on the last page of a book—are lost. Because the history of the Arabic script is still being written, even the most expert scholars are unable to agree on the date of a written document just by looking at the style of its writing.

A third reason why the Islamic contribution is underappreciated is that where Islamic civilization flourished, in the vast region between China and Europe, the introduction of printing did not follow quickly on the heels of paper, as it did in China and Europe. Although Muslims knew about printing as early as the tenth or eleventh century, and occasionally used it to make inexpensive amulets or to decorate cotton cloth, book printing came to the Islamic lands a full millennium after the introduction of paper in the late eighth and ninth centuries. Apart from Iran and Syria, where Armenian and Melkite Christians had respectively established printing presses in the seventeenth and early eighteenth centuries, there were no printing presses in the Islamic lands until the Ottoman convert Ibrahim Müteferrika established one in Istanbul in the second decade of the eighteenth century. Before it closed in 1742 he had printed maps, dictionaries, and other secular works, but the printing of the Koran and other religious texts remained forbidden. The first printed edition of the Koran was published not for Muslims but for Christian missionaries by the Venetian Paganino de' Paganini in 1538; the first Koran printed by Muslims for Muslims was not published until 1787, in St. Petersburg, followed by another in 1803, in Kazan.

Fourth, because most scholars have considered the history of paper to be a chapter in the greater history of printing and disseminating knowledge through printed books, the history of paper in the Islamic lands has not held their interest. But paper itself is a powerful medium for the transmission of knowledge, and the effects of the diffusion of paper and papermaking—normally hidden by the shadow of printing—can be seen in the enormous and revolutionary changes to such diverse realms of human activity as literature, mathematics, geography, commerce, and the arts in the Islamic lands between the eighth century and the fourteenth. Like the introduction of printing with movable type to fifteenth-century Europe, the introduction of paper to the Islamic lands spurred a conceptual revolution whose effects are still being felt today.

Finally, some of this neglect of the Islamic role in the history of paper may be due to a pernicious tendency to disregard the seminal contributions of Islamic civilization—in this case, as a transmitter of ideas—in favor of a search for ultimate origins elsewhere. Paper may have been invented in China, but if Muslims had not brought papermaking to Spain, Europeans would not have learned about it before the seventeenth century. If Gutenberg had been forced to print his books only on parchment, they would have been almost as expensive as the handwritten manuscripts they were meant to replace, and it would have taken much longer for Europeans to realize the benefits of printing. According to J. M. Roberts's recent book, *A History of Europe,* the impact of the world of Islam on European civilization was far greater than its impact anywhere else. Although Westerners are all too willing to accept the primacy of China in such inventions as paper, printing, and gunpowder, the vast distances that separated Europe from China, Japan, and India before the modern era meant that "few innovative ideas reached Europe from Asia . . . unless like Indian mathematics they had undergone refinement in the Arabic crucible." For the history of paper in the West, the ultimate origin of papermaking in China is, therefore, somewhat beside the point. The history of how Muslims made paper and what they did with it had, in contrast, an enormous impact on how Western civilization developed.

The importance of Islamic paper was brought to scholarly attention a century ago by the Austrian scholar Josef von Karabacek. In 1877–78 archaeologists discovered more than 100,000 documents on papyrus and paper at the Egyptian sites of Akhmim, Arsinoë, and Ashmunayn. Most were acquired by Archduke Rainer of Austria in 1884 to form the basis of the great Vienna papyrus collection, and Karabacek was appointed curator. Whereas Archduke Rainer was principally interested in the ancient papyri, Karabacek—an Arabist by training—was interested in the twenty thousand documents on paper. With the help of the chemist Julius Wiesner, Karabacek was able to perform the first technical analyses of Islamic papers and prove that they had been made largely of flax fibers from linen rags.

Although Karabacek's research on Arab paper is still being cited a hundred years later, knowledge of Islamic history, culture, and the arts, as well as of the larger history of paper itself, has increased greatly. Since the 1950s the French scholar Jean Irigoin and his colleagues have produced pioneering work on the identification and categorization of non-watermarked papers, both European and West Asian. Irigoin's work has been complemented since the 1970s by greater popular and scholarly interest in Islamic art, which has brought more dated examples of books and paintings to public attention. Don Baker, the English paper conservator, examined several thousand Islamic manuscripts and leaves in the course of his career. He published very few articles before his death, but the publication of his research notes by his successor, Helen Loveday, has provided a new standard against which specialists measure their studies of Islamic papers.

The history of paper in Islamic civilization is not, however, just about the transfer of papermaking technology from China to the West and the use of rags instead of bast fiber. The introduction of paper in the eighth century had a transformative effect on medieval Islamic civilization, spurring an extraordinary burst of literary creativity in virtually all subjects from theology to the natural sciences and literature. Religious scholars collected and codified the traditions of Muhammad, which had been preserved orally following his death in 632, and committed them to ink and paper. New types of literature, such as cookbooks and the amusing tales we now know as *The Thousand and One Nights,* were copied on paper for sale to interested readers. Scholars and copyists translated Greek rolls and manuscripts written on parchment and papyrus into Arabic and transcribed them onto sheets of paper, which were then bound into books. As paper became more common, new scripts more suited to the characteristics of the medium were developed, and eventually the scripts were deemed appropriate for copying the Koran.

The new availability of paper also encouraged new approaches to old subjects. At the same time that paper was being disseminated across the Islamic lands, the Hindu system of reckoning with decimal numbers (what we call "Arabic" numerals) was spreading from India westward. Before the Hindu system of reckoning was introduced, people in the Islamic lands, as elsewhere, did their calculations mentally and recorded them either on a dustboard—which could be repeatedly smoothed blank as they added the sums—or by the position of their fingers ("finger-reckoning"). The first manual of Hindu reckoning in Arabic was written in the ninth century by Muhammad ibn Musa al-Khwarizmi, whose name has given us our word *algorithm* (via the medieval Latin *algorithmus,* referring to the process of reckoning with Arabic numerals). Al-Khwarizmi still did his reckoning on a dustboard, but a century later the mathematician Abu'l-Hasan Ahmad ibn Ibrahim al-Uqlidisi ("the Euclidian") had altered the Indian scheme of calculation to suit the use of ink and paper.

Like the Muslims, Christians and Jews had access to paper as soon as it was made in the Islamic lands. One of the earliest surviving examples of "Arab" paper is a Greek manuscript on the teachings of the church fathers, probably copied at Damascus around 800, only a few decades after Muslim papermakers had set up shop in Baghdad. In the nineteenth century some 300,000 documents, the vast majority of them on paper, were discovered in a storeroom (known in Hebrew as a *geniza*) of the Palestinian Synagogue in Fustat (Old Cairo). The Geniza documents, largely from the mid-tenth to the mid-thirteenth centuries, pertain specifically to the Jewish community but have enormous implications for understanding medieval Islamic commercial society. The documents show how paper supplanted papyrus, which had been used in Egypt for four millennia, and became an indispensable medium of commercial communication. Medieval merchants in the Islamic lands regularly used paper for bills of exchange, orders of payment, and similar documents to foster trade between communities located as far apart as Spain and India.

The import of European watermarked paper in the fourteenth century caused some consternation, as some Muslims, particularly in North Africa, were uncomfortable with writing God's word on a surface marked with pictures and symbols—even crosses. Elsewhere, particularly in Iran, papermaking was at its apogee, and the production of large sheets of fine white paper in Iran spurred a second revolution in the Islamic book, the effects of which were felt for another two centuries there, as well as in Egypt, India, and the Ottoman empire.

Until the thirteenth century most books had been written on sheets about twice as large as a sheet of modern office paper; the sheets were made in molds that could easily be held between the papermaker's hands. Larger sheets of paper were significantly more difficult to make and consequently too expensive to use freely. Even when important people, like caliphs and sultans, needed long scrolls for documents and decrees, they had to make do with smaller sheets pasted together. From the thirteenth century, however, the size and quality of paper available in Iran for books and other uses increased dramatically, as seen in the numerous large luxury books that have survived from this period. These extraordinary changes were probably due to increased contact between Iran and China. In China papermaking techniques had improved over the centuries in response to the development of printing there, and beginning in the early thirteenth century the Mongol dynasties descended from Genghis Khan ruled China, Central Asia, southern Russia, Iran, and Iraq. The Mongol rulers of Iran even briefly (and disastrously) introduced printed paper currency in 1294. Simultaneously, techniques for processing the pulp improved.

The larger sheets of paper not only allowed for larger and more monumental examples of the calligrapher's art but also for books with large illustrations; beginning in the early fourteenth century the illustrated book became a major art form in the Islamic lands, eventually giving rise to what is paradoxically known today as Persian miniature painting. In previous centuries scientific and technical books had been illustrated with relatively small drawings and paintings to clarify specific points in the text. A few literary works were illustrated in the thirteenth century, but it was not until the fourteenth century that large volumes of history and literature were prepared with hundreds of generous paintings. The artwork did not simply illustrate the text but elaborated on it by using, for example, complex landscapes to enliven settings, or dramatic facial expressions and gestures to portray human emotions. Although Persian painters did not continue to use these pictorial devices in later centuries, the ideal of the heavily illustrated luxury book copied on large sheets of exquisite paper lived on for generations.

Along with the bigger size and better quality of the paper made in Mongol and post-Mongol Iran came wider availability, which spurred an artistic revolution in the Islamic lands from the thirteenth century. Architects and artists exploited the medium, working out designs on paper and transmitting them from one place to another. The most obvious new role for paper was in architectural plans. Builders in antiquity had sometimes used plans and drawings, and there are occasional references to plans in the first seven centuries of Islam, but most construction was based on empirical knowledge relayed from one builder to another by gesture and words and from one site to another by observation and memory. From the fourteenth century, however, builders in the Islamic lands took full advantage of plans and drawings to supplement their traditional skills. The result was an increased uniformity in architecture, for written plans allowed someone working in the capital to design a building for a provincial city he might never have visited.

The availability of paper in the Islamic lands also spurred changes in other arts—metalwork, ceramics, and particularly textiles—for artists could create designs on paper that artisans could apply to their work. In traditional craft practice throughout the first centuries of Islam, the artisans had also been the designers, working out the design of a piece as they went along. The increased availability of paper led some artisans in the Islamic lands to work in different ways: potters learned their designs from pattern books, and weavers learned to decode the instructions in large cartoons or smaller graphs. Not only did this development signal a break in the unity of artist and artisan, but it meant that old and new designs could be attached to whatever medium the artisan chose: similar designs, for example, might now appear on textiles, ceramics, metalwork, and illuminated books, creating the consistency in decoration that characterizes much Islamic art after 1400.

The consistency and repetition of messages and motifs found in the writing and arts of the Islamic lands after 1400 are usually associated with European culture after Gutenberg invented printing with movable type in the middle of the fifteenth century, and great portions of European society were exposed to the written word for the first time. The long reluctance in the Islamic lands to accept printing despite the widespread and enthusiastic acceptance of paper indicates that the humble material may have been as responsible for the reluctance as for the development of printing. In any event, Gutenberg's invention did not come out of nowhere. Although posible connections between his invention and movable type in fifteenth-century Mainz or the earlier invention of printing with movable type in eleventh-century China remain unexplained, movable type in Gutenberg's case resulted from several other developments in European technology of the late Middle Ages, including new techniques of finely cutting and casting metal, new oil-based inks, which would stick to the metal type better than the water-based inks used for printing woodcuts, and the invention of a machine that could evenly and quickly impress the image of the composed form of type onto sheets of paper. In the end, it comes back to paper—a simple material that truly changed the course of history.

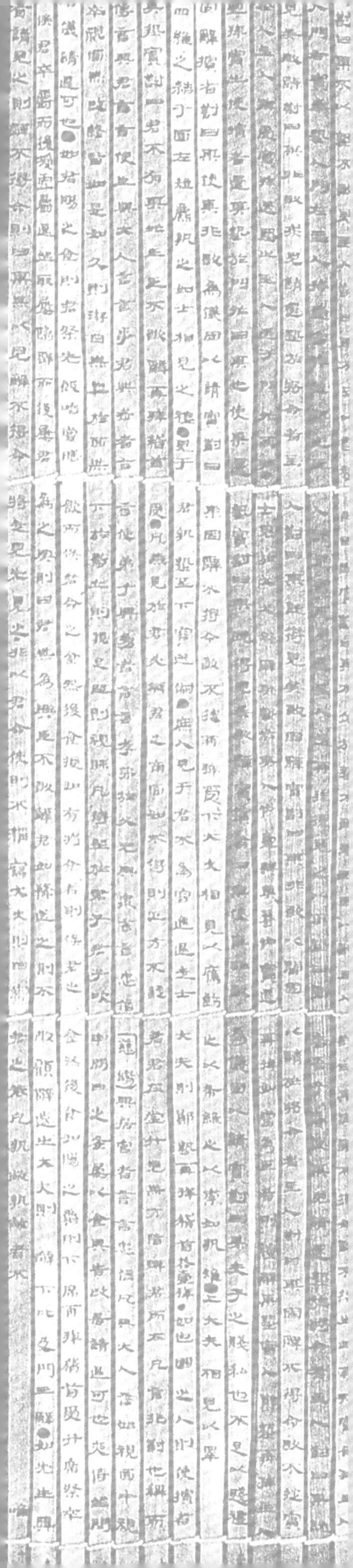

CHAPTER 1

In ancient times writings and inscriptions were generally made on tablets of bamboo or on pieces of silk. But silk being costly and bamboo heavy, they were not convenient to use. Cai Lun then initiated the idea of making paper from the bark of trees, remnants of hemp, rags of cloth, and fishing nets. He submitted the process to the emperor in the first year of Yuan-xing (105 C.E.) and received praise for his ability. From this time on, paper has been in use everywhere and is universally called the paper of Marquis Cai. —*Hou Han shu* (History of the Later Han Dynasty)

Humans have been around for five million years. For 99.9 percent of that time, or until about five thousand years ago, they did not write at all. The invention of writing around 3000 B.C.E. transformed human society by enabling people to transmit greater quantities of knowledge more accurately across vast distances of space and time. In spite of the power of writing, however, or perhaps because of it, for many centuries writing and reading were skills limited to a relative few. Truly literate societies, where a significant proportion of the people regularly read and wrote, did not evolve for several thousand years. Writing developed in some centers of ancient civilization, but the transformation to literate society was accomplished only with the help of paper, a writing material invented in China about two thousand years ago. Nevertheless, it was not the Chinese who exploited the potential of paper in this way, but the Muslims of West Asia, beginning in the ninth century. Their use of paper for writing inaugurated "a new era of civilization, the one we live in now," as the historian Alfred von Kremer wrote more than a century ago.

Paper, now used universally to write and print any language or message because it is light, flexible, strong, and inexpensive, was invented not for writing but for wrapping. The discovery that it was suitable for writing took many years. Before that discovery—namely, for the first three thousand years of writing—most writers used styluses, reed pens, brushes, stamps, or impressing tools to write on clay tablets, papyrus sheets, and bamboo strips. Writers certainly used other materials to write on, including bark, leaves, cloth, and skin, but these, being more fragile, have not survived the centuries, and we know about them only indirectly. The nature of the materials—soft, flexible, or absorbent—and the different tools developed for marking them gave the first writing systems—those of the Mesopotamians, the Egyptians, and the Chinese—their distinctive characteristics. These characteristics differentiated the scripts and the ones that evolved from them even after all the scripts came to be written on paper.

CLAY TABLETS AND PAPYRUS ROLLS

The earliest known writing system was invented in Mesopotamia in the fourth millennium B.C.E., and other scripts were invented apparently independently in the Indus Valley in the third millennium B.C.E., in China in the second millennium B.C.E., and in Mesoamerica in the first millennium B.C.E. Writing developed in Mesopotamia—in the southern part, Sumer—at a time of rapid urbanization, population growth, the division of labor, and the evolution of political systems. To write, the Mesopotamians impressed soft clay tablets with signs for words and syllables using a wedge-shaped stylus. The signs were laid out in horizontal rows, which were read, like English and many languages today, from left to right and top to bottom. The shape of the tip of the stylus gave the script its characteristic appearance as well as its modern name, *cuneiform* (wedge-shaped; fig. 3). The tablets were dried and, depending on the importance of the inscribed text, sometimes baked in a kiln. Although cuneiform script evolved for use on soft clay, from earliest times it was imitated in formal writings cut into stone or metal, but there is no evidence that it was ever written with a pen or a brush.

In Egypt, by contrast, the development of writing was not associated with the use of a particular tool and a particular material. Although Mesopotamians

FIG. 3. *Mesopotamian clay tablet impressed with cuneiform writing, Uruk, c. 1750 B.C.E. British Museum, London [ANE 33236]*

seem to have inspired Egyptians to take up writing and even though plenty of clay was available in the Nile Valley, Egyptians did not generally use clay tablets or the wedge-shaped styluses used for writing in clay. Nor did they imitate the Mesopotamian system of writing with signs and syllables. Instead, they developed the picture writing known as *hieroglyphic* (from the Greek meaning "sacred carving"). The earliest evidence for hieroglyphic writing is found on a group of stone cosmetic palettes carved in low relief. One of them, the Narmer Palette in the Egyptian Museum in Cairo, which is dated 3000 B.C.E., is decorated with several registers of scenes celebrating the triumph of Narmer, the last predynastic king of Egypt, over his enemies. On either side, at the top, is a hieroglyphic representation of the ruler's name flanked by horned heads.

The full hieroglyphic writing system, which combined logograms or pictures with determinatives to indicate grammatical function or pronunciation, seems to have emerged about this time, and examples of it are found on different materials: roughly incised on stone with details supplied in paint, delicately carved in stone (fig. 4), molded in relief on plaster, or drawn and painted in two dimensions on walls or papyrus rolls. Unlike cuneiform, hieroglyphics could be written (and read) from left to right, right to left, or top to bottom, with the characters facing either right or left, depending on the con-

FIG. 4. *Hieroglyphic texts running in different directions on the funerary stela from Tjetji's tomb-chapel in Thebes. The horizontal text is an autobiography, recounting his achievements and good character; the vertical text is a funerary prayer. First Intermediate Period (c. 2150– c. 2018 B.C.E.). 59½ x 43 in. (151.5 x 109.5 cm). British Museum, London [EA 614]*

The ancient Egyptians prepared a writing material from the stalks of the papyrus plant (*Papyrus cyperus*), a member of the sedge family, which grew in the uncultivated marshy areas of the Nile Delta. With increased cultivation of the land, by the nineteenth century the native reed had died out in the Nile Valley, although it flourished—and still flourishes—in the Sudan. The papyrus strain currently grown in Egypt was introduced from the botanical gardens of Paris in 1872.

Papyrus plants, Sicily. After Corrado Basile and Anna di Natale, Il Museo del Papiro di Siracusa *(1994)*

Under good conditions, Egyptian papyrus can grow to a height of 16 feet (5 meters), and its stems reach a thickness of 2 inches (5 centimeters). Under less favorable conditions elsewhere, the plant yields stems of only modest thick-

. . . continued

text in which they were used—for example, on a flat wall or a three-dimensional statue. Hieroglyphic writing and figural representations were organically linked, and there was little distinction between a bas-relief and the accompanying text, for the depiction could be read as an ideogram of sorts for written names and titles.

Hieratic (priestly) script was a simplified version of hieroglyphic developed for use in daily life. In contrast to hieroglyphic, which could be carved or painted on a variety of materials, hieratic was intended for use on papyrus; it was written in carbon ink with a reed pen (fig. 5). Only rarely and at a late date was hieratic ever engraved in stone. Whether written horizontally or vertically, it was always written from right to left; eventually it came to be written only in horizontal lines. A third form of Egyptian writing, *demotic* (popular), was even more scribal, in that it used many abbreviations and ligatures—ways to shorten words and tie them together. Commonly used from the seventh century B.C.E. to the fifth century C.E., demotic script was derived from the "business" style of handwriting used in the Nile Delta. It was the presence of Greek, demotic, and hieroglyphic inscriptions on the Rosetta stone, discovered in the Nile Delta region, that enabled Jean François Champollion to begin the decipherment of hieroglyphic in the nineteenth century.

Although Egyptians wrote on many different surfaces, the distinctive way their writing evolved was mainly a consequence of how they chose to handle papyrus. Strips of papyrus reed were made into rectangular sheets, which were then pasted together into long rolls. The sheets were pasted right over left so that the scribe's pen would not catch where the sheets overlapped. As papyrus sheets were relatively fragile at the edges or when folded, the roll format reduced the ratio of edge to surface and avoided folds altogether, although it allowed only one side of the sheet to be used. For rolls that received regular handling or for luxury projects, Egyptians also used leather, which was more durable.

FIG. 5. *Fragment of a papyrus roll inscribed in hieratic with a healing text, Ramessid Period (c. 12th century B.C.E.). Height 7½ in. (19 cm). British Museum, London [BMEA 10105]*

The unusually dry climate of Egypt has preserved enough early artifacts that we have a remarkably complete overview of Egyptian writing. In addition to inscriptions on walls and statues and writing on papyrus rolls, texts were inscribed on woven linen used for offerings, shrouds, or mummy wrappings. Students normally practiced on rectangular wooden writing boards coated with a thin layer of plaster, which allowed them to erase their writing easily. They also used potsherds and flakes of limestone (*ostraca*) for practice or for writing brief memoranda and accounts. Although scribes strove to write a well-formed and legible hand, Egyptians do not seem to have cultivated an aesthetic appreciation of calligraphy, or "beautiful writing."

Egyptians exported papyrus to most literate societies of the ancient Mediterranean world, but few examples have survived outside the arid Egyptian climate. The oldest preserved papyrus from outside Egypt is a Hebrew scroll of about 750 B.C.E., found in a cave by the Dead Sea. Hebrew is one of the scripts that evolved from the Phoenician alphabet, which was developed in West Asia during the second millennium B.C.E. The alphabet, a system in which each sound in the language is represented by a sign, was revolutionary because it could be applied to any language, not just the Semitic languages for which it was invented. Early in the first millennium B.C.E. the Greeks adopted and modified the Semitic alphabet of the Phoenicians for writing their language. Not only did they reverse the direction of their writing so that it now read from left to right, but they also began representing all their language sounds, not only the consonants and long vowels, as the Semitic alphabets had done (and continue to do). This made for a crucial gain in legibility and accuracy in the transcription of sounds.

Classical authors suggest that Greeks were using papyrus rolls by the sixth century B.C.E., but the oldest archaeological evidence is some burnt fragments discovered in an Athenian tomb dated a century later. Because Greek was written from left to right, papyrus rolls were prepared for Greek writing by overlapping the left sheet over the right sheet to accommodate the direction of the script. The Greeks knew papyrus as *khartes,* but a papyrus roll was known in Greek as *biblion* (book) from the Greek word *biblos,* meaning "papyrus pith." The Greek word is the root from which such English words as *bible* and *bibliography* derive. The Romans later called the same form of book a *volumen,* a term seen now in such English words as *volume* and *volute.* Like Egyptian literary texts, Greek ones were often written on the roll in columns (known in Latin as *pagina,* from which our word *page* derives) perpendicular to the length of the roll. In contrast to literary texts, documents were normally written in an entirely different format, known as a *rotulus,* or roll. A rotulus had a single long column of text parallel to the length of the roll; it was unrolled and read vertically.

ness, impractical for making writing materials. The manufacture of papyrus thus was effectively an Egyptian monopoly. Indeed, the papyrus plant became the emblem of Lower Egypt and was regarded as so typically Egyptian that it could be a metaphor for the entire country.

Papyrus was used to make many things, including baskets, ropes, and boats, but from about 3000 B.C.E. its most important use was as a writing material. The earliest surviving example is a blank papyrus roll found in the tomb of Hemaka, an official of King Den of the First Dynasty (c. 2925– c. 2775 B.C.E.), at Saqqara. The quality of the manufacture is already so fine that Egyptians must have been making papyrus rolls for some time.

Although the first-century Roman writer Pliny the Elder described the manufacture of papyrus sheets in his *Natural History,* the description has given rise to varied interpretations. Examination of surviving papyri gives a better indication of how sheets of writing material were actually prepared. The papyrus stems were cut into manageable lengths, and the outer layer was removed from the pith, which was then sliced or peeled into very thin strips, normally $^4/_{10}$–1¼ inches (1–3 centimeters) wide. The strips were arranged on a smooth surface in parallel lines, just touching or slightly overlapping each other,

. . . *continued*

and another layer, with the strips running at right angles to the first, was laid on top. Pressing or hammering brought the strips together, and the gluey sap of the freshly cut papyrus assured adhesion until the whole had dried into a strong and flexible sheet measuring between 16 inches (40 centimeters) and 8 inches (20 centimeters) wide. Dried papyrus sheets were attached end to end with flour paste to form a roll, the edge of one sheet covering that of the next, usually by about ¾ inch (2 centimeters). The edges were smoothed so that the joints were barely visible and offered no resistance to the pen. Normally a roll consisted of about twenty sheets; the Great Harris Papyrus (c. 1166 B.C.E.) is exceptional, being about 134 feet (41 meters) long.

The thinness of the papyrus strips determined the thickness of the sheet, and their quality determined its color and flexibility. The ideal sheet was thin and white, according to representations of papyrus in Egyptian paintings, but sheets yellowed with age. Egyptians soon realized this: the walls of the tombs of Amenhotep II and Thutmes III in the Valley of the Kings were painted with a yellow background to represent aged papyrus texts.

Papyrus rolls were prepared so that the fibers ran parallel to the length on the inner surface and perpendicular to the length on

. . . continued

These two distinct formats correspond closely to the types of scrolls used in East Asia: the horizontal handscroll and the vertical "hanging" scroll

Rolls had several disadvantages, however. Only one side of the surface could be used for writing, and because there was a practical limit to the length of text that could reasonably be fitted on one roll, long texts had to be copied on several separate rolls, any one of which could easily become lost. Whereas reading a roll from beginning to end was easy, finding a particular passage meant scrolling through the whole.

When Alexander the Great liberated Egypt from Persian rule in 332 B.C.E. and appointed his general Ptolemy I Soter as its governor, Greek became the main administrative language of Egypt and the language used by Egyptians to write on their papyri. Ptolemy is famous for founding the great library in Alexandria, which was expanded by his son and successor, Ptolemy II. Thought to have contained more than half a million volumes, or papyrus scrolls, it was the intellectual center of the ancient world. Because Greek writers used a stiffer type of pen than Egyptian writers did, when it was used on unsupported papyrus, it was more liable to puncture the fragile writing surface; so Egyptian papyrus makers learned to manufacture thicker sheets to accommodate the Greeks.

WOODEN TABLETS AND PARCHMENT CODICES

The horizontal roll was the most common form of book in antiquity, but other forms were also known. One was the writing tablet, which consisted of one to ten pieces of wood or ivory held together by a clasp or hinge or joined by a cord strung through holes drilled in the edges. A scribe could write directly on the tablets with ink or chalk, but in many cases the tablets were slightly hollowed out to hold a thin layer of wax into which writing could be impressed with the pointed end of a stylus (the other, rounded end was used to erase the wax surface by smoothing it). The edges and occasionally a small area in the center of the tablet were left raised to protect the text when the tablets were closed together (fig. 6). A pair of tablets that could be folded together to protect the waxed surface is known as a *diptych*. A multileaved tablet was known in Latin as a *codex*. Although the term was first used to describe a bound set of waxed tablets, it later came to refer to any collection of folded sheets of pliable material—whether parchment, papyrus, or, later, paper—joined along one edge.

Tablets were also known to the Hebrews, and the tablets of Moses, on which the God of Exodus wrote the Ten Commandments, have traditionally been imagined as a diptych. The Greeks, who may have learned about tablets from the Hittites of Asia Minor, used them before they acquired papyrus from the Egyptians. The oldest extant set of tablets was long believed to be an ivory set in the British Museum found at the Assyrian site of Nimrud, in northern Iraq,

F I G . 6. *Wooden writing tablet discovered at Vindolanda, a Roman frontier post in the north of England, late 1st or early 2d century C.E. British Museum, London*

F I G . 7. *Pair of boxwood writing tablets hinged with ivory, discovered in the Uluburun shipwreck off Turkey, 14th century B.C.E. 3½ x 5 in. (8.9 x 12.5 cm). Courtesy of the Institute of Nautical Archaeology, Texas A & M University [KW 4370]*

the outer surface. This arrangement minimized strain and fraying, for when rolled, the inner fibers would be compressed and the vertical fibers on the exterior stretched apart. It also helped scribes to write straight, for they could use the lines of the fibers as guides. Scribes preferred to write on the inside surface of a roll because the exterior could be smudged easily. When read, the roll was held in the left hand and unrolled into the right, as we can see from images of seated and standing scribes. If only a small surface of the roll was exposed, the papyrus was sufficiently stiff to allow the scribe to write without resting it on a hard surface.

and dated to about 707 B.C.E. Recently, however, archaeologists exploring a shipwreck off the coast of Turkey from the late fourteenth century B.C.E. found a pair of small (2 by 3 inch; 50 by 80 millimeter) hollowed tablets of wood held together by an ivory hinge (fig. 7). Writing tablets therefore were used centuries earlier.

Although the ancient Greeks used both writing tablets and papyrus rolls, the tablets were mainly for recording more transitory or mundane information, such as letters, memoranda, bills, accounts, exercises, and drafts of texts. Whether of wood, ivory, or baked clay, tablets were inherently unsuitable for recording lengthy texts, particularly literature, because a work of even moderate length would require many tablets, which would then need to be kept and read together. The Mesopotamians had maintained archives—for example, at the palace of Assurbanipal in Nineveh, where as many as twenty-six thousand clay tablets were stored in baskets, bags, and jars and on shelves—but storage and reference were always a problem with tablets, and outside Mesopotamia they were rarely collected in libraries. Writing tablets are documented from the earliest period in Rome, where they served to record legal documents and official certificates, and the wax tablet remained a common writing surface through much of the Middle Ages for initial composition, correspondence, notes, or business correspondence. Around the year 600, Pope Gregory the Great, for example, preached a series of sermons on the Book of Job that a stenographer took down in shorthand on wax tablets; the text was then transferred to thirty-five papyrus rolls, and the wax tablets were smoothed down for reuse.

Rolls were also prepared from parchment—a light-colored, stiff, and relatively inelastic material made from animal skins that have been scraped, soaked, and dried. Its Latin name, *pergamena*, from which our word *parchment*

Seated scribe, 5th Dynasty (c. 2465– c. 2325 B.C.E.). Musée du Louvre, Paris [E 3023]

The surface of the prepared roll was quite smooth despite the visually prominent lines of papyrus fibers, and the lines do not appear to have bothered

. . . continued

Egyptian scribes. The dried plant sap was a natural size; it prevented ink from penetrating the surface, so the scribe could erase by wiping or washing away the wet ink or using a stone scraper to abrade the dried surface. The scribe's kit consisted of a pen case, with slots for reed or rush pens; cakes of pigment (red, black); and a pot to hold water. The rush pen was cut obliquely and often chewed to achieve a stiff but brushlike point.

derives, comes from the city of Pergamon, in western Anatolia. The Roman author Pliny claimed that parchment had been invented when the Pergamene ruler Eumenes II Soter had to invent a new writing material in the second century B.C.E. because the Ptolemies, jealous of Pergamon's growing library, had embargoed shipments of papyrus from Egypt. Other classical sources, however, indicate that parchment and leather had long been the principal writing materials in the lands east of the Mediterranean. Since antiquity the Jews have copied the Torah on one side of parchments made from the skins of ritually permitted and slaughtered (kosher) animals. The prepared sheets are sewn together with sinews from similar animals to form a long roll on which the text is copied in black ink. The roll itself may not be touched, but it is manipulated by two wooden rollers, and the reader's place is kept with a pointer known as a yad, or "hand" (fig. 8). Corroboration for the use of parchment in the eastern Mediterranean region is provided by the Dead Sea Scrolls (second century B.C.E.–first century C.E.), some of which were written on this material.

At first, the Romans regarded parchment as inferior to papyrus, a writing material sanctioned by some three thousand years of use, and they deemed it suitable only for use in notebooks, not rolls. Although parchment was more expensive than papyrus—primarily because the animal had to be killed to make it—it could be made anywhere animals were available—everywhere, in effect. Nor did parchment fray or split when folded, a distinct advantage as the codex form of book, previously used only for tablets, became more popular.

FIG. 8. Parchment Torah scroll with wooden rollers projecting from the ends. The reader keeps his place in the text with a yad, or pointer

FIG. 9. *Writing on both sides of this papyrus fragment from an anonymous Latin work,* De bellis macedonis, *indicates that it once was a page from a codex, c. 100 C.E. British Library, London*

The increasing popularity of the codex in late antiquity is usually associated with the adoption of parchment, but the two developments were probably independent. The codex offered several improvements over the roll. In addition to the reduced production costs (because a writer could use both sides of the material, not just one) and the ability to accommodate even the lengthiest texts, codices are easier to handle, use, and store. To refer to a passage in the middle of a codex, one needed only to flip it open at that point.

The Romans began using parchment codices by the first century C.E. The Spanish-Roman poet Martial, though not using the word *codex,* referred to pocket editions of his poems on parchment, which were undoubtedly in codex format. The first extant fragment of a codex, an anonymous Latin work, dates from 100 C.E. and is actually on papyrus (fig. 9). Nevertheless, it was not until the third century that codices were accorded the official status of *liber,* or book, a position previously reserved only for the papyrus roll. Codices are scarcely mentioned in Greek literature before the third century, but by the fourth century they seem to have gained parity with papyrus rolls.

Scholars have been tempted to associate the ultimate success of the parchment codex over the papyrus roll with the contemporary growth of Christianity, particularly because virtually all early Christian texts survive as codices. The Nag Hammadi library, for example, is a cache of Greek texts discovered in Egypt in 1945. They had been translated into Coptic and transcribed as codices in the fourth century. Scholars have hypothesized that because most early Christians belonged to the lower classes, they would have preferred humble notebooks to noble rolls. Elaborating this thesis, the British scholar C. H. Roberts ingeniously argued that Mark originally write his Gospel in Rome in a

PARCHMENT

Parchment is a writing material made from animal skins that have been soaked, scraped, and dried. The result is a taut, stiff, and relatively inelastic sheet. Its Latin name, *pergamena,* from which our word *parchment* derives, comes from the city of Pergamon, in western Anatolia, where Romans believed it was first made in the second century B.C.E., although it had long been known in the Middle East and Egypt. *Vellum* refers specifically to calfskin prepared for writing and drawing; the word is often (and incorrectly) used instead of the more inclusive *parchment,* which does not indicate the kind of animal—kid, lamb, gazelle—whose skin was obtained. The finest skins come from young or even fetal animals.

The hair color of the animal affects the color of the parchment: the whitest parchments come from animals with white hair, whereas animals with brown, black, or variegated hair tend to produce darker parchments. The flesh side of the finished parchment is generally whiter and softer than the hair side, which is generally darker and smoother and often carries speckled traces of the hair follicles.

The laborious transformation of the pelt into a writing material begins with soaking it in lime and water, a slow ten-day process in antiquity and medieval times but one that modern chemicals have

. . . continued

Der Permennter.

Ich kauff Schaffell/Böck/vñ die Geiß/
Die Fell leg ich denn in die beyß/
Darnach sirm ich sie sauber rein/
Spann auff die Ram jeds Fell allein/
Schabs darnach/mach P. Permennt darauß/
Mit grosser arbeit in mein Hauß/
Auß ohrn vnd klauwen seud ich Leim/
Das alles verkauff ich daheim.

*"The Parchment-Maker" by Jost Amman.
From Hans Sachs,* Eygentliche
Beschreibung aller Stände auff Erden
(1568)

hastened. The softened skin is
laid on a curved surface, and the
hair and any traces of flesh are
removed with a knife. The skin is
then washed in water and tightly
stretched on a wooden frame to
dry slowly. Drying reorganizes and
aligns the fiber network of the
skin to give it a hard, gluelike consistency. While drying, the surface
is scraped with a curved knife to
free residual hair, pigment, fat,
and flesh and expose the smooth
boundary surface of the corium
layer. The rate at which the skin
dries and the degree to which the
surface is worked, as well as the
residual presence of fats, oils, or
chemicals, all affect the quality of
the product. After the parchment

. . . continued

FIG. 10. *Page from a blank papyrus codex later inscribed with a Greek grammar, a Greek–Latin lexicon, and a Latin calligraphic alphabet, c. 400 C.E. Reproduced by kind permission of the Trustees of the Chester Beatty Library, Dublin [CBL Pap. Ac.1499]*

parchment notebook; later, Egyptian Christians would have recopied it as a papyrus codex, thereby creating a vogue for codices among Christians.

Roberts changed his mind, however, suggesting (with T. C. Skeat) that the origins of the codex lay instead in the Jewish habit of recording oral law in bound tablets or leaves, as opposed to their tradition of copying the written law (the Torah) on rolls. According to this hypothesis, eastern Christians would have recorded Jesus' deeds and sayings (the Gospels) following the Jewish tradition for writing oral law. Scholars have raised objections to this theory, too.

More recently, James O'Donnell has argued that Christianity was "the high-tech religion of late antiquity, using the written word resourcefully to create and shape itself." In this context, small, easily concealed books would have been an appropriate technology for a mobile, persecuted religion, and the codex page lent itself to admirably new, nonlinear methods of reading and reference.

Whatever the truth of the matter, books from early Christian times are exceedingly rare, and most of the surviving fragments have been found in Egypt, which was just one of the many provinces of the Roman empire. The exceptional climate of Egypt may explain the unusual rate of survival there, but that reason is external to this discussion. Egyptian evidence does not necessarily represent or explain what happened everywhere else.

By the middle of the fourth century the codex had become the accepted form of the book throughout the Christian empire: the emperor Constantius

II instructed the scribes of the library at Pergamon to transcribe texts preserved on papyrus rolls onto parchment codices. Between the second and fourth centuries, Egyptians made their codices mostly from papyrus, even though the codex format exposed two of the weaknesses of papyrus: it is damaged by creasing, and it frays easily at unprotected edges. Papyrus codices were made up as blank books for later use, to judge from an example in the Chester Beatty Library dated to about 400 C.E. and inscribed later with a Greek grammar, a Greek-Latin lexicon, and a Latin calligraphic alphabet (fig. 10).

Elsewhere codices were made from parchment sheets. Among the earliest surviving manuscripts of the Christian Bible are the Codex Sinaiticus, perhaps copied at Caesarea, in Palestine, during the late fourth century, and the Codex Alexandrinus, copied at Alexandria in the late fourth or early fifth century. The Codex Sinaiticus, which included the complete New Testament and part of the Old Testament, would have contained nearly eight hundred leaves measuring 15 by 13 inches (370 by 320 millimeters), with four columns of forty-eight lines per page. Assuming that each sheet of parchment could have produced between two and four leaves, several hundred animals must have been slaughtered for the the writing surface. The scribe's use of multiple narrow columns is a holdover from the earlier practice of writing *paginae* (columns) on papyrus rolls (fig. 11).

Papyrus retained its importance even after the Arabs conquered Egypt in the seventh century C.E., although they adopted the Jewish and Christian practice of using parchment for copying scripture; the Koran, God's revelations to the Prophet Muhammad, was always transcribed as a parchment codex. The Arabs called papyrus *qirtas,* a word derived from the Greek *khartes,* and they continued to export it not only to Byzantium and Rome but also to other parts of the empire, where it was used, along with parchment, for keeping tax and payment records. Arabic papyri dated as late as the mid-ninth century have been discovered in Syria and Israel. Some papyrus was grown along the Euphrates in Mesopotamia, for Caliph al-Mutasim is said to have established a papyrus mill staffed by Egyptians at his capital, Samarra, in 836, but production there was insignificant. The tenth-century Sicilian geographer Ibn Hawqal indicates that papyrus was grown in Sicily, but most of it was used to make cordage for ships, and the small amount of writing material produced was reserved exclusively for the chancellery.

Papyrus remained the principal writing material in Egypt until the mid-tenth century. The vast majority of Arabic papyri to survive are fragments of rolls containing official and commercial documents, such as tax registers, accounts, orders, notarial deeds, deeds of purchase and lease, legal acknowledgments, marriage contracts, and private letters, but some literary papyri survive as well (fig. 12). As had been the practice since antiquity, nearly all Ara-

is dry, the surfaces can be further worked with pumice, which gives a fine nap, or they can be whitened with chalk.

Although the Roman writer Pliny stated that parchment was invented in the second century B.C.E., the material is known to have been used in Egypt for drumheads as early as 1900 B.C.E. or so, and it was the preferred writing material of the ancient Hebrews. Whereas papyrus could be made only in Egypt, parchment could be made virtually anywhere. Furthermore, the optimum conditions for the preservation of parchment are cooler and more humid that those appropriate to papyrus. Parchment was therefore suitable for use and preservation in a wider range of climates, although at low levels of humidity parchment becomes brittle, and at high levels it cockles, or wrinkles. The original parchment copies of the Declaration of Independence, the United States Constitution, and the Bill of Rights are now stored in an atmosphere of argon gas with 40 percent relative humidity, much higher than that needed (or appropriate) for paper.

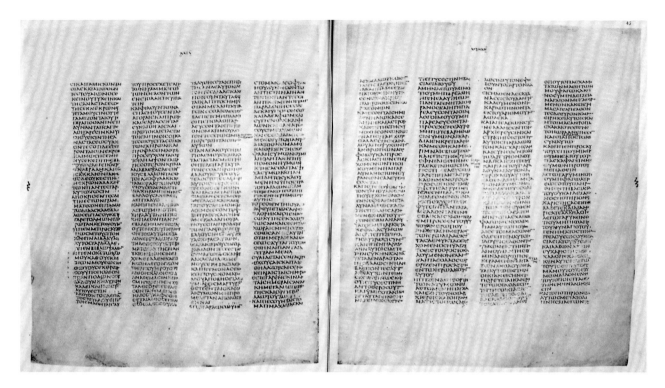

FIG. 11. *Pages from the Codex Sinaiticus written in Greek on large sheets of parchment, late 4th century C.E.*
Each page measures 15 ¼ x 13 ½ in. (38.8 x 34.4 cm). British Library, London

FIG. 12. *Papyrus sheet inscribed with a financial reckoning on one side and an autobiographical account on the other. Egypt, 9th century C.E. The Nasser D. Khalili Collection of Islamic Art, London [PPS 411]*

bic documents were written in long columns on one side of the papyrus roll;
the rolls were held vertically to read. Literary texts, on the other hand, were
normally written as codices, following the Late Antique tradition of using the
codex form for transcribing literary works. At least two examples are known to
survive: the stories of the prophets in the style of Wahb ibn Munabbih, dated
844, and a collection of Prophetic traditions by the Maliki traditionist Abdallah
ibn Wahb, copied at Isna, in Egypt, in 889.

The historian al-Masudi wrote in 956 that papyrus manufacture was not
completely defunct in Egypt, but Ibn Hawqal, who visited Egypt a few years
later, in 969, made no reference to the use of papyrus as a writing material,
although he did mention the papyrus plant. Egyptians still used papyrus in
preparing amulets and for medical treatment, but by the late tenth century it
had been decisively replaced by paper, the writing material invented a thousand years earlier in China. The papyrus industry, which had survived in Egypt
for four thousand years, ground to a halt, and whatever papyrus was around
was used by bookbinders to make pasteboard for book covers.

The decline and death of the ancient papyrus industry is not discussed by
medieval Arab authors. Egyptian manufacturers of papyrus sheets must have
known for several centuries—ever since writers began to prefer codices and
parchment—that their long monopoly over writing materials in the Mediterranean region was at an end. Although parchment had the great advantage over
papyrus that it could be made virtually everywhere, paper had the even greater
advantage that it could be made everywhere cheaply and in industrial quantities.
Although Byzantine administrators were undoubtedly happy to keep ordering
supplies of papyrus from Egypt, and Egyptian papyrus makers were undoubtedly
happy to keep supplying them, the growing use of paper by a burgeoning
bureaucracy in Iraq surely decreased demand for Egyptian papyrus by the
beginning of the ninth century. The papyrus beds were abandoned or turned over
to other cash crops, such as sugar cane or flax, and the native plant eventually
died out in Egypt. Eventually paper came to be manufactured in Egypt itself.

BAMBOO STRIPS AND SILK CLOTH

The earliest writing to survive from China dates from the end of the second
millennium B.C.E. The Chinese system of writing is generally believed to have
been invented independently of early Mesopotamian writing, although the
spread of sheep raising from Mesopotamia across Central Asia may have provided a means by which the concept of writing was brought to China: with the
sheep came people and ideas. According to Chinese tradition, preserved in the
Judgments appended to the *I Ching* (Book of Changes) prior to the invention of
writing, "government was achieved with the help of knotted cords," presum-

ably a reference to a mnemonic device similar to the *quipu* used by the Incas of pre-Hispanic Peru. As in Egypt, the development of writing in China was unconnected to the medium on which writing was done. Unlike Sumerian and Egyptian, which used both pictographs and syllable signs, or Hebrew, Greek, Latin, and Arabic, which used alphabets, ancient Chinese writing expressed words only in pictographs, one character corresponding to one word.

The earliest Chinese writings to survive are tens of thousands of questions to oracles incised on the shoulder blades of animals (largely oxen) and tortoise shells during the Shang dynasty (c. 1600–c. 1050 B.C.E.). These inscribed objects were subjected to heat; the resulting cracks in the bones or shells were read and interpreted. Other inscriptions, with the names of ancestors and supplications for protection, long life, and blessings, have been found on bronze vessels, as well as on stone and jade artifacts. By placing these inscriptions on durable materials that would not rot, the Chinese hoped to assure that their descendants would receive blessings.

Before being incised, the pictograms on the oracle bone inscriptions could have been painted with a brush, and brushed characters have been found on potsherds discovered at Shang archaeological sites. These remnants hint at a parallel—if now lost—Chinese tradition of writing with a brush and ink on flat surfaces. The earliest reliable literary evidence for such writing dates from the

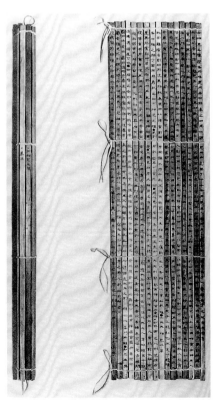

FIG. 13. *Bamboo tablets inscribed in ink with part of the* Book of Rituals, *discovered in Wuwei, Gansu Province, 25–220 C.E. 21 x ½ in. (54 x 1 cm). From* Wu-wei Han chien *(1964), fig. 1058*

late sixth or early fifth century B.C.E., when books were normally written with ink on narrow strips of bamboo or wood or on lengths of silk. The best and most complete extant examples, however, date from the first three centuries C.E.

Some forty thousand ancient bamboo and wooden strips have been discovered since the nineteenth century. Long and very narrow (20 by ½–1 inch; 50 by 1–2 centimeters), these strips, often called tablets, owe their shape to the bamboo from which they were normally made. They were bound together in books by means of interlaced cords strung through holes pierced in the tablets; the books look somewhat like bamboo blinds (fig. 13). Each tablet was inscribed vertically with about thirty characters, although some tablets contain as many as eighty. The medium determined the form of the message, for the use of such narrow material probably led to the distinctive organization of Chinese script in vertical columns that has continued to the present day.

Woven cloth of silk, which had been made since the late fourth millennium B.C.E., provided a much more generous surface for writing, but silk was far more expensive than bamboo or wooden strips because it was so laborious to produce: the silkworm cocoons had to be boiled, their filaments had to be unraveled and gathered together into threads, and the threads had to be woven into cloth. Silk cloth, therefore, was used only where bamboo or wood did not suit a particular purpose: for final editions of books that required a more gen-

FIG. 14. *Silk map discovered in Mawangdui, 2d century B.C.E. 28 pieces; the whole originally measured 39 x 31 in. (98 x 78 cm)*

erous surface, for illustrations appended to books written on tablets, for maps, or for projects for which cost was no object. Three silk maps dating to the second century B.C.E. were recently found in tombs at Mawangdui (fig. 14). Silk was also used for more elevated forms of writing, such as copying texts on divination and occultism, recording the sayings of kings for posterity, commemorating achievements of statesmen and military heroes, and writing messages to be sacrificed to spirits and ancestors. But, as Fan Yeh, author and editor of the *History of the Later Han Dynasty*, wrote in the mid-fifth century, "Silk was expensive and bamboo was heavy," so the Chinese came to use a light but less expensive material called *zhi* as a medium for writing: paper.

THE INVENTION OF PAPER

The invention of paper in the late first century C.E. was commemorated in the story of Cai Lun, or Marquis Cai, a eunuch who served at the imperial court during the reign of the emperor Hedi. According to a story in circulation some 350 years later, Cai Lun made zhi from the bark of trees, remnants of hemp, rags of cloth, and old fishing nets and used it for writing. The emperor praised him for his invention, and it was called the "zhi of Cai Lun." Archaeological and literary evidence suggests that paper had already been known for several centuries and that the story of Cai Lun is a pleasant fiction made up long after the events in question to add color to a long and obscure process.

Zhi was defined in a Chinese dictionary compiled around the time when Cai Lun lived as "a mat of refuse fibers" (*xu yi zhan ye*). The word *xu* refers to fibrous remnants obtained from rags or from boiling silkworm cocoons, and the word *zhan* refers to a mat made from interwoven rushes used for covering something. Since such processes as the treatment of refuse silk, the reuse of old fibers in quilted clothes, and the washing of hemp and linen rags are attested in China as early as the sixth or fifth century B.C.E., it is possible that someone accidentally placed wet refuse fibers on a mat and dried them. This might have then suggested the idea of forming them into a thin sheet, although the earliest surviving papers were made not from refuse silk but from hemp fibers. As silk fibers have neither the physical nor chemical properties of the cellulose fibers that are essential to papermaking, true paper could not have been made from silk refuse, even though the Chinese character for *zhi* (paper) bears the silk radical at its left.

Over the past century, archaeologists have discovered very early specimens of paper at several arid sites in western China. The technical analysis and dates proposed for these specimens have engendered a vigorous controversy, although none would deny Chinese preeminence, and most agree that paper had been invented by the second century B.C.E.—a full two, if not three, cen-

---

FELT

The random organization of matted cellulose fibers that characterizes paper invites a comparison with felt, which is a textile made from wool fibers physically matted by the application of friction, pressure, moisture, and heat. In felt, however, the woolen fibers are linked only by physical means, not by the chemical bonds of paper.

Felting is one of the oldest methods of making fabric, dating back to prehistoric times among the inhabitants of northern and Central Asia. The oldest surviving felts were found at the frozen burial mound at Pazyryk, in Siberia, which is conventionally dated to the fifth century B.C.E., and their fine quality suggests that felting had been known in Central and East Asia for centuries.

Although the techniques of papermaking and felting are somewhat comparable, and although both are first attested in East Asia, there is no reason to believe that papermaking derived from feltmaking. Historically, the two technologies have been quite distinct, and the feltmaking nomads of Central Asia live apart from the papermaking village dwellers. Modern developments in the nonwoven textile industry, particularly synthetic fibers and chemical bonds, as well as the suspension of fibers in water before collecting them on a screen, are, however, tending to blur the tra-

. . . continued

turies before Cai Lun. Perhaps the oldest fragment yet discovered is the coarse hemp paper found at Ejin Banner in Inner Mongolia. Dated to the Western Han period (206 B.C.E.–9 C.E.), it is too coarse to be suitable for writing. Specimens discovered in Baqiao (Ba Bridge), in the Chinese province of Shaanxi, in 1957, including one piece about 4 inches (10 centimeters) square, were made from hemp (*Cannabis sativa*) and dated no later than the reign of the Western Han ruler Wudi (141–87 B.C.E.). Said to be light yellow, thick and uneven, coarse and crude, the pieces show the impressions of weaving on the surface, undoubtedly from the woven cloth mold in which they were made. One of the specimens revealed some microscopic loops of fiber, and another contained a small remnant of thin, two-ply hemp cord, suggesting that they had been made from reused fibers. Another fragment, measuring 4 by 1½ inches (10 by 4 centimeters), was found in the ruins of a watchtower at Lop-nor, in Xinjiang, by members of the Mission of the Northwestern Expedition of China in 1934 and dated on circumstantial evidence to about 49 B.C.E. A few other fragments of paper, most attached to a lacquer utensil found alongside some coins of the time of the Han emperor Xuandi, who reigned in the first century B.C.E., were discovered in an underground vault unearthed in Zhongyan, Shaanxi Province, in 1978. None of these was suitable for writing, and it is unlikely that any of them were made in the remote regions where they were discovered. Rather, the origins of papermaking must lie in the more temperate, indeed tropical, regions of southern and southeastern China.

Literary evidence confirms the utilitarian role to which paper was put in early times. A Chinese story set in 93 B.C.E. records the first use of facial tissue—an imperial guard advised a prince to cover his nose with a piece of zhi—and another story mentions poisonous medicine wrapped in *he-ti*—the word is glossed by a second-century C.E. commentator as a thin piece of red zhi. By the first century C.E., however, well before Cai Lun supposedly invented the material, paper was already used for writing, indicating that papermakers had discovered how to surmount one of its few disadvantages: unless the surface is treated in some way, it absorbs ink like a blotter. Specimens from the third century indicate that papermakers had a range of sizing techniques, from coating the surface with gypsum to treating it with gum, glue, or starch, to prevent the ink from spreading. Already in the official history covering the reign of emperor Guangwu in the early first century C.E., the Assistant of the Right was responsible for supplying paper, brush, and ink. By 76 C.E. a scholar was able to instruct students by using copies of the classics written on (wooden or bamboo) tablets as well as zhi, so paper must have become reasonably common.

These reports have also been confirmed by archaeological finds in western China. In 1942, for example, investigators from the Academia Sinica found a

ditional distinctions between paper and felt so that it becomes difficult to say whether a particular material is a felt-like paper or a paperlike felt.

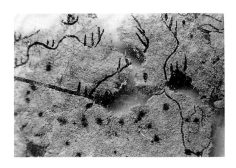

FIG. 15. *Fragment of hemp paper bearing traces of a map, discovered at Fangmatan, near Tianshui, Gansu Province, c. 150 B.C.E.*

specimen of coarse, thick paper inscribed with about two dozen readable characters under the ruins of an ancient watchtower near Juyan (formerly Karakhoto), in Inner Mongolia. Because this watchtower was abandoned by its Chinese defenders between 109 and 110 C.E., the specimen has been dated on historical grounds to the early second century (and it might be earlier) and has been considered the earliest sample of paper with writing on it. In 1974, two larger pieces of paper dated to 52 B.C.E. were found in another watchtower in Juyan, along with twenty thousand inscribed wooden tablets. In the same year several inscribed specimens were found in a pre-220 C.E. Han tomb discovered at Hantanpo, near Wuwei, in Gansu Province (fig. 15). Made of hemp, the specimens are said to be more technically advanced than other examples, being white and much thinner, and perfectly suited to writing with brush and ink. In 1991, paper dating from the time of the Han emperor Xuandi, in the first century B.C.E., was discovered between Anxi and Dunhuang, in Gansu Province. Two well-preserved sheets of flexible yet strong white paper of a uniform thickness were unearthed at the Eastern Han tombs on Fulong Plain near Lanzhou, also in Gansu Province.

From these early examples, we can tell that the first papermakers formed sheets by pouring a pulp made of rags and textile waste onto cloth molds floating in a pool of water, but as they became more proficient and the use of paper expanded, they developed different techniques and new sources of fiber. In particular, they began to use a new type of mold, which was made in two pieces and could be dipped in a vat of pulp. Because the damp sheet of paper could be removed from the screen once it was formed, this sped up the process considerably, for the same mold could be used immediately to make another sheet.

Chinese papermakers also began to abandon waste materials as the source of paper and to make their pulp from the bast fibers of such plants as hemp, jute (*Corchorus capsularis*), rattan (*Calamus* spp.), and bamboo or from the inner bark of paper mulberry (*Broussonetia papyrifer*) or mulberry (*Morus alba*). They used the fibers and barks either alone or in combination, and the choice and relative amounts seem to have varied from region to region, depending on what was locally available. Paper made from mulberry was used for public records, unearthed at Lopnor, during the Wei (220–65) and Western Jin (265–317) dynasties. Paper made from rattan was used during the Western Jin, and by the time of the Southern and Northern dynasties (317–581) rattan paper produced in Shanxi, in Zhejiang Province, was known as Shan paper.

Because molds had to be of manageable size, sheets of paper were, like Egyptian papyrus and Chinese silk, typically pasted into rolls for writing. Individual sheets averaged about 1 foot wide by 2 feet long (30 by 60 centimeters), so the mold must have been conveniently small to handle. The size of the mold gradually increased from the sixth century to the tenth, but the typical long scroll was still pasted up from ten to as many as twenty-eight sheets of paper. The beginning of the scroll was usually covered with a thicker sheet, much like the *protocollon* of Egyptian papyri, which protected and provided information about the contents; the other end was attached to a wooden roller. (This format is quite distinct: the papyrus roll of the Mediterranean world had no rollers, and a Torah roll has two.)

Under the Tang dynasty (618–907), paper manufacture became so specialized that papers were manufactured for particular purposes, and some of the special characteristics of paper were exploited. Paper made from the bark of paper mulberry, for example, which grows in mountainous areas of northern and southern China, was snowy white when the shrub had been nurtured in rich soil and the paper prepared with pure water. Pure Heart Hall paper, praised as the best paper of the time, was made that way and prepared in scrolls more than 50 feet (17 meters) long. Excavations at the Temple of Auspicious Brightness (Ruiguang si) in Suzhou uncovered specimens of magnificent green writing paper dated to the tenth century and possibly made from mulberry bark; the paper was smoothed with wax to give it the glossy finish popular with calligraphers. White rattan paper was used for official Inner Chamber edicts from the Tang government; bluish-green rattan paper, for literary documents. Bamboo paper was first made during the Tang period, and the calligrapher and landscape painter Mi Fu used it effectively in his impressionistic ink washes in creating soft and misty effects. Paper made from jute was first used in 715 for an imperial edict of the emperor Xuanzong; imperial edicts thus became known as "jutes." Sandalwood (*Santalum album*) was also used for the manufacture of paper. Paper made of a mixture of two types of bark—paper mulberry and bamboo, bamboo and hemp, or hemp and paper mulberry—was popular. Paper made from grass, abundant everywhere, was used by the common people.

The Chinese soon discovered that paper was suitable for purposes other than wrapping, writing, and painting. They used it for ceremonial offerings, household articles, clothing, hats, and kites—which the Chinese firmly believe were invented in China. General Han Xin (d. 196 B.C.E.) is said to have had a paper kite flown over a palace under seige so that he could gauge the length of tunnel his troops would need to dig under the palace defenses for a surprise attack, but the early date of this story may reflect wishful thinking. By the early seventh century paper kites were certainly employed for military signaling and for weather forecasting, and the nobility began to use them for amusement, often in a form incorporating a lantern.

Toilet paper was used by the sixth century, or so we can gather from a report about the noted scholar Yan Zhidui. Two years before his death he instructed his family not to use for toilet purposes paper on which quotations of commentaries from the Five Classics or the names of sages had been written. This suggests that at least some types of paper were cheap enough to use in such a way. Yan Zhidui's report is confirmed by that of a ninth-century Arab traveler to China. The traveler, who was used to Islamic traditions of personal hygiene, commented disapprovingly that the Chinese "are not careful about cleanliness, and they do not wash themselves with water when they have done their necessities but only wipe themselves with paper."

Perhaps the most important new use of paper in China was for printing, the reproduction with ink of reverse or negative images. Carved bronze and stone seals, from which impressions were made on clay and silk, had been used in China for millennia, and the process of taking inked rubbings from stone and bronze reliefs may have been another impetus to develop printing by the seventh century. The oldest example of Chinese woodblock printing is believed to be a miniature charm scroll, made of thick mulberry paper, about 20 feet long and 2¼ inches wide (6 meters by 60 centimeters), impressed with twelve woodblock prints (fig. 16). Containing the text of a Buddhist sutra in Chinese, the scroll was discovered in a pagoda at Pulguk Temple near Kyongju, Korea, in 1966. Several peculiarities suggest that the original Sanskrit text had been translated into Chinese by 704, and, because the style of calligraphy is similar to that found in Chinese manuscripts of the period, it is believed that this specimen was printed in Tang China in the early eighth century and brought to Korea no later than 751, when it was placed in the pagoda.

The oldest printed book in the world is a printed paper copy of a Chinese translation of the Diamond Sutra dated to 868 and found at Dunhuang, a major Buddhist site on the Silk Road (fig. 17). Seven sheets of white paper, each measuring 10½ by 30 inches (26.6 by 76.2 centimeters), were pasted together to form a scroll 17½ feet (5.33 meters) long. The scroll has a woodcut frontispiece and a colophon stating that "Wang Jie recently made this for universal distribution to gain blessings to his parents on the thirteenth of the fourth moon of the ninth year of *Xiantong*." Other books from the later Tang period were prepared on a regularly folded roll, a format often known as

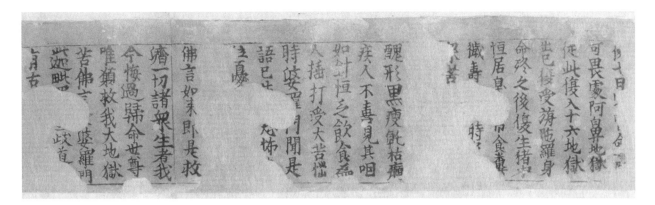

FIG. 16. *Detail of early 8th-century miniature printed charm scroll discovered in a pagoda in Pyongju, Korea, in 1966. This section shows how the scroll was pasted up from several sheets of paper. Height 2 ¼ in. (5.7 cm). Cultural Properties Administration of the Korean Government*

FIG. 17. *Block-printed frontispiece and beginning of the text from the Diamond Sutra, discovered in the Cave of the Thousand Buddhas in Dunhuang, 868 C.E. British Library, London*

"accordion" style. The form, though using only one side of the paper, allowed for convenient consultation of long texts and has remained in use in East Asia to the present day.

The Chinese may have invented movable type as early as the mid-eleventh century, but they did not use it widely, and woodblock printing remained the principal vehicle of traditional Chinese printing. This was probably because movable type did not save much labor when printing Chinese. Written Chinese is composed of thousands of ideograms, and since several copies, or sorts, would be needed for each character (twenty or more for the commoner ones), a font of some 200,000 sorts would not be unusual. The labor of making so many individual characters was not significantly less than carving entire woodblocks, and woodblock printing remained popular for centuries. Once printing became more widespread in the Song period (960–1279), the need for more paper on which to print more books stimulated the development of the paper industry, and the history of printing and paper was forever after intertwined in China as in Europe, but not, as we shall see, in the Islamic world.

THE DIFFUSION OF PAPER

China played the primary role in the diffusion of Buddhist scholarship throughout Asia in the first millennium of the Common Era, and Buddhism was the means by which paper, too, was spread throughout Asia. All students of Buddhism would have learned the Chinese crafts of making brushes, ink, and paper to spread Buddhist teachings more efficiently. Paper and papermaking skills were thereby exported from China to other lands, perhaps beginning as early as the third century. The closer a country lay to the centers of Chinese Buddhism, the sooner paper was used and made there. Because the main center of Buddhism remained in India, Chinese Buddhists traveled between the two countries, taking the Silk Road across western China. The extremely dry climate of the west allowed the preservation of specimens that would have been lost elsewhere, and indeed, this is where most early specimens of Chinese paper have been found—including the largest and most spectacular collection of medieval Chinese paper, consisting of more than thirty thousand paper rolls, found at Dunhuang. The greater part of the texts are written in Chinese, but some are written in Sanskrit, Soghdian, Middle Persian, Uighur, and Tibetan, showing the strong interregional connections in this now-remote corner of the globe.

Most of the papers found at Dunhuang were made from hemp and paper mulberry fibers, with a few made from ramie and mulberry fiber. Although Chinese literary sources indicate that bamboo and rattan were also used at this time, these materials were not found among the Dunhuang papers, perhaps

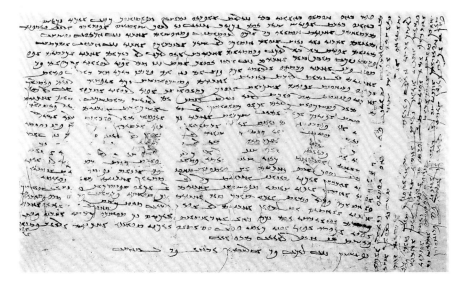

FIG. 18. *Letter in Soghdian script written on paper sometime during the 4th—6th centuries, discovered by Sir Marc Aurel Stein near Dunhuang. British Library, London [Or. 8212/98 plate CLVII]*

because bamboo and rattan did not grow in the colder and drier climate of eastern Central Asia, although it is unlikely that all the Dunhuang papers were made locally. Papers from earlier periods at Dunhuang, especially those made in the seventh and eighth centuries, are generally thin, of even thickness, highly finished, well sized, and stained yellow or brown. Those of the tenth century are of poorer quality, being mostly coarse, drab-colored, and thicker than early Tang papers. This change reflects more on Dunhuang's declining fortunes than on any deterioration in Chinese papermaking technology, which continued to improve.

In the early twentieth century the explorers Sven Hedin and Sir Marc Aurel Stein found paper fragments datable to the third century in the Loulan region of western China, and Prussian and Japanese expeditions found paper dating back to the fourth and fifth centuries in the Turpan and Gaochang area. In Hotan (Khotan), Stein also found paper manuscripts in Chinese, Tibetan, Sanskrit, and ancient Khotanese datable to the eighth century. Although some of these papers must have been brought from elsewhere in China, some may have been manufactured locally. Among the documents found at Turpan in 1972, one dated 620 bears the name of a *zhishi,* or papermaker, and another mentions sending prisoners to work in paper factories at an unspecified location. The preparation of the fiber for papermaking, particularly the laborious beating and hydrating of the stuff in mortars, must have been arduous, low-status work. It is no surprise that prisoners were compelled to do it.

The ancient letters in a mailbag discovered by Stein in a ruined watchtower between Dunhuang and Loulan (fig. 18) were written in Soghdian, probably no earlier than the fourth century, and perhaps as late as the sixth, although

JAPANESE PAPER

Modern Japanese papermakers use two methods, the older *tamezuki* (dip-and-drain) technique, which was introduced from China, and the *nagashizuki* (dip-and-cast) technique, which evolved from the tamezuki method in the eighth century and eventually became more common. The mold cover, made of fine bamboo strips held in place by silk threads, is placed between two rigid rectangular wooden frames. With the dip-and-drain technique, the wooden frames are dipped in a vat of pulp, and the water is allowed to drain away and the sheet of paper thus formed to dry. With the dip-and-cast technique, a forming aid, such as mucilage, is added to the pulp to make it more viscous, to delay draining time, and to permit greater control over the thickness of the finished sheet of paper. Once sufficient pulp covers the mold, the surplus is cast back into the vat with a wavelike action, hence the name of the technique. The pulp-filled mold is shaken to align the fibers, and the results of this technique of shaking remain a distinguishing characteristic of all Japanese and Japanese-style papers. Adding the forming aid allows the paper to be pressed flat without interleaving felts, because the damp sheets do not stick together, and after pressing and drying, no subsequent sizing is necessary.

. . . continued

Stein initially dated them to the second century. Whatever their date, however, they indicate that in addition to Buddhist monks, Silk Road merchants throughout the oasis cities of Central Asia used paper well before the coming of Islam to the region in the early eighth century. Chinese merchants—and paper—made it much farther west, for several pieces of paper inscribed in Chinese with notations of purchases were discovered at the eighth-century site of Moshchevaya Balka, in the Caucasus Mountains of southern Russia.

On the other side of China, the Chinese probably introduced paper to Korea by the third century, but no specimens that early have been found there. The northern part of Korea was under Chinese control from 108 B.C.E. to 210 C.E., toward the end of the Han period, and Chinese Buddhists probably brought paper inscribed with Buddhist texts to Korea during these years. It is not known exactly when the Koreans began manufacturing paper themselves, but, as elsewhere, it is likely that Buddhist monks and students who had studied in China brought papermaking to Korea.

The earliest Korean papers to survive include a glossy white paper made of hemp fibers discovered at a North Korean site dating to the Koguryo era (37–668 C.E.). They show that Korean papermakers followed Chinese precedents, using the same raw materials, tools, and techniques. Korean paper, known as *jilin zhi* (paper from the Silla Kingdom), was an item of tribute to China and received high praise from Chinese literati and artists for its qualities. Thick, strong, whitish, and glossy, it was especially prized for calligraphy and painting.

Koreans in turn introduced paper and papermaking to Japan. Already in the second half of the fourth century a Korean scholar, Wani, who served as tutor to the crown prince of Japan, presented several Chinese books, presumably copied on paper, to the Japanese court. During the sixth century Korean kings sent books, also presumably on paper, to the Japanese on several occasions, and in 610 the Korean monk Damjing went to Japan, where he was known as Doncho. Like all Buddhist monks educated in China, Doncho would have been trained to make brushes, paper, and ink. His arrival has been traditionally understood to mark the beginning of papermaking in Japan, but Korean immigrants may already have introduced papermaking to Japan in the fifth century. In time Japanese paper developed its own characteristics and came to rival the paper of China.

Papermaking was probably introduced in Vietnam, which had close political and cultural ties with China, as early as the third century, about the same time that it was introduced in Korea. In 284, thirty thousand rolls of "honey fragrance paper" (*mi xiang zhi*) were brought to China from "Da Qin," presumably Vietnam, and this paper, made from garco wood (*Aquilaria agallocha*), is said to have been shipped by Alexandrian merchants. Sometime between 265 and

FIG. 19. *Leaves of the talipot palm inscribed with the text of* Astasahasrika Pajnaparamita, *12th century C.E.* *2½ x 16 in. (6.8 x 41 cm). British Library, London [Or. 6902]*

290 the district of Nan-Yue, located in present-day southern China and northern Vietnam, sent China a tribute of more than ten thousand rolls of "intricate filament paper" (*ce li zhi*), perhaps made of fern or seaweed.

Oddly, although Chinese Buddhist monks traveled along the Silk Road to India in the first centuries of the Common Era, there is no evidence that Indians made paper until Muslims introduced the craft to the subcontinent perhaps a thousand years later. Writing had been used in India since the second half of the third millennium B.C.E.; various materials, including leaves, wooden boards, bamboo chips, and metals, were inscribed. The leaves of the talipot palm, native to south India, came to be preferred for books, but any kind of broad leaf was probably acceptable, and until recently, leaves of the plantain and *sala* trees were used in village schools (fig. 19).

The poor initial reception of paper in India is an enigma, for writing was used there, and the raw materials from which paper was made in East Asia were readily available. The hot and moist climate in much of India is, however, unsuitable for the long-term preservation of paper documents, as are the many insects that find cellulose a good meal—hence the invocation "O King of the Cockroaches!" in some medieval Arabic manuscripts, made to keep the ruler's "subjects" from eating the book. Some scholars have blamed the tradition-bound caste system for discouraging the adoption and development of new techniques, such as papermaking. Possibly, high-caste Indians, precisely those people most likely to be literate, thought that they could be polluted from contact with paper made from recycled rags.

The earliest recorded use of paper in India dates to the eleventh century, when Jewish merchants—and presumably Muslim merchants as well—exported it from Egypt and Arabia to their colleagues in Gujerat. Even today, papermaking

The earliest known paper manuscript extant in Japan is a commentary on the Lotus Sutra, reportedly written or annotated by Prince Shotoku between 609 and 616 on Chinese paper. The oldest specimens of Japanese-made paper, preserved in the Shoso-in Imperial Repository in Nara, are fragments of household registers from three provinces, dated 701. The paper, made from paper mulberry, is inferior in quality to contemporary Chinese paper.

Increased demand for documents and copies of Buddhist sutras led to an expansion of Japanese paper manufacture in the seventh and eighth centuries. Between 806 and 810 a papermill was established to supply the court at Kyoto.

Eighth-century texts refer to several hundred varieties of paper: most were made of hemp, which produced the best paper, some of fiber from two types of paper mulberry (*kozo* and *kajinoki*) and *gampi* (*Wikstroemia sikokiana*). Hemp fell into disuse some time after 800, but *mitsumata* (*Edgeworthia papyrifera*) was introduced by the sixteenth century, and its fibers are still the principal ones used in Japanese papermaking.

Dutch and other European merchants active in East Asia used Japanese paper for recordkeeping but did not export it to Europe. The Dutch East India Company, which had exclusive access to Japanese ports between 1639 and

. . . continued

by hand is largely associated with Muslims. The first papermills are attested only in the fifteenth century, when a sultan of Kashmir, returning from Samarqand, brought along artisans to establish a papermaking industry there.

THE INTRODUCTION OF PAPER IN THE ISLAMIC LANDS

The story that paper was introduced to the Islamic lands when Muslim soldiers captured Chinese papermakers at the battle of Talas in 751 is just that—a story—but the details illuminate some historical facts pertinent to the diffusion of paper. The army of the Arab commander in Central Asia, Ziyad ibn Salih, routed the Chinese army of Gao Xianzhi, and, according to the story, returned to their base at Samarqand with one, two, or several captive Chinese papermakers. There the captives would have used local supplies of hemp and flax, as well as the abundant water from irrigation canals fed by the Zarafshan River, to start a paper industry, for which the city remained famous for centuries.

The city of Talas, in southern Kazakhstan, formerly known as Awliya Ata and Dzhambul, sits on the Talas River where it is crossed by the Silk Road. In the seventh century, after the collapse of the Western Turkish and Sasanian empires, the Chinese had taken advantage of the power vacuum in the region and expanded their authority over Transoxiana, whose rulers had long dispatched embassies to China and received titular honors from the Chinese. In 659, Chinese forces reached Samarqand and Bukhara.

Meanwhile, Muslim rulers had also turned their attention to Transoxiana. After the death of the prophet Muhammad in 632 and the rule of the first four caliphs from Arabia, the governor of Syria seized power and established his family as the Umayyad caliphs, with their capital at Damascus. In the following decades, Umayyad military successes in the east, particularly the conquest of Iran and Transoxiana, led Muslims to look increasingly away from the Mediterranean lands and toward Iran and Central Asia. This shift intensified, particularly as dissatisfaction with Umayyad rule grew under the direction of the Abbasids—descendants of the Prophet's uncle Abbas—until they led an army from the northeastern Iranian province of Khurasan against the Umayyads. The Abbasid revolution in 749–50 resulted not only in the fall of the Umayyads and the further displacement of the Islamic capital from Syria to Iraq but also in a new eastward outlook, as the once peripheral provinces of Khurasan and Transoxiana became central to Abbasid politics and culture.

Like the story about Cai Lun, the story about captured papermakers is probably false for several reasons. As I mentioned in the Introduction, it is first reported three centuries after the events in question by the Arab historian Thaalibi, in his *Book of Curious and Entertaining Information*. Among Thaalibi's chap-

1854, shipped Japanese paper only twice, in 1643 and 1644. One of these lots probably reached Holland and included the paper that Rembrandt got his hands on. From about 1647, Rembrandt frequently printed his etchings on papers of non-European origin, most of them Japanese, although a few were Indian. Most Europeans, however, remained ignorant of Japanese paper until the mid-nineteenth century, when artists like J. A. M. Whistler, Edouard Manet, and Edgar Degas found Japanese paper for sale in London and Paris.

ters is one enumerating the specialities of different lands. One of the specialities of Samarqand, he wrote, is paper, which looks better, is more supple, is
more easily handled, and is more convenient for writing on than either Egyptian papyrus or parchment. On the authority of a certain *Book of Roads and
Provinces,* a text, now lost, probably written by the vizier to the Samanid rulers of
Transoxiana a century earlier, Thaalibi reported the Chinese prisoner story.

Thaalibi's entertaining book belongs to a popular genre of Arabic literature. In it he sought to match every place with its specialty and a colorful anecdote.
Earlier Muslim historians had ignored the battle of Talas and its repercussions
and instead focused their attention on other events in West Asia. There are,
consequently, no contemporary Arab accounts of the battle, which turned out
to be of inestimable importance: it ultimately determined that Islamic civilization would dominate in Turkestan. Later Arab historians, such as Ibn al-Athir
(d. 1233), report that fifty thousand Chinese were killed and about twenty
thousand taken prisoner, but the figures must be fiction. Chinese accounts
contemporary with the battle suggest that the Arab accounts were embellished
and exaggerated over time, for they state that the Chinese army had no more
than thirty thousand troops. Papermakers may have been conscripted into the
Chinese army, however, although only the late Arab sources mention them.
One Chinese source, Du Huan, who was taken prisoner but returned to his
homeland a decade after the battle, mentions only weavers, painters, gold-
smiths, and silversmiths among the prisoners taken.

In any case, papermaking would have been practiced throughout Central
Asia by the eighth century; captured prisoners need not be credited with introducing it. Paper was used in Samarqand—and probably made there—decades
before the battle. Quite apart from the Ancient Letters, one of which was
addressed to Samarqand some centuries before, several paper documents were
discovered at Mount Mugh, a mountain stronghold near Pendzhikent (Panch)
in Tajikistan, where Devastich, "king of Soghdia and lord of Samarqand," had
sought refuge from the Arab invaders in 722–23. In the 1930s a shepherd discovered a cave in Mount Mugh containing seventy-six texts in Soghdian, Arabic, and Chinese and written on several kinds of material—including paper,
cloth, leather, and wood (fig. 20). Although there is no way to know where the
Mount Mugh papers were made, it is likely that they were local and that, as elsewhere, Buddhist monks, who had been active in the region, had brought
papermaking to Transoxiana well before the Muslim conquest.

Al-Nadim, the tenth-century Baghdadi author of a book known as the
Fihrist (Index), which deals with writers and their books, lived somewhat earlier
than Thaalibi, and his near-contemporary account of the origins of paper is
more circumspect. He certainly believed that it was associated with Khurasan,

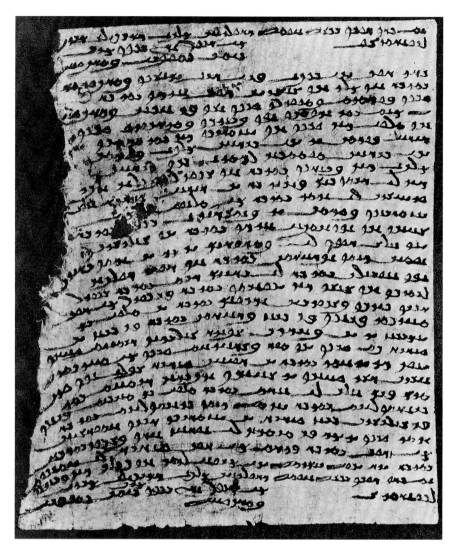

FIG. 20. *Early 8th-century letter written in Soghdian on paper from the state archive of Devastich, king of Soghdia, discovered at Mount Mugh. 11½ x 10 in. (29.5 x 25.5 cm). Institute of Oriental Studies, Academy of Sciences, St. Petersburg*

the province in northeastern Iran adjacent to Transoxiana. "Then there is the Khurasani paper made of flax, which some say appeared in the days of the Umayyads, while others say it was during the Abbasid regime. Some say that it was an ancient product and others say that it is recent. It is stated that crafts-men from China made it in Khurasan in the form of Chinese paper." His ref-erence to Chinese craftsmen may be convention, for Chinese artisans had long been famed in the Islamic lands, and Chinese paper remained esteemed for centuries.

The most convincing argument against the presumed role of Chinese papermakers is technical. By the eighth century papers from western China were made primarily from bast fibers—mulberry, paper mulberry, and ramie—

occasionally combined with hemp, waste fibers from linen (that is, flax), and ramie rags. Raw fibers always predominate, and rag fibers were always only a supplement. Although texts like al-Nadim's mention making paper from flax, examination of "Islamic" papers shows them to have been made predominantly of rag fibers, with the occasional admixture of raw fibers. Had captured Chinese papermakers been the first to introduce papermaking in Samarqand, they could hardly have perfected using waste fiber so quickly. It is easier to imagine that papermakers had been active in Central Asia for quite some time, where they had learned to use rags rather than bast fiber as their primary raw material. The chief contribution of papermakers working under Arab rule was the perfection of rag paper through improved techniques for beating the fibers and by preparing the surface for writing by sizing it with starch.

The likelihood that anonymous Central Asian papermakers invented rag paper well before the Islamic conquest and that when Central Asia became Islamic, the technology was transferred to the Islamic lands need not entirely discredit the anecdote alleging that Chinese captives brought papermaking technology to Samarqand in 751. But its message should be understood in a metaphoric rather than a literal sense. Much as Cai Lun's invention of paper remains a convenient metaphor for the underlying truth that paper began to be used for writing in early second-century China, the story of captured Chinese papermakers metaphorically describes how paper was introduced to the Islamic lands through Central Asia just at the time when, under Abbasid rule, this region began to play an increasingly important role in Islamic civilization.

CHAPTER 2

Thus, paper was used for government documents and diplomas. Afterwards, people used paper in sheets for government and scholarly writings, and the manufacture [of paper] reached a considerable degree of excellence. —I B N K H A L D U N, *The Muqaddimah*

The unification of West Asia under Islam in the eighth century meant that once Muslims encountered paper in Central Asia, its use spread rapidly across Iran, Iraq, Syria, Egypt, and North Africa to Spain. For papermaking to travel from its place of origin—China—to Samarqand, in Central Asia, had taken about five centuries, but a mere two centuries after Muslims encountered paper in Central Asia they were using it in Spain, on the Atlantic fringe of Eurasia. Just as the swift spread of Islam in the seventh century was unprecedented in human history, so the introduction of paper and papermaking across the Islamic lands in the ninth and tenth centuries was a remarkable historical and technological achievement that transformed society in its wake.

Before Islam, paper was entirely unknown to the empires of Sasanian Iran and Byzantium, which stood at the western termini of the Silk Road. Iranians are said to have copied the *Avesta,* the sacred book of Zoroastrianism (the main religion of pre-Islamic Iran), on twelve thousand skins. Paper was also unknown in early seventh-century Arabia, to judge from the evidence of the Koran and the biographies of the prophet Muhammad; no word for it appears in either source. When the Arabs eventually encountered paper in eighth-century Central Asia, they called it *kaghad* (sometimes *kaghid* or *kaghadh*), borrowing the Persian word *kaghaz,* itself derived from the Soghdian *kygdyh*. All these words, as well as the Uighur word for paper, *kägdä* or *kagda,* are phonetically derived from the Chinese word *guzhi,* meaning "paper made from paper mulberry [bark]," although the paper mulberry (*Broussonetia papyrifera*) grows nowhere in the region.

The Arabs also called paper *qirtas,* a word they had originally used for papyrus, papyrus rolls, and even parchment (also known as *riqq*). The word *qirtas* appears in the Koran in this sense, referring to writings on separate sheets. Perhaps the most common Arabic word for paper, however, was *waraq,* meaning "leaf," probably from the expression *waraq qirtas,* "a leaf or sheet of paper." From this usage in turn derive the words *warraq*—the common term for stationer, papermaker, paper merchant, and by extension copyist—and *wiraqa,* "papermaking," as well as many modern compound expressions referring to paper money, lottery tickets, commercial papers, banknotes, and the like.

I R A Q

Although paper was used earlier in Central Asia and Iran, let us look first at Iraq, the heartland of the empire, because the decision by the Abbasid bureaucracy to use paper was instrumental in its acceptance everywhere else. Bureau-cratic necessity led Muslims to adopt paper. The second Umayyad caliph, Umar I (r. 634–44), who ruled from Arabia, had established the first govern-ment office to organize payments, register the army, and regulate the treasury, and he needed account books for this purpose. Such documents—known in Arabic as *daftar* (from the Greek word *diphthera,* meaning "skin; hide")—were, strangely enough, initially kept on papyrus, which became the normal writing material used in caliphal offices following the conquest of Egypt in 641.

Early Islamic papyrus documents survive from Egypt as quires (booklets), rolls, and loose sheets, but the sheet format seems to have been most common. In contrast, Byzantine bureaucrats in Egypt and Syria had used papyrus rolls, and Sasanian bureaucrats in pre-Islamic Iran had kept their records on codices of prepared animal skins. According to later secretarial tradition, during the reign of the first Abbasid caliph al-Saffah (r. 751–54), who was responsible for moving the capital of the empire from Syria to Iraq, his vizier Khalid ibn Bar-mak ordered the loose sheets replaced with codices. These were possibly made of parchment, following Persian precedent, although papyrus continued to be used during the reign of al-Saffah's son al-Mansur, the founder of Baghdad. Assuming that the format of the account book was more important than the material on which the records were kept, the new codex format would have exposed two of papyrus' greatest weaknesses, just as it had in early Christian times: its edges were easily frayed and it was damaged by repeated folding. In both ways, paper was noticeably superior.

According to the thirteenth-century encyclopedist Yaqut, the first paper-mill in Baghdad was established in 794–95 during the reign of the Abbasid caliph Harun al-Rashid, and enough paper was made available for bureaucrats to replace their papyrus and parchment records with paper ones. Bureaucracy begat more bureaucracy, and in addition to recording such traditional infor-mation as landholdings, the assessment and levying of taxes, and army service, a host of new offices were established. The War Office (Diwan al-jaysh) now had two branches for recruitment and payment. The Office of Expenditure (Diwan al-nafaqat) dealt with requirements of the expanding court, covering salaries, provisions, supplies, contingency planning, and copying. The State Treasury (Diwan bayt al-mal) provided monthly (and later weekly) accounts to the vizier. The Board of Comparison (Diwan al-musadarin) made duplicate orders for payment. The Office of Correspondence (Diwan al-rasa'il or Diwan al-insha') wrote the caliph's letters and drew up documents and letters of appointment. The Post Office (Diwan al-barid) supervised the post roads and personnel, as well as a network of informants about conditions in the empire. The Cabinet (Diwan al-tawqi) received petitions, the Office of the

Signet (Diwan al-khatam) applied the caliph's seal to his orders, and the
Office of Letter Opening (Diwan al-fadd) received the caliph's official correspondence. The Caliphal Bank (Diwan al-ghibta) changed coins and received
fines, and the Office of Charity (Diwan al-birr wa'l-sadaqa) collected taxes!

Virtually none of the documents these offices produced has survived, but
vast quantities of writing materials were undoubtedly used. It is no surprise
that scarce Egyptian papyrus and expensive parchment were quickly replaced by
paper, which could be produced in virtually unlimited quantities anywhere.
Contemporary observers, however, ignored the triumph of paper. Like all
medieval Islamic historians, they were interested in recording the responsible
acts of particular individuals and not cultural and technological developments.

Only in retrospect did some perspicacious historians realize that something momentous had happened in the eighth century. One of the earliest was
the tenth-century Iraqi historian al-Jahshiyari, who was in a position to know,
for he had served as chamberlain to an Abbasid vizier and written a book on
the history of viziers and state secretaries in the Abbasid period. Al-Jahshiyari
noted that paper had been introduced during the reign of the caliph al-
Mansur (754–75), founder of Baghdad. The great Iraqi theologian Abu'l-
Hasan al-Mawardi (974–1058), quoted by the fifteenth-century Egyptian historian al-Maqrizi, ascribed the change to the famous caliph Harun al-Rashid.
Ibn Khaldun, the North African historian and philosopher (and one of al-
Maqrizi's teachers), was even more specific, indicating that the manufacture of
paper had been introduced by the Barmakid vizier al-Fadl ibn Yahya, who
served the caliph Harun, when insufficient parchment was available. "Thus,"
Ibn Khaldun wrote in his *Muqaddima* (Introduction [to the Study of History]),
"paper was used for government documents and diplomas. Afterwards, people
used paper in sheets for government and scholarly writings, and the manufacture [of paper] reached a considerable degree of excellence." Ibn Khaldun
neglected to mention an important reason why bureaucrats would have been
attracted to paper over parchment or papyrus: Because paper absorbs ink,
writing on it could not be erased easily. Paper documents were therefore far
more secure from forgery than those written on papyrus and parchment; from
them the writing could be erased by scraping or washing the surface.

Ibn Khaldun's association of paper with the Barmakid family of viziers is
intriguing, if unprovable. The charismatic Barmakids were descended from
the chief priest (*parmak*) of a large Buddhist temple at Balkh, capital of ancient
Bactria and now a city in northern Afghanistan. After the Arab conquest of
Central Asia, the family threw in their lot with the Arab conquerors, and
Khalid ibn Barmak (d. 781–82), apparently the first member of the family to
convert to Islam, served the first Abbasid caliph in the powerful role of admin-

MILLS

Three basic types of waterwheel were known in the medieval Muslim world: the undershot wheel, the overshot wheel, and the horizontal or Norse wheel. The undershot wheel is a paddle wheel mounted vertically on a horizontal axle; its power derives almost entirely from the velocity of the water flowing past it, and the power it produces is affected by both the water level and the rate of flow. Like the undershot wheel, the overshot wheel is also mounted vertically on a horizontal axle, but it has bucketlike compartments along the rim into which water is discharged from a reservoir above. Because the overshot wheel is unaffected by water level or rate of flow, it can be three times as efficient as the undershot wheel, but it is consid-

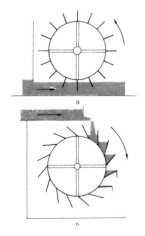

Undershot and overshot waterwheels

. . . continued

istrator of army and land-tax records. In spite of court intrigues, he remained in the administration, and his grandson, al-Fadl ibn Yahya, was foster brother to the future caliph Harun. The family revived interest in the literary masterpieces of Iran and India, as well as in various eastern philosophical and religious doctrines. Al-Fadl was appointed governor of the western provinces of Iran, then governor of the province of Khurasan, and eventually he was sent to pacify the region of Kabul. His successes and his family's notwithstanding, in early 803 the Barmakids fell into disfavor and disgrace. Several family members were executed, and their half-century of ascendancy was over. Their Central Asian and Buddhist antecedents, their experience in Khurasan, and their special interest in administration may well have familiarized them with paper and could have made them appreciative of its potential role for the burgeoning Abbasid bureaucracy.

Whatever the Barmakids' actual responsibility, Baghdad soon became a center of papermaking, and some considered paper made in Baghdad to be the best. Byzantine sources sometimes refer to paper as *bagdatixon,* which clearly refers to the city of Baghdad, but medieval Islamic sources mention many types and sizes, which can only rarely be identified or localized. The encyclopedist al-Nadim, for example, mentions Sulaymani paper (named after Sulayman, Harun's financial officer in Khurasan), Talhi (after Talha ibn Tahir, governor of Khurasan), Nuhi (after Nuh ibn Nasr, Samanid ruler of Transoxiana), Jafari (after Jafar ibn Yahya, one of the Barmakids), Tahiri (after Tahir ibn Abdallah, another governor of Khurasan), and Firawni (pharaoh-type, perhaps comparable to papyrus).

When papermaking flourished in Baghdad, stationery was big business. The Stationers' Market (Suq al-warraqin), in southwest Baghdad, was lined with more than one hundred shops selling paper and books. The population of the capital city would have provided a ready supply of rags, and its rivers and canals sufficient water, for papermaking. In the tenth century, ship-mills—floating mills powered by the flow of the current—were moored on the Tigris above the city, although the sources do not specify what product the mills processed, for example, grain or pulp.

Perhaps the earliest specimen of paper that can be associated with Baghdad is a ninth-century letter from the members of the Babylonian Jewish academy to their colleagues at Fustat, Egypt, now in the Cambridge University Library. The thick but unusually even paper suggests the proficiency of Baghdadi papermakers from an early date, as well as the availability of the material beyond the caliphal bureaucracy. Another specimen that can be associated with Baghdad is the small, 7-by-5-inch (17.5 by 13.5 centimeter) copy of the Koran that was prepared more than a century later by the noted calligrapher Ibn al-

Bawwab in 1000–1001. The paper, which has browned and stained with age, is thinner and more consistent than the letter paper, indicating not only that different qualities of paper were available but also that the finest available was used for transcribing the word of God (fig. 21).

The great Islamic theologian Ibn Hanbal (d. 855) is reported to have said that he preferred to write with "a reed pen, shining ink, and parchment," but by the middle of the ninth century—barely a century since Muslims had first encountered paper—many, if not most, lettered Muslims, as well as Christians and Jews, were using it for writing letters, keeping records, and copying liter-

FIG. 21. *Page from a copy of the Koran on paper transcribed by Ibn al-Bawwab in Baghdad, 1000–1001. Reproduced by kind permission of the Trustees of the Chester Beatty Library, Dublin [Is. 1431, fol. 286r]*

erably more expensive to install. When either type of vertical wheel is used to grind grain, a pair of gears is needed to transmit the energy to the millstones, which turn at right angles to the waterwheel.

Vertical wheels were known to the Roman architect, engineer, and writer Vitruvius in the first century B.C.E. They were most common in the Mediterranean region. Mills powered by undershot wheels were often mounted on the banks of swiftly moving streams and rivers and even in tidal pools. Some of the most famous are the huge norias in Hama, in Syria, which raise water from the Orontes River into aqueducts to irrigate the nearby fields.

Floating mills, a variant of the undershot wheel, were mounted in boats moored in rivers to take advantage of rapid currents. The Byzantine historian Procopius wrote that General Belisarius invented the floating mill when the Goths besieged Rome in 537 and cut the aqueducts. By the tenth century large ship-mills were moored along the banks of the Tigris and Euphrates Rivers between Mosul or Raqqa and Baghdad, but we do not know what they produced.

The horizontal wheel, in contrast, has propellers or scooped vanes radiating from a vertical axle that are driven by a jet of water directed from a reservoir. Some

. . . continued

say the horizontal wheel was a Greek invention, although the geographer Strabo wrote in the first century B.C.E. that the Parthian (Iranian) king Mithridates was the first to build such a mill, for the palace he erected in Asia Minor in the year 65. Archaeologists have discovered horizontal mills in the eastern Mediterranean region that date back to the fourth century C.E.

That the rotary energy of the horizontal wheel was in the same plane as the turning millstone meant that no gearing was needed, as for vertical mills. Horizontal mills enjoyed a further advantage, particularly in the eastern Islamic lands where they were most popular: they could run on the potential energy of slowly moving water gathered into tanks or reservoirs. Thus, they were perfectly suited to water coming from *qanats,* the underground aqueducts of Iran primarily used for irrigation, and many horizontal mills were built underground to operate in conjunction with qanat systems.

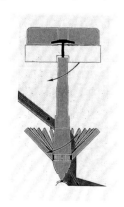

Horizontal waterwheel

ary and theological works. Byzantium itself was slow to adopt paper, but other Christian communities within and on the fringes of the Islamic empire were not. Syrian Christians used paper by the early ninth century, and Assyrian Christians in Egypt soon followed (although Egyptian Copts continued to use papyrus). Armenians used it by the tenth century—an extant manuscript is dated 961—and Georgians perhaps even earlier, although the oldest surviving Georgian manuscripts on paper date from the eleventh century.

All of these Christian communities appear to have been reluctant to use this material for copying Scripture. In this regard, Christians may only have been emulating Muslims and Jews, who continued to copy their scriptures on parchment. By the middle of the tenth century, although Jews held fast to copying their scriptures only on parchment, Muslims began to copy their Korans on paper, first in Iran and Iraq, much later in the western Islamic lands. By about the year 1000 paper appears to have been acceptable for all types of manuscripts, including the Koran, in Iraq, Iran, and Syria.

A book by the eleventh-century secretary Hilal al-Sabi, *Rusum dar al-khilafa* (The Rules and Regulations of the Caliphal Court), contains a chapter entitled "The Sheets of Paper [*turus*] Used in Writing to or from the Caliphs, the Envelopes Used to Hold Letters to or from Them, and the Seals Used in Them." In it Hilal describes the elaborate protocol surrounding the use of special paper for particular purposes. He specifies that Egyptian paper, for example, was used until the Fatimids took control of Egypt in the mid-tenth century. When this kind of paper was no longer imported into Iraq and became scarce, it was replaced by the wide Sulaymani paper. Such paper was used for letters of investiture and entitlement, as well as for correspondence between provincial governors and the caliph. But for letters from the caliph or petitions submitted to the vizier, half-size (*nisfi*) paper was preferred.

Over the following centuries, paper became finer and whiter, and the books made from it steadily larger, as we can see in manuscripts produced in Iraq. In contrast to the Koran penned by Ibn al-Bawwab, the celebrated copy of al-Hariri's *Maqamat,* probably made in Baghdad in 1237, is written and illustrated on whiter and larger (15 by 11 inch; 37 by 28 centimeter) pages, and a contemporary copy of the same text, now in St. Petersburg, which measures only half that size (10 by 7½ inches; 25 by 19 centimeters), is still larger than al-Bawwab's Koran. The pages of the dispersed twenty-volume manuscript of the *Kitab al-aghani* (Book of Songs) made at Mosul, Iraq, in the early thirteenth century are only slightly smaller, measuring 12 by 9 inches (30 by 22 centimeters). This trend toward larger paper in the last century of Abbasid rule continued in the late thirteenth and fourteenth centuries, when the Mongol dynasty of the Ilkhanids was ruling both Iraq and Iran.

A variety of sizes of paper were produced in Baghdad. The Egyptian historian al-Qalqashandi (d. 1418) enumerated nine sizes of paper, of which the two largest were the standard, full-sized Baghdadi sheet, measuring one (Egyptian linen) cubit (approximately 29 inches, or 73 centimeters) high by one and a half cubits (approximately 43 inches, or 110 centimeters) wide, and the reduced Baghdadi sheet (26 by 39 inches; 65 by 98 centimeters). The pages of an early fourteenth-century manuscript penned by Ahmad al-Suhrawardi measure approximately 20 by 28 inches (50 by 35 centimeters). This implies that they were folded from a sheet twice as large, or approximately 20 by 56 inches (50 by 70 centimeters)—in other words, about half the full-Baghdadi size. An even more magnificent manuscript made for the Ilkhanid sultan Uljaytu in 1306–7 was copied in thirty volumes, each averaging sixty-eight pages, with the pages having a trimmed size of 26 by 19 inches (66 by 48 centimeters). The two thousand pages would have measured 28 by 20 inches (70 by 50 centimeters) before trimming; they were folded from approximately one thousand full sheets measuring 28 by 39 inches (70 by 100 centimeters). This sheet size must be the "full Baghdadi" sheet mentioned in the sources.

The fine quality of Baghdad paper was celebrated despite the Mongols' reported destruction of the city in 1258. Nevertheless, as the city's fortunes ebbed in the following century, production of paper there declined. Al-Qalqashandi said that Baghdad paper (*waraq al-baghdadi*) had become rare by his time and was used exclusively for copying such important documents as treaties, acts of investiture, and writings from princes. At one time all princely correspondence had been written on this type of paper, and to keep it available, al-Qalqashandi said, a factory was established at Damascus that made an equally good product.

Al-Qalqashandi's judgment about the high quality of Baghdad paper is confirmed by a magnificent large manuscript of the Koran copied in Baghdad in 1307 for an anonymous patron by the noted calligrapher Ahmad al-Suhrawardi. The paper looks snowy white, smooth, and even, with a surface that allowed the calligrapher's pen to glide across it. Viewed under a microscope, the paper shows extremely well beaten long white fibers under a flawless size and glaze (fig. 22).

The art of papermaking died out centuries ago throughout most of the Islamic lands, and there is virtually no reliable evidence—apart from surviving sheets of paper themselves—about how paper was actually made. Nevertheless, papermakers must have found it extremely difficult to make excellent paper of a considerable size, particularly in large batches of even quality. Surviving manuscripts from earlier periods show that pages of such size were not made before the fourteenth century. Quite apart from the difficulties of preparing

MILLING

Most medieval Islamic watermills were used to grind grain, but other watermills crushed sugar cane and beat rags into pulp for papermaking. Sugarmills, used in those regions of Iran, Syria, Egypt, and Sicily where sugarcane was grown, relied on rotary motion, the kind used to grind grain. Rotary motion, however, would not transform rags into pulp suitable for papermaking. Rather, the rags had to be beaten in water with mechanical hammers, known as stampers. Unlike millstones, these mechanical hammers were activated by the conversion of the rotary motion of the millwheel—whether horizontal or vertical—into reciprocal motion by means of cams. Cams are projections attached to a rotating wheel or axle. When the wheel or axle was turned, the cam forced a trip-hammer (a pivoted arm) to lift; once the trip-hammer was raised, the cam released it, and gravity brought it down to do its work. The milling was done as the working end of the arm—in this case, a heavy wooden hammer—fell upon the wet rags. The cam was known as early as the first century, as we can tell from the inventions of Hero of Alexandria, but its practical applications did not flourish until medieval Europeans used trip-hammer mills for, among other things, transforming rags into paper pulp,

. . . continued

beating flax, fulling woolen cloth, hammering iron and copper, and making tanbark.

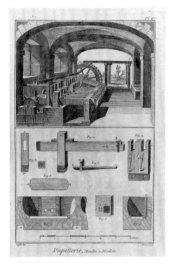

Cams and stampers in a papermill. From Denis Diderot and Jean d'Alembert, Encyclopédie (1765)

The history of the trip-hammer mill in the Islamic lands is largely a matter of speculation. Its prototype is the Chinese water-driven mill for husking rice, used from the first century C.E. and undoubtedly powered by a vertical waterwheel. The cultivation of rice had slowly spread from China and India to Iran and the Mediterranean region in pre-Islamic and Islamic times; by the tenth century there are numerous references to the cultivation of rice in Spain. In most of the Islamic lands, however, rice never enjoyed the popularity of other cereals, like wheat, sorghum, and barley,

. . . continued

FIG. 22. *Detail of figure 45, the colophon page from the "Anonymous" Baghdad Koran, showing the long fibers and smooth surface of the paper. The Metropolitan Museum of Art, New York*

appropriate molds and mold covers of fine grass or flax, plus horsehair—not to mention assembling sufficient quantities of pulp to assure reasonable consistency of quality—it would have taxed the physical ability of the strongest papermaker to repeatedly bend over to dip and lift a pulp-filled mold nearly a yard square without assistance and without spoiling the just-formed sheet. A mold that measured 28 by 39 by 1 inches (70 by 100 by 2 centimeters) would contain nearly 1,100 cubic inches (14,000 cubic centimeters) of water and pulp when full. This quantity would weigh nearly 31 pounds (14 kilograms), although the mold would quickly lighten as the water drained out. To get around the problem of weight, Chinese papermakers developed ways of making large sheets by attaching the mold to a system of counterweights, thereby making it easier for the papermaker to lift the mold repeatedly.

The speed with which the production of large sheets of paper resumed—indeed, increased—after the Mongols conquered Baghdad in 1258 suggests that the damage said to have been suffered by the city may have been overstated. Strong Mongol connections with China, however, may have encouraged Baghdadi papermakers to adopt Chinese techniques, such as the use of counterweights. We know, for example, that in the early fourteenth century the Ilkhanid vizier Rashid al-Din had Chinese papermakers working for him at Tabriz, in northwestern Iran. Whatever the technique used for producing such large sheets, however, the difficulty must have made them unusually expensive, even in prosperous times, and ample pages inscribed with only five lines of text would have connoted luxury as surely as did the majestic gold script and gold and lapis lazuli decoration.

The expense of even smaller sheets can be judged from a copy of the Koran transcribed by the famous calligrapher Yaqut al-Mustasimi in 1286. On one leaf of the 201-page manuscript, which measures 10 by 14 inches (24.5 by 34.5 centimeters), the calligrapher left out a single word in the twelfth verse, about

FIG. 23. *Manuscript of the Koran transcribed by Yaqut al-Mustasimi in 1286 with correction in left margin. Iran Bastan Museum, Tehran*

halfway down the page. Although neither the marginal rulings nor the illumination had yet been added, the calligrapher decided to insert the equivalent of an asterisk and write the missing word vertically in the left margin rather than recopy the text (fig. 23). Yaqut's great predecessor, Ibn al-Bawwab, had done much the same thing nearly three centuries earlier, when paper was theoretically much more expensive.

With the collapse of the Ilkhanid state in the 1330s, the market for such luxuries seems to have collapsed, and the papermakers of Baghdad were no

perhaps because in many places conditions were unsuitable for growing it. In the well-watered regions of southern Iraq and southwestern Iran, however, rice bread—made from ground rice—was the staple of the poor, and in many Islamic lands rice flour was used as a thickening agent for savory and sweet dishes in medieval cooking. Several medieval Arabic cookbooks describe rice dishes that resemble a pilaf; to make them grains of husked rice were boiled and steamed. The Chinese type of trip-hammer mill must have spread across Eurasia along with the cultivation of rice; otherwise, it would not have been practical to prepare dishes of husked rice. This type of mill is not attested in Iran before the seventeenth century, however.

The Iranian polymath al-Biruni, in discussing the extraction of gold from its ore, establishes unequivocally that water-driven trip-hammer mills existed in Samarqand in the late tenth and early eleventh centuries. He wrote that "gold can be united with the stone as if it is cast with it, so that it needs pounding. Rotary mills can pulverize it, but pounding it with trip-hammers is more correct and is a much more refined treatment. It is even said that this pounding makes it redder, which, if true, is rather strange and surprising. The trip-hammers are stones fitted to axles which are installed on

. . . continued

running water for pounding, as is the case in the pounding of flax for paper in Samarqand."

This crucial text shows not only that water-driven trip-hammer mills were used in Central Asia at virtually the same time that they first appear in western Europe (and centuries after they were first noted in China) but also—a crucial detail—that they were used for papermaking. It seems highly improbable that such a complex device could have been known in China, Central Asia, and western Europe and unknown in Iran and the Mediterranean Islamic lands where rice was grown. It is likely, therefore, that the water-driven trip-hammer mill spread through all the Islamic lands along with the cultivation of rice and the manufacture of paper.

longer called on to produce such large sheets. That several behemoth copies of the Koran were penned in either Damascus or Cairo in the third quarter of the fourteenth century suggests that some of these papermakers might have moved to Damascus, as al-Qalqashandi suggests, or even Cairo itself. The decline of Baghdad papermaking in the mid-fourteenth century may also explain why some Muslims were receptive to imported European paper. The earliest known manuscript of the Koran copied on European paper was produced just after the fall of the Ilkhanids, probably in Baghdad in the 1340s. It bears an Italian watermark of a double-key design surmounted by a cross (fig. 24). By the middle of the fourteenth century many Arabic, Persian, and Armenian books were being copied on Italian paper. Although it may not have been better than the local product, it was cheaper, particularly since Italian merchants seem to have been willing to sell it at an artificially low cost. Furthermore, the sack of Baghdad by Timur (r. 1370–1405), better known to the West as Tamerlane, in 1401 and the massacre of its population was a devastating blow to its culture, and, despite brief revivals under the Jalayirids and Turkmens in the fifteenth century, the city never regained its prestige. Iraqi papermaking had come to an end.

SYRIA

The Abbasid caliph Harun al-Rashid, who disliked Baghdad, established an alternative residence in the twin cities of Raqqa and Rafiqa, in northern Syria, on the middle Euphrates, in the late eighth century. The largest metropolis in all of Syria and northern Mesopotamia, and nearly as large as Baghdad, Raqqa remained Harun's base until his death in 809, when his successors retreated to the older capital in Iraq. While resident in Raqqa, Harun built enormous palaces and a huge city, which became not only the stage for world-changing political events but also the temporary military and administrative center of the vast Abbasid empire. It was from Raqqa, for example, that the Barmakids managed the empire's affairs, and to Raqqa that knowledge of paper and papermaking must have been brought from Mesopotamia at this time.

Syria's importance in the history of papermaking is confirmed indirectly by Byzantine sources, which called Arab paper *bambuxinon, bombuxinon, bambaxeron,* and sometimes, in late texts, *Bambaxeros kartis*. Nineteenth-century scholars thought the term *bambuxinon* referred to *bombax*, which means "cotton" or "silk" in Greek, and supposed that the Byzantines had been the first to invent a substitute for papyrus by making "bombycin" paper from raw cotton fiber. Although some cotton was grown in Syria during the Middle Ages, it was a relatively rare fiber in West Asia until modern times, and Julius Wiesner's analyses of early Islamic papers showed that cotton played an insignificant role in Islamic

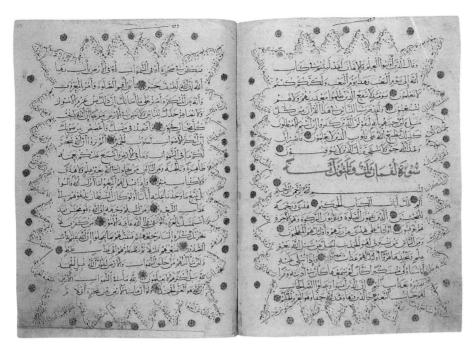

FIG. 24. *Manuscript of the Koran copied on European watermarked paper; the watermark is not visible in the photo. Iraq or Iran, c. 1340. The Nasser D. Khalili Collection of Islamic Art, London [QUR 561, fols. 72b–73a]*

papermaking. The few cotton fibers he found, like the occasional wool fibers, had been accidentally introduced in the ragbag from which the pulp was made.

The Greek word *bambuxinon* and its variants actually referred to the Syrian city of Manbij, which was known to the Byzantines as Bambyke, and the Greek expression referred to the paper's place of origin rather than the material of which it was made. Manbij, located in a fertile region on the Sajur River northwest of Raqqa, had an abundant supply of water, and paper seems to have been manufactured there at least from the tenth century. The Palestinian geographer al-Muqaddasi, who lived then, writes of paper being exported from Tiberias and Damascus as well; fine papers were associated with Syria for centuries. In the Latin West, paper was sometimes known as *charta damascena*.

From the ninth century geographers note the existence of papermills outside the walls of Damascus on a branch of the Barada River. Other papermills existed in the cities of Hama and Tripoli, but there were none in the major city of Aleppo, because no stream was strong enough to power the mills. Quantities of mass-produced Syrian paper were sent from Damascus to Egypt, particularly during the eleventh century. An Egyptian merchant is known to have put down a deposit of 250 dinars, a princely sum, for twenty-eight camelloads of paper bearing the trademark of a certain Ibn al-Imam of Damascus. The same trader is also known to have sent thirty bales of Damascus paper by sea via the port of Tyre. Because this was long before the invention of watermarks, the trademark must have been an extra leaf pasted to the bundles or rolls, much like the protocollon, the thicker sheet pasted to the beginning of papyrus rolls in antiquity and early Islamic times.

The oldest surviving manuscript written on Syrian paper is a Greek text, in the Vatican, of miscellaneous teachings of the church fathers, *Doctrina patrum* (fig. 25). On the basis of its script, the manuscript has been ascribed to Damascus in the early ninth century. The yellowish brown paper is remarkably smooth and even, despite the occasional clumps of fiber. The sheets, though flexible and soft, vary in thickness from one to another, suggesting that quality control was still a problem. The distinctive page size (10 by 6 inches; 26 by 15 centimeters) and narrow format of the manuscript show not that paper-makers used molds of that size but that the paper sheets were trimmed, probably to imitate the standard format of books written on papyrus.

A damaged bifolio (sheet folded once), roughly the same size, of brown-ish paper made from linen was discovered in Egypt and is now in the Oriental Institute, Chicago (fig. 26). It bears the beginning of the text of the *Thousand Nights*—the well-known collection of stories was originally known by that title— as well as several other phrases, texts, and a drawing. The arrangement of the writing indicates that the original sheet once formed the first pages of the ear-liest known manuscript of the *Thousand Nights*. The original manuscript fell apart, and the first four pages were used as scratch paper in October 879, when a cer-tain Ahmad ibn Mahfuz practiced copying legal phrases in the margins. Nabia Abbott, who first published the fragment, ascribed it on historical grounds to Syria in the first quarter of the ninth century, making it contemporary with the Greek text in the Vatican (of which she was apparently unaware) and making it as well the earliest surviving fragment of an Arabic book written on paper.

The oldest dated complete book in Arabic copied on paper that we know is a manuscript dating to 848, recently discovered by accident in the regional library of Alexandria, Egypt; it awaits complete publication. The second old-est surviving Arabic book on paper is generally believed to be a fragmentary copy of Abu Ubayd's work on unusual terms in the traditions of the Prophet, dated Dhu'l-Qada 252, or November–December 867 and preserved in Lei-den University Library (fig. 27). It bears no indication of where it was copied. The opaque stiff paper has turned dark brown and has a tendency to split along the edges. This feature has led some observers to suggest that the pages of early manuscripts were pasted together, back to back, from two separate sheets made in floating molds, which leave one side rougher than the other and unsuitable for writing. This tendency for the pages to split is actually a result of delami-nation, a condition seen in many early papers, such as the Vatican manuscript. When the pulp was not sufficiently beaten, the outer layers of the cellulose

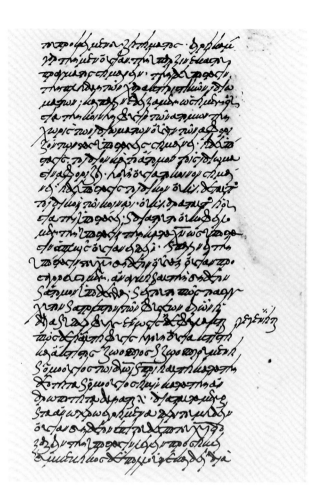

FIG. 25. *The Greek text of*
the Doctrina patrum, the earli-
est surviving manuscript on Arab
paper. Damascus, early 9th
century. 10½ x 6 in. (26.4 x 15
cm). Vatican Library [Gr. 2200]

FIG. 26. *Paper fragment from*
the 9th century, discovered in
Egypt, that contains the opening
text of the Thousand Nights *on*
the left. Folded dimensions 9½ x 5
in. (24 x 13 cm). Courtesy of the
Oriental Institute of the Univer-
sity of Chicago [no. 17618]

FIG. 27. *Manuscript of Abu Ubayd's* Gharaib
al-hadith, *the oldest Arabic manuscript on paper
in Europe, November–December 867. Legatum
Warnerianum, Leiden University Library*

fibers did not detach and form physical and chemical bonds with adjacent
microfibrils, and the resulting paper has weak internal cohesion. This condition was exacerbated when the paper was given a hard surface with the application of size. The weaker interior splits easily in two, revealing a rough, woolly,
and feltlike inner surface.

By the twelfth century, papermaking had become a major industry in
Syria, and paper was made in a range of sizes and weights. Perhaps the most
delicate was *waraq al-tayr* (bird paper), a thin, light sheet, which al-Qalqashandi
said was only three "fingers" wide (approximately 2½ inches; 6–7 centimeters)
and which was perhaps 3½ inches (9 centimeters) long. The ruler Nur al-Din ibn
Zangi used carrier pigeons for airmail service during the period of the Crusades, and this practice continued under the Mamluk sultans in the thirteenth
and fourteen centuries, when Syria and Egypt were governed as one. Pigeon stations were established in Syria a distance of three ordinary post stations apart.
A message was written on small sheets of this lightweight paper and attached to
one of the bird's rigid feathers in order not to disturb its flight. When the bird
arrived at a station, the dispatch was removed and tied to the wing of another
bird, and it was sent off to the next station. When the last pigeon arrived at the
sultan's palace, within the citadel of Cairo, an official would take the bird to
the head of the messenger service, who would remove the dispatch and read it.
In this way the sultan received daily reports from the provinces.

Papermakers were still active at Damascus in the thirteenth and fourteenth centuries, for the authors of several texts insist that papermakers be careful to keep their paper pure by not recycling papers on which sacred texts or names were written. This attitude is strikingly similar to Jewish concerns, as well the Chinese concern about toilet paper, and led to the preservation of many medieval documents in Cairo. What remained of the Syrian papermaking industry after the ravages of the plague in the middle of the fourteenth century and after economic mismanagement by the Mamluk governors and amirs seems to have collapsed after Timur sacked Damascus in 1401 and took its best artisans to Samarqand. At the same time Europeans began to export their own products to the Middle East in earnest, and Syrian papermakers could not stand up to the competition. The industry never revived.

IRAN AND CENTRAL ASIA

Although paper was introduced to the Islamic lands through Central Asia and Iran, little direct evidence survives for its use there in the first three or four centuries of Islam. The unparalleled prestige of Arabic, the language of Islam and of Iran's new Muslim rulers, put an end to Middle Persian, used under the Sasanian dynasty, as a written language, and New Persian, which was written in Arabic script, did not emerge as a literary language until about 1000. In the early twentieth century, Sir Marc Aurel Stein discovered a fragment of paper at Dandan Uiluq, in Chinese Turkestan, which had been inscribed in Judeo-Persian (Persian written in Hebrew characters) in the year 718. Otherwise, the oldest paper manuscript in the Persian language to survive is believed to be a copy made in 1055 of a treatise composed a century earlier by Muvaffaq ibn Ali of Herat.

Iranian scribes, however, used paper in the tenth century—and undoubtedly earlier—to copy manuscripts in Arabic. The oldest dated Koran manuscript on paper to survive was copied by Ali ibn Shadan al-Razi (whose name indicates that he came from Rayy, near modern Tehran) in 971–72, and the same calligrapher also copied an Arabic text some fifteen years later. Although there is no indication where this calligrapher worked, an anonymous calligrapher is known to have transcribed another copy of the Koran at Isfahan, in central Iran, in October–November 993 (fig. 28).

Medieval Persian authors mention papers of different qualities and types, as well as the professions and locations associated with papermaking. In the tenth century the Iraqi scholar al-Nadim had noted that the province of Khurasan was a center of papermaking, and the anonymous Persian author of the geographical work *Hudud al-alam* (The Regions of the World), written in 981–82, states that a monastery of Manichaeans in Samarqand made paper that was exported throughout the (Muslim) world. One eleventh-century

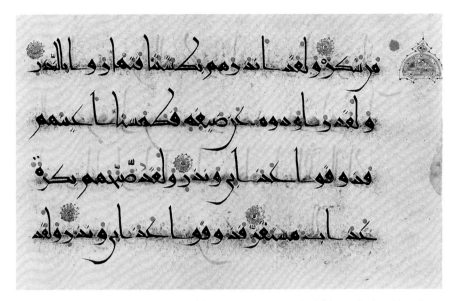

FIG. 28. *Page from a dispersed manuscript of the Koran on paper, copied in Isfahan in October–November 993. The Metropolitan Museum of Art, New York, Rogers Fund, 1940 (40.164.5r)*

Iranian source mentions that sheets of old manuscripts were used as linings for hats or as pasteboard for bookbindings, indicating that old paper remained a valuable commodity. By the eleventh century papermaking must have been common for the Persian poet Manuchihri to expect readers to understand a metaphor likening the snow-covered desert to ground covered with damp sheets of paper to dry: "The land from Balkh to Khavaran has become like the workshop of Samarqand / The doors, roof and walls of that workshop are like those of painters or paper-makers."

In the early fourteenth century Rashid al-Din, vizier to the Ilkhanid (Mongol) rulers of Iran and Iraq and one of the most powerful men of his time, is known to have established a *kaghaz-khana* (papermill) along a stream flowing through the grounds of the Shahristan-i Rashidi, the charitable foundation he established in a suburb of Tabriz. The paper, intended to supply the scriptorium that Rashid al-Din established there, was of the Baghdadi type and size, which is not surprising, because Baghdad was one of the Ilkhanids' winter capitals. In the endowment deed for the foundation, Rashid al-Din stipulated that the Korans copied in the scriptorium should be done on Baghdadi paper and that collections of hadith, or Prophetic traditions, should be copied "in the suitable format."

Rashid al-Din was also open to other aspects of papermaking. From information given in his treatise on agriculture, he is known to have brought Chinese artisans to work at his papermill. This is not as far-fetched as it sounds, for the Mongol domination of Iran had opened up easy communication across Central Asia. From the Chinese, Rashid al-Din learned about making paper from mulberry bark, writing on only one side of a sheet of paper, and wrapping many goods in paper. Mafarrukhi's late eleventh-century Arabic text about the wonders of the city of Isfahan, which was reworked in Persian in the fourteenth century, mentions that paper of the Rashidi type, presumably similar to that made for Rashid al-Din, was made in Isfahan, too. Mafarrukhi (or probably his anonymous translator) praises this paper, which was used for copying literary works and reviving the books of past scholars: "From the point of view of clarity of sheet, size and format, softness and cleanliness, firmness, evenness and sizing, paper of such quality does not, and did not, exist in any kingdom beyond Isfahan." It goes without saying that Mafarrukhi and his translator were natives of that city: chauvinism is a timeless trait.

FIG. 29. *"Noah's Ark," from Rashid al-Din's* Compendium of Chronicles, *fol. 285a.*
Tabriz, 1314. The Nasser D. Khalili Collection of Islamic Art, London [Ms. 727]

The profligate use of big sheets of paper was a prerogative of power. Both the sultan Uljaytu and his vizier Rashid al-Din consistently preferred that their scribes use high-quality paper in ostentatiously large sizes and quantities. In addition to ordering copies of the Koran and the hadith, the vizier ordered that every year the resident scribes should use large sheets of good Baghdadi paper to prepare copies of his own literary work, the *Jami al-tawarikh* (Compendium of Chronicles), in Arabic and Persian.

Several of Rashid al-Din's manuscripts survive. The single surviving volume, dated April 1315, from a thirty-volume Koran manuscript that he ordered made measures 21 by 14 inches (52 by 37 centimeters), approximately the same size as the one copied a decade earlier in Baghdad by Ahmad al-Suhrawardi and equivalent in size to the "half Baghdadi" sheet. The pages of the Arabic copy of the *Compendium of Chronicles* now measure 17 by 12 inches (43 by 30 centimeters), but the margins have been trimmed, perhaps by more than 1 ⅕ inches (3 centimeters) from each side (fig. 29). The original pages would then have measured at least 20 by 14 inches (50 by 36 centimeters), corresponding to sheets of the same half-Baghdadi size. The Persian version of the same text preserved in Istanbul was copied on pages measuring 22 by 15 inches (54–56 by 38–39 centimeters). The slightly larger dimensions suggest that the manuscript was rebound fewer times and consequently trimmed less. A copy of Rashid al-Din's theological works, *Majmua al-Rashidiyya,* originally measured 20 by 14 inches (50 by 37 centimeters), and an anthology of poetry associated with the Rashidiyya scriptorium was written on the same large sheets.

The preference for ostentatiously large sheets continued after Rashid al-Din was put to death in 1318. The pages of the Great Mongol *Shahnama* (Book of Kings) were similarly large; that book has been associated with the patronage of his son Ghiyath al-Din about two decades later at the revived Rashidiyya scriptorium (fig. 30). The manuscript has been extensively refurbished, and the margins have been replaced, probably in the nineteenth century; but because the text panels themselves measure 15 by 11 inches (40 by 29 centimeters), and original margins of 4 inches (10 centimeters) on at least three sides are not improbable, the original pages must have been at least of the half-Baghdadi size, if not somewhat larger.

The collapse of the Ilkhanids in mid-fourteenth-century Iran meant that, as in Iraq, there were few, if any, patrons still able or willing to commission manuscripts of such generous proportions; and some papermakers, along with calligraphers and other artists, probably migrated to such intellectual centers as Cairo and Damascus. Nevertheless, Iranian papermakers continued to produce fine, if smaller, sheets, or so we can judge from the paper used for illustrated manuscripts made in such provincial cities as Shiraz. Indeed,

FIG. 30. "Salm and Tur slay Iraj," from the Great Mongol Shahnama. Tabriz, c. 1335. Reproduced by kind permission of the Trustees of the Chester Beatty Library, Dublin [Pers. Ms. 111.3]

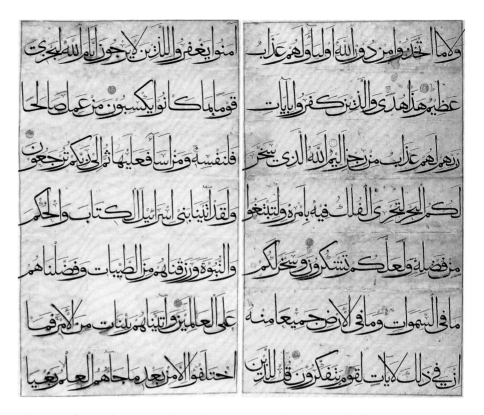

FIG. 31. *Two pages from a mammoth copy of the Koran, presumably commissioned by Timur for a mosque he built in Samarqand between 1399 and 1404. Art and History Trust, courtesy of the Arthur M. Sackler Gallery, Smithsonian Institution, Washington, D.C. [LTS1995.2.16.1, LTS1995.2.16.2]*

the quality of the paper appears to have gradually improved over the second half of the century.

Papermaking, as well as all the other arts of the book, was transformed after Timur began to re-create Genghis Khan's Mongol empire in the second half of the fourteenth century. Timur rapidly conquered Central Asia, Iran, Iraq, Syria, Anatolia, the Caucasus, and southern Russia, returning to his capital at Samarqand with not only immense wealth but also thousands of captured artisans. They were set the task of beautifying his capital. Among the greatest of Timur's projects just before his death was the construction of a colossal mosque in Samarqand, now known as the Mosque of Bibi Khanum. The mosque was larger than any in Central Asia, able to hold ten thousand worshipers, and it seems likely that it was Timur who commissioned for it the largest Koran manuscript ever produced in medieval Iran and Central Asia—and probably in the entire medieval Muslim world (fig. 31). Eventually it was displayed in the mosque on an enormous stone lectern, measuring more than 2 yards square and nearly as high, commissioned by Timur's grandson Ulughbeg.

On the basis of the surviving pages and fragments of this gargantuan manuscript, each page originally measured just over 7 by 5 feet (2.2 by 1.55 meters), or eight times larger than a full-Baghdadi sheet of paper. The gigantic size of the sheets required that the paper be heavier and stronger than usual, so that it would not tear when the leaves of the book were turned. Since the surviving pages have seven lines of text each, the complete Koranic text would have required approximately sixteen hundred sides, or 29,000 square feet (about 2,700 square meters) of paper—two-thirds of an acre.

Oddly, none of the surviving pages has any text on the back, which is unusually rough and unsuitable for calligraphy. The absence of text on the reverse, combined with the unusual thickness of the sheets, indicates not only that the papermakers had to make at least twice as much paper than if they had used the backs but also that they used a different technique. Had they used the normal technique of dipping two-piece molds of the appropriate size in a pulp-filled vat and removing the just-formed sheet from the mold, the mold would have had to be deeper to make the thicker sheet. If the mold was at least 2 inches (5 centimeters) deep to collect sufficient pulp, a reasonable assumption, the filled mold would have weighed nearly a staggering 390 pounds (172 kilograms). The papermakers must have resorted instead to the older process of ladling pulp into floating molds, which rested in a basin of water. Making the paper in this fashion would have required more molds, for each sheet of paper had to dry before it could be removed from the mold and a new sheet formed, but it obviated the need to dip and lift a pulp-filled mold of backbreaking weight. This process must have been the only one available in Samarqand that allowed papermakers to make the sheets of the colossal size the patron required. Although the paper of Samarqand had long been renowned, it is tempting to imagine that the papermakers responsible for this feat were Damascenes captured by Timur and brought back to his capital.

Chinese papermakers had developed a different technique for making extra-large sheets of paper by the tenth century, but these techniques do not seem to have been known in Ilkhanid Iran. And because Timur had not yet conquered China—he was just setting off on campaign when he suddenly died in early 1405—these techniques were not known in Samarqand. Su Yijian, the tenth-century author of the *Wen fang si pu,* the earliest Chinese treatise on paper and papermaking, described papermakers in Huizhou making a sheet of paper some 50 feet (17 meters) long. The hold of a ship was used as a vat, and fifty or so workers lifted the enormous mold in time to the beating of a drum. This paper was dried horizontally over a big brazier, instead of on the usual wall, to make the sheet even. The rough reverse sides of the leaves in the great Timurid Koran manuscript indicate that Timurid papermakers did not use this technique. Even had they known of it, it might not have suited their purposes, for

MOLDS

The first sheets of paper were probably formed using a floating mold—a woven cloth stretched on a wooden frame. To make paper this way, the mold is floated in a shallow vat of water, and the prepared pulp is poured into the mold. When the mold is lifted from the vat, the water drains slowly through the interstices of the cloth, leaving behind the fibers in a thin, moist mat. The entire mold, with its deposit of fibers, is placed in the sun to dry. When it is dry, the mat of fiber can be separated from the woven screen, whose faint regular impression is visible on one surface of the paper, and the mold can be used again.

Woman in western Nepal making paper with floating mold. From Silvie Turner, The Book of Fine Paper, pl. 13

. . . continued

Although a second type of mold, the dipping mold, seems to have been developed as early as the third century C.E., the floating mold continued to be used—and it is still used in parts of China and Southeast Asia. The eleventh-century North African prince Ibn Badis describes using a floating mold, although physical examination of contemporary paper from that region shows that the dipping mold was commonly used. The use of short fibers extracted from rags—rather than long ones extracted from bast—may explain the preference for the dipping mold in the Islamic lands and eventually Europe, presumably because of the different draining properties of the fibers. The use of one type of mold did not preclude the use of the other, and the floating mold might have been used where its special properties—for example, that the sheet had to be kept in the mold until it dried or that the mold did not need to be dipped and lifted—were no hindrance or were even an advantage. Indeed, the modern Fourdrinier papermaking machine is based on the technology of the floating mold, for the pulp is poured onto an endless screen belt through which the excess water drains away.

The invention of the dipping mold sped up papermaking because the just-formed sheet of paper could be removed from the

. . . continued

the Chinese mold was undoubtedly long and very narrow—ideal for making a long strip of paper to use in a roll but quite inappropriate for making a book in codex format.

Timur's mammoth Koran manuscript was still famous nearly two centuries after it was made, for the Safavid chronicler Qadi Ahmad was familiar with the manuscript and attributed it to the calligrapher Umar-i Aqta (Umar the Amputee), who had lost his right hand and wrote with his left: "He wrote a copy of the Koran in *ghubar* [minuscule] script: it was so small in size that it could be fitted under the socket of a signet ring. He presented it to the Lord of the Time, but as Umar had written the divine word in such tiny characters, Timur did not approve of it or accept it and did not deign to favor the calligrapher. Umar then wrote another copy, this time extremely large, each of its lines being a cubit or more in length. Having finished, decorated, and bound the manuscript, he tied it on a barrow and took it to the palace of the Lord of the Time. Hearing that, the sultan came out to meet him, accompanied by all the clergy, dignitaries, amirs, and pillars of the state, and rewarded the calligrapher with great honors, marks of respect, and endless favors."

Qadi Ahmad's amusing story notwithstanding, it is inconceivable that any Timurid calligrapher would—or could—have ordered thousands of such large sheets of paper on his own. Rather, the sheer magnitude of the project indicates that it was a royal commission from the start, requiring a substantial portion of the resources available even to the experienced papermakers of Samarqand. This great manuscript, however, apparently remained unique, for other patrons in the fifteenth century, though bibliophiles, chose not to emulate their ruler's example. Rather, they encouraged papermakers to produce sheets of more modest dimensions but of extremely high quality.

By the fifteenth century Iranian papermakers had perfected their art. They could make paper of virtually any size, strength, or texture, and calligraphers and painters appreciated the qualities of the different papers they used in producing some of the most elegant and splendid manuscripts yet made anywhere in the Islamic lands. The years when Timur's successors ruled in Central Asia and Iran were the classical moment for the Persian arts of the book, as exquisite illustration was integrated into a harmonious ensemble of paper, calligraphy, illumination, and binding. Technical examination shows that papermakers were able to beat the pulp so thoroughly that the resulting paper had few visible fibers. The improved processing gradually allowed them to make thinner and finer sheets without any loss in strength. Although consistency between individual sheets was valued, calligraphers were still prepared to use papers of somewhat varying thickness in a single volume.

That the finest paper for calligraphy and painting should be thin, strong, and sized with rice starch was mentioned in Jamal-i Yazdi's encyclopedia *Far-rukhnama-i Jamali*, written centuries earlier, in 1184–85. In the thirteenth and fourteenth centuries, thanks to improvement in the quality of materials, calligraphers brought their art to new heights, developing scripts of breathtaking beauty. To create a smooth surface on which their reed pens could leave a flawless trail of ink, calligraphers preferred to glaze their paper by burnishing the already-sized surface with a hard, smooth stone. The eminent calligrapher Sultan-Ali Mashhadi (d. 1520) devoted several couplets of his treatise on calligraphy to sizing and glazing paper by hand:

ON SIZE PASTE

Prepare the size (*ahar*) from starch

Learn these words from an old man (repeating) ancient words

First make a paste, then pour in water,

Then boil this for a moment on a hot fire;

Then add to this starch some glue.

Strain [so that it is] neither too thin nor too thick,

Spread it on paper and see

That the paper should not move from its place;

When you are applying size to your paper

Moisten the paper slightly with water, carefully.

ON POLISHING PAPER

The paper must be polished so

That no creases appear in it.

The board for polishing should be wiped clean

With a strong hand, but neither hard, nor softly.

In addition to glazing, paper for calligraphy was often tinted. A taste for colored paper had long existed in the eastern Islamic lands. Simi Nishapuri, a librarian in the city of Meshed, in Iran, and an expert in the arts of the book in the fifteenth century, wrote, "It is better to give paper a slight tint because white is hard on the eyes and the master calligraphic specimens that have been observed have all been on tinted paper." Simi offered various recipes for dyes. For him, the most popular colors were reddish yellow, reddish orange (henna), lime green, pistachio, and buff. In the era before the discovery of chemical bleach, although papermakers were proud of being able to make very white paper, calligraphers seem to have preferred tinted paper, and the distinct tan or beige tone of many medieval Persian manuscripts may reflect that

sieve or strainer while still moist, and other sheets could be formed while the first sheet was dried. In some parts of the world, the moist sheet was placed vertically on a smooth wall to dry; in Europe, the wet sheets were normally or couched (pronounced "cooched")—interleaved with woolen felt—placed in a press, and squeezed of the remaining water. The damp sheets were then hung on lines to dry.

The dipping mold is a rectangular wooden frame. When the mold was large, supplementary ribs connecting the longer sides were sometimes added to give the mold dimensional stability and to keep it from warping. The edges of the mold (and ribs) supported the sieve, which might be made of grass or strips of rounded bamboo laid side by side. Whatever the material, the strips were fastened together at regular intervals with strings of silk, flax, or animal hair. In some of the Islamic lands where bamboo was not available, the screen may have been made of flax fibers stiffened and strengthened by being boiled in oil, but fiber screens tended to sag with use and eventually resulted in an uneven sheet. Once Europeans had sufficiently developed the technology of drawing fine wire, the screen was normally woven from bronze wire, which would not rust from continued exposure to water.

. . . *continued*

The modern paper mold consists of a fine screen laid on a frame and surmounted by a second, removable frame. The second frame, called a deckle, helps to regulate the amount of fiber collected on the screen. The two-part mold is introduced vertically into the vat containing the pulp and brought up horizontally, allowing it to fill with a measured amount of fiber and water. The water drains through the screen, leaving a mat of fiber. Because the screen is both smooth and firm, once the deckle is removed, the moist fiber mat can be released, the sheet of paper laid to dry, and the entire mold reused immediately.

Japanese papermaking mold. The deckle is hinged to the ribbed mold and holds the bamboo screen in place. From Sophie Dawson, The Art and Craft of Paper-making, *p. 20*

taste rather than the unwanted effects of age. Surviving manuscripts from the fifteenth and sixteenth centuries include papers in a broad range of colors, including blue, pink, salmon, and pale green, in addition to the more common tans and beiges.

Many Persian calligraphers considered the finest paper to be Chinese (*khitai*). Already in the tenth century, Ibn al-Nadim had met a bibliophile who collected Chinese paper. The fourteenth-century litterateur and chancellery scribe Hindushah Nakhchivani mentions sixty sheets of "Chinese" paper among a list of gifts included in the collection of private and official letters that he compiled for the Jalayirid ruler Uvays. The calligrapher Sultan-Ali Mashhadi thought Chinese paper the best for quality and color, and this sentiment was repeated by several contemporary and later poets.

Just as *Baghdadi* became a generic term for fine and large sheets in the fourteenth century, the term *Chinese* may have taken on a generic meaning as well. Still, Chinese paper was expensive; some idea of its value is given in a document bearing the name of Sultan Husayn Mirza, ruler of Herat in the late fifteenth century. The document contains estimates of the expense of copying a manuscript of the *Shahnama*: 42,450 dinars, of which 12,000 dinars (28 percent) went for "Chinese" paper at 20 dinars a page. Some 15,570 dinars (37 percent) was paid to the calligrapher, who got 250 dinars for copying every thousand couplets. The rest of the money went to illuminators, marginators (people who drew the margins), and painters. The exact figures cannot be trusted because the document is probably a forgery intended to increase the value of the manuscript when it was resold in the sixteenth century, but the relative percentages must have been reasonable enough to fool the contemporary eye. That paper accounted for 28 percent of the total cost indicates that the material was still far more expensive than it is today, when the cost of paper is usually a small fraction of the total cost of producing a book.

Chinese paper was made from fibers entirely different from those used in Iran, and it was given a much softer finish because it was prepared for writing with soft brushes, not reed pens. Not only was it valued for its fine quality, but it was also prized for the various decorative treatments that Chinese paper-makers had developed over the centuries, including dying, marbling, and sprinkling and painting it with gold. Some of these techniques appear in the oldest surviving examples of identifiably Chinese paper used in a Persian manuscript: two volumes of the poetry of Farid al-Din Attar, prepared in Herat in 1438 for the library of the Timurid ruler Shahrukh. The manuscripts were copied on sheets of thin Chinese paper tinted various colors, sprinkled with gold flecks, and painted with gold designs. Another manuscript, a small copy of Mir-Haydar Khwarazmi's *Makhzan al-asrar* (Treasury of Secrets), was copied in Tabriz in 1478 by the calligrapher Sultan-Ali Qaini on sheets cut from two Chinese rolls. Careful examination of the manuscript has allowed scholars to reconstruct the rolls from which the sheets were cut. Both rolls measured 17 inches (44 centimeters) wide, but one was twice as long as the other (110 versus 57 inches; 280 versus 144 centimeters). The paper, dyed light blue, had been sprinkled with gold flecks and painted in gold with flowers and birds, as well as landscapes (fig. 32). Presumably the Persian calligrapher had to size the Chinese papers with starch before writing the Persian verses on them with reed pens, unless starch had already been used to make the gold adhere.

Such decorated Chinese papers had probably been brought to Iran as gifts from the numerous embassies exchanged between Timur and his successors and the Ming emperors of China. One caravan of merchants from the Timurid lands arrived in Nanjing in 1413 bearing presents for the Yongle emperor. The emperor sent a return mission to Samarqand, which arrived in 1414, bearing gifts of plain and patterned silk. Persian sources mention another Chinese embassy arriving in 1417 bearing gifts of falcons, brocades, porcelains, and paper.

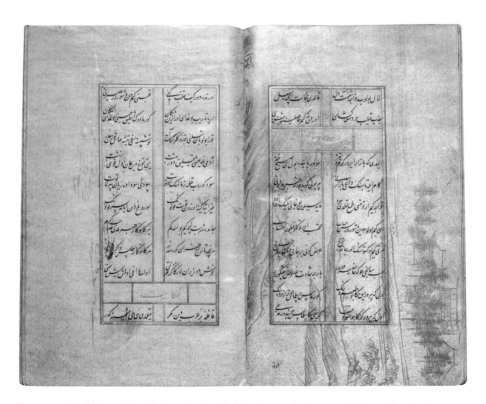

FIG. 32. *Blue Chinese paper with decoration in gold of* Landscape of a River and Hills *and* Two Birds in a Flowering Tree. *Inscribed in* nastaliq *script by Sultan-Ali Qaini with Haydar's Chaghatai poem* Makhzan al-asrar. *Tabriz, 1478. Spencer Collection, The New York Public Library, Astor, Lenox and Tilden Foundation [Pers. Ms. 41, fols. 21b, 22a]*

Iranian artisans soon developed their own techniques for speckling and painting paper with gold (*zarafshan*), and this technique became very common when collectors developed a taste for binding together specimens of calligraphy —and eventually paintings—in albums. The specimens of various sizes were mounted on standard-size sheets of fancy paper before being bound together in books. Several medieval writers give directions for decorating paper with speckles in sizes ranging from "dust" to "coarse." The paper was first starched and then sprinkled with gold particles—made by grinding pure gold leaf— using either a horsehair brush or sieves of this or that degree of fineness, depending on the effect desired. Next, the paper was burnished with a hard stone to make the gold adhere and develop its metallic luster. Simi also gives recipes for making suspensions of gold, silver, bronze, and copper to paint on decorative papers.

Marbling was another Chinese technique adopted and developed by Persian artisans, and marbled papers were used in the same ways as gold-sprinkled ones. As early as the tenth century Chinese artisans had developed various ways for decorating paper with mottled or marbled designs, to which they gave such colorful names as "fish-eggs notepaper" and "drifting sand notepaper." Although no early examples of these papers are known to survive in Iran, they were probably brought to the Timurids as gifts, for it is at that time that Iranian artisans first developed their own techniques for achieving similar effects. They called this paper *kaghaz-i abri* ("clouded" or "variegated" paper).

The Persian marbling technique was based on suspending ground colors in a medium lighter than water, normally oil. A vat large enough to hold the sheets of paper was filled with water that had been thickened with a mucilaginous substance. The colors were gently poured or dropped at random or in a desired pattern onto the surface of the thickened water, and a sheet of prepared paper was laid carefully down. The designs could be infinitely modified with the help of rods or combs to manipulate the colors. At first the effects were simple, but the colors and patterns became increasingly complicated. From Iran the technique of marbling spread to India, the Ottoman Empire (where it is known as *ebru*), and eventually Europe, where it enjoyed enormous vogue, particularly in the nineteenth century.

Iranian papermaking improved remarkably in quality, size, and decoration between the thirteenth century and the sixteenth. Before then, books written on paper had been relatively small, having likely been made from small sheets. (Before the advent of printing, there would have been no economic advantage to making large sheets of paper and then cutting them up into small pages.) In addition, the older papers are thicker, softer, and more floccular (a technical term meaning "fluffy") and have relatively poor internal cohesion.

They are usually brownish or tan, not from intentional tinting but from the difficulty of bleaching the fibers. Over the course of the twelfth and thirteenth centuries, papers from the eastern Islamic lands became distinctly whiter and finer, and they were, or could be, manufactured in larger sizes. The best-quality paper of the fourteenth and fifteenth centuries is thinner and stronger and, for the finest calligraphy and painting, was normally glazed. By the fifteenth century, the papers used in Iranian books were better than ever before: they were thin, strong, very smooth, and highly polished, allowing artists to use them for exquisitely delicate calligraphy, illumination, and painting characteristic of the period.

Although some of these technical improvements resulted from Persian papermakers perfecting their own techniques, the markedly improved quality of paper in the eastern Islamic lands during this period must have been due to direct and repeated contacts with China following the integration of Iran into the Mongol sphere of influence. Chinese paper and papermakers had played little or no part in the introduction of papermaking in the Islamic lands in the eighth century, but they apparently played a far greater role from the thirteenth century on as papermakers and artists became familiar not only with specimens of Chinese paper but also with Chinese papermakers and their techniques. Chinese papermaking itself had improved dramatically between the eighth and thirteenth centuries, because printing, which the Chinese had invented in the eighth century, eventually led to an increased demand for paper. In response, Chinese papermakers developed more sophisticated methods of producing greater quantities. Iranian papermakers' contacts with China provided the impetus for them to improve their own products in terms of size, thinness, strength, and decoration.

The high standard of Iranian papermaking continued into the sixteenth century, as Safavid patrons continued their predecessors' interest in the arts of the book. By the eighteenth century, however, the industry had fallen on hard times, for the Indian paper industry provided stiff competition. A Safavid work on administration from 1725 or thereabouts specifies that the chancellery secretary received thirty reams of paper from Dawlatabad, in the western Deccan, which had become an important papermaking center. By the nineteenth century Russian papermills were also supplying Iran, and many old manuscripts were refurbished using machine-made Russian paper.

All told, the tradition of papermaking in greater Iran between the ninth and the seventeenth centuries was the longest of any in the Islamic lands, and papermaking there reached the most advanced levels. The papers made there, particularly from the late thirteenth century to the late sixteenth, were of extraordinarily high quality and—when necessary—of a large size, and the best papers of the fifteenth and sixteenth centuries, which were exceedingly smooth and strong and sometimes remarkably thin, played an essential role in the florescence of the decorated luxury book as the major art form there. The paper-based arts of calligraphy, ruling margins and columns, gold sprinkling, illumination, illustration, doublures (endpapers), and binding were symphonically combined: in the final works the exquisite whole was far greater than the sum of the beautifully made individual parts.

EGYPT

Paper had been introduced to Egypt from Syria in the ninth century, and it was manufactured there by the tenth. Although papyrus, which had been made in Egypt for more than four thousand years, was still being made in the early tenth century, the geographer Ibn Hawqal, who visited Egypt in 969, makes no mention of it as a writing material, and the geographer al-Muqaddasi, writing in 985–86, mentions paper as one of Egypt's products. The shift to paper is confirmed by archaeological evidence: during the archaeological season at Fustat (Old Cairo) in 1980, for example, 441 documents dating from 950–1050 were found; of them, 399 (90 percent) were on paper, 35 (8 percent) on parchment, and only 7 (2 percent) on papyrus. In 1216 a traveler to Egypt explicitly declared that the manufacture of papyrus was by then quite forgotten.

In contrast to other regions of the Islamic lands, where physical evidence for the early history of paper is lacking, Egypt's unusually dry climate, like western China's, has preserved an abundance—indeed, a plethora—of paper from medieval Islamic times. Twenty thousand paper fragments dating from the ninth to the fourteenth centuries were among the more than 100,000 papyrus and parchment documents found in excavations in the Fayyum in 1877–78. These documents were acquired by Archduke Rainer of Austria in 1884 for his papyrus collection and examined by Josef von Karabacek and Julius Wiesner at the end of the nineteenth century. The sheets, made almost entirely from linen rags, had all been made in molds and sized with starch to render them suitable for writing. According to Karabacek, the earliest dated paper was a letter of 874, although he claimed that two letters on paper could date from a century earlier—which is conceivable, if not very probable. It has been impossible to determine where the papers were manufactured or the letters composed; it seems likely that some of the early ones, like the *Thousand Nights* fragment in Chicago, were brought from Syria.

Nearly 300,000 more paper documents, including trousseau lists, commercial documents, and personal letters relating to the Jewish community and dating mainly from the mid-tenth century to the mid-thirteenth, were among the Geniza documents found in the Palestinian Synagogue in Fustat (fig. 33).

FIG. 33. *Geniza document on paper. Egypt, 1151. Freer Gallery of Art, Smithsonian Institution, Washington, D.C. [F1908.44—7]*

Largely written in Judeo-Arabic—the vernacular Arabic (Middle Arabic) spoken by all medieval Cairenes, which Jews wrote in Hebrew characters—the documents had been placed in the synagogue storeroom to await proper disposal by burial, because it is an article of Judaic belief that inscribed papers should not be desecrated if it is at all possible that they bear God's name. The storeroom and the papers it contained were forgotten until the nineteenth century, when their importance for medieval social and economic history began to be appreciated. A very few Geniza documents predate the year 1000, but there are hundreds, if not thousands, of dated or datable documents from almost every year between 1002 and 1266, after which use of the storeroom seems to have declined. Together the Geniza and Vienna documents are particularly important because—oddly enough—very few books survive from this period in Egypt, even though the libraries of the Fatimid caliphs, who ruled the country at this time, are known to have contained hundreds of thousands of books.

In contrast to the Vienna papers, in which paper and content alike have been scrutinized, the Geniza documents have been analyzed only for their literary and historical content. Nevertheless, their often precise dates and specific localization should allow scholars to understand better the development of the medieval paper industry and the varied uses of paper. A cursory

examination of some Geniza documents suggests some preliminary generalizations. We see various shades of beige and light brown, which indicates
incomplete bleaching of the fibers used for inexpensive papers, as well as natural discoloration over time. The rather spongy and floppy papers are somewhat cloudy (floccular) when held up against the light, a result of the fibers
from an incompletely beaten pulp clumping on the screen. One document,
dated 1084, contains a tiny fragment of woven cloth, which proves that the
pulp was made from rags.

Ibn Said, the Andalusian poet, historian, and geographer who visited
Egypt in the 1240s, remarked that papermills were confined to Fustat and not
found in Cairo itself; an ample supply of running water for the papermills
would have been available along the banks of the Nile in Fustat, but not in
Cairo itself, which was built on higher—and drier—ground. Papermills also
needed copious quantities of fiber. Flax (*Linum usitatissimum*) had been one of the
major agricultural products of Egypt since prehistoric times; it was valued not
only for its fiber but also for its seed, which was pressed for oil. Grain, however, had been the major crop in Pharaonic, Roman, and Byzantine times, for
the empires depended on the surplus grain provided by Egyptian farmers. In
Islamic times, the caliphs and their governors replaced wheat with flax as the
main cash crop of Egypt. The major industry of medieval Egypt thus became
the manufacture of linen textiles, and flax supplanted grain as the primary
Egyptian export, supplying the looms of North Africa, West Asia, and Europe.
This shortsighted policy led to food shortages and epidemics, which contemporary authors blamed on the Nile's failure to flood the fields rather than on
their rulers' mercenary policies.

Although paper can be made directly from the fibers of the flax plant,
making it out of waste fibers is easier—particularly rags and old paper, which
have already been processed and bleached in the sun. Some of the bundles of
paper and textile fragments excavated at Fustat in modern times may therefore
have been left by ragmen who had collected them for papermakers to recycle.
The 1980 excavations at Fustat, for example, yielded approximately three
thousand textile fragments, most found in refuse heaps near the top of the
mound and attributed to the eleventh century. Roughly 70 percent of the textiles found were relatively coarse undyed linens woven in a balanced plain
weave, representing the most common type of textile. About 12 percent were
linens dyed medium blue with indigo, and another 5 percent were striped,
checked, or plaid linens of blue and white. About 8 percent were heavy fabrics
of hemp or reed woven with undyed linen. The remaining 5 percent included
textiles of wool, silk, cotton, hemp, and reed. Virtually all but the wool and silk
would have been appropriate raw material for Fustat's paper mills. Micro-

scopic examination of medieval Islamic papers shows the occasional presence of colored fibers, often blue, probably from indigo-dyed rags or patterns that slipped into the paper miller's vats.

In addition to recycling rags from the living, Egyptian papermakers were said to make a coarse wrapping paper for grocers by recycling shrouds collected by graverobbers. The Iraqi scholar Abd al-Latif al-Baghdadi visited Cairo in the late twelfth century and reported that graverobbers there looted tombs for bodies wrapped in hempen winding-sheets, but the story sounds like something told by a tour guide to a gullible traveler. According to Abd al-Latif, the shrouds sometimes measured over one thousand ells long, which is clearly an exaggeration. The graverobbers, he said, removed the shrouds and sold the ones in good condition to the poor, who made garments from them; otherwise, they sold them to papermakers. Perhaps this ghoulish report inspired I. Augustus Stanwood, a nineteenth-century Maine papermaker, to make a coarse brown paper from the wrappings taken off mummies he imported for this purpose from Egypt.

As elsewhere, Egyptian paper was traded and used in different sizes. The court records from the Geniza documents are remarkably uniform in size, suggesting that Jews, like their Muslim counterparts, sometimes used specific sizes for specific purposes. Mostly, however, scribes cut paper to size, according to their needs, and very little of a sheet was left blank. S. D. Goitein, a scholar who devoted his entire life to the study of the Geniza documents, believed that this practice was partly aesthetic: he felt that medieval writers regarded blank space as an offense to the eye, so they filled the margins on the front of a sheet with writing before they turned it over. It seems equally likely that thriftiness played a role and that medieval writers regarded blank space as an offense to the pocket. Small pieces of paper were used (and reused) for important purposes: the typical Geniza order of payment measures half the size of a modern check (less than 3 by 3½ inches; 7.5 by 9 centimeters).

Large sheets of paper were available when necessary. One document, dated 1027, measures an unusual 28 ¾ inches (73 centimeters) long, apparently the full width of the original sheet. Others, such as a responsum (a nonbinding Jewish legal opinion equivalent to a Muslim *fatwa*) dated around 1000 and a document dated 1018, were written on long (up to a yard) but narrow (7½ by 28 inches; 19–35 centimeters) sheets pasted up from smaller pieces of paper. To prevent fraudulent additions or omissions, Geniza documents were normally written on only one sheet of paper. When multiple sheets had to be pasted together, the copyist arranged his writing so that a line straddled the join between two sheets, and sometimes a word like *emeth,* "truth," was written across the join. Muslim scribes did likewise, running the text or impressing a seal across the join to prevent forgery.

The varying sizes and generally coarse quality of the Geniza documents suggests that, as is true today, different qualities of paper were used for different purposes. Letters and comparable documents were not normally written on fine polished paper, which was undoubtedly more expensive because of the increased processing involved. People were sensitive to the variations in quality: one writer apologized for using inferior paper by saying he was unable to find better. Most Egyptian writing paper was neither heavily sized nor burnished, and this lack of processing can be seen by the way the paper soaked up ink. Some paper documents were inscribed twice, first with brown ink of a type normally used on parchment, then with a black (carbon) ink; the gall-based ink tended to eat through paper eventually, whereas the carbon ink did not.

Letters and bills found in the Geniza collection indicate that Egyptians exported their paper to North Africa, Yemen, and India. Syrian paper was imported into Egypt, and Egyptian paper was exported to Iraq. According to the Geniza documents, one Tunisian merchant ordered five thousand sheets of fine paper and one thousand of the *talhi* type, which was apparently made in Egypt. The Geniza correspondence of Ben Yiju, an eleventh-century Jewish trader from Tunisia resident in India, shows that the most important of his imports was paper; along the Malabar coast, as elsewhere in India, the most common writing material remained palm leaf, paper being rare and difficult to obtain. Once Ben Yiju moved to India, his Egyptian friends kept him well supplied with paper, including packages of it in virtually every shipment they sent to him from Aden. His friends normally sent him somewhere between twelve and thirty-six sheets at a time.

Like the Abbasid rulers of Baghdad, the Fatimid caliphs in Egypt used paper lavishly for their decrees and documents, but in Egypt, unlike Iraq, several decrees of the Fatimid period have survived intact. The documents, preserved in St. Catherine's Monastery in Sinai, are rolls measuring as much as 33 feet (10 meters) long; they vary between 8 and 18 inches (21 and 45 centimeters) wide. Each roll is composed of several sheets pasted end to end. In contrast to the densely written Geniza documents, these official decrees show a profligate use of space between the lines of writing (fig. 34). Wide spacing was characteristic of documents produced in the Fatimid and Abbasid chancelleries: the ability to waste so much expensive paper was a prerogative of power. Logically enough, letters and petitions submitted to the caliph were spaced "normally," without such expanses of blank paper between the lines.

Later letters and decrees from the Ayyubid and Mamluk chancelleries are also long, narrow, and widely spaced. A letter to the king of Aragon dated 29 January 1292, for example, is a long narrow strip (5 by 79 inches; 13 by 201.6 centimeters) pasted up from sheets of unsized, yellow hempen paper, each

FIG. 34. *Section of a decree
issued by the Fatimid caliph
al-Hafiz in 1134. Church of St.
John in the Balat, Istanbul. From
S. M. Stern,* Fatimid Decrees,
pl. 8

measuring 5 by 13 inches (13 by 32 centimeters). Six other letters from Egypt
in the Aragonese archives dating from 1292 to 1300 are also in the form of
long (maximum 79 inches; 200 centimeters), narrow (11 inches; 28 centimeters) scrolls, pasted up from similar sheets of paper 18–19 inches (46.5–48.5
centimeters) long. This format continued to be used under the Safavids and
Ottomans, but it was not followed farther afield, in North Africa or Spain,
where by the fourteenth and fifteenth centuries chancellery documents were
often crammed onto one sheet.

Paper was already cheaper than papyrus by the mid-ninth century in
Egypt, but it was still not cheap, and writing materials remained relatively
costly. In the late ninth century pages from discarded books, such as the *Thousand
Nights* fragment in Chicago, were used as scratch paper, and many of the other
scraps found in the Fustat dumps had been repeatedly reinscribed. This is not
surprising, given that paper at this stage was still an imported item, but even
after paper began to be manufactured in Egypt, it was still saved for reuse and
recycling. A Geniza fragment first inscribed on 26 April 987, for example, was
reinscribed nearly two centuries later, on 21 December 1085. According to one
tenth-century source, 125 sheets cost six and two-thirds dinars, a sum sufficient
to support a lower-middle-class family for more than three months. As in Iran,
old paper was used for stuffing and stiffening caps and other garments, and
sheets of old paper were pasted together to make cardboard for bookbindings.

Such practices continued well into modern times, according to a long but extremely revealing description by Ameen Rihani of how daily affairs were transacted in early twentieth-century Yemen. It is quoted by Nabia Abbott, in her book on the rise of the Arabic script, to make the point that Arabs were not "naturally fond" of recordkeeping. Although this idea now seems remarkably out-of-date, the anecdote serves to remind us how precious paper remained for centuries.

The economy of paper in the Imamdom reaches the sublime. Seldom one sees an envelope, seldom a full sheet of stationery—the scrap is the rule, and very rare is the exception. . . . Evidently the Imam Yahya, who won "a wealth" of guns and cannons from the Turks, turned their archives also into service. Books, coupons, petitions, documents of every sort, they have all been cut into scraps to be used in every department of the Government.

Only in foreign correspondence are envelopes and regular stationery used. But in the country, the Government itself has set the example—a Government without red tape, without pomp, without official affectation, without luxuries. A messenger brings you "a cigarette" [a document rolled up tight], which you find is from the Imam, and in his own hand. After reading it, you tear off the blank portion and write your reply upon it. Should you ever receive a communication in an envelope, you cut it up and use the inside part for correspondence, and should your correspondent be an intimate friend, and his message written on a slip as big as a visiting card, you write your answer in the blank space, though it be as small as a thumb-nail, and send it back to him. Waste is reprehensible; extravagance is condemned. This economy in paper teaches also an economy in words. Some of the petitions which the Imam receives from his subjects are not more than three or four lines. . . .

The Chamberlain Saiyed Ali Zabarah, who was visiting us one day, lingered a while to overhaul his papers. He took out of his bosom pocket about twenty little "cigarettes" and as many out of the folds of his turban, where he also sticks his fountain pen and his tooth brush. He then began to separate the white portion from the written, and tear up the latter. . . . One of the papers which Saiyed Ali showed me was a line from the Imam ordering him to pay 200 *reals* to a certain Government official. "Are you not going to destroy this too?" I asked. "If I pay two thousand reals," he said, as he tore it up, "no one will question." "But the Imam is likely to forget, and he will ask you to produce the order." "He forgets not," the Chamberlain replied, "and he questions not." "And does not the Government keep any records at all?" Saiyed Ali looked at me, while still destroying his own private and public documents, and said: "There is very little worth keeping." A soldier then came in with a message from the Imam, written on a scrap 3 inches square, and Saiyed Ali replied to it on a scrap not as big. His Eminence is laconic, and his officials, if they want to rise in his favour, try to emulate him. The standard model is the thumbnail note, with just enough blank space on the sides—the Imam is very fond of writing in circles—for the reply.

In fourteenth-century Egypt the use of paper still seems to have been associated with people of quality. According to Ibn Battuta, the Moroccan globe-trotter who visited Egypt in 1327, none might enter the city of Damietta without the governor's seal. Persons of repute had the seal stamped on a piece of paper, which they showed to the gatekeepers; all others had the seal stamped on their forearms.

In spite of the increasing availability of paper in medieval Egypt, other writing materials were still in demand. The Jews continued to use parchment for Torah scrolls, as did the Coptic Christians for their Gospel manuscripts. Book lists found among the Geniza documents and other surviving manuscripts show that Jews also used parchment for transcribing many other religious, scientific, and literary works. Certain types of documents, such as marriage contracts and bills of divorce and manumission, were normally written on parchment, as were the circular letters of religious authorities, which were meant to be handed around among a wide audience and needed to be especially durable. Among Muslims, documents such as marriage contracts were written not only on parchment but also on leather and silk. A particularly magnificent example on white silk survives from the reign of the Fatimid caliph al-Mustansir, in the eleventh century.

As in Ilkhanid Iran, the arts of the book flourished in Egypt during the fourteenth century, although most of the effort seems to have gone into making fine, large manuscripts of the Koran for the Mamluk rulers' pious and charitable foundations rather than illustrated books of epics and poetry. The Ilkhanid taste for large Koran manuscripts had been brought to Egypt, whose Mamluk rulers, despite waging nearly continuous war against the Mongol rulers of Iraq and Iran, emulated the latest styles of Iranian art. In 1304, the Mamluk sultan Baybars al-Jashangir commissioned a seven-volume manuscript of the Koran for the Sufi convent he was building in Cairo. Each volume has 155 folios and measures 12½ by 19 inches (32 by 48 centimeters), approximately the same size as the untrimmed half-Baghdadi pages used for the *Compendium of Chronicles.* According to a later source, the manuscript was actually written on Baghdadi paper; the calligrapher was Ibn al-Wahid, who had trained in Baghdad under Yaqut al-Mustasimi, and it was illuminated by three assistants. The unusually large size and multivolume format of the manuscript, as well as its splendid calligraphy and illumination, brought it to contemporary attention. As far as we know, the size and scale of the Baybars Koran were not immediately reproduced in Cairo, although in 1326 a Mamluk amir bequeathed the enormous thirty-part manuscript made for the Mongol sultan Uljaytu in 1313 to the amir's mausoleum in Cairo.

The production of large-format manuscripts reached its apogee in the Mamluk domains toward the middle of the fourteenth century under Sultan Hasan, his wife Khwand Baraka, and their son, al-Ashraf Shaban II. The manuscripts made under their patronage are all large, and some are huge, measuring approximately 20 by 27–30 inches (50 by 70–75 centimeters), the sheets being full-Baghdadi size and folded in half. The ability to order manuscripts of such dimensions was a prerogative of great wealth. For the incompetent Hasan the Black Death helped in realizing his dreams of glory, for the estates of those who died intestate passed to the government.

In Cairo the book crafts were localized near the Azhar mosque, the center of Cairene intellectual life. In the fifteenth century, according to the historians al-Maqrizi and al-Sakhawi, the stationers' market, *suq al-warraqin,* was near the madrasa, or theological college, founded by al-Malik al-Ashraf Barsbay. Al-Maqrizi also mentions a *khan al-wiraqa* (papermakers' warehouse) near the Bab al-Futuh, one of the gates of Cairo, but paper was probably not made on this spot, so far from the Nile. By the sixteenth century, according to the historian Ibn Iyas, the paper market was being used by textile merchants, a trenchant comment on the decline of the industry in Egypt.

Paper had always been relatively expensive in Egypt, but at the beginning of the fifteenth century, living costs rose considerably in the Mamluk realm, and customers found it difficult to afford good Syrian or Egyptian paper. They turned instead to Italian paper, made from linen rags, which had become increasingly available in the late Middle Ages. Egyptians had continued to produce great quantities of linen, but at the beginning of the fifteenth century, Egyptian habits of dress changed. The Egyptian textile industry was in the midst of a serious decline, largely as a result of depopulation following the Black Death, technological stagnation, and the Mamluks' mismanagement of the economy. Native Egyptian linen became increasingly expensive, and for the first time upper-class Muslims wore garments made from European woolen broadcloth, known as *jukh,* rather than from domestic linen. Euro-

peans were able to produce cheap woolen broadcloth not only because they had
access to English wool but also because they had adopted several technical
innovations, including the spinning wheel, the treadle loom, and the water-
powered fulling mill, which lowered the cost of production. The increased
availability of European woolens, combined with declining Egyptian demand
for linen, meant that fewer linen rags were available for Egyptian papermakers
to turn into paper. Thus Italian papermakers could flood the market, and
their paper was cheaper than the local product.

The Italian merchants who brought paper to Mamluk Egypt returned from
commercial ventures there with paper playing cards, which had been introduced to Egypt and Syria from Asia in the medieval period. Playing cards had
been used in China before the ninth century and had been disseminated over
much of Asia before the time of the Crusades. After merchants brought them
to Italy, they spread quickly throughout Europe. The oldest playing card
known from west of China is a fragment, decorated in black ink with blue, red,
and gold, said to have been found in the Fustat dumps. It is dated to the thirteenth century. Although only the right half of the card remains, it clearly represents the four of the suit of cups, or goblets (fig. 35). Although the paper is
fragile, it is probably an actual card, not just a design for one; before the
mechanical reproduction of designs, it would have made little sense to draw
and color a design from which to copy other hand-drawn designs. Because the

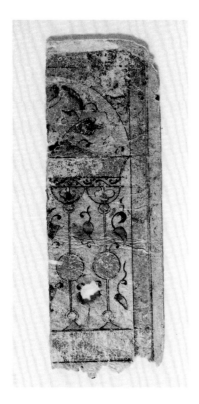

FIG. 35. *Fragment of a playing card (the four of
cups). Egypt, mid-13th century. Courtesy of the Keir
Collection, England [I.27]*

BODY LINEN

Habits of dress changed in many
parts of Europe during the thirteenth and fourteenth centuries as
linen became more widely used,
making greater quantities of linen
rags available to papermakers.
Europeans replaced their traditional woolen undergarments with
body linen not only because linen
was more comfortable to wear than
wool (it did not scratch) but also
because it was easier to wash, a
property that seems to have encouraged better personal hygiene and
improved health. Britons continued to wear woolen underwear
longer than elsewhere.

The wearing of linen was
encouraged by two late thirteenth-
or early fourteenth-century inventions. The first was a mechanical
flax breaker, perhaps invented in
Holland. Until the later Middle
Ages, flax fibers had to be separated
from the retted (soaked and fermented), dried flax stalks by
pounding them with a wooden mal-
let. With the new flax breaker—an
arrangement of two parallel wooden
planks standing on edge, with a
third plank pivoted between them—
a person could process greater
quantities of flax more quickly.

The second invention was the
spinning wheel, which sped up the
transformation of fiber into yarn.
Previously, all thread was spun by
hand with a spindle. The spinning
wheel, which was known throughout Asia, was probably invented in

. . . continued

fragment has nothing on its back, the sheet was probably intended to be (or once was) pasted to a stiffer backing of paperboard.

An almost-complete pack of hand-painted cards dating to the fifteenth century survives among the extraordinary collections of the Topkapi Palace Museum in Istanbul. As reconstructed, the pack consists of fifty-two cards in four suits: swords, polo sticks, cups, and coins. Each suit consists of numerals from one to ten, and court cards labeled *malik* (king), *naib malik* (deputy king), and *thani naib* (second deputy). This arrangement is virtually identical to the Italian variety of Latin-suited pack, and the early date of the Fustat fragment clinches the argument that cards arrived in Europe through Egypt. Furthermore, the Arabic word *naib,* or deputy, is the source of both the Italian word *naibbe* and the Spanish *naipes* for the "Game of Deputies."

Paper made in such Italian towns as Treviso and Fabriano was another of the European manufactured goods that Italian merchants traded for the Oriental spices and silk they bought in Cairo's bazaars. One Johann Lio claimed in a lawsuit against the widow of Lorenzo Bembo, his agent in Alexandria in 1412, that he had sent the deceased *carta da scriver* (writing paper); in 1417–19 the same man entrusted one Giacomo di Zorzo with the sale of a quantity of paper he had shipped to Alexandria. In 1441, according to another lawsuit, a certain Michiel Michiel claimed that he had sent the Venetian merchant Nicolo de Nani six bales containing sixty-eight reams of paper (a total of thirty-four thousand sheets) to be exchanged in Egypt for spices. European paper was also sent to Tripoli and other Syrian cities, where it was exchanged for native cotton. Good-quality European paper was initially more expensive than that produced locally in Syria or Egypt, but Italian merchants mostly exported cheap paper into those Muslim countries where paper was still produced; elsewhere, they also exported the better kinds. Given a choice, Muslim writers may have used these cheaper papers not for books and manuscripts, many of which have been preserved, but for notes, letters, and bills, which have largely disappeared. A contemporary Egyptian writer, al-Qalqashandi, claimed that the European paper imported into Egypt was "of the worst kind."

Some paper continued to be made in Egypt until the seventeenth century, but from the sixteenth century French and Italian papers were dominant there. The few dated documents in the Geniza collection from the second quarter of the sixteenth century, for example, are on European, rather than locally made, paper. By the eighteenth century the role of Cairo in the paper industry had declined considerably; now it was merely a redistribution point for the export of European paper to Arabia. In the seventeenth and eighteenth centuries, the stationers' market in the Ashrafiyya quarter sold almost exclusively European products. Nearby were the inkmakers (*habbirun*) and those in

India and came to Europe via the Middle East. It is mentioned around 1280 in a German regulation permitting wheel-spun yarn to be used in the warp—but not the weft—of textiles.

These two inventions increased the production of cloth and clothing, particularly the more economical linen. As more people wore linen, more linen rags became available to make paper; and as rags became cheaper, so did paper itself. Papermakers usually set up shop near urban centers to be close to the supply of rags, or near ports, where they could collect discarded linen sails and hempen ropes and nets to make paper.

the book trades (*kutubiyya*), including binders, bookcover makers, pasteboard makers, and booksellers. The seventeenth-century Ottoman traveler Evliya Chelebi mentions only thirty booksellers working in twenty bookshops, a sad testament to the mediocre level of intellectual life in Ottoman Cairo, as well as the decline of papermaking in Egypt.

THE MAGHRIB (NORTH AFRICA AND SPAIN)

Unlike all the other Islamic lands, writers in the Maghrib used parchment when elsewhere it had been abandoned in favor of paper. The major reason was that the provinces of Ifriqiya (corresponding to modern Tunisia) and Sicily were centers of sheep raising, and the manufacture of leather and parchment, as well as the export of hides, remained an important industry. The oldest surviving Maghribi Koran manuscript on paper is dated 1139–40, but scribes used parchment well into the fourteenth and even fifteenth centuries. Scribes also continued to use parchment for other types of manuscripts long after paper had become common elsewhere. For example, one Muhammad ibn Hakam ibn Said transcribed a copy of Abu Hatim al-Sijistani's *Kitab al-nakhl* (Book of the Palm) in a distinctive North African (Maghribi) script on twenty-seven small parchment folios; he completed his work on 26 March 1004, a date by which such a book produced elsewhere would have been copied on paper. Private letters and accounts sent from Tunisia found among the Geniza documents were written on parchment well into the middle of the eleventh century; Egyptian writers had made the transition to paper about a century earlier. Geniza documents also indicate that Tunisians got whatever paper they used from Egypt. Nevertheless, paper was known in North Africa perhaps as early as the ninth century, and papermaking was practiced there from the eleventh century, if not earlier.

Paradoxically, the only medieval account of Arab papermaking to survive anywhere is the eleventh-century treatise on bookmaking by the Zirid prince Tamim ibn al-Muizz ibn Badis, who ruled a small principality in northeast Algeria. He makes no mention of the preparation of parchment, although he does give recipes for making special colored inks to use on it. According to Ibn Badis, to make paper

you soak the best white flax repeatedly in water and quicklime, rub it with your hands, and then dry it in the sun until the plant stalks release the fibers. Next you soak the fibers in fresh water to rinse away the lime and then pound them in a mortar until they are very fine. You then dissolve the pulp in water and make it into sheets on molds. These are made from straw used for baskets, and nails, and the walls are col-

lapsible. Under it [the mold?] is an empty rib. The flax is beaten vig-
orously with the hand until it is mixed. Then it is spread with the hand
flat in the mold so that it will not be thick in one place and thin in
another. When it is evened out, it is [allowed to partly] dry properly
in its mold. When the desired [result] is attained, it is adjusted on a
flat tablet. Then it is bound to a wall and straightened with the hand.
It is left until it is dry, when it separates [from the wall] and falls off.

The rest of his description refers to the sizing of the paper with equal quantities of
chalk and starch, or with rice starch, and to dyeing paper different colors.

Taken as a whole, Ibn Badis's text is remarkably out-of-date, for he ne-
glects to mention the use of rags, which we know were added to the vat, and he
describes the floating screen, which most papermakers had long abandoned
except for special jobs. Because his text is the only one to survive on the subject, it has been treated with reverence, but the author's ignorance of basic
facts raises questions about the reliability of his information. In sum, Ibn
Badis's book is comparable to many medieval Islamic how-to manuals: long on
theory but short on practical advice.

The fourteenth-century writer Ibn Abi Zar reports that by the end of the
twelfth century, that is, during Ibn Badis's lifetime, the city of Fez, in
Morocco, had 472 papermills. Whatever the accuracy of the numbers, the
presence of papermills in Fez was encouraged by the swift stream that still flows
through the industrial center of the city, even now supplying dyers and tanners
with running water. Documents show that as late as the fourteenth century, Fez
shipped fine paper to Majorca and Aragon.

Nevertheless, as in Egypt, by the middle of the fourteenth century Maghribi
chancelleries began to use European papers. A letter dated 8 December 1350
from the sultan of Tunis to Peter IV of Aragon-Catalonia was written on paper
bearing a griffin watermark, a sign of European manufacture. Because watermarks had been invented in Italy in the late thirteenth century, the paper is
probably of Italian manufacture and would have been exported to Tunis in
trade. Genoese merchants, among others, had been resident in Tunis
throughout the thirteenth century, and the Pisan merchant Leonardo
Fibonacci had lived there before writing his treatise on Arabic numerals in
1202. Another paper document, dated 23 February 1360, is written on a sheet
bearing both a watermark and a zigzag, the distinctive mark of Spanish papers.
It was probably made in Italy especially for the North African or Catalan market.

Muslims were troubled about using these European products, some of
which bore images that conservatives found objectionable. In Tlemcen, a city
now in western Algeria, the noted jurisconsult Abu Abdallah ibn Marzuq

delivered a long fatwa, or legal decision, on 21 August 1409. Entitled *Taqrir al-dalil al-wadih al-malum ala jawaz al-naskh fi kaghid al-rum* (Decision . . . Concerning the Permissibility of Writing on Paper Made by Christians), it indicates that Italian paper had entirely supplanted local production by the beginning of the fifteenth century. According to the document, paper had once been made in Tlemcen, as well as in Fez and the Muslim regions of Spain, but no longer was. Pious Muslims were therefore forced to write on European paper bearing watermarks that they found offensive because the designs often contained a cross or an image of some living being. According to Ibn Marzuq's decision, which saw the problem in terms of ritual purity, writing in Arabic over the idolatrous designs rendered them invisible. Writing God's name (and message) on such papers, Ibn Marzuq argued, replaced falsehood with truth. The situation, he said, was comparable to transforming a Christian church into a mosque.

Paper had been introduced to the Iberian Peninsula in the tenth century, probably as a result of the trade described so vividly in the Cairo Geniza documents. The first Spaniard to mention paper was the Spanish Muslim poet and encyclopedist Ibn Abd Rabbih. In his encyclopedia *al-Iqd al-Farid* (The Unique Pearl), he discusses the different kinds of reed pens most suitable for writing on parchment, papyrus, and paper. Considering the time when he wrote—in the late ninth and early tenth century—he probably encountered paper on his pilgrimage to Mecca rather than in Spain itself. By the middle of the tenth century, however, substantial quantities of paper must have been available for the lexicographer Ibn Hani al-Andalusi to give his students paper on which to copy books from his private library. The library of the Umayyad caliph and bibliophile al-Hakam II was said, perhaps incredibly, to contain 400,000 volumes. Only one manuscript from al-Hakam's library is known to survive, a copy of the *Mukhtasar* (Summary) of Abu Musab Ahmad ibn Abi Bakr al-Zuhri, now in the library of the Qarawiyyin Mosque in Fez. It bears a note saying that it was copied by Husain ibn Yusuf in Shaban 359 (June–July 970).

As elsewhere in the Muslim world, religious affiliation was no impediment to using paper. The earliest Spanish Christian manuscript on paper is believed to be the Mozarabic Breviary and Missal in Silos, which has been dated on paleographic grounds to the second half of the tenth century. Of the 150 leaves, the last 38 are of strong and thick paper made from linen rags well sized with rice starch; the rest are of parchment. It seems that the scribe ran out of parchment and had to substitute what he considered an inferior material. The early thirteenth-century catalogue of the monastery's manuscripts refers to it as a Toledan missal on "rag parchment [*pergamino de trapos*]."

Papermills were established throughout the Iberian Peninsula in the eleventh century. The first specific mention of a papermill dates from 1056,

WATERMARKS

The unusually rapid development of the Italian paper industry in the second half of the thirteenth century is attested by a group of dated Greek manuscripts copied on paper made in Fabriano. As in Valencia, copper or brass wire came to replace the brittle bamboo or oiled flax from which molds were traditionally made in the Islamic lands. In Fabriano paper, the laid lines, left by the mold, became finer and more closely spaced, the pulp became increasingly well beaten, and the sheet became whiter. In the late thirteenth century, Italian papermakers also discovered that they could put faint watermarks, or papermarks, in the finished sheets. Scholars have now studied and catalogued thousands of these watermarks, allowing them to date watermarked paper with relative ease.

Watermark of a bunch of grapes on a copy of the forty-two-line Bible printed by Gutenberg. From Dard Hunter, Papermaking *(1947), fig. 217*

. . . continued

Watermarks on papers used along both shores of the Adriatic indicate their origin in or around Fabriano at the end of the thirteenth century. Watermarks—more properly called papermarks because they have little to do with water—are one of several technical developments credited to early Italian papermakers. Fabriano papermakers probably invented watermarks in the late thirteenth century, for the oldest example dates from 1282.

All papermakers knew that the mold left impressions on the finished paper, and even a few drops of water could leave unwanted blemishes on a finished sheet. Spanish papermakers had already used this knowledge to put zigzags in their sheets. Once molds were made of brass wire, papermakers realized that they could work a design in wire and attach it to the mold so that a faint impression would be left on the finished paper. These impressions might indicate who had made the paper and thereby serve as a sign of quality. In contrast, Muslim papermakers appear to have identified their paper by pasting some sort of trademark on the outside of a bundle. The earliest Italian watermarks were simple designs, for the wire would not allow much twisting into fancy shapes, but the designs grew fancier as finer wires became available.

when a certain Abu Masafya (or Mescufá) is reported as owning one "next to the old irrigation-channel" near the city of Shatiba (now Játiva or Xàtiva), located southwest of Valencia. Already in Roman times, the city of Saebtis had been famous for its fine linen cloth, which was woven from flax grown in fields irrigated by the many rivers flowing through the region. The same rivers provided abundant water for the preparation of flax fibers and, eventually, for powering papermills. Around 1150 the geographer al-Idrisi praised Shatiba for its magnificent paper, which was of a quality found nowhere else and which, he said, was exported to the East and the West. The paper, known by the generic term *shabti,* from the Arabic name of the town, was famed throughout the Mediterranean for its weight as well as its smooth and glazed finish.

In 1094, nearly forty years after Abu Masafya's mill at Shatiba is mentioned, his son Matumín fled Valencia to establish another papermill in Ruzafa. In 1085, the year in which Christian forces retook the city of Toledo, a "rag-paper mill" is mentioned there. Ibn Abdun, supervisor of markets for the Almoravids in Seville around 1100, noted in his manual of market regulations that "papermakers must make their paper somewhat larger and glaze it a bit more," which tells us not only that paper was made there at that time but also that papermakers, like many other artisans, tried to cut costs.

Spanish paper was well regarded, especially for copying books, and was exported throughout the Mediterranean. According to the Geniza correspondence of the twelfth-century Spanish Jewish poet Judah ha-Levy, he sent five hundred sheets of Toledan paper to his friend Halfon ben Nethanel in Egypt around 1125. Another letter in the Cairo Geniza collection, written from Granada in 1130, is on unusually white, strong, and "pleasantly smooth" paper—we can see why this Andalusian export was in wide demand.

As in Iran, colored papers were popular in the Maghrib. Ibn Badis gives recipes for dyeing paper in the eleventh century, and the Nasrid sultans of Granada used colored papers varying from red or vermilion to purple or pale pink for their correspondence. Known by the generic term of *nasri* after the dynasty, which presided over its export from the late thirteenth century, nasri sheets are smaller than Játiva paper, measuring approximately 11 by 14 inches (27 by 36 centimeters). Perhaps the most striking example of nasri paper in the Aragon archives is a blood-red paper made equally of linen and hemp, which bears a letter written in 1418 by Muhammad VIII of Granada to Alfonso V. It has been suggested that the vivid color was intended to symbolize the wrath of the writer, although the Nasrids and the kings of Aragon did not necessarily share a common language of color symbolism.

Considering the importance of paper in Islamic Spain, it is surprising that its history there, as in Egypt, must be reconstructed largely from official doc-

F I G . 36. *"The Woman speaking with the
Old Lady about Riyad, while Riyad is
stopped near the pool with blood pouring
from her face,"* from the romance Bayad
and Riyad. *Vatican Library [Vat. Ar. 368,
fol. 13r]*

uments rather than books. Whereas the lack of Egyptian books from the
Fatimid period remains something of a mystery, the absence of Spanish Arabic
manuscripts is a direct consequence of the *reconquista*. To eliminate all copies of
the Koran from the formerly Muslim areas of the peninsula once the Moors
were driven out, the Catholic church and state ordered the wholesale destruction
of all Arabic manuscripts. The book burners' success was virtually complete, and
the only manuscripts that survive are those carried to safer havens. Among the few
literary works to have survived the flames is the illustrated manuscript of the
romance *Bayad and Riyad,* probably produced in early thirteenth-century Seville.
The manuscript, copied on paper, measures 11 by 8 inches (28.2 by 20 centimeters). The first and last pages of the text are missing, but fourteen graceful illustrations in a unique style are preserved, and testify to the extraordinary richness of
the vanished culture of the book in Islamic Spain (fig. 36).

In sum, although paper had been used in Central Asia and Iran before it
was used in Iraq, the heartland of the empire, the decision by the Abbasid
bureaucracy in Iraq to use paper was instrumental in its acceptance everywhere
else. Iran, which at times encompassed parts of both Iraq and Central Asia,
remained at the forefront of paper technology, particularly as a result of
repeated contact with China in the later Middle Ages. On the other hand, the
Maghrib was initially slow to accept paper. Once it did, however, this was the
region that was ultimately responsible for the transfer of the technology to
Europe. But it transferred paper, not printing. It was bookmaking by hand
that reached a high art in the Islamic lands.

CHAPTER 3

Stories which were written had a higher status than those which continued to be transmitted orally. Remarkable stories deserved something better than oral transmission. That the story is so good that it must be written down is in fact a recurring topos in the *[Arabian] Nights*: "Your story must be written down in books, and read after you, age after age." Only writing guarantees survival, and writing makes the best claim on the attention of those who should marvel at or take warning from the stories. —ROBERT IRWIN, *The Arabian Nights*

Western historians have often argued that Islamic civilization made its greatest mistake in the fifteenth century when it refused to accept the printing press, for this failure supposedly condemned Islamic civilization to isolation from the mainstream of knowledge. Although Muslims did not use the printing press until the eighteenth century, and then only tentatively, they had other means of transmitting knowledge effectively and broadly, and for the preceding eight centuries the inhabitants of the Islamic lands—not only Muslims but Christians and Jews as well—controlled the sluicegates of the very same stream of knowledge at which thirsty Europeans repeatedly came to drink.

Bureaucratic necessity may have led Muslim officials to adopt paper, but the availability of paper in the Islamic lands also encouraged an efflorescence of books and written culture incomparably more brilliant than was known anywhere in Europe until the invention of printing with movable type in the fifteenth century. In spite of the absence of printing in the Islamic lands, the spread of written knowledge there was comparable to—and may have surpassed—the spread of written culture in China after large-scale printing developed there in the tenth century. Even with printing, Chinese books were published in relatively small editions of perhaps a hundred copies, a number easily attained by the unique system that Muslims developed for transmitting knowledge. The real distinction between all these cultures lay not in technology but in their attitude toward books and book learning, and ultimately in the different roles which they accorded writing and the written word.

The importance of writing in Islamic civilization is usually ascribed to the centrality of the Koran, revered as the revelation of God delivered in Arabic to the prophet Muhammad early in the seventh century of the Common Era. As Muslims brought Islam and the Koran to the lands they conquered, Arabic became the lingua franca from Spain to Central Asia, uniting vast populations in a single linguistic commonwealth. Even nonbelievers within the Muslim community used the Arabic language. The Jewish merchants of Egypt and North Africa spoke the same Arabic as their Muslim brethren, although they wrote it in Hebrew characters. The power of the Arabic script was so strong that eventually even linguistically unrelated languages spoken by those living under the banner of Islam, such as Persian and Turkish, came to be written in modified Arabic scripts.

The extensive use of Arabic writing is surely one of the most distinctive features of Islamic visual culture. Writing was used not only to create documents and books but also to decorate virtually everything from the humblest everyday object to the most sophisticated edifice (figs. 37–38). Few other cultures have elevated the art of writing to the position it occupies in Islam, and the ubiquity of writing in Islamic civilization suggests that medieval Muslims were more likely to be literate—or at least familiar with writing—than members of contemporary societies elsewhere.

Under Islamic rule Arabic, like Greek and Latin before it, quickly became a language of imperial administration, and the administrative bureaucracy that Muslim rulers created came to require vast quantities of writing materials—at first papyrus or parchment and then paper—for keeping records. Apart from caches of paper documents discovered in the Egyptian desert, the Cairo Geniza, the Monastery of St. Catherine, and the crown archives of Aragon,

FIG. 37. *Oil lamp inscribed ". . . do not extinguish and may the light be clear." Egypt, 8th–11th century. Molded and glazed earthenware, length 3 ¾ in. (9.8 cm). Benaki Museum, Athens [inv. no. 12275]*

FIG. 38. *Detail of Koranic inscription on the facade of the Taj Mahal, Agra, completed in 1647*

relatively few documents have survived from the period before about 1500, and the general picture of the history of writing in this era is normally sketched out from books rather than documents. Whether medieval Islamic civilization used more paper for documents or for books is impossible to say, but Islam certainly became a culture of books, particularly in comparison with Byzantium and western Europe at the time. One estimate, for example, is that 600,000 Arabic manuscript (hand-copied) books survive from the period before printing was introduced, and they must represent only a minute fraction of what was originally produced.

In Islamic societies the most important and venerable book was and remains the Koran, and consequently much of our knowledge of medieval Islamic writing and bookmaking is derived from manuscript copies of it. After the Koran was revealed orally to Muhammad, as tradition has it, the words were transcribed onto parchments and meticulously recopied to preserve the integrity of the initial revelation. Surviving Koran manuscripts, however, represent only one element in the entire range of medieval Islamic book production, for copies of the Koran were normally written with greater care and employed costlier materials than were used for most other books. Koran manuscripts were also more likely to have been treasured and preserved.

The extraordinary importance of writing in Islam combined with the primacy of the Koran as scripture has fostered an impression that Islam always was—and remains—a text-based culture. The importance of the written word in Islam is undeniable, but since the time of the revelation, Muslims have learned and experienced the Koran primarily as an oral text—not as a written one—and memory and gesture have persisted as equally important means for the transmission of Islamic culture, even if they have not always been recognized as such by Western scholars.

Current impressions of the past are also skewed by later reinterpretations. Early Muslims lived in an intellectually dynamic and fluid milieu, with many different communities of interpretation and schools of thought. The eventual success of the text-focused Sunni society that evolved under the patronage of the Abbasid caliphs of Baghdad in the ninth century has encouraged scholars to paint a monolithic picture of early Islam at variance with the evidence gleaned from other sources. Similarly, the text-focused, typographic nature of Middle Eastern culture today may lead us to overemphasize the textual aspects of Islamic culture over its oral and aural ones, particularly since most historical records—at least in the eyes of traditional historians—are written documents. Nevertheless, as documents, books, and other forms of graphic notation—all of which represented distinctly new ways of thinking—spread through Islamic society, the increased availability of paper encouraged the transition in medieval Islamic times from a culture based on memory and gesture to one grounded in the written record.

THE KORAN AND ORAL CULTURE

Pre-Islamic culture in Arabia was largely oral and aural, and although writing was known, it played a relatively unimportant role. The highest form of art was poetry, and the poet was often likened to a prophet or king. Poetry was the summit of Arabic eloquence, and the *qasida,* or ode, was the supreme verse form. Pre-Islamic Arabs spoke many dialects of Arabic, but every tribe used and understood the same poetic language, which was characterized by an extremely refined grammar and vocabulary. The poems celebrated the gods, their own social affairs, their exploits, including raids and battles, and their genealogies. Poems were usually short, especially in comparison to those of Homer or Chaucer, and were composed to be recited in public, either by the poet or by a professional reciter, who would add details and background. The idea that there was a single authentic version of a particular work did not exist, because poems were constantly reworked and embellished by the transmitters. Professional reciters relied on their prodigious memory, and the great pre-Islamic poems were not written down until several centuries after their composition.

Yet Arabs had used writing for centuries before Islam. In Yemen, archaeologists have found inscriptions in South Arabian script dating from long before the Common Era, and in northwest Arabia and Syria they have found Arabic inscriptions in other alphabets. A funerary inscription dated 328 from al-Namara, in Syria, contains Arabic words written in the Nabatean alphabet of Petra (now in Jordan), but the oldest examples of Arabic texts written in Arabic script are three brief historical inscriptions, dating between 512 and 568, found near Damascus and a trilingual one in Greek, Syriac, and Arabic found near Aleppo. For the Meccans, who engaged in long-distance trade before the rise of Islam, writing would have been essential to record debts and credits, control inventories, and instruct agents. Merchants would have used materials such as palm fronds, wood, bone, pottery, and stone for personal notes and jottings, but they would have found papyrus, parchment, or leather more suitable and durable for business correspondence. As mentioned earlier, the Jews and Christians of pre-Islamic Arabia would have copied their scriptures on parchments. Nevertheless, writing did not play a very important role in pre-Islamic Arabia.

God's first revelation to Muhammad (Koran 96.1–2) opens with the phrase "Recite (*iqra*) in the name of thy Lord," and reciting the words of this revelation has been a central part of Muslim worship from the beginning. Given the oral nature of pre-Islamic literature in Arabia and the oral nature of the revelation, the primary means of understanding, transmitting, and preserving the revelations was, naturally enough, aural and mnemonic. The very word *al-quran,* from which the English word Koran derives, is a verbal noun whose Arabic root basically means "to recite, read aloud." Contemporaries therefore conceived the revelations to be oral texts intended to be rehearsed and recited, not read from a book.

The desire to preserve the Koranic text intact eventually developed into a discipline known in Arabic as *ilm al-qiraat,* usually rendered as "science of readings." A more accurate rendering would be "science of recitations," for the discipline has remained fundamentally oral and mnemonic to the present day. Even when the Egyptian "standard edition" of the Koran was prepared in the 1920s, it was the oral tradition—supported by the literature on the science of recitation—that served as the authority for determining the written text. In this respect, Koran studies differ from Bible studies, which rely on compilation and comparison of manuscript evidence.

For modern literates, reading is a silent, wholly mental process, but until quite recently reading in all cultures was a vocal and physical activity. Reading aloud also gave nonliterates access to writing, and most literates preferred listening to a statement rather than perusing it in script. Medieval Arabic documents confirm the persistence of orality in medieval Islamic society. Four Egyptian documents dating from the tenth century—more than three centuries after the Koran was revealed—concern the sale of residential property from several villages in the Fayyum. The documents expressly state that the contract in question had been "read to the seller in Arabic and explained to him in the 'foreign language,'" meaning Coptic, the language of the Egyptian peasantry. The legal document was written, but the power of writing was activated only by reading it aloud.

In medieval Islamic society the written text, therefore, was not an end in itself but served primarily as an adjunct to memory. A modern Western scholar confronted with a page from a medieval copy of the Koran written in the angular "Kufic" script might puzzle out the individual letters and words to decipher the text (fig. 39). In contrast, a traditionally educated Muslim who had since childhood committed large blocks of the Koran to memory might be unfamiliar with the stylized script but would need to recognize only one group of letters to recognize the entire text. Indeed, the Koran is not normally read like normal prose, but is chanted or recited in techniques known in Arabic as *tilawa* and *tajwid,* which move between stylized speech and artistic singing. Koranic cantillation has always been transmitted orally from master to pupil, which has led to the evolution of innumerable personal and regional variations. Even in the twentieth century the clergy of the Azhar mosque in Cairo, the preeminent cen-

FIG. 39. *Page from a Koran manuscript in Kufic script, 9th century (?). Ink and gold on parchment. Freer Gallery of Art, Smithsonian Institution, Washington, D.C. [F1930.60]*

ter of Sunni religious opinion, remained opposed to transcribing cantillation into notation.

Recitation of the Koran is the backbone of Muslim education, and innumerable anecdotes recount how Muslims at all times and at all levels of society learned the Koran through oral transmission. The Abbasid caliph Harun al-Rashid made his son al-Mamun recite the Koran for the scholar al-Kisai. While al-Mamun recited, al-Kisai sat with his head bowed until al-Mamun made a mistake, whereupon the scholar raised his head and the young man corrected himself. Eleven centuries later, during the 1940s, the Moroccan sociologist Fatima Mernissi learned the Koran from her *lalla* (aunt) in much the same way. "For you see, most of the time, Lalla Tam did not bother to explain what the verses of the Koran meant. Instead, we copied them down into our *luha,* or tablet, on Thursdays, and learned them by heart on Saturdays, Sundays, Mondays, and Tuesdays. Each one of us would sit on our cushion, hold our *luha* on our lap, and read out loud, chanting back and forth until the words sank into our heads. Then on Wednesdays Lalla Tam would make us recite what we had learned. You had to put your *luha* on your lap, face down, and recite the verses from memory. If you did not make any mistakes, Lalla Tam would smile. But she rarely smiled when it was my turn."

As a book, the Koran runs about the length of the New Testament, and memorization of the text has always been an accomplishment of pride and status among Muslims. The *hafiz* (one who "knows by heart") might be young or old, male or female, a layperson or a scholar. The fourteenth-century Persian poet Shams al-Din Muhammad Shirazi, who is loved as perhaps the greatest lyric poet of all time, received a thorough classical education and by an early age had memorized the Koran. This feat earned him the nickname Hafez (*hafiz*), by which he is universally known. In all Islamic societies memorization of the Koran was assumed to be a prerequisite for higher learning. Consequently the training of memory was a constant feature of medieval Islamic education, in particular, which was based not only on knowledge of the Koran but also on reports of Muhammad's words and deeds (the hadith), as well as on the *sharia*—scholars' interpretations of the Koran and the hadith.

The typical hadith takes the form "I heard from so-and-so, who heard from so-and-so, who heard from so-and-so, that the Prophet did (or said) such-and-such," and consists of two parts, the chain of transmission (*isnad*) and the text itself (*matn*). At first, as the chain of transmission indicates, hadith were transmitted only orally, perhaps out of fear that written hadith might be confused with the Koran. From an early date, however, some scholars were driven to prepare critical written editions of the hadith because the texts (and the chains of transmission) were subject to pious falsification. Nevertheless, students had to memorize the hadith (and the accompanying chains of transmission), and repetition was the best way to commit texts to memory. Scholars regularly repeated memorized texts fifty, seventy, or one hundred times. The famous preacher and encyclopedist al-Khatib al-Baghdadi advised students to repeat to each other what they had learned in class and quiz each other on it. Once learned by heart, the lesson should be written down from memory, he said, the written record only serving as a reference when the student's memory failed.

People with prodigious memories were often the subject of popular anecdotes. The young poet al-Mutanabbi won a thirty-folio book written by al-Asmai by memorizing its contents after a single reading. The theologian al-Ghazali is reported to have been robbed of his books while traveling. When he cried out to the robber to take everything but leave him his books, the robber retorted, "How can you claim to *know* these books when by taking them, I deprive you of their contents?" Al-Ghazali took the theft as a warning from God and spent the next three years memorizing his notes. Such masters of the hadith as Ahmad ibn Hanbal, Bukhari, and Muslim were said to have memorized hundreds of thousands of traditions along with their accompanying chains of transmission. Abu Hanifa the Younger was able to quote hadith in support of any aspect of the law without reference to a book. Jurisconsults referred to him and based their opinions on what he said; in his day hadith were transmitted on his authority alone.

Even though Muslim scholars emphasized stocking and maintaining one's memory, from early times they also believed that writing had an important role to play in transmitting and preserving knowledge. Some scholars did, however, prefer oral transmission to written texts and produced prophetic traditions to support their views. Muhammad is reported to have said, for example, "Do not write anything about me except the Koran, and if anybody has written anything, he is to erase it." Mentions in early Arabic literature to *kutub,* which is the modern word for "books," certainly do not refer to books in a literary sense, but to "writings," notes or collections of sayings written down for the sake of accuracy. In later times books were deemed indispensable for refreshing one's memory, but learning a hadith from a book was still less authoritative than hearing it directly, even if it was read aloud from a book. One unusual account concerns the early philologist and lexicographer Ibn Durayd, who neither dictated hadith from a book nor recited them from memory. Instead, he would write them down from memory in his own hand and give his notes to his students for them to copy. When they had done so, he would tear up his copy and throw it away.

In his *Introduction to the Study of History,* the great fourteenth-century philosopher-historian Ibn Khaldun underscored the value of writing in Islamic society. He wrote that scholars and bureaucrats concentrated on accuracy in writing by establishing a chain of transmitters leading back to their writers and authors, because

that is the most important element in establishing a correct and accurate text. Statements are thus led back to those who made them, and decisions are led back to the persons who decided in accordance with them and were able to pronounce them by means of independent judgment. Wherever the correctness of a text is not established by a chain of transmitters going back to the person who wrote that particular text, the statement or decision in question cannot properly be ascribed to its (alleged author). This has been the procedure of scholars and experts in (all matters of religious knowledge) in all times, races, and regions, so much so that the usefulness of the craft connected with the transmission of traditions came to be restricted to this aspect (of the process of transmission). The main fruit of (the craft concerned with the transmission of traditions) is the knowledge of which traditions are "sound," which are "good" . . . etc.

Despite such concentration on accuracy and the obvious value of written documents, Islamic law developed an ambivalent attitude toward them. Two passages in the Koran (2:282 and 24:33) prescribe written documents for certain cases, but legal scholars usually interpreted these verses as only recommendations. In general, legal theorists ignored written documents and considered them merely aids to memory or evidence, but only insofar as they were confirmed by the verbal testimony of witnesses. Muslim jurists tended to view written documents with a generous measure of suspicion, primarily because the written word could be manipulated in a manner impossible with the oral testimony of trustworthy people; for instance, important clauses in a document could "accidentally" be torn away. Thus, in law the effective legal instrument remained the verbal agreement made in the presence of witnesses, who, when necessary, could reiterate and verify what they had seen. Still, the *qadi,* or judge, kept written records, and customary commercial law relied on written documents. They proved indispensable, theory aside, and remained in constant use, becoming a normal accompaniment of every important transaction and engendering a highly developed branch of practical law.

WRITTEN ARABIC

Writing played a central role in all the religions of West Asia from ancient times. For the Jews, the Torah, or written law, was imbued with God's sanctity to such an extent that even the slightest scrap of sacred text or text bearing a sacred name was treated with reverence. This attitude to the written word lies behind the preservation of the Dead Sea Scrolls and the Geniza documents. The Koran, despite the oral nature of its revelation, also asserts the authoritative nature of written documents. God's revelations to Moses are said to have been copied on sheets (*qirtas;* Koran 6:91); elsewhere (6:7) God says to Muhammad that even if he sent down sheets of writing for Muhammad's adversaries to hold and feel, they would still reject the revelation.

In several places the Koran refers to itself as *kitab,* "writing" or "book" (from the Arabic verb "to write"), and Muslims believe that the earthly Koran is a manifestation of God's heavenly scripture preserved for eternity. Just as God's first revelation to Muhammad emphasizes the importance of recitation, it also makes explicit the central role of writing, for the text continues:

> Recite in the name of thy Lord,
> Who taught by the pen,
> Taught man what he knew not. (Koran 96:3–5)

The pen, which is mentioned several times in the Koran, was, according to later commentators, either an actual reed or a metaphoric shaft of light. They reasoned that it had to be the first thing God created so that he could record events to come.

Muslims began to transcribe the revelations in order to forestall the corruption of the sacred text, a perpetual danger with oral transmission. The written text of the Koran may have initially served as a memory aid, but in all cultures documents tend rapidly to replace rather than to support memory, and a culture of writing emerged in the years immediately following Muhammad's death in 632.

It is said that only seventeen Meccans knew how to write in the time of the Prophet. Muslim tradition holds that Muhammad himself was illiterate, for Muslims understand the Koranic phrase *al-nabi al-ummi* to refer to the "unlettered Prophet." Following this interpretation, Muhammad would have repeated the revelations to his equally unlettered followers, who would have memorized the texts. Later secretaries would have transcribed the texts on materials ranging from palm fronds to potsherds and thin stones. Western Orientalists, however, usually interpret the same Koranic phrase somewhat differently and take it to mean the "Prophet of the common folk." They see no reason why Muhammad, who spent his early life as a merchant, should not have known how to write.

For fourteen centuries scholars have studied the text of the Koran, but they have found no great variety in the wording of the texts as preserved by one transmitter or another, although the early transmitters did not fix the order in which they arranged the revelations. Slight variations in readings and interpretations did result, however, from the ambiguities of the early Arabic script in which the text was transcribed. Arabic script, which is derived from either Nabatean or Syriac writing, uses only a cursive form—many of the letters are connected by ligatures—for all types of writing. Unlike many other scripts, Arabic cannot be written with the letters always separated from each other, as they are in "monumental" or "printed" Greek, Latin, Hebrew, Russian, or English. Because of the ligatures that allow some letters to be connected, the letters themselves may change their shape depending on their position in a word. Thus, the same letter can have one form when it stands alone, another at the beginning of a word, another in the middle of a word, and yet another at the end of a word. Because not all letters can connect, breaks in the *ductus*, or line of writing, can occur just as easily within a word as between words. Early writers did not differentiate the space between nonconnecting letters from that between words, and in texts spread over several lines, breaks occur as often between the letters of a word as between the words themselves. All of these peculiarities, which make reading extremely difficult and slow, indicate that all early Arabic texts were meant to be read aloud by readers who already had some expectation of their contents.

A further difficulty with the Arabic script is that it imperfectly represents the sounds in the Arabic language. The language has twenty-eight phonemes, or distinct sounds, but the script uses only eighteen characters to represent them. From an early date, however, extra strokes or marks were sometimes used to differentiate phonemes sharing the same letter shapes. The letters *ba, ta, tha, nun,* and *ya,* for example, share the generic letter shape, a single "tooth" in the *ductus,* but can be differentiated from each other by one, two, or three strokes or dots above or below the line. Like Hebrew, Arabic script records only the three long vowels; the three short vowels, silences, and case endings are normally interpolated by the reader from the context and form of the word. Nor did writers use punctuation marks until modern times. All of these characteristics made it extremely difficult to reconstruct a verbal utterance from a written text without knowing beforehand what the text says. Thus, transcriptions of the Koran could have served as memory aids only to those who had already memorized it.

The first complete transcriptions of the text may have been made in the time of Muhammad himself, but the third caliph Uthman (r. 644–56) ordered Muhammad's revelations collected and collated in order to produce a uniform written text. The revelations were transcribed onto sheets (*suhuf*) of equal size, presumably made of parchment, which were then gathered in codices (*mushaf*). Copies of this authoritative text were distributed to the congregational mosques in the major cities of the realm, where they were preserved as references. Since medieval times people have claimed that a few tattered parchment folios in one mosque or another are fragments of one of Uthman's codices, but none has been authenticated, and the dating of early manuscripts of the Koran remains a matter of lively scholarly debate. Putting aside these purportedly Uthmanic codices, the earliest date proposed for surviving fragments is the late seventh or early eighth century. Certainly, Koran manuscripts existed then, but the oldest securely dated or datable manuscripts were not produced until the ninth century.

The importance of Uthman's collation of the text should not be overestimated, because knowledge of the Koran still remained more a matter of memory than of reading. Even at best, a text written in the often ambiguous and "defective" Arabic script could have served as little more than a mnemonic device for people who had already committed it to memory. No seventh- or eighth-century manuscripts of the Koran are known to have survived, but somewhat later sources indicate that within decades of Muhammad's death scribes and calligraphers had regularized and modified the styles of handwriting current in Arabia for transcribing the Koranic text. In addition, the Umayyad caliph Abd al-Malik made Arabic the official language of the realm, and inscriptions and coins were produced in the new regularized script.

By the late seventh century the city of Medina was home to a group of pro-fessional calligraphers who produced fine copies of the Koran, although descriptions of their styles of writing are too vague to allow a reconstruction. Al-Nadim, who wrote his *Fihrist* in the late tenth century, records that a certain Khalid ibn Abu'l-Hayyaj was a calligrapher and epigrapher (a designer of inscriptions) for the Umayyad caliph al-Walid, who reigned in the early eighth century. Khalid was the first to calligraph the Koran, and he also designed the inscription with a Koranic text that once decorated the mihrab (the niche in the Mecca-facing wall) at the mosque of Medina.

Even if the exact nature of Khalid's calligraphy remains a mystery, some early Arabic inscriptions, such as those on coins and particularly the one encircling the interior of the Dome of the Rock in Jerusalem (692) show the impact of scribal techniques. As with later calligraphy, the text is written in groups of connected letters separated by spaces; isolated letters are treated as groups, being preceded and followed by spaces of the same width. Close exam-ination of the mosaic inscription band shows the varying width of the calligra-pher's ductus reflected in the varying width of the individual letters, which take from three to five or even six mosaic tesserae (cubes). Furthermore, some let-ters are stretched horizontally to fill the available space, showing an early use of *mashq,* the aesthetic principle of elongation (fig. 40). A calligrapher must have painted the inscription on the underlying plaster using a brush (a pen

FIG. 40. *Detail of the glass mosaic inscription band in the interior of the Dome of the Rock, Jerusalem, begun in 692*

FIG. 41. *Portion of a document recording receipt of payment. Egypt, 723. Black ink on papyrus. The Nasser D. Khalili Collection of Islamic Art, London [PPS 185]*

would not have been wide enough). The mosaicists, who were not necessarily literate and may very well have been Greek-speaking Christians used to decorating churches, would then have outlined the calligraphed letters in gold glass tesserae, filled in the outlines with more gold glass tesserae, and finally filled in the background with blue glass tesserae.

Early Arabic handwriting was quite different in style from the well-formed artistic writing used on buildings and coins (and presumably on Koran manuscripts as well), as we can tell from eighth-century papyrus documents found in Egypt (fig. 41). More spontaneous, the writing used on these documents reflects the specific situations in which the documents were produced. Most are private and commercial letters and accounts; only a few are literary or legal works. The few papyrus fragments bearing Koranic verses were personal anthologies of verses rather than copies of the complete text, which was always transcribed on parchment, at least until the tenth century. Nevertheless, whether documents or literary texts, the handwriting on Arabic papyri was a utilitarian cursive script markedly different from the artistic script used for Koran manuscripts and state documents.

The first manuscripts of the Koran that can be dated with some certainty were copied on horizontal-format ("landscape") parchments in one of several angular scripts, commonly called Kufic—a convenient, if modern, misnomer —during the mid-ninth century. These early scripts are characterized by relatively simple geometrical shapes, harmonious proportions, and wide spacing between groups of connected letters. Most early manuscripts of the Koran have a horizontal format, where the page is broader than it is tall, although a few are in vertical format. No contemporary source explains the scribal preference for the horizontal format, although modern scholars have often noted that the distinctive shape served visually to differentiate the scriptures of the Muslims from those of the Christians (who used vertical-format codices) and the Jews (who used horizontal rolls).

The remarkable conservatism of Koranic calligraphy in the first three centuries of Islam is shown by the copy of the text made for Amajur, governor of Damascus for the Abbasid caliphs between 870 and 878; this text provides one of the few fixed points for dating early Koran manuscripts (fig. 42). Originally comprising thirty volumes of perhaps two hundred parchment leaves each (a total requiring the skins of around three hundred sheep), the manuscript was endowed to a mosque in Tyre, Lebanon, in 875–76. The script shares many calligraphic features with the inscription on the Dome of the Rock done over 150 years earlier, such as the constant spacing between letter groups rather than words.

At the time this manuscript was produced, copyists were developing new scripts for different purposes. The earliest of these—known quite confusingly by such names as Qarmatian (or Karmathian) Kufic, broken Kufic, eastern Kufic, Kufic-*naskhi,* New Style, *warraq* (stationer's) script, or broken cursive— has an accentuated angular character and a deliberate contrast between thick and thin strokes; in some samples the script is quite vertical and elongated. Spaces between the nonconnecting letters of a word are differentiated from those between words, and the different letters sharing the same shape are distinguished from one another by diacritical points. In contrast to Kufic, which was used only for Koran manuscripts, this new script was used for a wide variety of texts, both secular and religious, Muslim and Christian, over an enormous geographical area, from the ninth century, as demonstrated by the Leiden *Gharaib al-hadith* (see fig. 27) to the early thirteenth.

Most scholars have attempted to explain the appearance of the new script as a logical outgrowth of earlier Kufic scripts used for copying the Koran. It seems much more likely, however, that it was developed by professional secretaries and copyists who regularized the cursive styles of handwriting they used for copying documents onto paper into a new and more legible script appropriate for copying books, now made of paper as well. The emergence of this

FIG. 42. *Page from a manu-script of the Koran copied for Amajur, Abbasid governor of Damascus, 870—78. Brown ink on parchment, 5 x 7 in. (12.7 x 19.3 cm). Türk ve Islam Eserleri Müzesi, Istanbul [inv. SE 5643]*

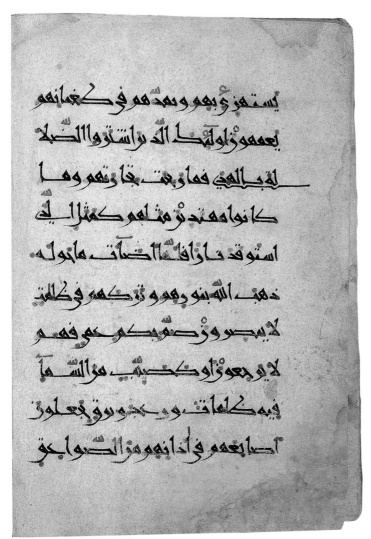

FIG. 43. *Page from a dispersed manuscript of the Koran copied on paper by Ali ibn Sadan al-Razi, 971—72. Black ink on paper, 10¼ x 7 in. (26 x 17.8 cm). Reproduced by kind permission of the Trustees of the Chester Beatty Library, Dublin [CBL Is. 1434, fol. 4b]*

new script can be linked, therefore, to the secretaries' familiarity with paper as the principal material for writing.

As the Abbasid empire had grown in the ninth century, the bureaucracy had burgeoned, and secretaries, known in Arabic as *kuttab* ("writers"), became important and powerful. Some, as officials and linguists, merely gave written documents the appropriate form, but others served as their masters' advisers and confidants and rose to positions of influence. In this bureaucratic world, official documents were increasingly judged not only by their contents but also by the elegance of the wording and the cleverness of hidden allusions in the text. Successful government secretaries had to be thoroughly grounded in Arabic grammar and vocabulary, familiar with proverbs and tales, widely read in all branches of prose and poetry, soundly informed about the theory of state and administration, impeccably versed in the Koran and the traditions of the Prophet, and knowledgeable of prosody and poetics. All of this knowledge had to be conveyed in an elegant hand, so the art of fine writing moved from the exclusive domain of Koran copyists and became a necessary part of state correspondence and documentation and the growing world of books.

This would explain why the broken cursive script was used for many other texts well before it was adopted for copying manuscripts of the Koran. Broken cursive, for example, is the script used for one of the earliest surviving books copied on paper in Arabic script, the fragment, dated 866, of Abu Ubayd's work on unusual terms in the traditions of the Prophet (see fig. 27). The script, with its system of spacing designed for easy reading and its pointed letters, was far more legible than Kufic. Legibility was of primary concern when copying literary texts, as opposed to the Koran, because the writer could not assume that the reader would already know their contents.

When calligraphers eventually used the new script to copy the Koran, they did so when they began to use paper instead of parchment for manuscripts of the holy text. The oldest dated Koran manuscript in broken cursive script is also the oldest dated copy on paper. Copied in 971–72 by the Persian calligrapher Ali ibn Shadan al-Razi, the four-volume manuscript is divided between Istanbul University Library, the shrine at Ardabil, Iran, and the Chester Beatty Library, Dublin (fig. 43). Fifteen years later, the same scribe copied a tenth-century secular text, *Kitab akhbar al-nasriyyin al-bahriyyin* by Abu'l-Said al-Hasan al-Sirafi, in a combination of the broken cursive and other more rounded scripts. Another paper manuscript of the Koran (see fig. 28) was copied in an elegant broken cursive script at Isfahan, Iran, in 993. The horizontal format of this manuscript, its large size (9½ by 13½ inches, or 23.9 by 33.8 centimeters—twice that of the previous manuscript), and the large size of the script—each page has only four lines 1½ inches (4 centimeters) high—are all more

FIG. 44. *Two pages from a manuscript of the Koran copied on parchment in broken cursive script. Palermo, 982–83. The Nasser D. Khalili Collection of Islamic Art, London [QUR 261, fols. 8b, 9a]*

commonly associated with parchment codices and show that by the end of the tenth century the new breed of calligraphers were learning some lessons from the conservative Koran copyists.

The advantages of this new script, which was legible and easy to write, made it widely popular among Christians as well as Muslims. They used it to copy the Gospels almost a century before the first extant paper Koran was copied at all— the evidence, a manuscript dated 897 preserved in the library of the Monastery of St. Catherine, Mount Sinai. Fragments from a horizontal-format parchment manuscript of the Koran copied at Palermo, Sicily, in 982–83 show how quickly the broken cursive script had reached the Mediterranean lands even in areas where parchment still held sway. The transitional character of this manuscript, however, is evident in the black carbon-based ink with which it was copied (fig. 44).

Black ink, prepared from lampblack bound with plant gum and known in Arabic as *midad,* was appropriate for use on papyrus, but it had notoriously poor adhesion to parchment and tended to flake off. Kufic manuscripts of the Koran were normally copied on parchment in the brownish ink known in Arabic as *hibr,* which was made from metal tannates prepared with gallnuts. The metal tannate ink actually penetrated the surface of the parchment like dye. When used on paper, however, the mixture of metal salts and tannins in tannate ink produced acids that eventually destroyed the paper. Carbon ink, by contrast, had no chemical effect on the surface to which it was applied; it was the type of ink secretary-copyists normally used on papyrus and paper. The Palermo manuscript, like most manuscripts in broken cursive script, was copied in carbon ink.

Secretary-copyists preparing Koran manuscripts in broken cursive script had no reason not to emulate and adapt certain attractive features of Korans written in archaic Kufic, such as material or format. The conservative Koran calligraphers never emulated the work of the copyists in turn, and there are no Kufic manuscripts of the Koran copied on paper, nor was carbon black ink normally used on parchment. As the brown tannin ink faded on some parchment Koran manuscripts, however, later calligraphers sometimes retouched the writing with carbon-black ink.

In sum, the development of the new broken cursive script went hand in hand with the adoption of paper and carbon-black ink. These three features encouraged the proliferation of books from the ninth century. Paper would have been cheaper and more widely available than parchment or papyrus. The carbon-based ink was easier to prepare and did not eat away at the underlying surface. Compared to the earlier Kufic scripts, the broken cursive script—apart from stylized variants used for the fanciest copies of the Koran and literary works—was relatively fluent and thus easier and faster to write.

Although broken cursive continued to be used for several centuries in particular situations, its success paved the way for the development of rounded styles of Arabic handwriting in the tenth century. Normally known as *naskh,* this group of related scripts remains common to the present day, being the type of script most familiar and legible to ordinary readers. Naskh was taken as the exemplar for modern Arabic typography. As with the broken cursive script, the origins of the rounded style are obscure, but tradition reports that the Abbasid secretary (and later vizier) Ibn Muqla introduced a new method of writing known as "proportioned script" (*al-khatt al-mansub*). Ibn Muqla, originally a tax collector in the Iranian province of Fars, was made secretary in the central administration and put in charge of opening and dispatching official letters. From the early tenth century he served as vizier to three Abbasid caliphs. Although no genuine samples of his writing are known to survive, Ibn Muqla is famed for developing a system of calculating the size of letters based on the rhombic dot formed when the nib of a reed pen is applied to the surface of the paper. Ibn Muqla calculated the height of an *alif,* the first letter of the Arabic alphabet, in terms of these dots and then calculated the size of all other letters in relation to the alif. The first script he regularized was known as *muhaqqaq* ("accurate," "well-organized," or "ideal"); in it the alif was nine dots high.

Ibn Muqla's skill in writing passed on to the next generation in the person of Ali ibn Hilal, known as Ibn al-Bawwab, who began his career as a house-painter but soon turned to calligraphy, where he added elegance to the system developed by his predecessor. An intimate in court circles in Baghdad, Ibn al-Bawwab was appointed librarian to the Buyid ruler of Shiraz. He is said to have copied the Koran sixty-four times, but only one of his manuscripts is known to survive, a small volume (trim size 7 by 5 inches; 17.5 by 13.5 centimeters) of 286 folios, copied in Baghdad in 1000–1001 (see fig. 21). On each page of

this manuscript are fifteen lines of a rounded (naskh) hand of uniform thickness, except where titles and headings occupy more space. His script—an elegant distillation of everyday handwriting—is still perfectly legible to the modern reader a thousand years after it was done. In contrast, European readers
usually find it challenging to read any handwritten text more than two or three
centuries old.

The various styles of handwriting used during the lifetime of Ibn Muqla
(885–940) were eventually codified into six round hands, consisting of three
pairs of large and small scripts (*thuluth-naskh, muhaqqaq-rayhan,* and *tawqi-riqa*),
known collectively as the Six Pens. Just as the first regularization of Arabic
calligraphic norms since the late seventh century had occurred in conjunction
with the increased use of paper in the tenth century, these six scripts were
themselves regularized in thirteenth-century Iraq and Iran in conjunction
with the extraordinary improvement in papermaking technology seen under
the Mongols. The master calligrapher Yaqut al-Mustasimi had served the last
Abbasid caliph al-Mustasim as secretary and reportedly survived the Mongols'
sacking of Baghdad in 1258 by seeking refuge in a minaret. He is famed for
perfecting Ibn Muqla's system of calligraphy by replacing the straight-cut nib
of the calligrapher's pen with an obliquely cut one, thereby creating a more
elegant ductus and earning such epithets as "sultan," "cynosure," and "*qibla*" of
calligraphers; the last—which indicates that he was like the direction of Mecca,
to which all Muslims turn in prayer—is equivalent to calling him the polestar.

Yaqut's Koran manuscripts, although small in size, are notable for the
spaciousness of their layout, an effect that he achieved by using an extremely
delicate script (see fig. 23). A script of such delicacy was possible only on the
smoothest paper of the finest quality, and contemporary papermakers were
able to meet the demand by producing extremely white strong paper that
acquired a flawless, smooth surface when polished. Such calligraphy would
simply not have been possible on the browner, coarser papers of the eleventh
century. Yaqut himself had six famous pupils; the list varies in different
sources, but the most famous include Yahya al-Sufi, Haydar, and Ahmad ibn
al-Suhrawardi, calligrapher of the "Anonymous" Baghdad Koran (fig. 45).

Just as the widespread use of paper in the ninth century had encouraged
such masters as Ibn Muqla and Ibn al-Bawwab to regularize handwriting in
books in the tenth century, so the improved quality of paper in the thirteenth
century, particularly in the lands under Mongol rule, encouraged such masters
as Yaqut and his followers to take the art of Arabic calligraphy to new heights.
But the steady refinement of calligraphy and the growth of a more popular style
of writing are only part of the story. They accompany an exponential increase
in the demand for books.

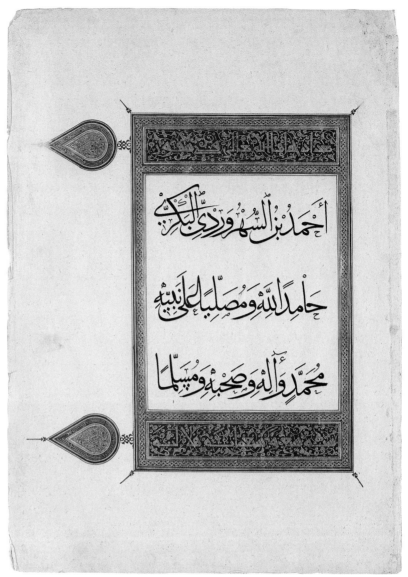

FIG. 45. *Colophon page from a copy of the Koran transcribed by Ahmad al-Suhrawardi. Baghdad, 1307. The Metropolitan Museum of Art, New York, Rogers Fund, 1955 [55.44]*

AN EXPLOSION OF BOOKS

Ibn al-Bawwab's signature in the colophon of the Chester Beatty Library man-uscript and the absence of a dedication, combined with the legibility of the manuscript and its small size and single-volume format, suggest that the cal-ligrapher copied this volume not on commission for a mosque or other insti-tution but on spec. That someone in early eleventh-century Baghdad might have wanted (and been able!) to buy a manuscript of the Koran copied by the most famous calligrapher of his day is eloquent testimony for the explosion of books and book learning brought about by the introduction of paper in the late eighth century, the concomitant development of new, quicker, and more legible scripts in the ninth century, and the increased conversion to Islam and familiarity with the Arabic language in the lands where Islam held sway. Conversion to Islam resulted in larger numbers of people involved in or expecting to be involved in the dominant culture. It has been estimated, for example, that half the population of Iran had converted to Islam by the 820s–860s; of Iraq, Egypt, and Syria, by the 880s–960s; and of Spain, by the 960s–1100s. These dates correspond remarkably well with the florescence of medieval Islamic literary culture in these regions.

The Umayyad caliphs had encouraged some kinds of literature, notably hadith and poetry, but with the rise of the Abbasid caliphate in the middle of the eighth century, books and book knowledge became a general aim of Islamic society. New kinds of literature were encouraged. In addition to studying the Koran, religious scholars wrote about theology, hadith, and *fiqh* (religious law). Early Islamic law had been based on oral transmission, and it combined aspects of Koranic law with pre-Islamic practices. Ibn al-Muqaffa, vizier to the caliph al-Mansur, had unsuccessfully attempted to assert the power of the new Abbasid state by codifying and regularizing Islamic law as practiced by individual judges. Although Ibn al-Muqaffa himself was unable to put together a unified legal code before he was put to death in 756, the "literary period" of Islamic law began in the second half of the eighth century and flowered in the ninth when such scholars as Abu Hanifa, Malik ibn Anas, Shafii, and Ahmad ibn Hanbal compiled the legal collections that remain the basis of Islamic law to this day.

Doctrinal differences among Sunnis, Shiis, Ibadis, and other Muslim sects led to the writing of theological works, Koranic exegeses, and philosophical literature. A desire to understand the words and linguistic structure of the Koran motivated scholars to write on Arabic philology, lexicography, and grammar. The need to identify the individuals who had transmitted hadith and make sure they had been where they were reported to have been brought an upsurge in biographical writing. Even the conception of history expounded in the Koran, which traced history back to Creation, provided a justification for historians to write about history in a new way, and many now began their works with the Creation itself.

Not all learning was religious. Expansion of the government encouraged the production of legal and administrative texts, and general curiosity impelled authors to write works on poetry, philosophy, geography and navigation, mathematics and applied science, astronomy, astrology, medicine, and alchemy. At the same time there was a veritable explosion in the compiling of collections of stories and other works of fiction in Arabic. The earliest evidence that the stories of the *Thousand Nights* were written down, for example, is the early ninth-century paper fragment from Syria, now in Chicago (see fig.

THE ISLAMIC BOOK

Because Arabic script reads from right to left, the typical format of the Islamic book is the reverse of that commonly used for left-to-right scripts, such as English, and the book opens from what English readers would consider the back. The spine of the book is therefore on the right when the book is about to be opened. The text normally begins at the top of a right-hand page (the back, verso, or "b" side of the first leaf). The text continues onto the left-hand page (the front, recto, or "a" side). The text, or sometimes just a section of the text, often ends with a colophon giving the name of the copyist, the place the copyist worked, and the date.

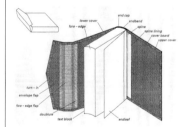

Parts of the typical Islamic book

Early manuscripts, particularly of the Koran, were copied on folded parchment sheets. These were either gathered loosely in soft leather covers or protective boxes or sewn together in quires, or gatherings, and kept within a stiff binding, often made of molded leather on board. After paper replaced parchment as the

. . . continued

usual material on which the text was written, the second method prevailed: the pages were sewn together in gatherings, consisting of sets of folded sheets nested within one another: usually three sheets (trinions), four sheets (quaternions), or five (quinions).

Because larger sheets of paper were more difficult (and more expensive) to produce than smaller ones, it made little economic or practical sense to copy out books on large sheets of paper cut into halves or quarters. Thus, the sheet of paper on which a book was copied usually measured approximately twice the size of the the individual page. The largest sheets of paper used in medieval Islamic manuscripts were sometimes known as "full Baghdadi" sheets. These expensive sheets—used, as far as we know, only for special manuscripts of the Koran—measure approximately 28 by 39 inches (70 by 100 centimeters) and produce a page size of about 20 by 28 inches (50 by 70 centimeters). The deckle (outer) edges of the sheet being constantly exposed to wear, they were often trimmed when a manuscript was bound or rebound. It is therefore difficult, if not impossible, to establish the original size of a trimmed sheet with certainty.

To protect the text, Islamic bindings often have a flap attached to the outer edge of the back cover; it has a fore-edge flap

. . . continued

112

26), and this fortuitously preserved single sheet must represent only a fraction of what was produced and lost.

Another unusual genre that enjoyed popularity was the cookbook. Although cookbooks existed in antiquity, they began to be produced in quantity in the ninth and tenth centuries. Al-Hamdani, who died in 945, alludes to a complex culinary literature in his aphorism "The food and drink of the Yemen are preferable to [all the] recipes from cookbooks," and al-Nadim, the tenth-century author of the *Fihrist,* mentions the existence of several books about cooked food (as well as an equal number about concocting poisons and drugs, amulets and charms). None of these early texts has survived, but they are known to have been written not by cooks but by courtiers, musicians, poets, and librarians, which indicates the importance and literary nature of the genre.

The earliest Arabic cookbooks to survive date from the thirteenth century. One was written in 1226 by Muhammad ibn Hasan ibn Muhammad ibn al-Karim al-Katib al-Baghdadi. The author divides pleasure into six classes: food, drink, clothes, sex, scent, and sound. Of these, the noblest and most consequential is food, the discussion of which he divides into ten chapters, including sour dishes (six milk dishes among them); plain dishes; fried and dry dishes; *harisa* (porridge) and baked dishes; fried, pickled, and upside-down dishes; fish dishes; sauces, relishes, and savories; *judhab* and *khabis* (sweet dishes with almonds or sesame seeds); sweet desserts; and pastries. The author gives more than 150 recipes, and they are specific enough for a modern cook to follow. His recipe for apricot stew (*mishmishiyya*) reads:

Cut fatty meat into small pieces, put into a saucepan with a little salt, and cover with water. Boil, and remove the scum. Cut up onions, wash them, and throw them in on top of the meat. Season the mixture with ground coriander, cumin, mastic, cinnamon, pepper, and ginger. Take dry apricots, soak them in hot water, then wash them and put them in a separate saucepan and boil lightly. Take them out, wipe them dry with the hands, and strain them through a sieve. Take the puree and add it to the saucepan with the meat mixture to form a broth. Take sweet almonds, grind them fine, moisten them with a little apricot juice, and throw them in to thicken the broth. Some cooks add a pinch of saffron to color the stew. Spray the saucepan with a little rosewater, wipe its insides with a clean rag, and leave it to simmer over the fire.

Another cookbook from thirteenth-century Syria, *Kitab al-wusla ila'l-habib fi wasfi'l-tayyibati wa'l-tib* (Book of . . . Descriptions of Good Dishes and Perfumes), exists in at least ten manuscript copies following several rescensions, showing its widespread popularity in the Middle Ages. The French scholar Maxime Rodinson, who studied and published this text, interpreted the existence of such books as a sign of conspicuous consumption in the late Abbasid period, as the products of an extraordinarily wealthy society where every activity was regulated by a complex system of rules. Although the cookbooks and other books certainly testify to the social and cultural complexity of medieval Arabic life, they should also be understood as the practical result of quite another mentality at work, prompted by the proliferation of paper in the medieval Islamic lands—namely, that writing something down ensures its survival.

Islamic society fostered such a respect for book learning and scholarship that rulers and the wealthy opened their doors to the learned and lavished large sums of money on them. Caliphs, governors, courtiers, gentlemen-scholars, and physicians sponsored new books as well as translations of Christian and Jewish works written in Syriac and Greek. The translators themselves sometimes took on disciples, scribes, and amanuenses.

People wrote books simply because they wanted to or because patrons or rulers suggested they do so. Writers expected to be paid with honors, presents, and often cash. Others, such as secretaries and judges in state chanceries and offices, wrote books in their spare time. Unlike modern authors, writers in the medieval Islamic lands seldom, if ever, chronicled their personal revelations; rather, they normally presented their own selection of a chain of opinions and traditions on a particular subject handed down from one source to another. When the selected pieces presented different points of view, an author might conclude with the phrase "*Wa'llahu alam*" (And God knows [the truth]). Like the transcriptions of hadith, such books still represent the continuous and unbroken oral tradition of knowledge. Because oral transmission was deemed far superior to reading something in a book, people traveled widely to hear eminent scholars speak about or "read from" their own works. If being in an audience was not possible, however, reading a book could be an acceptable substitute. A writer of history, for example, might search out a copy of a work dealing with the period and subject that interested him.

The publication of books was itself an oral procedure, for a work was first recited and written down to dictation, usually in a mosque. The mosque remained the center of most literary activity, although the range of knowledge pursued in medieval Islamic society went far beyond the Koran and the religious sciences. From the early years of Islam, mosques had been used not only for strictly religious purposes, such as daily and Friday communal worship, but also for public announcements, judicial proceedings held, and classes, so the use of the mosque as a publishing center was appropriate.

covering the block of text and a pentagonal pointed envelope flap that comes over part of the front cover. The title of a book is often written on the spine, and books are normally stored horizontally on shelves.

Rashid al-Din, the fourteenth-century Ilkhanid vizier, stipulated in the endowment deed to his charitable foundation in Tabriz that his collected works were to be copied by scribes "who possess good, legible hands" and, when finished, "brought to the large *suffa* in the *rawda*," a mosque in the complex, "and each shall be placed on a raised platform between the pulpit and the mihrab, and there the following prayer for the donor shall be recited." The superintendent was to inscribe each book with an attestation and show the copies to the judges of Tabriz, who would record the physical condition of each manuscript.

Even poets published their works in mosques, and even privately commissioned works had to be published there. The author would sit crosslegged with his auditors seated in a circle before him. His most intimate associate or pupil might sit close by to act as intermediary with the audience. These activities are depicted in the frontispiece to the *Rasail ihwan al-safa* (Epistles of the Sincere Brethren), copied in Baghdad in 1287 (fig. 46). Normally the author himself wrote out his work and followed the draft manuscript in dictating, which was often done from memory. Many anecdotes center on scholars' phenomenal feats of memory. The tenth-century traditionalist Abu Bakr ibn al-Anbari is

FIG. 46. *Authors, scribes, and attendants. Right half of a double-page frontispiece from a manuscript of the* Epistles of the Sincere Brethren. *Iraq, 1287. Süleymaniye Library, Esad Efendi, Istanbul [3638, fol. 3b]*

FIG. 47. *Two students presenting their books to the author for check-reading. Double-page frontispiece to a manuscript of the Arabic translation of Dioscorides'* De materia medica. *Northern Iraq or Syria, 1229. Ink and opaque pigments on paper. Topkapi Palace Library, Istanbul [Ms. Ahmet III, 2127, fols. 1b, 2a]*

said to have dictated forty-five thousand pages by heart; his contemporary the philologist al-Bawardi dictated thirty thousand pages on linguistics. Authors might stop dictation in the middle of a book for one reason or another, and auditors who were taking dictation had to be content with truncated works.

A copy of a book could not be considered genuine unless it had been authorized by the lecturer, and just as the authenticity of a hadith rested on the chain of its transmitters, the guarantee of the authenticity of a copy rested on a chain of authorizations going back to the author himself. An author might himself produce authorized copies, but normally he authorized transcripts of public readings by having copyists read the transcripts back to him for accuracy. Scholars' biographies constantly state not only that "he heard [a particular book] from so-and-so" but also that "he read it to so-and-so." The copyist had to read the copy aloud in order to obtain the authorization, and an author might save time by assembling an audience for check-reading in the same way he had assembled one for dictation. A famous double-page frontispiece to a thirteenth-century manuscript of the Arabic translation of Dioscorides' *De materia medica* is usually interpreted as an Islamic rendering of the classic author portrait, but with the author and his inspiring muse replaced by the author instructing and certifying his students (fig. 47). The prevalence of check-reading may explain why medieval Western manuscripts, in contrast to medieval Islamic ones, are so often a tissue of scribal errors by successive generations of copyists.

The origins of this publication procedure probably lie in the tradition of orally transmitting the Koran, although dictation to a group of scribes was quite common in the ancient world. In the medieval Islamic lands, once the necessary materials and scripts were available, the system resulted in an explosion of books. In contrast to the situation in medieval Christendom, where a single scribe made a single parchment copy of the single parchment manuscript on the desk before him, one author in the Muslim world could generate a dozen paper copies from a single reading, and each of these authorized copies could generate another dozen. Within two "generations" of readings, well over a hundred copies of a single work might be produced. This ingenious and efficient system was extraordinarily effective in increasing the circulation of books. It explains how, in a society without printing, medieval Islamic libraries could have had so many books.

Besides expanding interest in book learning, the explosion of books resulted in new professions; people earned their living copying books commercially in writing rooms, dealing in paper or books, or working as bookbinders. The multiplication of books also led to the creation of both public and private collections of books, for books were not confined to schools and learned institutions, but were widely disseminated. A modestly small, but lavishly gilded, thirty-part manuscript of the Koran was made specifically for the library (*khizana*) of Qutb al-Din Muhammad, Zangid ruler of the small city of Sinjar in northern Mesopotamia from 1198 to 1219, and several surviving illustrated manuscripts made at virtually the same time for the Artuqid court in the nearby city of Diyarbekir argue for the existence of a similar library there. Books and book learning permeated medieval Islamic society.

COLLECTIONS AND LIBRARIES

Western sources generally dismiss the extraordinary numbers of books cited for medieval Islamic libraries as examples of "Oriental" exaggeration, although they accept that the ancient library of Alexandria contained somewhere between 100,000 and 700,000 volumes. All sources agree that the libraries of medieval Christendom were uniformly small. In 841 the monastery library at St. Gall, in Switzerland, held 400 volumes; in the early 1100s the monastery of Bobbio, in Italy, held 650 volumes; by the early 1110s the monastery of Cluny, in France, held 570 volumes in its main library. The inventory of the library of the Byzantine monastery of Michael Attaleiates, written in 1077, lists eight books on paper and six on parchment, for a total of 14 books. In the fourteenth century, the papal library at Avignon had barely

2,000 volumes. Even after the invention of printing, books remained scarce: an inventory made at the great monastery of Clairvaux in 1506 records 1,788 manuscripts and only three printed books. The richest library in Christendom was said to have been the library of the Sorbonne, in Paris; in 1338 it had only 338 books for consultation, chained to reading desks, and 1,728 works for loan in its registers, 300 of which were listed as lost. The collections of other European colleges of the period often included no more than 300 works, among them the basic religious and philosophical texts.

In contrast, there were private and public libraries all over the Islamic lands. Shops in the Suq al-Warraqin (Stationers' Market), the street in Baghdad for paper sellers and booksellers, served somewhat like private research libraries; the polymath al-Jahiz used to rent shops by the day in order to read the books they kept in stock. Stationers like Ahmad ibn Abi Tahir, a teacher, writer, and paper dealer, were men of learning. Abu'l-Faraj Muhammad ibn Ishaq, known also as Ibn Abi Yaqub al-Nadim al-Warraq ("the Stationer"), used his extensive professional knowledge to compile the *Fihrist,* his encyclopedia of contemporary books and writers, which remains a mine of information about medieval books and writing. The lexicographer al-Azhari reports that a predecessor, the Andalusian lexicographer Abu Abd al-Rahman Abdallah ibn Muhammad ibn Hani al-Andalusi, owned an extensive private library that was housed in a structure built for the purpose, where he received all those who came to study with him. He lodged the students and gave them paper with which to copy from his great collection of books. When he died, the collection was sold for 400,000 dirhams, suggesting that he had somewhere between four hundred and four thousand books. At that time an ordinary book cost ten dirhams, and a fine one ten times as much.

The first public collections of books were assembled under the Abbasids, either during the reign of al-Mansur (754–75), the founder of Baghdad, or his successor Harun al-Rashid (786–809). Although the earlier, Umayyad caliphs had collected writings about principal branches of knowledge, such as hadith and poetry, these were hardly more than collections of notes and single sheets kept under covers or in chests. During the reigns of the early Abbasids and the ascendancy of the Barmakid viziers, translation of Greek, Persian, and Indian works into Arabic became a regular state activity, for the Barmakids, with their literary and administrative interests, had extensive knowledge of what other civilizations could offer. Rich manuscript collections were won as booty in the victories over the Byzantines at Ancyra (806) and at Amorium (838). Al-Mansur sent to the Byzantine emperor requesting copies of Euclid and Greek books on the physical sciences. The caliphal library at Baghdad became a reference center for physicians and astronomers; Harun appointed al-Fadl ibn Nawbakht, the son of the Persian astrologer who had helped al-Mansur found Baghdad, as librarian and Persian translator.

The caliphal collection underwent its greatest development when Harun's son, the caliph al-Mamun, created the House of Wisdom (Bayt al-hikma), which served as the official translating institution in Baghdad. It and the associated library, Storehouse of Wisdom (Khizanat al-hikma), were created in imitation of the pre-Islamic Iranian academy at Jundishapur, whose director, the Christian Jurjis ibn Bakhtishu (or Bukhtishu), and his descendants had served the caliphs as physicians. The caliph sent Salman of Harran, the Sabian curator of the House of Wisdom, a translator of Aristotle who was also conversant with Middle Persian, with a delegation of scholars to purchase philosophical and scientific manuscripts in Constantinople.

In an episode prefiguring the modern academic star system, al-Mamun repeatedly, but unsuccessfully, tried to hire the brilliant Byzantine polymath, Leo the Mathematician, after one of his former students, who had been captured by the Arabs and set to work in al-Mamun's academy, apprised the caliph of his teacher's knowledge. The caliph's repeated requests only led the emperor Theophilos to offer his mathematician a position in Constantinople, and Leo was eventually named director of a philosophical school founded privately around 855. Under al-Mamun's patronage, Greek scientific texts, including Ptolemy's *Syntaxis* (*Almagest*), were translated into Arabic, and the earliest known Arabic treatise concerning astrolabes was written at his court. Astronomical observatories in Baghdad and near Palmyra were attached to the House of Wisdom; scholars were charged with devising new astronomical tables to correct those furnished by Ptolemy.

The House of Wisdom was apparently destroyed during the period of orthodox reaction under the caliph al-Mutawakkil (r. 847–61), but Ali b. Yahya al-Munajjim ("the Astronomer"), a man of letters and a friend of al-Mutawakkil and his successor al-Mutamid, built his own private library, which was open to scholars of all countries. Similar libraries were established at Mosul, Basra, Hormuz, and Rayy. In the tenth century, the Buyids, a Shii dynasty of condottieri from northern Iran, became "protectors" of the Abbasid caliphs, and several of the Buyid rulers built their own libraries. In Shiraz, the Buyid capital in Iran, the geographer al-Muqaddasi saw a huge library that had been built by the Buyid ruler Adud al-Dawla. It was a large free-standing building consisting of a long vaulted hall on three sides of which were series of rooms. According to the chief official, who took the geographer around, there were 360 rooms, "one for every day of the year." The main hall and the side rooms contained carved wooden bookcases with doors; the books lay on shelves, one atop the other. Yahya al-Wasiti's illustration of a library painted some two centuries later, in the copy of al-Hariri's *Maqamat* (Assemblies) that he prepared in Baghdad in 1237, gives some idea of what a medieval Arab library might have looked like (fig. 48).

Libraries not only collected books; they also produced them. Baha al-Dawla,the Buyid ruler of Shiraz in the early eleventh century, appointed the calligrapher Ibn al-Bawwab to be superintendent of his library. The calligrapher found, scattered among the other manuscripts in the library, twenty-

FIG. 48. *A medieval Arabic library as depicted in a copy of al-Hariri's* Assemblies, *transcribed and illustrated by Yahya al-Wasiti. Baghdad, 1237. Ink and opaque pigments on paper. 14 ½ x 11 in. (37 x 28 cm). Bibliothèque Nationale de France, Paris [Ms. Arabe 5847]*

nine of the thirty volumes of a manuscript of the Koran penned by the great Ibn Muqla, but a prolonged and careful search failed to locate the thirtieth and last part of the set. The calligrapher reproached the ruler for treating the precious manuscript so carelessly, and the prince asked Ibn al-Bawwab to make a replacement for the lost volume in Ibn Muqla's handwriting. The ruler said that if he failed to detect the forgery, he would give the calligrapher one hundred dinars and a robe of honor. So the calligrapher "went to the library and searched among the old paper for a paper resembling that of the Koran manuscript. There were several sorts of old Samarqand and China paper in the library—very fine and admirable papers. I took what suited me and wrote out the missing volume. Then I illuminated it and gave the gold an antique appearance. Then I removed the binding of one of the [genuine] parts and bound the part which I had written in it. Finally, I made a new binding for the genuine volume and made it appear old." It was nearly a year before the ruler remembered the incident. He inquired whether Ibn al-Bawwab had fulfilled his promise and was shown the complete Koran manuscript in thirty parts, but he was unable to distinguish the replacement from the original. Baha al-Dawla, however, showed no haste in fulfilling his part of the bargain, so the calligrapher finally asked the prince's permission to help himself to sheets of "China" paper kept in the library. The request was granted, and the calligrapher was kept in paper for years.

Perhaps the most important Abbasid library was the one built in Baghdad in 991 by the Persian Sabur ibn Ardashir, Baha al-Dawla's vizier. Known variously as the House of Knowledge (Dar al-ilm) or House of Books (Dar al-kutub), it contained over ten thousand volumes on a range of scientific subjects. Over the six decades of its existence, several notable scholars were appointed librarian, and many consulted its volumes and added to its collection. It was burned during the Saljuq invasion of Baghdad in 1055–56, and only a handful of its books were saved.

The Abbasid libraries were models for libraries in distant provinces, even when the rulers of these regions did not look to Baghdad for political leadership. The second Umayyad caliph in Spain, al-Hakam II (r. 961–76), whose ancestors had been massacred by the Abbasids, established an enormous library in Córdoba on the model of the great libraries of Baghdad. Al-Hakam's main interest was books, and he seems to have been a greater scholar and bibliophile than he was a leader and ruler. The son of Abd al-Rahman III, whose long reign had been marked by the efflorescence of Córdoba as a cultural center, al-Hakam had been tutored by the best scholars of his time and began to study and collect books in his teens, long before his accession to the throne at the relatively advanced age of forty-six. Al-Hakam's library served as the focus of a whole set of cultural activities that helped to lay the foundations for the burst in literary production in Islamic Spain during the century and a quarter following his death.

Al-Hakam's library is said to have contained 400,000 books. The catalogue of titles alone is said to have filled forty-four volumes, each with twenty folios. This works out to an unlikely 227 items per page, so the actual numbers may be somewhat inflated. Still, even at one-tenth the size, it would have been larger, by a factor of fifty or more, than any contemporary library in Christendom. The Córdoba library lent out books, and outsiders appear to have had some degree of access to them. Librarians, different types of translators, and numerous copyists were employed, as well as checkers to verify the accuracy of copies. After al-Hakam's death, his successor, the generalissimo al-Mansur, burned the philosophical and theological works that he and his associates considered heretical, and the rest of library was dispersed.

In Egypt, the Fatimids, who also disputed the Abbasids' claim to the caliphate, established several major institutions of learning in Cairo modeled on those in Baghdad. Just as the number of books in al-Hakam's library at Córdoba seems exaggerated, the numbers of books in the Fatimid libraries seem incredible. Nevertheless, even if these libraries only held a fraction of the books they are reported to have contained, the collections would still have been impressive.

Some of the numbers seem quite reasonable. For example, it is said that in 993–94, the caliph al-Aziz was able to produce from his library thirty copies of al-Khalil ibn. Ahmad's lexicographical masterpiece *Kitab al-ayn,* including one in the hand of the author, as well as twenty copies of al-Tabari's multivolume *Tarikh al-rusul wa'l-muluk* (History of Prophets and Kings), including an autograph copy, plus one hundred copies of the *Jamhara* of Ibn Durayd. Given how Arabic manuscripts were normally copied and transmitted, such numbers are not as improbable as they might seem.

The Fatimid caliphs maintained their own House of Knowledge (Dar al-ilm; sometimes also known as the House of Wisdom, Dar al-hikma) in their palace in Cairo. It contained a library and reading room and served as a meeting place for scholars of hadith, jurists, grammarians, doctors, astronomers, logicians, and mathematicians. The historian al-Maqrizi has preserved the annual budget for the library during the reign of al-Hakim (r. 996–1020). The total was 207 dinars, of which the largest single expense, 90 dinars, was on paper for the copyists. (A lower-middle-class family could survive on 24 dinars a year.) The next largest expense, 48 dinars, was for the librarian's salary, with lesser amounts for the attendant's wages (15 dinars), wages for the keeper of paper, ink, and pens and wages for the person who repaired books (12 dinars each); floor mats and drinking water (10 dinars each); felt carpets and blankets for winter (5 and 4 dinars, respectively); and repairing the curtains (1 dinar). When a new catalogue was prepared in 1045, the library was said to contain sixty-five hundred volumes on various subjects, an unexceptionable number.

Over the course of the year 1068–69 the Fatimid palace was looted by hungry troops, who took whatever they thought they could sell for cash or food. The accounts of the fabulous treasures the troops found are mind-boggling. One storeroom yielded eighteen thousand volumes on the "ancient sciences," and another contained twenty-four hundred boxed manuscripts of the Koran written in "proportioned scripts," that is, the kind developed by Ibn Muqla. An eyewitness saw twenty-five camels laden with books valued at 100,000 dinars headed to the house of the vizier Abu'l-Faraj Muhammad ibn Jafar ibn al-Muizz al-Maghribi, who had taken them in lieu of the 5,000 dinars in salary he was owed. A month later, the same books were looted from the vizier's house and dispersed.

At his death in 1121, the powerful Fatimid vizier al-Afdal left a library of half a million books; the caliph al-Amir moved them to the palace and then endowed many of them for public circulation. The late Fatimid historian Ibn al-Tuwayr reports that the library contained more than 200,000 bound volumes on such subjects as *fiqh* (jurisprudence), hadith, theology, grammar, lexicography, history, biography, astronomy, and chemistry. According to the historian Ibn Abi Tayyi, when the Fatimid dynasty fell to Saladin in 1171, the caliph's library contained 1,200 copies of al-Tabari's *History,* along with an estimated 1.6 million other books, many of which Saladin sold. In apparent confirmation of these incredible numbers, Ibn Abi Tayyi claims that at least 100,000 volumes were transferred to the new Sunni madrasa (theological college) established by al-Qadi al-Fadl, and the rest were sold over the next decade. Just as only one manuscript has survived from al-Hakam's library in Spain, only two manuscripts have survived from the incredible Fatimid royal libraries.

A CULTURE OF WRITING

The period between the emergence of Islam in the seventh century and the Mongol invasions of West Asia in the thirteenth was the golden age of Islamic civilization. During that time the culture evolved from largely oral to scribal— a momentous change. Writing came to play a crucial and pervasive role in virtually every aspect of life. Although all sorts of reasons have been adduced to explain the change, I believe that the increased availability and use of paper served as a catalyst.

In the greater history of world civilization, the shift from oral to scribal culture was as important to the flowering of medieval Islamic civilization as was the later shift in Europe and elsewhere from a scribal culture to a typographic one. The shift from scribal to typographic culture in Europe, which was marked by the invention of printing with movable type, has received more attention from historians than the earlier shift from oral to scribal culture, but the earlier transformation, marked by the introduction of papermaking to the Islamic lands, may have been at least as important. The intellectual act of remembering is essentially different from the act of referring to a written record, whether copied by hand or printed. As writing penetrated society, mnemonic systems for preserving traditions gave way to physical texts that could be referred to independently of their human transmitters.

The changes in modes of thinking brought about by dealing with written texts are not the result of underlying differences between the mental capacities of oral and literate peoples; rather, they stem from a fundamental alteration in the tools available to each. The graphic representation of speech is a tool that encourages reflection on information and the organization of information; it also changes the nature of representations of the world, even for those in the culture who cannot write. Just as a text written in codex format was easier to access than the same text written on a roll, information is often far easier to access from writing than from memory, particularly when the sequence or accuracy of items, rather than their general content, is essential. To remember a passage of music or the sequence of some lines of poetry, one often has to "scroll down" from some beginning to the appropriate point. Leafing through a written text, no matter what its format, can be far faster and is usually more reliable.

In medieval Islamic civilization, however, the shift from reliance on memory to a comparable reliance on the written record was never completely accomplished. Indeed, in some regions and in some areas of knowledge, such as learning and reciting the Koran, mnemonic systems persist to this day. Nevertheless, a watershed seems to have been crossed by the twelfth century, when the general availability of paper allowed early patterns of oral transmission of authority and knowledge to be altered; what took their place was increased use of a corpus of Islamic texts, declared authoritative by professors teaching in new government-sponsored institutions. The fateful shift from memory to written word had other repercussions, because paper and ink could be used for more than the mere representation of speech; they had important contributions to make in other fields of human endeavor, such as mathematics, geography, commerce, and the arts.

CHAPTER 4

The scribes in the administration refrain, however, from using Indian numerals because they require the use of paper; they think that the system of finger-reckoning, which calls for no materials and which a man can use without any instrument apart from one of his limbs, is more appropriate in ensuring secrecy and more in keeping with their dignity. —AL-SULI, *Adab al-kuttub* (Handbook for Secretaries)

The spread of paper from Baghdad, the Abbasid capital, in the late eighth and early ninth centuries coincided not only with expanded literary production on many subjects and an absolute increase in the number of books but also with the development of several systems of notation. The attempt to create graphic analogues of human activities was in itself nothing new in human history, but the introduction of paper to the Islamic lands offered new possibilities for expanding the application of older systems of notation and developing new ones. Some of the systems, particularly mathematical, commercial, and geographical notation, came to be widely adopted, whereas others, such as culinary and musical notation, remain historical curiosities. Scholars have long recognized most of them individually as major achievements of intellectual life under the Abbasids, but these achievements were not accidental. Rather, they were tied to the introduction of paper: they were a product of both increased intellectual curiosity— itself fostered by the growth of learning made possible by the explosion of books—and attempts to exploit the potential applications of paper.

Why develop systems of notation? There are several motivations. Notation aids memory. It expands communication with others, allowing someone to compose a message and send it elsewhere in time or space. It allows access to a far greater repertory of ideas than a person might otherwise be able to retain in memory alone. It provides a framework for improvisation and allows the relations between parts to be visualized in new ways. Basically, it enables conceptualization at a level of sophistication that is impossible in a tradition based on memory alone.

MATHEMATICS

We instinctively reach for pencil and paper whenever we are faced with a mathematical problem, yet during the early years of Islam—as in antiquity—all people did their arithmetic mentally. When the sums became too large or the problems too complex to keep in memory, reckoners could hold intermediary results by various means. They could represent the numbers by using counters, by positioning the fingers, or by employing an abacus or dustboard. Whatever the means of calculation, once writing was invented the results could be written either in words ("five") or, somewhat later, in numerals (V or 5).

The use of counters—whether notches on a stick, pebbles in a pile, or similar tokens—appears to be as old as counting itself. Archaeologists have discovered bones and sticks, some more than twenty thousand years old, cut with notches that they regard as the earliest known representations of numerals. They have also found small clay objects bearing stylus marks and seals at many Middle Eastern sites. Dated as early as 8000 B.C.E., these objects may have been the simple counters used by early farmers and herders to count their harvests and flocks. Pebbles have also been used for numerical recordkeeping for millennia; the English word *calculate* derives from the Latin *calculus,* referring to a small stone used for reckoning. The pre-Islamic Arabs also counted by means of pebbles, which they called *hasa.* From *hasa* derives the Arabic verb *ihsa,* "to count or enumerate."

The ancient Mesopotamians used several different systems of counting during the protoliterate period but eventually came to use their cuneiform writing system to express a sexagesimal (base 60) number system, which persists to this day in our division of a circle into 360 degrees. The Egyptians, in contrast, used a decimal (base 10) system, which they expressed in hieroglyphics. The ancient Greeks also used a decimal system, which they initially represented by an acrophonic system of numerals; that is, they used the first letter of the words *pente* (π), *deka* (δ), *hekaton* (η), *khilioi* (χ), and *myrioi* (μ) to represent five, ten, one hundred, one thousand, and ten thousand, respectively. Then they developed an easier alphabetic system, which gave a numeric value to each of the letters of the alphabet, corresponding to the three series of one to nine, ten to ninety, and one hundred to nine hundred (a= 1, β = 2, γ = 3, etc.; ι = 10, κ = 20, λ = 30, etc.; π = 100, σ = 200, τ = 300, etc.). Following the Greek example, those who used other alphabets, eventually including writers of Hebrew, Gothic, Georgian, Syriac, and Arabic, also began to use letters as numerals.

The equivalent system of employing the letters of the Arabic alphabet as numerals is known as *abjad,* after the series of mnemonic nonsense words— *abjad hawwaz hutiy kalamin,* and so on—that reminds the reckoner that the letter *alif* stands for 1, *ba* for 2, *jim* for 3, *dal* for 4. This system, however, created many problems because several Arabic letters share the same letter shape and are differentiated only by diacritical points, which are often omitted in writing. Thus, the letters *jim, ha,* and *kha* (which in abjad represent 3, 8, and 700) all share the same shape, although the first and last letters are distinguished from the middle letter, which has no points, by points respectively above and below the letter. Eventually abandoned in favor of other systems for general use, the abjad system remained popular for specific purposes: marking scientific

instruments, such as astrolabes, numbering verses in manuscripts of the
Koran, carrying out divinatory practices and composing talismans, and making versified chronograms, in which the sum of the values of the letters in a
word or phrase gives the date of some event. Even in modern times abjad numbers are sometimes used for the pagination of the front matter in books, where
American and European typographers would use Roman numerals.

Perhaps the most familiar ancient system of representing numbers is that
of the Romans, which combines features of several systems. The numerals I, V,
and X (representing 1, 5, and 10) are not letters but symbols derived from
counting with the fingers and hands. Higher values are made by adding the
numerals like counters (III = 3; XX = 20) or even subtracting them (IV = 4; IX
= 9). In contrast, the larger numerals (C for 100; M for 1000) appear at first
to be acrophonic (*centum, mille*), as in the early Greek system. Neither L (50)
nor D (500) are acrophonic, however, and because the larger numerals were
at first represented in other ways, the system must have had other—as yet
undetermined—origins.

It is commonly said that Roman numerals are relatively easy to add and
subtract and impossible to multiply and divide. For big tasks, virtually all
ancient peoples turned to some form of the abacus, which was originally a flat
surface ruled or slotted with columns in which to place *calculi,* identical counters used to represent numbers. (The familiar Oriental type of abacus with
beads strung on rods or wires is a relatively late invention.) The abacus made
it possible to do multiplication and division using Roman numerals by translating them into a decimal place value array. The advantages of the abacus
meant that it was used throughout ancient and medieval Eurasia. Although it
is now commonly identified with Japan, the abacus was introduced there only
in the sixteenth century, and it remained popular and competitive despite the
invention of the electonic calculator.

Dactylonomy, or expressing numbers by the position of the fingers, was
also known in classical antiquity, although its origins are obscure. The Greco-
Roman author Plutarch, in his *Lives,* mentions the practice as being used in
Persia in the first centuries of the Common Era, so the origins of the system
may lie in Iran. The Arabs called it both the "reckoning of the Greeks and the
Arabs" (*hisab al-rum wa'l-arab*) and the "arithmetic of the knots [finger joints]."
Several verses of the Koran seem to refer to the practice of counting on the
fingers, suggesting that it was already used in Arabia before the coming of
Islam. Early Muslims described or interpreted certain gestures made by the
prophet Muhammad as indicating numbers, although the traditional accounts
do not agree with later practice. Muhammad is said, for example, to have
extended his right forefinger while pronouncing his profession of faith—"I

bear witness that there is no god but God and that Muhammad is his prophet"—because the extended forefinger means "one," signifying God's unity.

Finger reckoning was widely used in the medieval Islamic lands. The polymath al-Jahiz advised schoolmasters to teach the "arithmetic of the knots," which he placed among the five methods of human expression as the one needing "neither spoken word nor writing." Similarly, al-Suli, in his *Handbook for Secretaries,* wrote that scribes working in the administration preferred dactylonomy to any other system because it required neither materials nor an instrument, apart from a limb. Furthermore, it ensured secrecy and was more in keeping with the dignity of the scribe's profession.

Books dealing with dactylonomy, such as a treatise by the mathematician Abu'l-Wafa al-Buzajani, gave rules for performing even complex arithmetical operations using the fingers, such as the approximate determination of square roots. The mathematical operations were performed mentally and the fingers held in certain positions to retain partial results obtained in the process of reaching the final solution of a problem. Because of these features this arithmetic came to be known as hand or mental ("air") reckoning.

Dactylonomy was also used in early medieval Europe, for the system described in various Muslim treatises is curiously reminiscent of that expounded in the seventh century by the Venerable Bede, the Anglo-Saxon theologian, in the first chapter of his *De temporum ratione,* entitled "De computa vel loquela digitorum." Using Bede's technique a person could express and calculate with numbers between 1 and 9,999, although it was seldom used for values with more than two digits. Bede's system, however, seems to have fallen into disuse in the West after the early Middle Ages, although a similar system continued to be used in the Islamic lands until modern times. Arab or Persian poets of the classical period could allude to someone's lack of generosity by saying that the person's hand made ninety-three (a closed fist, the sign of avarice). The system was still current in Ilkhanid Iran, for the fourteenth-century historian and finance minister Hamdullah Mustawfi credits the great Ibn Sina (Avicenna) with having invented calculation by dactylonomy in 1029. According to Mustawfi, accountants were thereby freed from the bother of using cumbersome counters.

A form of dactylonomy was still practiced until recent times in Algeria, along the Red Sea coast, and on the island of Bahrain. There the system was modified for commercial transactions involving pearls or other rare and costly merchandise. Because the buyer and the seller did not wish to reveal to bystanders the terms of the transaction, the two negotiators, sitting face to face, hid their right hands under a cloth and touched each other's fingers according to a precise code. Although the system did not distinguish between ones, tens, hundreds, and thousands, the parties involved in the transaction knew which sum was meant. A kind of finger reckoning even persists to this day in the United States. In the second grade my daughter learned how to use her fingers to multiply by nines. To multiply seven by nine, for example, she held up her two hands and counted off seven fingers from left to right, bending the seventh finger down: the six fingers to the left of the bent finger represented the tens, and the three fingers on the right represented the units, giving the result of sixty-three.

Although fingers are always available, calculation with an abacus or written numerals offers the great advantage that the calculator can stop work in midstream and resume later or check the work so far. The Latin word *abacus* actually derives from the Greek word *abakos,* which itself comes from the Hebrew word *abaq* (dust). In postbiblical usage, *abaq* meant "sand used as a writing surface," suggesting that the original form of the abacus was neither the familiar beads on wires nor the grooved or ruled board used with counters in medieval times, but rather a dustboard, that is, a board or slab spread with a fine layer of sand or dust in which designs, letters, or numerals might be traced and then quickly erased with a swipe of the hand or a rag. This type of temporary writing surface was known to the Babylonians and was commonly used by astrologers even in Islamic times to cast horoscopes. Apart from the simplest operations—such as adding tick marks—calculation on a dustboard, however, makes sense only when the calculator uses numerals, and the introduction of the Indian system of numerals to the Arab world made it even more advantageous.

The earliest reference in the Mediterranean world to the Indian system of numeration dates from the mid-seventh century, just after the rise of Islam. In a fragment, dated 662, of a work by Severus Sebokht, the learned bishop of the monastery of Qinnasrin (located on the Euphrates in Syria), the bishop expresses his admiration for the Indians because of their valuable method of computation "done by means of nine signs." Severus had probably learned about the system from Eastern merchants active in Syria. This ingenious and eminently simple system of representing any quantity by using nine symbols in decimal place value (there was originally no zero) arose in India perhaps as early as the fifth century. The Indian system seems to have been known in Baghdad as early as 770, or less than a decade after its founding, but it was principally diffused through the writings of the Abbasid mathematician and geographer Muhammad ibn Musa al-Khwarizmi (or al-Khwarazmi), who died around 846.

Al-Khwarizmi, a native of the Khwarizm region of Central Asia, which is located just south and east of the Aral Sea, was attached to the caliph al-Mamun's House of Knowledge in Baghdad. Although al-Mamun's institute was instrumental in preserving Greek scientific and literary texts, paradoxically none of al-Khwarizmi's Arabic mathematical works survive. The earliest known copy is a twelfth-century Latin translation, which opens with the words *"dixit Algorithmi"* (Algorithmi says). In this manner, the mathematician's epithet of origin came in the West to denote the new process of reckoning with Hindu-Arabic numerals, called *algorithmus* in medieval Latin and *algorism* in English, and even the entire step-by-step process of solving mathematical problems, *algorithm*.

Al-Khwarizmi's efforts in ninth-century Baghdad should be understood in the broader context of the enormous interest in learning and science that was encouraged by the wider availability of paper. By the end of the century, Abbasid mathematicians had acquired and translated from the Greek all the writings that were to have a decisive effect on the growth of Arabic mathematics —including the works of Euclid, Archimedes, Apollonius of Perga, and Ptolemy—as well as the great Sindhind astronomical work in Sanskrit and writings in Middle Persian by pre-Islamic Iranian mathematicians. By using Indian numerals, Abbasid mathematicians were able to combine all these to produce a new arithmetic based on the consistent application of the previously known concept of decimal place value.

Although al-Khwarizmi's original writings on the subject are lost, scholars have reconstructed the workings of his Hindu-Arabic system from the writings of some of his successors and followers, such as Abu'l-Hasan Kushyar ibn Labban al-Jili, who composed his *Principles of Hindu Reckoning* around 1000. In it the author says that calculations are performed on a dustboard, called by the Persian name *takht* (table; throne). Calculation involved rubbing out and displacing numerals; the result of a calculation replaced one of the given numbers. For example, to multiply 123 by 456 the following figures successively replace one another on the dustboard:

123
456

4 123 (multiply 100 by 400; insert 4 in the ten thousands' place)
456

45123 (multiply 100 by 50; insert 5 in the thousands' place)
456

45623 (multiply 100 by 6; erase 1 in the hundreds' place and replace with 6)
456

53623 (multiply 20 by 400; add 8000)
456

54623 (multiply 20 by 50; add 1000)
  456

54723 (multiply 20 by 6; erase 2 from the tens' place and add 120)
  456

55923 (multiply 3 by 400; add 1200)
  456

56073 (multiply 3 by 50; add 150)
  456

56088 (multiply 3 by 6; erase 3 from the units' place; add 18)
  456

As in earlier systems, the multiplications and additions are performed mentally, but in this case the interim results are entered and erased on the dustboard. This was still a tedious process, with plenty of room for error, because so much of the calculation was done mentally, making it difficult to check one's work. The handbook of arithmetic for government bureaucrats by the mathematician Abu'l-Wafa indicates that finger reckoning was still preferred for some operations. Nevertheless, Abu'l-Wafa sometimes employed Indian-type schemes and attempted to free them from the messy dustboard through, one may conjecture, the use of paper.

Already by the middle of the tenth century, several noted mathematicians had attempted to improve this cumbersome system by adapting it for use on paper. The Syrian mathematician Abu'l-Hasan Ahmad b. Ibrahim al-Uqlidisi ("the Euclidian"), writing at Damascus, applied Indian schemes of calculation to the old finger arithmetic as well as to sexagesimal (base 60) fractions. Al-Uqlidisi was also the first mathematician to alter the dustboard method to suit the use of ink and paper. Not only did he object to the awkwardness and messiness of dustboards, but he also frowned on their unsavory connotations, for most people still associated them with astrologers casting horoscopes. Significantly, al-Uqlidisi's method of calculation on paper showed separate steps, so revision was now possible. Although al-Khwarizmi's name is better remembered today, al-Uqlidisi's system of arithmetic is essentially the same as the one some of us were taught when young. We multiply each integer by each other integer, and then add up the results.

   123
  ×456
    18
   120

```
      600
      150
     1000
     5000
     1200
     8000
 + 40000
    56088
```

We can follow the same route half mentally:

```
      123
    x 456
      738
     6150
  + 49200
    56088
```

Like multiplication on the dustboard, multiplication with ink on paper is broken down into simple steps; unlike multiplication on the dustboard, the individual steps are permanently retained for verification.

In retrospect, the new approach to calculation using Hindu-Arabic numerals and pen and paper appears to be an easy leap of the imagination, but practically it was not. Although it was eminently superior to the old system, most people were conservative and continued to prefer mental arithmetic, finger reckoning, and dustboards. Al-Jahiz advised schoolmasters to teach finger reckoning instead of calculation by means of the "Indian" numerals, and al-Suli gave secretaries similar advice. Even the great mathematician Abu'l-Wafa preferred finger reckoning for most secretarial uses. Al-Nadim, the well-informed and generally reliable author of the *Fihrist,* the survey of Arabic literature, gives Indian numerals perfunctory treatment. He does not even list al-Khwarizmi's fundamental book, *Calculation of the Hindu Numerals,* among the list of the author's important works.

Similarly, mathematicians, astronomers, and astrologers continued in their writings to use words and the old abjad system of referring to numbers by the letters of the alphabet. Their writings, however, provide little evidence of how most mathematicians actually did their calculations, because the books are fair copies of finished works. It is likely that many mathematicians still used dustboards, despite their disadvantages, because paper remained too expensive to scribble on and throw away.

Nevertheless, some mathematicians may have used the new paper-based

system for purely mathematical work. Ibn al-Banna, for example, writing in
the early fourteenth century, does not mention dustboards at all, which suggests that he did his calculations on paper, but most mathematicians were not
"pure" mathematicians—they often earned their bread practicing the traditional sciences of astronomy and astrology, which remained staunchly attached
to the older systems. The Ilkhanid mathematician and astronomer Nasir al-
Din Tusi wrote an entire work on dustboard arithmetic at a time—the thirteenth century—when good paper was readily available for books. The erasable dustboard, like the hornbooks and slate tablets of later times, continued to
have the advantage of being cheap. Until the invention of the erasable pencil
in the nineteenth century, writing was difficult to erase from paper. Indeed,
one of paper's distinct advantages was that it provided a permanent record of
the reckoning.

Ordinary people, too, seem to have kept to the old ways of calculation.
Medieval Jewish traders, whose transaction records are preserved in the Geniza
documents, continued to represent their numbers with words as well as with
Hebrew and Coptic numerals, which are similar to the Arabic abjad system.
Because these alphabetic systems do not lend themselves to arithmetical operations, merchants must have performed their calculations in some other way,
but there are no traces in the Geniza materials of how merchants actually did
their arithmetic. They could have used mental computation, but finger reckoning, dustboards, or even pen and paper may also have been used, for there
would have been no reason to save in the Geniza storehouse a scrap of paper
inscribed only with numerals. At first merchants may have been reluctant to
use Hindu-Arabic numerals, but in the late fourteenth century, the historian
Ibn Khaldun noted that practical business arithmetic using them was being
taught in the schools of Islamic Spain.

Mercantile practice in the Islamic lands may have lagged far behind scientific theory, but despite scant initial interest in the new system, knowledge
of Hindu-Arabic numerals spread fairly quickly. Hindu-Arabic numerals are
first mentioned in the western Islamic lands about 950, when they were called
"dust" numerals (*huruf al-ghubar*). Much nonsense has been written about the
mysterious origins of dust numerals, but they are simply the type of Hindu-
Arabic numerals that were used in Spain on a dustboard, the standard tool for
computation at that time. Under the so-called Taifas, or Party Kings, successors to the Umayyad caliphate of Córdoba, which had collapsed in the early
eleventh century, Muslim, Jewish, and Christian scholars met together at centers like Toledo to study scientific writings, particularly in astronomy and
astrology, acquired from Eastern regions. The Hindu-Arabic system of calculation became unusually popular in Spain, thanks not to merchants who would

have recognized its inherent advantages but to mathematicians who owned or read copies of al-Khwarizmi's book *Calculation of the Hindu Numerals.* There, beginning in the twelfth century, it was repeatedly translated and adapted into Hebrew and Latin.

At the other end of Christendom, Byzantine mathematicians seem to have remained completely uninterested in the new system for several centuries. In the ninth century Abbasid mathematicians had been eager to acquire all the ancient mathematical knowledge they could from Byzantium, but the attitude was not reciprocal. Just as the Byzantines generally ignored the enormous opportunities afforded by paper, so Byzantine mathematicians failed to grasp the opportunity to learn about the new system directly from al-Khwarizmi's successors. The Byzantine emperor Michael III sent Photius, one of the most learned men of his time, on an embassy to Baghdad in 855, three years before Photius was named Patriarch of Constantinople, and Photius's interests, as well as his prolonged stay in Baghdad, enabled him to meet the major scientific personages in the city. Yet he apparently did not take knowledge of the new mathematics back home, for Hindu-Arabic numerals and the new method of reckoning with them remained unknown in Byzantium until 1252, when an anonymous work on Indian arithmetic was published. Maximus Planudes, who is generally credited with the introduction of Indian reckoning and the use of Indian numerals in Byzantium, is thought to have read this book.

In Spain, the transfer of mathematical knowledge from Muslims to Christians coincided with a sudden growth in the use of Hindu-Arabic numerals. European Christians, who since Roman times had done their calculations with movable counters on a type of abacus, began to inscribe the counters (apices) with the new numerals. The traditional Arabic numeral forms were rotated and transformed, first into the huruf al-ghubar, the dust numerals, and eventually into the "Arabic" numerals used universally in the West. A few numerals, such as 5 and 8, which is derived from a medieval scribal abbreviation of the Latin *octo,* replaced those commonly used by the Arabs (fig. 49). By the twelfth century, ghubar numerals had been absorbed into the Latin version of the algorism (system of numeration), as seen, for example, in the work of the translator John of Seville.

The new technique of calculating with Hindu-Arabic numerals therefore spread throughout the Muslim world at exactly the same time as the new medium of paper. Some medieval mathematicians were quick to realize that paper and ink provided a better way to calculate with the numerals than the dustboard did, because the method left a permanent record of the calculation and allowed results to be checked, not just immediately after the calculation but as long as the paper remained legible. It also had the further advantage of using relatively little space. But paper, for all its advantages, was still just too

[0]	[9]	[8]	[7]	[6]	[5]	[4]	[3]	[2]	[1]
	٩	٨	✓	٦	8 or ∅	٤	٣	٢	١
•	٩	٨	✓	٦	٥	٤ or ٤	٣	٨	١
	9	8	7	6	4	4	3	2	1
.0. or .٤.	9	8	٨	6	4	9	3	2	1

FIG. 49. *Chart comparing (top to bottom) the medieval Oriental, modern Oriental,* ghubar, *and* algorismus *forms of the Arabic numerals. From* Dictionary of the Middle Ages, *1:388*

expensive to use and throw away. The spread of these numerals, therefore, was not the result of practitioners writing them on paper, with one user of the new system teaching another. Nor did it depend on practitioners using Hindu-Arabic numerals on dustboards. Rather, as in other contemporary fields of knowledge, books written on paper provided the medium by which knowledge was disseminated throughout the Muslim world, in this case reaching Christian Europe through the crucible of Spain and eventually transforming the ways Europeans used numbers. European Christians were themselves at first as reluctant as their Muslim peers to adopt the new system, and a struggle ensued between the abacists, who preferred traditional calculation with counters, and the algorists, who preferred manipulating the new numerals on paper.

Italian merchants were the first to consistently use Arabic numerals for business. Although commercial contact between Spain and Italy could have brought knowledge of the new Hindu-Arabic numerals to Italian notaries by the late twelfth century, Spanish merchants did not yet use the system, and it was introduced to central Italy through North Africa. The merchant Leonardo Fibonacci of Pisa (Leonardo Pisano), whose father had had commercial contacts with the Arab world, lived in Tunis and became familiar with Arabic numerals there. In his *Liber abaci* (Book of Apices), despite its name, he rejected the use of the abacus in favor of the Hindu-Arabic method of reckoning. As a result of his treatise, written in 1202, the use of Hindu-Arabic numeration caught on quickly in the merchant communes of central Italy and supplanted the use of the abacus. By the fourteenth century, pen and paper had by and large replaced the abacus as a calculating tool in Italian banks, and in yet another odd twist of history, European merchants trading in West Asia and North Africa appear to have been responsible for introducing their Muslim partners to the benefits of the system that Muslim mathematicians—but few Muslim merchants—had known and used for centuries.

COMMERCE

Although Muslim merchants did not immediately adopt Hindu-Arabic numerals, paper nevertheless played an important role in the development of trade in the medieval Muslim world. Although we tend to think of the credit economy as a strictly modern development, medieval Muslim merchants conducted most economic activities on credit and recorded them on paper documents. The range of these documents—including but not limited to contracts, accounts, and letters of credit—shows that writing and written documents, particularly those on paper, were common at a time when the ideas of writing and written records were just beginning to enter the lives of Europeans and supplant the traditional reliance on memory and oral testimony. This is not to say, however, that commercial documents were written only on paper, for many ancient Babylonian tablets and Egyptian papyri record commercial transactions. Still, the quantity of commercial documents from medieval West Asia, especially those preserved for centuries in the Cairo Geniza, have allowed scholars to reconstruct much of the economic, social, family, and daily life of the time.

The demands of the state bureaucracy established by the Abbasids encouraged the use of paper for keeping government registers and accounts. Medieval historians report on the complexity of the recordkeeping. One tenth-century Khurasani tax collector kept accounts showing "the amount of assessed taxes, the amount paid by each taxpayer on account of the tax assessed, the journal containing daily income and expenditure, and the amounts totaled up at the end of every month. The yearly account was a register in which amounts paid in were systematically entered for easy reference. The statements were shown in three columns: first, the amount taxed; second, the amount actually collected; and third, the difference between the two. In most cases the amount paid in was less than the amount assessed. The quittance receipt for the tax. Final settlement. Release." Few, if any, of these government accounts have survived, so our knowledge of the workings of the medieval Muslim economy is often based more on interpretation of commercial papers, largely those preserved in the Cairo Geniza.

Trade in agricultural goods and the products manufactured from them, especially textiles, was the fuel that powered the medieval Muslim economy. Unification of the lands between the Atlantic and the Indian Oceans had created a vast common market the likes of which the world had never seen. Although the Koran and Islamic legal literature denounced all forms of lending money at interest, Muslim merchants had several other ways to acquire investment capital; and members of religious minorities were not prohibited from borrowing and lending with people outside their faith—the Geniza documents provide ample evidence of extensive trade and commercial relations between Jews and Muslims.

Trade between the furthest reaches of the Islamic empire was facilitated by the use of a single language (Arabic) and a single monetary system: the central government was, at least in theory, responsible for minting gold dinars, silver dirhams, and copper fals at fixed weights and standards of fineness. This was, of course, the ideal. Although government mints struck coins to a weight standard in principle, coins were actually weighed and their value determined at every transaction, because the weight and fineness of individual coins varied from mint to mint and with the length of time they had been in circulation; coins became thinner and less valuable through wear. Weighing and assaying coins were tedious tasks, so—as earlier in Roman times and subsequently in Christian Europe—money was often handled in sealed purses, the exact value of which was indicated on the outside of the purse. Thus when a commercial document speaks of "a purse from the Treasury" whose value was seventy-six and one-sixth dinars, it undoubtedly contained eighty gold coins of less than full weight.

The profession of money changing was related to weighing and assaying, for an enormous variety of coins circulated at any one time. The documents from the Cairo Geniza tell us of coins minted in Iraq, Egypt, Tunisia, Morocco, and Spain, as well as in Norman Sicily and on the Italian mainland. These all had to be converted into the local currency to be legal tender. Oddly enough, there was no abstract term for money, at least in the period covered by the documents, the mid-tenth to the mid-thirteenth centuries.

The large number of coins in circulation meant that the inhabitants of the medieval Islamic domains were probably more accustomed to using money as a medium of exchange than were their contemporaries elsewhere, certainly in Europe. This is revealed by the size, variety, weight, fineness, and design of medieval Islamic coins. Nevertheless, most wholesale and even retail commerce was mainly conducted through the use of credit, recorded on sheets of paper. Immediate cash payments were rare and were usually rewarded by a standard discount of 2 to 4 percent. According to the eleventh-century legal scholar al-Sarakhsi, "Selling on credit is an absolute feature of trade. . . In most cases, profit can be achieved only by selling for credit and not selling for cash."

A large number of the Geniza documents deal with credit—for example, in acknowledgment of a debt (explaining when and how a debt will be repaid)—or with settlements and special arrangements connected with previous obligations. Other types of documents, including wills, inventories, accounts, and letters, also deal with credit and mention that collateral was provided by real estate, jewelry, clothing, bedding, and even books. Although Muslim, Jewish, and Christian law all prohibited the charging of interest, the documents show that borrowers consistently paid back more than they had borrowed. Sale on credit was normal business procedure, and loans were often disguised as deferred payments. The borrowing of relatively small sums was relatively common; merchants—both Muslim and Jewish—regularly lent each other money.

Commercial "paper," in use from at least the eighth century, made possible the transfer of large sums of money over considerable distances without the use of specie. Paper, as bureaucrats had discovered, had the inherent advantage of being more difficult to erase than papyrus or parchment, an extra protection against dishonesty in financial transactions. This system could—and did—lead to some complicated transactions, which were dealt with by means of such credit instruments as the *hawala,* a payment of debt through endorsement or transfer of a claim. (The Arabic word lies behind the French word *aval,* "endorsement.") An Alexandrian merchant wrote that "the purchasers of the pearls transferred payment to those to whom they had sold aromatic balls." A statement of release from the summer of 1052 tells of a North African merchant who purchased forty dinars' worth of Egyptian flax on credit. He sold it in Tyre and Lattakiya (both now in Lebanon), promising to pay for it in Fustat (Egypt) by transferring his debt to one Nahray ben Nissim. This Nahray paid twenty-seven dinars, and the banker Abraham, "Son of the Scholar," paid the remaining thirteen dinars. One must assume that they both owed the North African merchant money or expected they could collect from him.

Another instrument of credit was the *suftaja,* a letter of credit or, technically, a loan of money to avoid the risks of transportation. In the vast stretches of the empire, there were bankers and banking but no banks, for there were no specialized institutions exclusively dealing in money. Well-known bankers usually issued letters of credit for a fee, and the suftaja could be drawn on like a modern money order, although they normally could not be transferred to another party. Around 1100 an Alexandrian merchant wrote to his correspondent in Cairo that he had sent the amount owed in cash because he had been unable to find someone willing to issue a suftaja. Suftajas could be sent over long distances, but only where direct and permanent business connections already existed. To illustrate: Geniza letters from Tunisia show that people anxious to send money to Baghdad had to send purses of coin to Fustat, where the suftaja might be issued.

Merchants also sent notes written on paper, known by the Persian term *sakk* or *sakka,* from which the European principle (and name) of a check is derived. At Awdagusht, in the western Sudan, the tenth-century geographer Ibn Hawqal saw an officially certified check for forty-two thousand dinars drawn by a man from Sijilmasa on one Muhammad ibn Ali Sadun in the same city. The piece of paper had traveled across much of the Sahara. Around the year 900, an important man paid a poet with a check, but when he presented it, the banker refused payment. The disappointed poet composed a verse to the effect that he would gladly pay a debt of a million dinars on the same plan!

Credit permeated all levels of society. According to the Geniza documents, one did not even pay the local grocer cash for daily supplies but sent written orders and settled after a certain figure—5, 10, or 20 dinars—had been reached. Even orders drawn on most bankers were relatively small, if we can judge from a collection of twenty orders drawn on a Fustat banker in 1140. Most of them ranged from one and a quarter to seven dinars; only one was for the relatively large sum of one hundred dinars. Orders of payment avoided cash transfers, and debts were endorsed over to other merchants, a religious foundation, or even a government office, although normally they were paid by a banker.

Cash discounts were granted when the payment was made promptly, a process called "speeding up" in the few Geniza documents that mention them. These discounts hovered around 3 percent, and were never granted on commodities that sold well. One Alexandrian merchant wrote his friend in Fustat, "Do not sell your caraway for less than three and one-half dinars per *qintar,* cash or credit; otherwise, keep it."

Although the suftaja has received scholarly attention, the paper economy reflected in the Geniza documents depended less on this device, whose role was rather limited, than on the pervasive *ruq'a,* which was both an order of payment or delivery given to a grocer, merchant or banker and a promissory note. A banker issued promissory notes only for people who had already made deposits, and the notes were issued in sums ranging from hundreds or thousands of dinars to fractions of a dinar. Promissory notes from established bankers were considered as good as cash. In one mid-eleventh-century case, a banker redeemed a suftaja for 44 dinars with promissory notes worth $20\frac{1}{8}$, 18, and $4\frac{1}{72}$ dinars; he paid the remaining sum of less than 2 dinars in coin. A century later, a man owed the administrator of a pious foundation twenty dinars, of which he paid seventeen dinars in bankers' notes and the rest in gold.

Although orders of payment dominated medieval economic life, actual paper money was tried only once—and disastrously. Paper money was used in China in a limited way as early as the ninth century. At first this "flying money" was more like a banker's draft, but by the eleventh century, the government had authorized sixteen private houses to issue notes and had even established an official agency to issue government notes, backed by cash reserves, in various denominations. Paper money circulated widely by the end of the Northern Song (1127) period, and Marco Polo described it with amazement. As a result of increased contact between China and Iran following the Mongol invasions of both countries in the thirteenth century, the Ilkhanid (Mongol) sultan of Iran Gaykhatu tried to introduce block-printed paper money in 1294. Gaykhatu's *chao* notes were introduced to the city of Tabriz, whose local population, even when threatened with death for their refusal, rejected them outright. The minister responsible for the disaster was eventually executed, and the Ilkhanids returned to minting coins of the traditional Islamic type.

That we have any knowledge of economic activity in the medieval Islamic lands is largely because of the survival of written documents. In addition to commercial paper, which permeated economic life in the medieval Muslim world, paper was also used to keep accounts. Some Geniza merchants balked at providing written accounts and viewed requests as expressions of their partners' mistrust, but in reality merchants regularly rendered exact accounts, often down to minute fractions of a dinar. Several types of accounts survive among the Geniza documents. They include reports to partners or customers about shipments, sales, purchases, and outstanding balances; accounts for specific connections or transactions, such as partnerships, sales, purchases, or transport; and accounts made for the writer's own use. Another type of account was that submitted by community officials, which, oddly enough, lack a reckoning of total revenues and expenditures.

Short accounts were often written on single sheets, like letters, and were sometimes made in several copies, either for safety or because several partners were involved in the transactions. Multiple copies were also required in special situations, such as statements of indemnities to be paid after a ship foundered. Longer accounts were normally written in a narrow booklet format known as a *daftar,* which typically measured between 3–4 inches (7–10 centimeters) wide and either 5½–6 or 7½ to 11 inches (14–15 centimeters or 19–28 centimeters) tall. The format allowed the merchant to carry a daftar in his sleeve, which was normally quite wide and served as a pocket, to be readily available for reference. The daftar consisted of a single sheet folded into a bifolio, creating four sides for writing. It could be punched with holes near the fold, so that it could be assembled, presumably with cords, somewhat like a modern loose-leaf binder, to continue a long record. Apart from those from Tunisia, where parchment remained popular longer than elsewhere, virtually all Geniza daftars were written on paper. Because paper itself remained expensive, the typical order of payment was half the size of a modern check.

The Geniza documents hardly provide a complete picture of the financial state of the complex businesses these merchants ran. Ledgers as such do not survive among them, for instance. Account books were files into which a merchant entered notes about his payments and receipts, as well as copies of any accounts submitted to a business correspondent. The copy was called the "root" or "original" because it could be admitted in court as circumstantial, if not formal, proof. Merchants, like Muslim legal scholars, had an ambivalent attitude toward written documents, exemplified in a court record that reports, presumably with approval, that "one of the witnesses remembers the fact, although it is not recorded in a daftar." Even though written accounts were essential to conducting business, skill and good memory remained equally important, even to merchants with complex commercial undertakings.

There is a close connection between the banking practices reflected in the Geniza documents of the eleventh century and those known from Europe two or three hundred years later. Accounting in the Geniza period followed well-established practices indicative of a long tradition and was a vital instrument in the maintenance of an orderly economy, although it did not attain the standards reached by the Italians in the late Middle Ages. The double-entry method of accounting used in late medieval Europe was, it has been suggested, of Arab or Indian origin. The suggestion, however, lacks supporting evidence, and it is safest to locate its origin in Italy toward the end of the thirteenth century, at a time when European merchants combined access to paper with calculation using Hindu-Arabic numerals; double-entry bookkeeping was, in fact, known throughout Europe as the "Italian" method. Later developments notwithstanding, financial procedure in the medieval Islamic lands was complex and sophisticated, and the whole complicated edifice depended on the availability of paper. It was used for communication over long distances, for recordkeeping, for transfer of cash, and for legal safeguards.

CARTOGRAPHY

Paper also played an important role in the development of medieval Islamic cartography, which inherited and expanded upon earlier traditions of Greek, Persian, and Indian cartography to create the most accurate representations of the world—and the heavens—before the development of modern cartography during the European Renaissance. The political and administrative requirements of Islam gave the ancient cartographic traditions a new impetus, but the flowering of Islamic mapmaking—like that of mathematics, new governmental administrative procedures, and complex intercontinental commercial enterprises—coincided with the expansion of a paper-centered culture in the ninth century. Greater interest in geography immediately resulted in a large number of geographical writings describing the world and its provinces and climates, although the earliest actual maps to survive date from after 1000.

Just as the explosion of writing and books in the Islamic Middle Ages should not hide the persistence of oral modes of expression among large segments of the population, the existence of maps does not signal the emergence of a map-reading public. Maps were neither available to nor meant for use by the masses; few people would have known how to read a map or even known that they needed one. Many medieval Islamic maps appear today to be particularly schematic and difficult to interpret (fig. 50). Nevertheless, the increas-

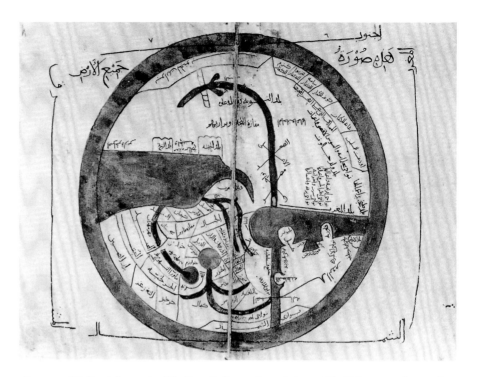

FIG. 50. *World map from a copy of Ibn Hawqal's* Geography *made in 1086. The Mediterranean Sea is on the right, with Europe below it and Africa above it. Ink and color on paper. Topkapi Palace Library, Istanbul [A 3346]*

ingly sophisticated techniques of representing the three-dimensional world on a two-dimensional surface should be understood in terms of two trends: a growing awareness of the possibilities offered by large sheets of paper and a raised level of visual sophistication. I will discuss the latter in the next chapter.

For Muslims, knowledge of geography was of central religious importance. One of the fundamental pillars of Islam is to worship God five times daily, facing the Kaaba in Mecca, a direction known in Arabic as the *qibla*. Thus Muslims have to be able to determine from any point on earth the sacred direction of Mecca in order properly to pray and perform certain other ritual acts, such as burying the dead, reciting the Koran, giving the call to prayer, and ritually slaughtering animals. Mosques and other buildings for religious purposes were oriented toward Mecca; profane structures, such as bathhouses or latrines, in other directions. The Islamic idea of a sacred direction is comparable to the Jewish custom of praying toward Jerusalem, from which Muslim practice derives, and to the Christian notion of orienting churches to the east. The idea of a sacred direction, however, plays a much more important role in Islam, for it ultimately determines the orientation of much secular as well as all sacred space. Correct orientation, moreover, is obligatory on all Muslims, not optional, as it is to Christians.

Other aspects of Islamic ritual practice, such as the use of a lunar calendar and the need to determine the correct time for the five daily prayers, promoted popular interest in observing the heavens. At a more scientific level, astronomers expanded classical traditions of mapping the stars and constellations and making astrolabes, the instrument used to calculate the position of heavenly bodies and ultimately one's position on earth. The earliest Islamic map of the heavens is the painted domed ceiling of the early eighth-century bathhouse at Qusayr Amra, in Jordan. The decorative scheme was derived not from a planar projection on parchment or papyrus but from a celestial globe. The oldest surviving astronomical manuscript having illustrations of the constellations is Abd al-Rahman al-Sufi's *Treatise on the Fixed Stars,* dated 1009–10 (fig. 51). The pictures show the configurations of the stars in the forty-eight constellations recognized by Ptolemy, but the figures are dressed in Oriental rather than classical Greek garb. Al-Sufi wrote in his text that although he knew of another illustrated astronomical treatise, he copied his illustrations directly from images engraved on a celestial globe, indicating that he was not working in a manuscript tradition. According to the eleventh-century scholar al-Biruni, al-Sufi explained that he had laid a very thin piece of paper over a celestial globe and fitted it carefully over the surface of the sphere. He then

FIG. 51. *The constellation Andromeda from al-Sufi's* Treatise on the Fixed Stars, *1009–10. Ink and color on paper. Bodleian Library, Oxford* [*Ms. Marsh 144, p. 165*]

traced the outlines of the constellations and the locations of individual stars on the paper. Al-Biruni later commented that this procedure "is an [adequate] approximation when the figures are small but it is far [from adequate] if they are large." The Oxford manuscript of al-Sufi's text was copied from the author's original by his son.

In the early years of Islam, when the community was small and restricted to Arabia, the relative direction of the Kaaba in Mecca was easy to determine. Any group who had traveled northeast from Mecca to Medina would know that the qibla was southwest, opposite from the direction in which they had traveled. As the Islamic world expanded to the shores of the Atlantic and the steppes of Central Asia, however, it became a greater challenge to determine the direction in which to pray. Medieval Muslims used two different approaches to determine the relative direction of Mecca: folk science and the mathematical traditions of classical and Persian scientific geography, which, unlike folk science, involved theory and computation.

Folk science divided the world into sections, which radiated from the Kaaba, and the qibla was determined by principles of folk astronomy. Thus, someone in the Maghrib prayed toward the "Maghribi" section of the Kaaba, which was defined by the rising or setting of some celestial body. By placing oneself in the opposite direction of the celestial body, one therefore faced toward the Kaaba. This easy approach was widely popular and advocated by most scholars of religious law. It is attested from the tenth century in treatises on folk astronomy and mathematical astronomy, almanacs, geographies, cosmographies, encyclopedias, histories, and legal works but was probably used much earlier.

Like scientific astronomy, scientific geography was the speciality of a select few. It was based on the application of mathematical principles of geometry and trigonometry to the determination of longitudes and latitudes, as well as on knowledge of geodesy (the measurement of distances on the curved surface of earth). Islamic geography incorporated several different geographical traditions, the most important being the classical tradition of the second-century Alexandrian geographer Ptolemy and his successors, who gave localities coordinates of longitude and latitude and divided the earth into zones, or climes, according to the length of the longest day in the center of the zone. Many mathematicians were naturally interested in the problems of geography.

From the very few and ambiguous references to geographical representations in early Islamic times, we can guess that maps were neither widely known or widely used. Around 702, for example, a "picture" of Daylam, the mountainous province to the southwest of the Caspian Sea, was prepared for al-Hajjaj ibn Yusuf, the Umayyad governor of the eastern part of the empire, so that he could better understand the military situation there. The same governor is also said to have ordered a picture of Bukhara so that he could prepare for its siege in 707. A picture of the swamps of al-Batiha, near Basra, was available during the reign of the Abbasid caliph al-Mansur to settle a dispute about water rights. We have absolutely no idea whether these pictures were actual maps, schematic plans, bird's-eye views, or something else, but they were rare enough for later historians to single them out for mention.

A consistent and coherent system of mapmaking did not evolve until the early ninth century, during the reign of the Abbasid caliph al-Mamun, when the House of Wisdom in Baghdad was in full operation. Scholars there translated and even improved on earlier Greek, Persian, and Indian geographical works, particularly Ptolemy's *Geography*. Al-Mamun himself is known to have commissioned a large colored representation of the world, known as the *mamuniyya,* "representation." A century or so after the events in question, the historian and geographer al-Masudi reported that the caliph had ordered a group of scholars to represent the world with its spheres, stars, lands, and seas, the populated and unpopulated areas, settlements, cities, and the rest. Al-Masudi said that the representation was better than anything that had preceded it, whether the map in the *Geography* of Ptolemy, his successor Marinus's map, or any other.

No trace of al-Mamun's map remains, and its actual form is uncertain, although it must have been quite large. On the one hand, al-Masudi's comparison with Greek maps suggests that it, like them, was built up from longitude and latitude tables on a gridlike projection. On the other hand, references to later, but equally lost, copies of al-Mamun's map suggest that it may have been based on the Persian geographical system of seven climes (*kishvar*), in which a central capital region is surrounded by six provinces. Topographical accuracy does not seem to have been of prime concern, for al-Mamun, like other rulers before and after him, probably ordered his "picture" to show that he, placed in the center, ruled over everything that mattered, which was spread around him.

Although al-Mamun's world map may have been designed primarily to massage the caliph's ego, it is still likely that the mathematician al-Khwarizmi was one of the group of contemporary scholars whom the caliph had chosen to make it. Al-Khwarizmi's fame in the West was established by his books on Indian numerals and algebra, but in the medieval Islamic world his astronomical and geographical works were at least as significant. Al-Khwarizmi wrote a book containing tables that located 2,404 localities by exact longitude and latitude. These corrected many erroneous values given by Ptolemy and gave the coordinates of many more locations.

Because Ptolemy's coordinates were given to mark places on a map, it seems likely that al-Mamun's map would have used a similar system of location by means of coordinates. The likelihood is strengthened by another connection: Al-Khwarizmi's tables provided a model for those of the geographer Suhrab ibn Sarabiyun, who did give detailed directions for producing a map on a rectangular grid from lists of coordinates. First, draw a rectangle, the larger the better, and then divide its edges into degrees, mark the equator, and insert the horizontal lines dividing the climes. To pinpoint features on the map, stretch a thread due north and south at the required longitude, and stretch another thread due east and west at the required latitude. Mark the point of intersection.

Suhrab's text suggests that al-Mamun's earlier map followed Greek precedent in yet another important way, for he indicates that east should be to the right and west to the left on the map. North would therefore be at the top of the map, following the Greek principles of orientation. By the time Suhrab's manuscript was copied in Arabic in the tenth century, however, normal Islamic practice put south at the top of maps, probably because Mecca was to the south of most localities represented on their maps. Although putting south at the top is also characteristic of Chinese maps, the Islamic development appears to have been independent.

It is thought that al-Khwarizmi derived the coordinates for his tables not by copying earlier tables but by placing a grid, like the one that Suhrab describes, over a Syriac version of a Ptolemaic map. This idea is supported by al-Khwarizmi's confusions and misreadings of certain place-names and coordinate values, which can best be explained by the difficulties of translating names and numbers from Greek and Syriac into Arabic. In all these languages, as we have seen, numbers were normally represented by alphabetic signs, and in the Semitic alphabets, the frequent omission of diacritical marks to distinguish letters of similar shape but different numeric value would have caused mixups and garbling of unfamiliar names and values. Sometimes, for example, geographical coordinates rendered in abjad could be read as unfamiliar place-names!

Texts do not specify the material from which al-Mamun's map was made. Because it was large, it may have been drawn on cloth, like other large maps from later times, for paper was not yet made in large sheets. In the tenth century, al-Nadim, the author of the *Fihrist,* saw a "description of the world" prepared by a Sabian from the city of Harran, in northern Mesopotamia. He noted that it was on linen, "unbleached, but with colors," which suggests that this description of the world was actually a map on cloth. At roughly the same time, in 964, the Fatimid caliph al-Muizz, who then ruled in Tunisia, ordered a "picture" woven of blue *tustari* silk, portraying the earth's climes, mountains, seas, cities, rivers, and roads. Representations of the two holy cities, Mecca and Medina, were prominent. Every detail was identified in writing, presumably embroidered, in gold, silver, or colored silk threads. The picture is reported to have cost the stupendous sum of twenty-two thousand dinars to prepare and seems to have been intended to fulfill much the same purpose as al-Mamun's representation: to exalt the caliph who commissioned it.

The earliest extant maps from the Islamic world, however, are on paper. They are included in a unique manuscript of al-Khwarizmi's geographical work discovered in Cairo at the end of the nineteenth century. This manuscript, dated 1037, contains four sketch maps showing the Island of the Jewel, the World Ocean, the Nile, and the Sea of Azov (fig. 52). Because the maps were made almost two centuries after al-Khwarizmi wrote the text, it is unclear to what extent they reflect al-Khwarizmi's original concept and to what extent they reflect a convergence with a second tradition of Islamic cartography, associated with the florescence of geographical writing in the tenth century.

Within little more than a century a new genre of Islamic literature had developed. Its practitioners were not merely geographers; their works contained much historical, economic, and sociological information. Maps were

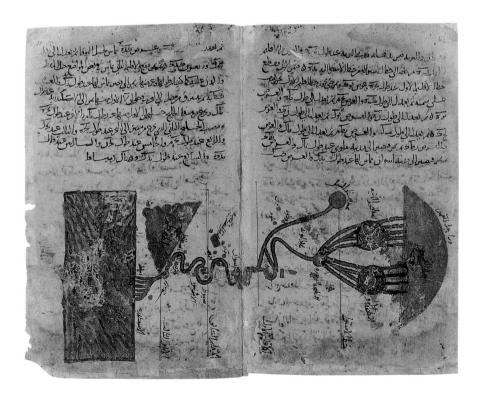

FIG. 52. *Map of the Nile from a copy of al-Khwarizmi's* Geography, *1037. Ink and color on paper. Collection of the Bibliothèque Nationale et Universitaire de Strasbourg [MS. 4.247, fols. 30b–31a]*

necessarily an integral part of this genre. Apart from the writings of Ibn Khurradadhbih, whose geographical manual was designed for use by secretaries in government administration, most of the geographical works produced in the tenth century belong to the genre of "routes and kingdoms" (*al-masalik wa'l-mamalik*). Their authors were largely travelers who had gathered firsthand documentation about the geography of the Islamic world. These include al-Yaqubi, who wrote the *Kitab al-buldan* (Book of Lands), al-Balkhi, who wrote the *Kitab suwar al-ard* (Book of the Depiction of the Earth), al-Istakhri, who wrote the *Kitab al-masalik wa'l-mamalik* (Book of Routes and Kingdoms), Ibn Hawqal, who wrote the *Kitab surat al-ard* (Book of the Picture of the Earth), al-Muqaddasi, who wrote the *Kitab ahsan al-taqasim* (Book of the Finest of Selections), and al-Bakri, who wrote the *Kitab al-masalik wa'l-mamalik* (Book of the Routes and Kingdoms). Rather than divide the world into climes, these authors distinguished large regions roughly corresponding to contemporary political entities (*mamalik*), about which they recorded general features, including the climate and people, and assessed how the details of each place bore on present life there. The relationships among the different authors, the many manuscripts, and the surviving sets of maps in these geographical works are extremely difficult for scholars to disentangle. Because al-Muqaddasi wrote that al-Balkhi's book (which has not survived) represented the earth with very carefully prepared maps, this tradition of mapmaking is commonly known as the Balkhi school. The number of surviving examples suggest that it was very popular in the Middle Ages.

Many, if not all, of these geographical works were—or were meant to be—accompanied by regional maps of the Islamic empire, and a complete set of maps contained between twenty and twenty-two separate representations. Indeed, the texts sometimes specify that they are meant to be read as accompaniments to the images, suggesting that authors were thinking in new, more graphic ways. We know that al-Mamun's map was colored, but we have no indication that the different colors used were linked to specific geographical features. A century and a half later, however, al-Muqaddasi explained that colors are significant on his map: "We have colored the familiar routes red, the golden sands yellow, the salt seas green, the well-known rivers blue, and the principal mountains dull brown." Al-Muqaddasi's text is particularly concerned with the relative importance of the features described. On his maps he indicates the relative importance of towns, for example, by varying the size of the circles that represent them.

A complete map set in the Balkhi school normally consisted of a world map, maps of the three seas—the Mediterranean, the Persian (Gulf), and the Caspian—and seventeen maps of "provinces," or regions. In complete contrast to maps based on the Ptolemaic system, the Balkhi set had no mathematical basis in latitude and longitude. The Balkhi world map should be understood, therefore, as an armchair attempt to see all the provinces set down relative to each other and fit them into a stereotyped idea of the world. The inhabited hemisphere is represented by a circle in which the Mediterranean and Persian Seas are complementary shapes.

This schema is somewhat comparable to, but quite different from, the tripartite "T-in-O" *mappae mundi,* or world maps, of the Western medieval tradition. In these, the *O* represents the ocean surrounding the disc of the earth. Within the circle, the vertical stroke of the *T* represents the Mediterranean Sea, which divides Europe on the right from Africa on the left. The horizontal stroke of the *T* is formed by the River Don on the left and the Nile on the right, which separate Asia (at the top) from Europe and Africa on the bottom left and right. This tripartite division, which conveniently places Jerusalem at the exact center of the map, also symbolizes the Trinity and the inheritance of Noah's three sons. The largest of these medieval mappae mundi to survive is a thirteenth-century example on parchment in Hereford Cathedral.

The number (normally thirteen) and consistency of the Balkhi school maps that represent the Persian-speaking regions show a distinct bias toward the Iranian lands, suggesting that the set derives from an earlier, perhaps pre-Islamic Iranian tradition of representation. In contrast, the maps of Egypt and the Maghrib—both Mediterranean regions—vary enormously from manuscript to manuscript, suggesting that the Balkhi geographers were quite unfamiliar with the Ptolemaic cartographic tradition. In no case can the individual maps be joined together, like the pieces of a jigsaw puzzle, into a larger whole.

Most Islamic maps followed the style of the Balkhi school, but the increasing availability of paper, particularly in the eastern Islamic lands, seems to have encouraged geographers and others to design their own maps. The Turkish grammarian al-Kashgari wrote a book on the Turkish language in 1076–77. The only surviving manuscript of his text is dated 1266 and contains an unusual map of the world, which may be a fair copy of the author's original design (fig. 53). Centered on the Turkish-speaking areas of Central Asia, with other countries receding in size as they approach the circumference, the map prefigures by some seven centuries Saul Steinberg's celebrated *New Yorker* cover, in which the lands west of the Hudson River recede into faint and provincial nothingness.

Around the year 1000, the polymath al-Biruni grappled with the most appropriate method of representing the spherical surface of a globe on a flat surface. He came to this problem in the context of his own scientific work in the plains of what is now Pakistan, where the slight curvature of the earth that he observed led him to the conclusion that the earth was round. Al-Biruni may

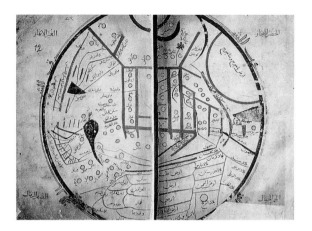

FIG. 53. *World map from a
copy of al-Kashgari's Turkish
grammar made in 1266. Ink and
color on paper. Millet Genel
Kütüphanesi, Istanbul [Ali Emiri
4189]*

have also been brought to this question because he had tried to determine the
correct length of one degree of latitude. In his book comparing the calendri-
cal systems used by different peoples of the world, he devoted one chapter
to several methods for projecting star maps, and a few years later he composed
a monograph on the same subject, probably for Abu'l-Hasan Ali, the
Khwarazmshah ruler of Central Asia who died in 1008–9.

Although al-Biruni mentioned terrestrial maps, his focus was on celestial
maps, and he described seven methods of projecting the celestial sphere onto
a flat surface. The first four of al-Biruni's methods were derived from earlier
sources, including Ptolemy's *Geography* and several Abbasid scientific works, but
the last three were quite original. The first of his original methods was a glob-
ular projection resulting in four maps; the second employed dividers to measure the distances between stars on a globe and transfer them to a map; and the
third involved marking the stars on a globe with a substance that would transfer to a flat surface when the globe was rolled with a circular movement, producing in effect a sort of monotype. Whatever the practicality or impractical-
ity of al-Biruni's seven celestial projections, they indicate an increased interest
in graphic modes of representation around the year 1000, encouraged, no
doubt, by the wider availability of and increasing familiarity with paper.

The outstanding figure in Islamic cartography is the Sharif al-Idrisi. Born
to a noble family in Ceuta in 1100, he traveled widely in Morocco and Spain
and even ventured to southern France and the English coast. Around 1138,
King Roger II of Sicily invited him to Palermo to construct a world map and
write a commentary on it. The map and the accompanying book, *Nuzhat al-mush-
taq* (Pleasant Journeys; also known as the Book of Roger), were completed in
January 1154. The irony is that al-Idrisi, who had been invited to Roger's court
because of his impressive genealogy, which went back to the prophet Muhammad (hence his title Sharif), had little knowledge of cartography at first. Even-

tually, however, he came to be regarded as one of medieval Europe's foremost geographers and cartographers, for his work combined knowledge of the Ptolemaic and Balkhi traditions with a distinctly new and graphic conception of the world.

Al-Idrisi's method was refreshingly practical and original, probably because as a novice in the field, he was unencumbered by generations of cartographic and geographical scholarship. For about fifteen years, according to his own account, he studied extant geographical writings. Finding the writings contradictory, he discussed the subject with scholars, but they were not much more help, so he talked with well-traveled people, who told him what he needed to know about foreign places. He collated the pertinent material by entering it on a "drawing board," using "iron instruments" to inscribe items mentioned in books, together with the more authentic of the scholars' and travelers' information. He then prepared a pure silver disk weighing four hundred Roman *ratl* (a measure somewhat equivalent to a pound), on which he engraved the design transferred from his drawing board. It showed the seven climes and their lands and regions, shorelines and hinterlands, as well as other details.

Neither al-Idrisi's drawing board nor his silver disk survives, but six later manuscripts of his *Pleasant Journeys* preserve a small circular world map, which appears to be a reduced version of the silver original. The earliest is a copy (on paper) dating to 1300 (fig. 54). Several features, such as the location of south at the top and the general shape of the continents, closely follow world maps of

F I G . 54. *World map from a copy of al-Idrisi's* Geography *made in 1300. Ink and color on paper. Bibliothèque Nationale de France, Paris [Ms. Arabe 2221, fols. 3b–4a]*

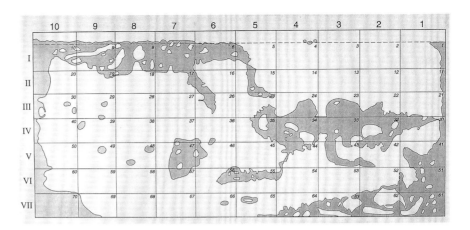

FIG. 55. *Index diagram showing the relation of the sectional maps in al-Idrisi's* Geography. *From Konrad Miller*, Mappae arabicae, *in J. B. Harley and David Woodward, eds.,* The History of Cartography, *vol. 2, p. 162, fig. 7.6*

the Balkhi school. New elements are the curved boundaries of the seven climes and the division of each clime into ten sections. Unlike the provincial maps of the Balkhi school, the sectional maps that survive in eight early al-Idrisi manuscripts can actually be fitted together into a grid, like maps in a road atlas (fig. 55). Because the cartographic style varies considerably between the different manuscripts, a consistent vocabulary of geographical representation seems not yet to have evolved, however.

Al-Idrisi's world map was unusual in combining the Islamic circular world map, ultimately derived from the idealized maps of the Balkhi school, with the coordinate system, or graticule, known to the Greeks. Although the graticule may have been used in al-Mamun's map, it was not widely used in the Islamic lands, even though geographers there did commonly use terrestrial and celestial coordinates to locate positions. Al-Idrisi's adherence to the old system of the seven climes made his attempt somewhat unwieldy, but his set of maps shows an increased graphic sophistication, with each small map keyed exactly to its position on the larger world map.

Al-Idrisi's original world map was engraved on silver to guarantee its preservation, but its production is inconceivable without the use of paper, for paper was perfectly suited not only to assembling all the relevant information but also to transferring it either from or to a rounded surface. In the end, the bullion value of the silver seems to have guaranteed just the opposite fate for the disk, and only paper copies of al-Idrisi's text and maps survive. Similar concerns about the durability of paper led the Norman rulers of Sicily to recopy paper records onto parchment, with better results.

The final development in Islamic cartography before it was transformed by the European cartographic tradition occurred in early fourteenth-century

Iran, another crucial period for the history and development of paper in the Islamic lands. Just at the moment when many types of books were becoming larger and illustration was taking on a new and important role, the Ilkhanid geographer Hamdullah Mustawfi prepared two world maps for his geography, *Nuzhat al-qulub* (Diversion of the Hearts). Although no copies of Hamdullah Mustawfi's maps survive from the author's lifetime, a later copy of his map showing the eastern Islamic lands takes off in an entirely new direction. The map identifies the climates according to the earlier system, but it differs completely from earlier maps in showing no linear features except for coastlines. Instead, the map is ruled into a graticule of squares, each one degree of latitude wide and one degree of longitude long. Localities are placed within individual squares (fig. 56).

This new type of map did not derive from the Islamic cartographic tradition but from the Chinese, a product of increased contacts between Iran and China during the thirteenth and fourteenth centuries. The date and place at which this gridded map appeared suggests that Mustawfi must have seen and been inspired by Chinese maps, which often used grids. Mustawfi's map differs, however, from Chinese grid maps, which are based on linear measurement on the ground and not, like Islamic maps, on the angular measurement of latitudes and longitudes. Still, Mustawfi's map is similar to Chinese

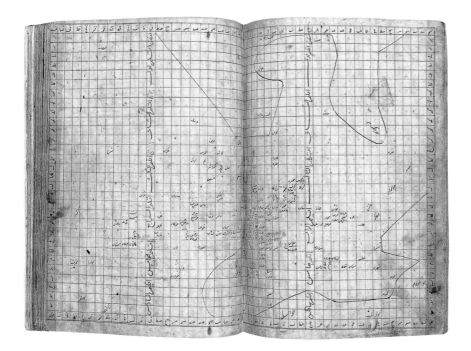

F I G . 56. *Graticule map of central and western Asia by Hamdullah Mustawfi, a 16th-century copy after a 14th-century original. British Library, London [Add. Ms. 16736, fols. 143b–144a]*

prototypes in placing the represented spot in the relevant square instead of on a particular point.

Similar gridded maps appear in the work of the Timurid geographer Hafiz-i Abru, but by the end of the fifteenth century, Islamic geographical cartography was in decline in face of the development of a more sophisticated European tradition; Europeans soon had direct knowledge of places that no Muslim geographer or traveler had ever visited. In the Ottoman world, cartographers participated in the explosion of European cartography, but outside it, most maps made later in the Islamic lands continued to reproduce, with lesser degrees of accuracy, the great achievements of the past.

Medieval Islamic geographers could have achieved their cartographic triumphs without paper. Earlier Greek geographers had created maps of lasting importance without even knowing about paper. Nevertheless, the easy availability of paper in medieval Islamic times encouraged new graphic modes of thinking, and the coincidence of papermaking with mapmaking in the ninth and again in the thirteenth to fourteenth centuries can hardly have been fortuitous. The connection becomes all the more convincing when we look at other contemporary systems of notation developed for use on paper.

MUSIC, GENEALOGY, AND BATTLE PLANS

In the medieval Islamic lands, as in the ancient world, music was closely related to mathematics. Not only were pitches and meters governed by mathematical principles, but, as in mathematics, the study and performance of music were largely anchored in memory and gesture—in other words, in a system in which one musician learned directly from another and played by ear. Although most West Asian musicians have transmitted their knowledge by memory and gesture to the present day, Arabic music underwent important developments as a substantial corpus of theory was written down and as musical theorists attempted to develop systems of notation. The first period of development occurred under the Abbasids in ninth- and tenth-century Iraq; the second, under the Ilkhanids in thirteenth- and fourteenth-century Iran. These two attempts to transcribe sounds and rhythms coincide with the two most important periods in the development of paper in the Islamic lands. It makes sense to think that individuals who already knew the possibilities of paper in one realm of knowledge were eager to realize its possibilities in others.

The ancient Egyptians, Hebrews, Chinese, and Greeks had all come up with very different systems to represent their music. Just as the ancient Greeks had used the built-in ordering of the alphabet to represent numbers, they represented pitch with a mixture of letters and signs. By the ninth century, many different systems were being used. The Byzantines used this ancient system of

ekphonetic notation, and Nestorian Christians may have transmitted their
own version of it as far as Tibet, where Buddhist monks employed it to notate
their chants. At the monastery of St. Gall, in Switzerland, monks used neu-
matic notation, with finely drawn lines, curves, and hooks representing the
rise and fall of the melodic line in their plainchants. This was also the time
when Arab musical theorists first developed an alphabetic system of notation
for Arabic music. Because of the differences between musical theory and practice, their system was never actually used in the ninth century, and other
attempts at notation were made in the thirteenth century.

The major figure in Arabic music of the early ninth century was the
philosopher Abu Yusuf Yaqub ibn Ishaq al-Kindi. Son of the governor of
Kufa, he was educated in Basra, a lively intellectual center, and became
attached to the Abbasid court in Baghdad during the reigns of al-Mamun and
al-Mutasim. There he studied Greek philosophy and wrote several short treatises on music, of which at least five have survived. Eclectic in approach, they
show his dependence on the Aristotelian and Platonic-Pythagorean traditions.
In his musical treatises he outlines melodic movement schematically in words,
implying visual metaphors with terms like *lawlabi* (spiral), *dafir* (braid), and
muwashshaa (girdled). His descriptive account of contemporary rhythmic cycles
is somewhat puzzling and imprecise, possibly because it was a pioneering
attempt quite independent of previous analytical models.

Al-Kindi is particularly interesting because he discussed a model of musical notation that several later theorists borrowed or even reinvented. He
denoted pitches with letters of the alphabet, ordered in the abjad sequence,
making his system alphabetic-numeric. It was, however, confined to purely
theoretical discussions, for when al-Kindi defined the pitch outlines of an
elementary lute exercise, he did not use notation to record them but preferred
verbal definitions of the frets used. Al-Kindi's efforts to write about music
derived in part from Greek traditions, but, like many of his contemporaries in
other fields, he was also encouraged by the flowering of books and book learning associated with the spread of paper use from ninth-century Baghdad.
Musical notation is scarcely conceivable without a writing medium, and paper
was readily available.

Al-Kindi's efforts apparently went nowhere, but some of his ideas reap-
pear in the late thirteenth century in the most influential of all later treatises
on music, the *Kitab al-adwar* (Book of Cycles) by Safi al-Din al-Urmawi, a native
of Urmiya, in northwestern Iran. The book gets its name from the author's
representations of the basic set of common rhythmic cycles in the form of a
circle. The perimeter of the circle is inscribed with the appropriate syllabic
sequences, which are qualified by a verbal statement of the number and posi-

tion of those time units marked by percussion. The circles are also used to indicate the number of consonant relations in some of the modes, which are shown as lines across the circle joining the notes in question inscribed around the perimeter. Because Safi al-Din uses letters for pitch and numerals for duration, his system also gives some indication of rhythmic structure. It defines rhythmic cycles and their variant forms in terms derived from prosody to specify the various internal divisions and accentual patterns. Such a scheme seems impossible to imagine without some writing material, and paper was readily available in thirteenth-century Iran.

Safi al-Din did not intend to provide an accurate record of the musical repertoire, which would have served no useful purpose in a tradition in which aural transmission and lengthy and free variations on simple themes were the norm. Rather, he aimed to represent the melodic structure of particular forms and demonstrate that a technique of notation was possible. His are the first precise depictions of musical meters; letters and numbers notate melodies. His book was the most popular and influential book on music for centuries, and no other Arabic (or Persian or Turkish) music treatise was so often copied, commented on, and translated.

Safi al-Din may have been prompted to develop his system by the peculiarities of his education, which deeply involved him in the paper-centered culture of his time. Born around 1216, he went to Baghdad in his youth, where he was educated in the Arabic language, literature, history, and penmanship. He studied Shafii theology and comparative law at the Mustansiriyya madrasa, eventually assuming a post in the caliph's juridical administration. He also made quite a name for himself as a calligrapher, working as a copyist at the new library built by the caliph al-Mustasim. His disciples included both Yaqut al-Mustasimi, the cynosure of calligraphers, and his famous student Shams al-Din Ahmad al-Suhrawardi. Safi al-Din also became known as a musician and excellent lutenist, talents he was able to exploit when he was accepted into the caliph's circle of boon companions. Safi al-Din wrote the *Book of Cycles* while he still worked in the library of al-Mustasim; the earliest known manuscript was finished in 1236, when the author was only twenty years old or so. Because the handwriting closely resembles Yaqut al-Mustasimi's, it may well be the author's own copy.

After the fall of the caliphate to the Mongols, the Ilkhanid governor of Iraq, Ala al-Din Ata-Malik Juwayni, and his brother Shams al-Din Muhammad Juwayni put Safi al-Din in charge of the chancellery of Baghdad. He was also appointed chief supervisor of charitable foundations in Iraq until 1267, when the noted astronomer Nasir al-Din Tusi took over the position. Safi al-Din's ample private fortune helped him survive the fall of Baghdad:

having graciously accommodated one of the Mongol officers, the officer introduced him to the new ruler, who was impressed by Safi al-Din's art and erudition and doubled his income. Safi al-Din's later musical career was supported
mainly by the Juwayni family, but after the demise of his patrons in 1286, he
fell into oblivion and poverty.

Safi al-Din's alphabetic and numeric representation of pitch and duration
was systematically expanded by his first great successor, the Persian Sufi polymath Qutb al-Din Shirazi. Qutb al-Din was born into a family of physicians
in 1236 but was not only a medical man; he also distinguished himself by writing on philosophy, astronomy, and religious problems. Sufis often flaunted
norms, and as a Sufi, he neglected some of his religious duties, drank wine,
and associated with people of ill repute. He played chess brilliantly and was also
skilled as a conjurer and musician. In a unique example of a fully notated piece
of music—a song by Safi al-Din—Qutb al-Din used a grid in which the divisions along the horizontal axis represent time units, and superimposed layers
provide for pitch, the text, a percussion part, indications of expression and
dynamics, and specifications of changes of mode. His use of a grid came at virtually the same moment that cartographers were beginning to use grids for
mapmaking, and, as we shall see in Chapter 5, builders were using grids for the
representation of architecture.

Qutb al-Din's unique effort was revisited a century later by the Persian
musician Abd al-Qadir ibn Ghabi. His major treatise, the *Jami al-alhan,* gives a
succinct description of the major structural features of each type of song, not-
ing any associations with particular rhythmic cycles and, more characteristi-
cally, with verse in a particular language or form. He also provided an extended
analysis of one piece of music, including skeletal notation; the various sections
are segmented, and aspects of verse setting are illustrated.

Another form of notation that developed as a function of the increased use
of paper was the genealogical tree. The study of genealogy, known in Arabic as
nasab, was fundamental to Arab society because it validated kinship and all that
kinship involves. Genealogical research was practiced from very early—even in
pre-Islamic times—although none of the earliest genealogical works has survived. The study of genealogies, like other sciences, flourished under the
Abbasids in the ninth century, when writers such as al-Baladhuri wrote *Ansab
al-ashraf,* a multivolume work concerning the genealogy of the sharifs, or
descendants of the Prophet. Far more interesting for our purposes, however,
is that genealogical writers began at the same time to present the essence of
their research in graphic form—a form known either as *tashjir* or *mushajjar,* from
the Arabic word for "tree." Some of the earliest examples appear in al-Hamdani's *al-Iklil* (The Crown), a tenth-century encyclopedia of south Arabian

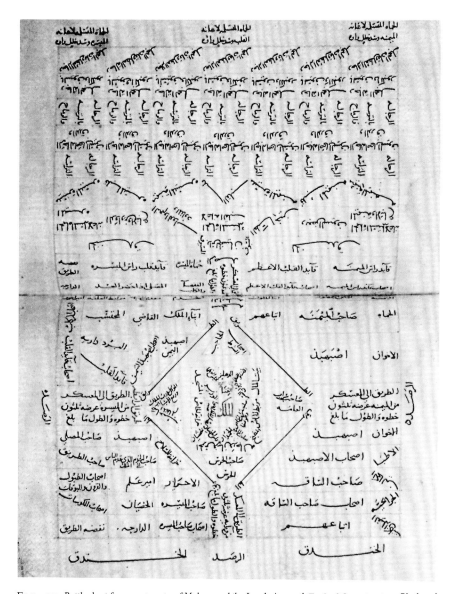

FIG. 57. *Battle chart from a 1371 copy of Muhammad ibn Isa al-Aqsarai's* End of Questioning. *Black and red ink on paper. British Library, London [Add 18866, fols. 209v–210a]*

archaeology and genealogy, known only (and incompletely) from later manuscripts. Once again, the introduction of paper and the development of new
graphic modes of representation coincided.

The use of genealogical trees became more frequent over time; trees did,
after all, provide an immediate understanding of relationships, as the fourteenth-century historian Ibn Khaldun averred. An example of a tree can be
found in the early fourteenth-century copy of the Ilkhanid vizier Rashid al-
Din's *Majmu'a al-rashidiyya,* a collection of his theological writings, where a graphic
genealogy beginning with Adam and ending with the family of Fatima, Muham-

mad's daughter, covers nearly twenty-five pages. Some of Rashid al-Din's historical works were illustrated with genealogical charts in which individuals were represented by more or less schematic portraits. The originals of these charts have not survived intact, for the portraits were later excised from the manuscripts and pasted into albums, but the charts are known from later copies.

Yet another form of graphic representation that developed in medieval Islamic manuscrips was the battle chart; such charts are sometimes found in manuals of *furusiyya,* or theoretical and practical equestrian knowledge. Ninth-century writers, such as al-Jahiz, explored the equestrian field, as they did other branches of science, but the full development of the equestrian manual did not occur until the thirteenth century, under the Mamluk rulers of Egypt and Syria. The later manuals described the skills necessary for a successful military career, including knowledge of horsemanship, archery, fencing, and games, ranging from polo to chess. Some of these manuscripts, such as the *Nihayat al-su'l* (End of Questioning) written by al-Aqsarai, have schematic illustrations and even charts that represent the tripartite battle formation, with the crack troops in the center under the personal command of the "king"; his royal banner flies above them. He is flanked by right (*maymana*) and left (*maysara*) wings (fig. 57). Because no earlier manuals of this type are known to survive, it is impossible to say whether such battle charts were used earlier, but the complexity of the chart is well served by the generous two-page spread in the manuscript, making the chart a full 16 inches (40 centimeters) wide.

All told, the convergence of so many new and transforming forms of notation in the ninth and the thirteenth to fourteenth centuries cannot be mere coincidence, especially since so many of the individuals involved in one were involved in another. Men of letters familiar with paper would have been quick to recognize its advantages in various areas of study. Paper was thus the catalyst for many of the intellectual developments of the Islamic Middle Ages. It was also the catalyst for many simultaneous developments in the visual arts.

CHAPTER 5

Then [Arthur Upham] Pope asked Ustad [a master mason from Isfahan] details of building a brick squinch. He seemed stumped. So I handed him a sheet of paper and a pencil. He held them at arm's length, a look of total hopelessness on his . . . face. . . . He was illiterate: more, he was incapable of presenting a three-dimensional object in two flat dimensions. He put the pencil aside, then folded the paper intricately to construct an actual squinch. —Jay Gluck and Noël Silverman, eds., *Surveyors of Persian Art*

Once paper was available in the Islamic lands, artists and artisans eventually came to exploit its possibilities, but they were somewhat slower to do so than were writers, mathematicians, geographers, and merchants. Before paper, artists and artisans worked directly with their chosen materials—clay, bronze, cloth, brick, plaster—relying on experience and practice to do what we would use instructions and drawings to do today. With the dissemination of paper this changed. Gradually some artisans developed vocabularies of representation, but learning how to do something by reading about it in a book remains a distinctly modern practice.

Paper began to be used as an adjunct in the production of art in the eastern Islamic lands—particularly northwestern Iran and Central Asia, the regions where it had been known the longest—as early as the tenth century, but it is only from the thirteenth century that paper became significant in the making of art and architecture. From this time on, increasing numbers of artisans and artists exploited the possibilities of paper for making preliminary sketches and plans for the production of finished works of art. Eventually many of the most characteristic features of later Islamic art, such as the ready transferral of designs from one medium to another, were developed through the use of paper and paper-based patterns.

The major reason that visual artists were so tardy to use paper was their low social status in Islamic culture. Calligraphers, who practiced the only form of visual art universally accepted in Islamic culture, were familiar with paper and highly literate, but weavers, metalworkers, potters, painters, and other craftworkers occupied a relatively low position in medieval times. Because paper was relatively expensive and necessarily restricted to the literate strata, artisans were no more likely than any other low-status and poorly paid individuals to have had much access to or familiarity with books or with the idea of executing drawings on the new medium. Indeed, they did not need paper to do their work. As paper became cheaper and increasingly available, however, they discovered and exploited new ways of using it, thereby transforming the visual world of Islam.

The slowness with which artists in the Islamic lands took up the use of paper reveals a process largely obscured in the West, where its use spread rapidly in the fifteenth and sixteenth centuries through its close association with printing. In the Islamic lands, in contrast, printing was not adopted until the end of the eighteenth and nineteenth centuries, so increased access to paper led only gradually to changes in the ways art was made.

That art could be, and sometimes was, figural. A popular Western misconception holds that Islam prohibits the representation of living beings in its art, but every public or private collection of Islamic art has scores of textiles, ceramics, metalwares, and pages from books bearing images of real and imaginary creatures. These images, made in many Islamic lands over the fourteen centuries since the rise of Islam, testify to a long and vibrant tradition of representation. It is religious art that is nonfigural, in contrast to Christian religious art, which is often figural and based on Christian Scripture. Muslims never illustrated the Koran, for the physical text itself was already the only conceivable representation of God's message. Therefore, although the art of book illustration in the Christian world—medieval Europe and the Byzantine empire—grew out of religious representations, the art of Islamic book illustration was an entirely secular development. The history of this art is quite distinct from the history of the Koran manuscripts copied on parchment and paper, already discussed in Chapter 3. Secular Islamic books were copied almost exclusively on paper, but the role of paper in the arts of the Islamic lands went far beyond books.

BEFORE THE THIRTEENTH CENTURY

The illustrated book is a characteristic type of later Islamic art, but the word *later* requires emphasis here. Although hundreds of Islamic manuscripts copied before the mid-thirteenth century survive, only about three dozen are illustrated, and of these only three date from before the twelfth century. Books and book learning may have flourished from the ninth century and inspired the development of systems of notation, but manuscripts illustrated for the sheer pleasure the art would provide—as opposed to scientific and technical works requiring illustrations—were quite rare in early Islamic times. The emergence of the distinctive visual language of representation used in Arabic manuscripts followed, rather than accompanied, the first flowering of book culture, because it was first developed not on paper but in other media.

Because geographical, scientific, and technical works were routinely illustrated in antiquity, it is logical to assume that writers and translators of such works in early Islamic times simply continued ancient tradition. Before the introduction of paper, authors in the Islamic lands may therefore have pro-

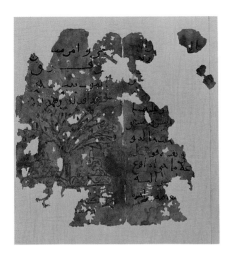

FIG. 58. *Final page of an anonymous popular romance with illustration of two tombs separated by a tree. Egypt, late 9th or early 10th century. Ink and color on paper. Nationalbibliothek, Vienna [Chart. Ar. 25612]*

duced illustrated texts on parchment or papyrus, although none has survived. If we consider, however, that Islamic interest in the ancient sciences did not burgeon until the ninth century, with the introduction and spread of paper, it is more likely that the development of scientific illustration in the Islamic lands was itself a function of the increased production of books and wider use of paper.

The three earliest illustrated books to survive are indeed all scientific texts in which the illustrations are essential for understanding the text. All were copied on paper. The oldest set of illustrations is found in the 1009–10 copy of al-Sufi's *Treatise on the Fixed Stars,* discussed in Chapter 4. The second oldest illustrated manuscript is the copy, dated 1037, of the geography written some two centuries earlier by the noted mathematician and geographer Muhammad ibn Musa al-Khwarizmi, also discussed in Chapter 4. Art historians usually ignore it because its pictures contain no people. The third illustrated manuscript is an Arabic translation, dated 1083, of *De materia medica,* written a thousand years earlier by the Greek physician and pharmacologist Dioscorides. Most of the pictures in this manuscript show just plants; the sole figural painting, demonstrating the pharmaceutical use of a plant, was modeled on a Greek prototype.

In addition to these three manuscripts, several fragments apparently from illustrated books have been discovered, primarily in the course of rogue excavations in the rubbish heaps of Fustat (Old Cairo) in Egypt. The earliest, a fragment in Vienna, has been dated on paleographic grounds to the late ninth or early tenth century, but the illustration is only a simple schematic drawing (fig. 58). Like the unillustrated *Thousand Nights* fragment in Chicago (see fig. 26), also discovered in Egypt, the Vienna fragment consists of a worn sheet of paper, measuring only about 6 inches square (16 by 14.5 centimeters) when open and representing, when folded, the first and last leaves of a gathering of

FIG. 59. *Drawing of a lion with three lines of text from a discourse on wild animals by Ka'b al-Ahbar. Egypt, 11th or 12th century. Ink and color on paper. The Metropolitan Museum of Art, New York, Rogers Fund, 1954 [54.108.3]*

pages. The text begins on the front of folio 1 with the standard invocation at the start of a written text and concludes on the back of the last folio with " . . . until death did them part. This is their tomb, may God have mercy upon them"; the text is followed by a crude painting of two stepped tombs separated by a tree. There is no way to tell how much text is missing between the first and last pages of the gathering—though probably not much, because of its size—or whether the booklet had any other illustrations. The simplicity of the image and its technique, combined with the small size of the text, confirm that this was a popular romance of no great artistic importance. The copyist probably inserted the illustration to fill up the blank space on the page. The text itself belongs to a well-known literary genre of stories concerning unhappy lovers united only in death. In the *Fihrist,* al-Nadim classifies this type of story in the genre of night entertainments and fanciful tales, and such works—although no others have survived—appear to have enjoyed great popularity under the Abbasids in the early tenth century, the time to which the fragment is gener-ally dated in the absence of any archaeological evidence.

Other fragments of paper found at Fustat bear more sophisticated draw-ings, which some scholars have interpreted as evidence for a lost early Islamic art of the book. In fact, few of them bear both text and pictures. For those that do, the only conclusions that can be drawn are equivocal, because none is dated, and many raise troubling questions about authenticity. One fragment, for example, bears an almost calligraphic drawing of a lion on one side. The drawing is accompanied by a few lines of text, which have been identified as part of a discourse on wild animals by an early Jewish convert to Islam, Kab al-Ahbar (fig. 59). The presence of this text suggests that the drawing comes from an early Islamic book about animals. The style of the drawing, however, sug-gests a twelfth-century date, indicating that the drawing comes from a copy of an early text illustrated at a later date. But the reverse of the same sheet bears a drawing of a hare accompanied by a text irrelevant to that on the front of the sheet, so it is difficult—indeed impossible—to imagine how this page could once have formed part of a book. Another painting purports to be the fron-tispiece to a collection of poems by a well-known Umayyad poet, but similar historical and technical problems raise doubts about the authenticity of this painting and several other related drawings. It seems best, therefore, to treat all these unauthenticated fragments with extreme caution and not base an argument on them.

Scattered literary references to illustrated manuscripts suggest that they did exist but were rare, for medieval authors noted such manuscripts precisely because they were unusual and had pictures. When the historian al-Masudi vis-ited the house of a notable in the Iranian city of Istakhr (near modern Shiraz) in 915, he reported that he was shown a manuscript about the Sasanian kings and their achievements. This luxury manuscript, a copy of which had also been sent to the Umayyad caliph Hisham, had supposedly been compiled two cen-turies earlier from sources found in the old Sasanian royal library. Embell-ished with twenty-seven "lifelike" portraits of rulers—twenty-five kings and two queens—painted with gold, silver, and ground copper, the manuscript had been copied on leaves of parchment tinted purple, a clear reference to Byzantine imperial manuscripts and an indication of its singularity.

At a more mundane level, al-Nadim indicates that his *Fihrist* was meant to be illustrated with images to clarify the meaning of the text, much the way a scientific book is illustrated with diagrams. Where he wrote, "It is said that this is the form of the idol that is at Multan [in India]," several copies of the text have a blank space intended for an illustration. One manuscript of the *Fihrist,* once owned by the Mamluk historian al-Maqrizi, is illustrated with purported specimens of ancient scripts discussed by the author. Similarly, according to a twelfth-century account, Mansur al-Suri, who wrote a book on botany, commissioned a painter to accompany him on his field trips and paint plants in color at the different stages of their growth; none of this work is known to survive.

Manuscripts of the book of animal fables known as *Kalila and Dimna* may have been illustrated from pre-Islamic times, but even if so, we should not assume that other texts were regularly illustrated in the first centuries of Islam. The *Kalila and Dimna* tales, which derive from the Indian *Pañcatantra,* a mirror for princes written around the year 300, were first translated into Arabic from a Middle Persian version by Ibn al-Muqaffa in the eighth century. The earliest extant Arabic manuscripts do not date from before the early thirteenth century, so there is no direct evidence that earlier manuscripts were illustrated. According to Ibn al-Muqaffa's introduction, however, "He who peruses this book should know that its intention is fourfold. Firstly, it was put into the mouths of dumb animals so that light-hearted youths might flock to read it and so that their hearts would be captivated by the rare ruses of the animals. Secondly, it was intended to show the images of the animals in varieties of paints and colors, so as to delight the hearts of princes and increase their pleasure, and also the degree of care which they would bestow on the work. Thirdly, it was intended that the book be such that both kings and common folk should not cease to acquire it; that it might be repeatedly copied and re-created in the course of time, thus giving work to the painter and the copyist. The fourth purpose of the work concerns the philosophers in particular." From this passage it would seem obvious that the book was always intended to be illustrated (unless the passage is to be understood metaphorically), but the matter is not quite so simple. Ibn al-Muqaffa's text was repeatedly edited in later times, so there is some question about whether this passage belongs to his original edition or was added to justify the inclusion of illustrations in a later edition. Although this question remains a matter for specialists to debate, the tales do seem to have been unusually popular in the Middle Ages, for medieval Hebrew, Latin, and New Persian translations are also known.

A fragment of an illustrated Greek version of *Kalila and Dimna* copied on parchment, which has been attributed to southern Italy between 980 and 1050, bears similarities to the illustrations in later Arabic and Persian manuscripts of the text (fig. 60). These similarities have led scholars to suggest that all the extant illustrated versions descend from a common, but lost, Arabic

FIG. 60. *"The Wolf-Parents complaining to Azacher, the Lion King, about the lion who devoured their young,"*
leaf from a Greek manuscript of Aesop's Fables *and* Kalila and Dimna. *Southern Italy, 980–1050. Ink and*
color on parchment. Pierpont Morgan Library, New York [MS 397, fol. 5v]

manuscript source dating as early as the tenth century and ultimately related,
like the stories themselves, to Central Asian and Indian prototypes. Such
hypotheses aside, this hypothetical illustrated *Kalila and Dimna* manuscript seems
to be the exception to the general observation that illustrated manuscripts were
rare in the first centuries of Islam.

   In imagining the early history of the illustrated book in the Islamic lands,
scholars have also tried to incorporate the evidence of images found on other
fragments of paper, most of which were found in Fustat and are convention-

FIG. 61. *Drawing of a seated figure on the back of
a luster-painted tile. Iran, 1265. Edward C. Moore
Collection, Bequest of Edward C. Moore, The Metropolitan Museum of Art, New York [91.1.105]*

ally dated between the tenth and twelfth centuries. Many of the drawings and
paintings that cannot be specifically identified as coming from books have
been taken to be preparatory studies for painters working on manuscripts or
even on pottery, ivory boxes, glass vessels, wooden panels, and the like. Other
drawings are thought to have been designs for the textile weaver or embroi-
derer, the bookbinder or metalworker. Yet there is no evidence at all that
muralists, potters, metalworkers, glassblowers, or most weavers worked from
designs on paper at this time, so the purpose of the drawings, as well as their
date, remains unclear.

Potters in ninth-century Iraq or eleventh-century Egypt would have
learned to draw on ceramics by practicing not with ink on paper—paper was
too expensive to use and throw away—but with a brush on unfired ceramics or
some other available surface. They would have stored their artistic repertoire
in their memory, not in pattern books, and maintained it in their muscles.
Occasionally, we find a drawing on the back of a tile, which demonstrates that
potters practiced a drawing on disposable or concealed surfaces (fig. 61). The
vast majority of their sketches, therefore, would have been either painted over
or thrown out, leaving little or no indication of how the artist had proceeded
to make the finished product.

The freshness of representation and execution in most media of early
Islamic art, whether ceramics, metal, or textiles, is further evidence for the use
of a direct technique (fig. 62). Had potters or metalworkers copied images
from another medium, such as paper, instead of drawing or working directly
on their medium itself, the resultant drawings would have lacked their charac-

FIG. 62. *Bowl with standing woman holding a goblet and flanked by two birds. Nishapur, Iran, 10th century. Glazed earthenware, diam. 7 ⅞ in. (20 cm). The Metropolitan Museum of Art, New York, Rogers Fund, 1950 [38.40.290]*

FIG. 63. *Plate inscribed "He who professes faith will excel, and to whatever you accustom yourself, you will grow accustomed. Blessing to the owner." Northeastern Iran or Transoxiana, 10th century. The Freer Gallery of Art, Smithsonian Institution, Washington, D.C. [F1952.11]*

teristic energy and individuality. In Islamic ceramics of this period, no two pots are exactly—or even nearly—alike, and the drawings are not rehashed but are fresh and quite independent of representations in any other medium. In short, the men who painted ceramics did not make—or probably even look at—designs appropriate for, say, metalware or carved wood.

There is a significant exception: a group of ceramics attributed to tenth-century northeastern Iran and Transoxiana, particularly the cities of Nishapur and Samarqand, inscribed with Arabic aphorisms in studied, elegant scripts (fig. 63). Unlike the other contemporary pottery attributed to the same region, whose designs were applied directly to the surface, the inscriptions on the plates and bowls were clearly planned in advance so that the calligraphy exactly fits the surface. The inscribed texts are sometimes religious, but for the most part they consist of proverbs of a secular nature, such as "Learning is at first bitter to the taste but in the end sweeter than honey" or "Patience is the key to comfort." One elegant plate, whose inscription reads "Planning before work protects you from regret" has a superfluous letter *kaf* added as a space filler to show what happens when one doesn't plan before work, very much like the once ubiquitous PLAN AHEAᴅ" signs. As a group, these ceramics show that at least some of the city dwellers were literate enough in Arabic to appreciate having their dinnerware decorated with aphorisms written in elegant script.

The spare and deliberate inscriptions on these ceramics are written in scripts close to those used on parchment manuscripts of the Koran attributed to the ninth century (see fig. 39). The styles are quite different from the broken cursive styles used on contemporary manuscripts, whether of secular or religious texts (see fig. 43). Considering the high status accorded calligraphers and the relatively low status of potters, it is unlikely that calligraphers would have deigned to decorate pots or even known how to handle a brush; it is equally improbable that potters were accomplished in the Koranic scripts or knew how to wield a calligrapher's pen. Rather, we must imagine that calligraphers prepared designs that potters copied onto plates and bowls, much as modern craftworkers in the souks of Isfahan, Cairo, and Marrakesh transfer calligraphers' designs to ceramics, metalwork, and embroidery. Although the scripts in which the aphorisms are written are comparable to those of Koran manuscripts on parchment, calligraphers probably prepared their designs not on expensive parchment but on paper, now cheaper and already widely used for other types of manuscripts. Several centuries of paper production in the cities of Central Asia and northeastern Iran made it likely that artisans serving the wealthy urban population who were able to afford fine wares were among the first to explore the artistic possibilities of this new medium.

Paper may also have been involved in the design and production of luxury

FIG. 64. *Linen textile with inscription band tapestry-woven in silk mentioning the name of the Fatimid caliph al-Zahir. Egypt, 1021–36. Royal Ontario Museum, Toronto [973.424.8b]*

textiles, which played an important economic role in medieval Islamic times, but our knowledge about how weavers worked then is based largely on extrapolation from surviving fragments, and these may not necessarily be representative. For most plain fabrics (and those with simple geometric patterns, like stripes and checks), which were the bulk of the textiles produced, weavers had no need of pictorial instructions. Tapestry weavers adding decorative bands may have used drawings under their looms to guide them when inserting colored threads to make their patterns, but the largely repetitive nature of most tapestry designs in this period—bands of small roundels containing geometric, plant, or animal motifs—suggests that all but novices could have produced many of the typical designs from memory or by using a woven sample as a model.

Cartoons on a material like paper, however, were probably required to produce those Islamic textiles inscribed with texts naming the ruler and indicating that they were made on his order. These *tiraz* textiles, produced from early Islamic times in Central Asia, Iraq, and Egypt, were an important sign of sovereignty, because the ruler seasonally gave lengths of the fabrics to courtiers, who had them made up into garments. The formulaic texts were either woven into the fabric using the tapestry technique or embroidered onto the finished fabric, depending on what was usual in the state or private workshop where the fabric was made (fig. 64). A court official prepared the texts, which were then copied into or onto the textile by the weavers or embroiderers, who were presumably illiterate—or so we can judge from the mistakes they often made. Although we can imagine weavers producing geometric, plant, and animal patterns in the borders from memory, the difficulty of inscriptions and their willful complexity point to the need for court officials to have used some portable medium to provide them with correct texts. This medium was probably paper in Central Asia and Iraq, papyrus in Egypt until the ninth century, and, possibly, parchment in North Africa.

Diagrams on paper or a similar medium were also needed to prepare drawlooms to weave luxury silks, which became increasingly popular in the Islamic lands from the tenth century. As we have seen, the older techniques of tapestry weaving and embroidery are dependent on the artisans' decisions as they work. If weavers find that threads are thicker or thinner than usual, they can adjust the pattern as they go along, and embroiderers can choose to create flowers, say, instead of birds. In contrast, with drawloom weaving, which was invented in China and brought to Islamic lands, the pattern has to be prepared in advance and entered on the loom prior to weaving, much the way a program must be installed on a modern computer before we can do anything useful. Entering the pattern on the loom consists of tying cords to each warp (lengthwise) thread; the cords are gathered in bundles, collectively known as a simple, which are pulled in a predetermined order, thereby regulating the pattern to be woven. In itself, the simple does not reveal how the finished textile will look, just as the program files on a computer do not show what a program will do. Once the pattern has been entered on the loom, the weaver and the weaver's assistant, or drawboy, can start weaving. The drawboy select bundles of threads in sequence, thereby raising and lowering the pattern warps, and the weaver inserts the wefts (crosswise threads) to make the cloth. As long as the weaver and the drawboy follow the instructions encoded in the bundles of cords, the designer's pattern will be reproduced in the weave, and very little is left to the weaver's volition.

We have no direct knowledge of how medieval Islamic weavers encoded their patterns, but analogies can be drawn from eighteenth-century France or even twentieth-century Iran, where similar results were obtained. The design for the finished textile is transferred to graph paper, each square representing a single warp step. The graph is transferred to the simple; now each square of the graph represents one tied warp thread. For fine silks, which might have 150 warps per inch (60 per centimeter), entering the pattern into the loom could take as little as a month or as long as a year, and the weaving could progress from half an inch to a yard per day (a centimeter to a meter), depending on the fineness of the pattern and the number of colors used. Given the demands of the technique, designers of drawloom textiles must have drawn preparatory gridded designs, because weavers could not have retained such complexity entirely in memory. No gridded designs for medieval textiles are known to have survived, but the use of grids in other contexts is first suggested by descriptions of Islamic maps from the early tenth century. In addition, we know that a system existed for notating the patterns used on medieval textiles—presumably a grid—because we have examples of complex textiles woven to identical patterns with different materials on different looms.

FIG. 65. *The Shroud of Saint-Josse. Iran or Transoxiana, before 961. Silk twill compound. Musée du Louvre, Paris [AO 7502]*

The complexity of drawloom weaving explains why this elaborate technique was used only for the finest silk textiles, such as the Shroud of Saint-Josse, which was woven in seven colors (plum, yellow, ivory, sky blue, light brown, copper, and golden brown) on red warps with a design of facing elephants with dragons between their feet, the whole surrounded by a train of Bactrian camels (fig. 65). An inscription in Arabic gives the name and titles of a Turkish commander active in northeastern Iran who was executed on the orders of his Samanid sovereign in 961. Because the commander must have been alive when the piece was made, it must have been woven in Khurasan or Transoxiana in the mid-tenth century. It is inconceivable that this splendid textile was prepared without a preliminary drawing to set up the loom, and it is likely, given the place and date of production, that the drawing was made on paper. Complex silks had, of course, been woven on drawlooms in pre-Islamic Byzantium and Sasanian Iran, where paper was not yet available, so the designs were undoubtedly prepared on some other writing surface, presumably parchment, whose expense would have been offset easily by the high cost of the finished goods. Paper was not, therefore, strictly necessary for the planning of drawloom silks, but it facilitated artistic creation and innovation.

Most scholars have assumed that builders in the medieval Islamic lands used plans and that once paper was available, these plans were drawn on paper. But no such plans have survived from the early medieval period, and the assumption is probably unwarranted. As in medieval Europe, architectural practice in the medieval Islamic lands was essentially traditional, empirical, and experimental, and it remained so until modern times, if the anecdote with which this chapter opened is indicative. With few exceptions, builders did not use plans—because they did not need them. Like potters and metalworkers, builders learned from other builders, using memory and gesture to preserve and transmit their plans and designs, as well as to estimate costs and quantities.

Close scrutiny of some exceptional buildings, such as the Dome of the Rock in Jerusalem, which was ordered by the Umayyad caliph Abd al-Malik in 692, admits the possibility that the designer used some graphic aids in setting out an extremely sophisticated plan, but the evidence is far from conclusive, and even here the complex plan may have been drawn out on the site. In any case, to generalize from an exceptional building like the Dome of the Rock could well be misleading, because most other early Islamic structures were far simpler in design and construction.

During the first five centuries of Islam most builders worked entirely without graphic representations, as when erecting the most popular type of mosque—a hypostyle structure, consisting of many columns or piers holding up arches that support vaults or a flat or gabled wooden roof (fig. 66). Hypostyle mosques could be large or small, but the repetitive nature of this type of structure meant that, as in medieval European churches with repeated bays, the first element erected—whether a column, arch, or vault—served as a full-scale model for erecting subsequent elements. Adjustments were easy but

FIG. 66. *Córdoba, interior of the Great Mosque, 10th century*

were also necessary to make, particularly since building materials did not come in standard sizes. Builders adjusted and fit all elements into place on site; plans were of limited value. At the Great Mosque of Tunis, built in the ninth century, the realization of the plan was so askew that none of the angles is even close to right, although this is hardly apparent to the casual observer; many modern plans of the site—even those prepared by qualified drafters—have missed this feature entirely.

Furthermore, most buildings, whether in the Islamic lands, Byzantium, or western Europe, were overbuilt. Buildings were usually far stronger than modern engineers calculate they needed to be, and this was in order to absorb any mistakes made in planning or estimation. It was far wiser, for both builders and clients, to be on the safe side and overbuild. Just as carpenters today know without calculation or reference to manuals what the acceptable span for a wooden beam is, or the appropriate pitch for a roof in a snowy climate, most builders in the medieval Islamic lands knew how to make buildings stand up without recourse to preliminary drawing.

That said sometimes people made drawings of buildings or parts of buildings. Scholars have collected scattered references to plans in early Arabic texts and concluded that plans were widely used, but whatever these plans may have been, they were not very sophisticated, nor were they systematic representations of architectural space. Contemporary geographers had far greater experience of mathematical theory and a far more pressing need to use graphic representation than did the practitioners of the wholly empirical practice of building. Yet even the most sophisticated geographical representations were still remarkably crude, or so we can judge from the surviving examples (see, e.g., fig. 52). It is not likely that builders were more sophisticated than geographers.

Builders may occasionally have made drawings or models to work out a particular detail or to convince a patron to spend money on a building, but most builders did not draw at all, and in any case, few patrons would have been able to read a drawing. Literate people today tend to forget that the ability to conceptualize and represent three-dimensional spaces on two-dimensional surfaces (and decode these representations) is an extremely sophisticated skill, one that has been honed in the West since the Renaissance. There is no evidence that medieval Islamic builders, much less ordinary or even exalted folk, were able to think of buildings and spaces in this way.

Some idea of how people thought about buildings is provided by what was written about them, but there are few such medieval Islamic texts. Not many of the people who wrote books, it would seem, thought much about architecture. The existing discussions of buildings are usually so obscure as to suggest that their authors were grappling to find an appropriate vocabulary with which to express their observations. Here is how the tenth-century historian al-Masudi, who is normally extremely clear, describes a palace erected in ninth-century Iraq:

> And in his day [the caliph] al-Mutawakkil created a building in a style that the people had not known, and it was the one known as "the *hiri* and two sleeves and porticoes." One of his companions in nightly entertainment related to him one night that a king of al-Hira of the Numaniyya [branch] of the Bani Nasr [family] created a building in his permanent residence, that is, in al-Hira, in the image of war and its form, because of his fascination with war and his leaning toward it, so that it would not slip from his memory as long as he lived. And the portico had in it the seat of the king, which is the chest, and the two sleeves to the right and left. And in the two *bayts,* which are the pair of sleeves, were those of his attendants who were close to him. And in the right one was the wardrobe store and in the left, what he needed of drink. And the portico's enclosure encompassed the chest, the two sleeves, and the three doors to the portico. And this construction has been called to this day "the *hiri* and the two sleeves," referring to al-Hira. And the people followed al-Mutawakkil's lead in this example, and it became famous thereafter.

Modern architectural historians have pondered over this text. Had al-Masudi known how to describe buildings as a succession of spaces or how to depict them graphically, he undoubtedly would have done so.

Another example is provided by an inscription on the Great Mosque of Taza, Morocco, which states that the thirteenth-century Marinid sultan Abu Yaqub Yusuf expanded the mosque by four *balat*—the word is normally understood to mean a bay or an area enclosed under a single rectangular vault or roof. Examination of the mosque shows that the sultan actually extended each of the nine aisles, which run perpendicular to the qibla wall, by four units. As we can deduce from the inscription, the contemporary audience was concerned only about the depth of the extension and not about the number of aisles or the direction in which they ran; both of these features are far more important when displayed on a two-dimensional plan than when viewed from inside the mosque.

Like the mason mentioned in the epigraph to this chapter, medieval builders did not need paper to teach them how to use materials and exploit their decorative potential. Masons simply manipulated the spaces between bricks and the way the bricks were laid to create patterns of light and shade, as we can see in the web of brick patterns enveloping the mausoleum erected for

FIG. 67. *Bukhara, tomb of the
Samanids, early 10th century*

the Samanid family in Bukhara (fig. 67). Although paper was certainly available and used in early tenth-century Bukhara, the builder had no need to draw
the geometric patterns that he proposed to use; rather, the ability to make such
patterns was an expected part of the builder's repertoire, learned from masters
and remembered.

In contrast to those who made and decorated buildings, philosophers and
mathematicians, seeing what builders and decorators had done with practical
geometry through empirical knowledge, developed models to explain and
reproduce the results. There is little, if any, indication, however, that artisans
thought or worked in such ways, or that they communicated with the intellectuals. Modern scholars have interpreted several treatises by such thinkers as the
extraordinarily curious and prolific polymath Abu'l-Wafa al-Buzajani and the
tenth-century philosopher al-Farabi as evidence that medieval architectural
practice had a theoretical basis. These works, however, attest more to the intellectual curiosity of the age than to the systematic practice of any art. Similarly,
contemporary manuals of calligraphy are not how-to books but treatises written to fit scripts into authors' theories. As in mathematics, there was a great
difference between the theoretical subjects about which the cultivated urban
elites wrote and the empirical practices of those who got their hands dirty.

The idea of learning how to do something by reading about it in a book is
distinctly modern. The medieval treatises that survive are not manuals but

attempts by intellectuals to give order to what seemed to them to be the chaotic and disorderly practices of artisans. It seems hardly likely that a work such as Abu'l-Wafa's *Book of the Things That Writers and Secretaries Need to Know About Arithmetic,* which is in any case known only from much later Arabic and Persian copies, was intended as a medieval version of *Popular Mechanics* or *Fine Homebuilding,* for medieval builders learned by following the example of their masters, not by reading instructions. Even if artisans could read the Koran or recognize the words in religious inscriptions whose text they already knew by heart, it is doubtful that they were sufficiently literate to read a book on geometrical constructions. Such books should be understood, therefore, in the context of the literary genre known in Arabic as *adab,* belles lettres dealing with knowledge of the nature and passions of human beings and their environment and material and spiritual culture, a subject of great importance in the Abbasid period. We can conclude that although paper was increasingly available to several segments of society from the ninth century, there is little evidence that architects and other artisans were fully alive to its extraordinary potential until three or four centuries later.

FROM THE THIRTEENTH CENTURY

Paper played a larger role in the arts in many of the Islamic lands toward the end of the twelfth century. Apart from a sudden increase in illustrated manuscripts, there is also evidence that artisans in other media used designs on paper for reference or for transfer to another medium, and evidence, too, that builders used paper for architectural plans. Unlike earlier drawings, those from this period had a clear purpose: they can easily be identified as preliminary sketches for more finished works.

But the principal evidence for the increased use of paper concerns books with paintings. Illustrated books burst on the scene in Iraq and Iran during the late twelfth and early thirteenth centuries, when new and different types of books were illustrated, apparently for the first time. In addition to scientific and technical treatises, which had long been illustrated with diagrams and maps, books of poetry and belles lettres now appear with frontispieces and with pictures in the text. But where scientific and technical illustrations had made the accompanying texts intelligible, the new pictures were quite unnecessary for understanding the text. Something new was going on.

Scholars have proposed various explanations for this phenomenon. Some, using pictorial evidence from the other arts, have argued that manuscripts had long been illustrated in the Islamic lands, but as we have seen, little direct evidence supports this hypothesis. Others have traced the explosion of illustrated books to external influences—perhaps, for example, artists in the Islamic lands copied Middle Byzantine or Syrian Jacobite painting—and still others have proposed the appearance of illustrated manuscripts as the result of an internal development within the Islamic lands, specifically the emergence of the bourgeoisie as patrons of this new art form. All of these explanations may be partly true, but they deal with the problem in a rather narrow way. From the broader perspective of the history of paper, it seems obvious that the illustrated book emerged as a major art form just at the time when larger sheets of fine-quality paper became increasingly available.

Northern and central Mesopotamia, the heartland of the old Abbasid caliphate, became the major centers of book illustration in the twelfth and thirteenth centuries. By the early fourteenth century, the center of innovation had shifted to northwestern Iran under the patronage of the Ilkhanids, and the art of the illustrated book remained a speciality of Iran, from which it eventually spread to the Ottoman empire and Mughal (Mogul) India. The Mamluks of Egypt and Syria seem to have been less interested in illustrated books, although a few such manuscripts were produced in either Cairo or Damascus. Only one illustrated manuscript, the romance of the lovers Bayad and Riyad, has survived from Islamic Spain, so it is difficult to generalize about the development of the illustrated book there (see fig. 36). Nevertheless, as the illustrations to this manuscript, which was copied on paper in the thirteenth century, clearly depend on Mesopotamian models, Spain may have enjoyed a parallel flowering of illustrated books from the thirteenth century.

Many of the texts chosen for illustration continued to be scientific and technical works, such as books on astronomy, pharmacology, mechanics, farriery, and the *Kalila and Dimna* animal fables. New works chosen for illustration included the *Book of Songs*, a twenty-volume collection of early Islamic poetry by the tenth-century anthologist Abu'l-Faraj al-Isfahani. A copy of the text was prepared for Badr al-Din Lulu, regent of Mosul in northern Mesopotamia in the early thirteenth century. Although the poems themselves are not illustrated, each volume has a dedicatory frontispiece showing the ruler engaged in a princely activity (fig. 68). These images have been linked to the classical tradition of frontispieces depicting the author or patron of a particular book, but their sudden appearance at this time demands some other explanation. The most likely one is that artists were beginning to realize the potential offered by paper. We know that several other poetical works were illustrated in a similar manner. The historian al-Ravandi mentions in his history of the Saljuqs, composed in 1202, that in 1184–85 the sultan Tughril III asked al-Ravandi's uncle to compile and transcribe an anthology of poems; when it was completed, the painter Jamal of Isfahan illustrated the volume with depictions of the poets cited.

FIG. 68. *"Badr al-Din Lu'lu'lu hunting with falcons," frontispiece to* Book of Songs, *volume 20. Mosul, 1219. Det kongelige Bibliotek, Copenhagen [Cod. arab. 168 fol. 1r]*

Other poetical works contained depictions of events described in the text. An undated manuscript of Ayyuqi's Persian verse romance, *Warqa and Gulshah*, is the earliest illustrated text in the Persian language to survive (fig. 69). The small manuscript has seventy-one striplike illustrations with small haloed figures. Scholars initially thought that the stylistic similarities between the illustrations and dated Iranian lusterware meant that the manuscript had been copied in Iran in the late twelfth century, but the painter's name, Abd al-Mumin ibn Muhammad al-Khuvayyi (which indicates that he came from Khoy, in north-western Iran), also appears on the 1253 endowment deed of the Karatay madrasa in Konya, Turkey. It now seems more likely that the manuscript was copied and illustrated in central Anatolia in the mid-thirteenth century.

One of the favorite texts to be illustrated in the period was the *Maqamat* (Assemblies), composed around 1000 by the Iranian al-Hamadhani but popularized in the version written maybe a century later by the Iraqi al-Hariri. Eleven illustrated copies of the text, a series of fifty picaresque tales set in different parts of the Muslim world, have survived from before 1350. Each recounts the adventures of the rogue Abu Zayd of Saruj as told to the merchant al-Harith. By overwhelming people with his eloquence and erudition, Abu Zayd gets them to reward him with money. The subject of the tales is not the rogue's adventures but the author's verbal pyrotechnics. The illustrated man-

FIG. 69. *"Warqa's father, Humam, dies in his arms," from* Warqa and Gulshah. *Konya, mid-13th century. Topkapi Palace Library, Istanbul, H 841, fol. 16b*

uscripts, however, emphasize an almost gratuitous aspect of the text: the var-ied settings of Abu Zayd's adventures. The most famous copy of the text, tran-scribed and illustrated with ninety-nine pictures by Yahya al-Wasiti in Bagh-dad in 1237, has particularly inventive and detailed illustrations (see fig. 48). Nevertheless, the colophon mentions no patron, so it, like most other manu-scripts of the text, was probably made for sale on the market to a well-educated and well-heeled buyer.

Even historical chronicles began to be illustrated in the late twelfth cen-tury, although no examples have survived. The illustrator of Rashid al-Din's *Compendium of Chronicles,* a multivolume universal history copied in Tabriz, in northwest Iran, in the 1310s, based many of his images on those found in ear-lier manuscripts. Because of the number and consistency of his images dealing with the Ghaznavid and Saljuq dynasties, he must have been copying now-lost illustrated histories of those dynasties. The manuscripts that he copied, and his own, had striplike illustrations scattered throughout, depicting the major battles and enthronements of the Turkish rulers. The illustrations would have been pretty but gratuitous additions to the text.

Illustrated books were not just growing in number and type; they were also increasing in size. Indeed, books of all kinds were being produced in larger formats; with improvement in papermaking techniques, paper in larger sizes became more widely available. The earliest known books with illustrations were very small, measuring only 6 by 3 inches (16 by 7 centimeters), or about one-quarter the size of a sheet of modern business paper. The manuscript of al-Sufi's *Treatise on the Fixed Stars,* dated 1009, measures 10 by 7 inches (27 by 18 cen-timeters; see fig. 51), and the pages of the *Book of Songs* made at Mosul in the early thirteenth century measure 12 by 8½ inches (31 by 22 centimeters; see fig. 68), just a bit larger than a sheet of modern business paper. The celebrated copy of al-Hariri's *Maqamat,* made in Baghdad in 1237, is on even larger pages (13½ by 11 inches; 37 by 28 centimeters; see fig. 48), although the contempo-rary copy of the same text in St. Petersburg is half the size (10 by 7½ inches; 25 by 19 centimeters). The pages in the early fourteenth-century copies of Rashid al-Din's *Compendium of Chronicles* were folded from sheets measuring some 20 by 28 inches (50 by 72 centimeters; see fig. 29), and even larger sheets were used to prepare the Great Mongol *Shahnama,* probably made in Tabriz around 1335 (see fig. 30). By the fifteenth century designers and calligraphers seem to have placed less emphasis on the sheer size of books, preferring to emphasize the qualities of the paper itself and the calligraphy, illumination, and illustra-tion. Nevertheless, particularly important manuscripts, such as royal copies of the *Shahnama* and Timur's mammoth manuscript of the Koran, were often made on unusually large sheets of paper.

F I G . 70. *"Bahram Gur kills the dragon," from the first Small* Shahnama *manuscript. Baghdad or*
northwest Iran, c. 1300. Reproduced by kind permission of the Trustees of the Chester Beatty Library, Dublin [CBL
Per. 104.61]

Small manuscripts must always have remained more common than those
of imperial scale because large sheets of paper were always more difficult to
make (and therefore more expensive). There are, for example, three fine but
small manuscripts of the *Shahnama,* known collectively as the Small *Shahnamas,*
which were produced, at a guess, in Iraq or Iran in the late thirteenth or early
fourteenth century (fig. 70). Although each manuscript is lavishly illustrated
with more than one hundred illustrations spread over three hundred folios,
the written surface of the largest measures only 10½ by 7 inches (25 by 18 centimeters), less than half the size of the Great Mongol *Shahnama.* That these

manuscripts are so consistent in size and scale also shows that they were products of commercial workshops, where ample supplies of good paper in standard sizes were readily available.

That more paper and larger sheets of it were available in the Mongol domains during the late thirteenth and fourteenth centuries placed this region at the forefront of artistic innovation in several respects. First, bigger books allowed artists to design larger and more complicated illustrations than had been previously attempted. The tiny sheets of the earliest illustrated book could not have afforded even the most talented artist much room to display his abilities. The unusually large pages of the 1237 copy of al-Hariri's *Maqamat,* probably made in Baghdad, offered the artist, al-Wasiti, generous spaces in which to create his unusually inventive and expressive compositions, but most contemporary books, especially ones produced in the provinces, where paper supplies were limited, must have been smaller, with space only for narrow striplike illustrations. The seventy-one illustrations in the *Warqa and Gulshah* manuscript measure only 2 to 3 inches (5 to 7 centimeters) high; even the most talented miniaturist would have little scope to show detail and setting. The larger format of Rashid al-Din's *Compendium of Chronicles,* dating from a half-century later, provided the illustrator with a larger surface on which to work, although most of the illustrations retain the striplike format of earlier manuscripts. The Rashid al-Din illustrations, which are typically 4–5 inches (10–12 centimeters) high, are more complex and detailed than earlier illustrations, for the doubling in height and width gave quadruple the area for complicated scenes and details of dress, landscape, and setting. As we might expect, the images in the contemporary Small *Shahnama*s retain the miniature scale of the *Warqa and Gulshah* illustrations.

The culmination of the trend toward larger illustrations on larger pages is the Great Mongol *Shahnama.* Its pages provided the most generous opportunities to date for introducing both spatial and psychological complexity into the picture space (see fig. 30). The images are as much as 8–10 inches (20–25 centimeters) high, and the finest are monumental in conception, in a mode quite at odds with traditional notions of Persian miniature painting. Other illustrations attributed to the same period, detached from manuscripts centuries ago and collected in albums (now in Berlin and Istanbul), are of a comparably generous size, indicating that the Great Mongol *Shahnama* was just one of many large-format manuscripts produced at the time. By the end of the fourteenth century, however, the taste for expansive compositions in early Persian book painting had given way to a preference for an exquisite miniature style in which composite vignettes and episodic lyricism replaced strong composition and emotional drama.

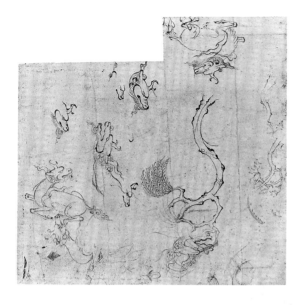

FIG. 71 *Sheet with sketches of mythical animals and trees. Iran, 14th century. Brush and ink on paper, 5 ½ x 5 ⅓ in. (14.5 x 13.5 cm). Staatsbibliothek zu Berlin — Preussischer Kulturbesitz — Orientabteilung [Diez A, fol. 73, S. 46, nr. 3]*

In a parallel development, illuminators began to take advantage of the expanded format of Koran manuscripts to decorate the opening pages with extraordinarily complex geometrical patterns. Pages at the beginning and end of a text decorated with geometric interlaces and arabesques had been popular additions to manuscripts of the Koran since earliest times, but the complexity of the compositions was limited by the relatively small size of the page and often by the reluctance of the designer to use all the space available. In the thirteenth and fourteenth centuries illuminators exploited the bigger pages, as well as the smoother surface of the available paper, to create designs of unparalleled complexity, detail, and elegance (see fig. 78). Thus it was not simply a matter of more and cheaper paper creating the conditions for the art of the book, although these were key factors. Larger and higher-quality sheets of paper were also a precondition for major changes in style and composition.

A second way in which the use of paper had an effect on the arts was that artisans of all types began drawing on paper, making it an important stage in artistic creation. The albums in Berlin and Istanbul also preserve ink drawings dated to the fourteenth century that were certainly preparatory sketches for some other work (fig. 71). Some of them must have been preserved in artists' or studio portfolios to maintain and transmit successful designs and compositions once a completed manuscript had been sent from the workshop to the patron's library. Other drawings may have been used to prepare designs for transfer to other media, such as ceramics or metalwork.

Preliminary drawings had already been used in the early thirteenth century, as we can see by charting the development of Iranian lusterware. The luster ceramic tiles and vessels, which often bear precise dates, display a variety of

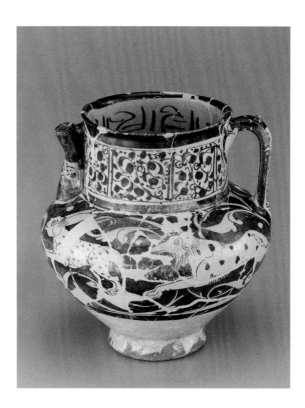

FIG. 72. *Luster-painted jug.
Kashan, 12th century. Glazed
fritware, height 7 in. (17.9 cm).
Freer Gallery of Art, Smithsonian
Institution, Washington, D.C.
[F1909.370]*

styles. Scholars initially associated the different styles with different centers of production, such as Rayy and Kashan, but more recent scholarship has shown that luster potting was a monopoly of the city of Kashan, in central Iran, and that all the styles were produced there. The earliest style of decoration is the "monumental" style, in which large-scale motifs were painted directly on the surface and kept in reserve against a luster ground—that is, the "subject" is left white, with a few details drawn in luster, while the background is painted (fig. 72). Dated to the twelfth century, this style bears many similarities to the type of painting found on Egyptian lusterware from about a century earlier, and it may have been introduced to Iran by immigrant Egyptian potters. In the second, "miniature" style, the ceramic surface was divided into panels or bands, and the designs were drawn on the glaze much as if the luster paint were a form of ink (fig. 73). In the third, "Kashan" style, figures are reserved against the ground as in the monumental style but are drawn as in the miniature style. In the Kashan style both figure and ground, however, are decorated with painted and scratched (reserved) spirals and surrounded by similarly decorated inscription bands (fig. 74).

The differently styled ceramics are usually explained as the products of different workshops or as the result of changes over time, but they also reveal that painters were using paper designs in the preparation of their work. The monumental style comes out of the traditional method of painting directly on

FIG. 73. *Luster-painted bowl. Kashan, March 1191. Glazed fritware, diam. 15 in. (38 cm). The Art Institute of Chicago, Logan-Patten-Ryerson Collection [1927.414]*

FIG. 74. *Luster-painted dish. Kashan, 1207. Glazed fritware, diam. 13⅘ in. (35 cm). Victoria and Albert Museum, London [C51-1952]*

the ceramic surface, whereas the miniature style, which has often been compared to contemporary manuscript painting, such as the *Warqa and Gulshah* illustrations (see fig. 69), shows that some painters were adopting for the ceramic surface techniques developed for drawing on paper. The Kashan style, which best displays the luster technique, is the work of master decorators who were comfortable not only with the ceramic techniques of reserve painting but also with the fluid drawing and calligraphy more suited to working on paper.

These master decorators of Kashan, unlike potters elsewhere, had high status. Earlier potters had occasionally signed their work with a name and perhaps a father's name (as in the case of the Egyptian luster potter Muslim ibn Dahhan), but some of these Kashan potters traced their lineages over several generations. They rose to positions of importance in the arts, as well as in government and religion, particularly under the Ilkhanids. One of the best known families of potters descended from one Abu Tahir, who must have lived around 1200. His grandson Ali ibn Muhammad ibn Abi Tahir was active in the middle of the thirteenth century, for he signed several luster mihrabs between 1242 and 1265. Ali's son Yusuf signed major luster mihrabs between 1305 and 1334.

Ali's sons—Yusuf's brothers—chose to enter other professions. One, Izz al-Din Mahmud, became a mystic in the ulema, or religious establishment—specifically, at the Suhrawardi Sufi hospice in Natanz. Another, Jamal al-Din Abu'l-Qasim Abdallah, became a scribe and accountant in the Ilkhanid bureaucracy. This second brother, Abu'l-Qasim, wrote a biography of the sultan, as well as a treatise on gems and minerals, a section of which remains the major literary source on the art of making ceramics in medieval Iran. Abu'l-Qasim's treatise, unlike earlier theoretical manuals—which show little familiarity with how things were actually done—is based on a firsthand knowledge of pottery, learned from his family. Clearly, by the early fourteenth century a new type of artisan had emerged in Iran who was able to move easily between the hands-on practice of ceramics and the text-based literary culture traditionally associated with the bureaucracy and the ulema.

At the same time, just when paper use was spreading, the quality of painting on Kashan ceramics declined. A century earlier the drawing on Kashan ceramics had represented the finest drafting skill in Iran; by the fourteenth century it had become clumsier and less inventive than in either earlier ceramic decorations or contemporary book illustrations. It is hardly a coincidence that painting on pottery declined as painting in books became more important, improved in quality, and increased in expressiveness. The growing prestige of book painting in the thirteenth and fourteenth centuries, fostered, as we now know, by the increased availability of paper, may have encouraged the best decorators of pottery to switch to paper. Dust Muhammad, the Safavid librarian and chronicler, looked back on this period as the source of the later Persian tradition of representation. He said that it was in the reign of the Ilkhanid Abu Said (r. 1317–35) that a certain painter, Master Ahmad Musa, had "lifted the veil from the face of depiction" and invented the style of depiction that was then current.

By the fifteenth century the idea of working from paper drawings was so common that they were regularly used and reused, or so we can infer from the many figures and compositions repeated and reversed in manuscript illustrations. Sometimes artists copied their models by eye, adding subtle changes of line and scale, but sometimes they used mechanical means of transferring designs. A scene of an open-air Mongol court in the *Anthology* prepared for Iskandar Sultan in 1410–11 appears to be based on an earlier, probably Ilkhanid painting (fig. 75). Close inspection reveals that the artist of the *Anthology* composition traced the outlines of the drawing following a row of tiny dots, still visible beneath his line. Dust or powdered pigment, called pounce,

FIG. 75. *"An open-air Mongol court," from an* Anthology *prepared for Iskandar Sultan. Ink and color on paper. Shiraz, 1410–11. Calouste Gulbenkian Foundation, Lisbon [L. A. 161 fol. 260b]*

FIG. 76. *Pricked drawing of
"a paradisiacal scene." Iran, 2d
half of the 15th century. Staatsbibliothek zu Berlin — Preussischer
Kulturbesitz - Orientabteilung
[Diez A Fol. 73, S. 39, nr. 1]*

was rubbed through a pricked design on paper or parchment to create a copy
of the original. Pouncing, which is related to stenciling, seems to have origi-
nated in China before the tenth century, for pounced drawings were used to
mass-produce wall paintings in Dunhuang; Sir Aurel Stein actually found
three heavily pounced paper drawings in the Cave of the Thousand Buddhas
there. The technique of pouncing was carried across Asia and surfaced in Iran
about 1400, although the pricked drawings still extant are of a somewhat later
date (fig. 76). The first appearance of pouncing in Europe is in Cennino
Cennini's *Libro dell'arte* (around 1390), where he recommends using it to repli-
cate complex brocade patterns in paintings. Although it is possible to make
stencils and pricked drawings on parchment or skin — and Cennini did so —
the dissemination of this technique across western Asia was closely tied to the
medium of paper. The similarity of design and scale on several vessels and tiles
produced at Iznik in the late fifteenth or early sixteenth century suggests that
potters in western Anatolia used pouncing for transferring patterns from
paper to the ceramic surface.

The first attempts at establishing a dynastic style may have been made
under the Ilkhanids. As early as the fourteenth century, the designs on metalware began to bear strong similarities to designs found in contemporary manuscript illustrations. No intermediary drawings survive, but it is more likely

that metalworkers and book illustrators were working from common design
sources than that one was dependent on the other. Similarly, the carved and
painted geometric patterns decorating the vaults of sultan Uljaytu's gargantuan
mausoleum at Sultaniyya, built in the early fourteenth century (fig. 77), share
many features with the geometric frontispieces decorating contemporary
manuscripts of the Koran (fig. 78). Unlikely though it may be that Ilkhanid
plasterers also worked with pen and ink, the similarities do indicate that, as
with metalwork and book illustration, architectural decorators and manuscript
illuminators worked from common sources. Although none is known to have
survived, these sources must have been drawings on paper that could be read
and interpreted by manuscript illuminators, architectural decorators in paint
and stucco, and metalworkers alike.

By the fifteenth century the evidence for the use of such drawings is
unequivocal, for significant numbers of preparatory drawings from this
period have been preserved. In addition, there is clear evidence for the existence of royal design studios. We know that the Timurid prince Baysunghur
placed the renowned calligrapher Jafar ibn Ali Tabrizi in charge of his court
workshop. In a celebrated letter, the calligrapher wrote to the prince detailing
progress on twenty-two projects, including manuscripts, designs, objects,
tents, and architectural work. At least twenty-three artists, painters, illuminators, calligraphers, binders, rulers, and chestmakers worked alone and in
teams within the royal studio. Unlike earlier times, when craftworkers would
have been responsible for reinterpreting what they had seen and remembered,
artisans now were charged with reproducing and executing designs created by
others. Furthermore, individuals engaged in different crafts worked from the
same or similar designs.

The medium of paper not only allowed designs to be conveyed from a
designer to an artisan but also served to convey designs from one medium to
another. Drafters could abstract a design from one place and apply it in an
entirely different setting. The scale, too, might also change dramatically. An
artist could, for example, draw a design observed on a Chinese carved lacquer
bowl and put the drawing aside in a portfolio or album. A bookbinder or plasterer might come upon the drawing and transfer the design by means of sten-
cil or pounce to another medium, perhaps a molded-leather book cover or a
carved and painted plaster panel many times the size of the original lacquer
bowl. The bookbinder or plasterer would never have seen the bowl, and the
intermediary drafter might have had no inkling that his drawing would be
translated into leather or stucco. Designs were divorced from their original
contexts, and this free-floating quality of design became a feature of later
Islamic art, particularly the art made for the court.

FIG. 77. *Gallery vaults of Sultaniyya, mausoleum of Sultan Uljaytu, early 14th century*

Paper also allowed artists to plan their work in new ways. In the fifteenth
and sixteenth centuries, the tile designs on buildings erected by Timurid and
Safavid patrons are so often exactly fitted to the space available that the designs
must have been worked out first on paper. After artisans in workshops made
tiles following the designs, the finished tiles were sent to the sites for installa-
tion. In another example, in the fifteenth-century Blue Mosque in Tabriz, an
unfinished inscription carved in marble indicates that the engraver must have
been working from full-scale drawings.

A third consequence of the increased availability of paper after 1200 was
the development of systems of notation that allowed designers to encode
specific instructions for later realization. A design for an inscription might be
only the outline of the letters drawn on paper at full scale. An architectural
plan on paper, on the other hand, is a complex system of representing three-
dimensional space at reduced scale on a two-dimensional surface. In spite of
occasional statements from rulers and philosophers that plans had been used
in earlier times, there is little direct evidence that architects and builders
worked with them. Later they did.

The earliest surviving architectural plan from the Islamic lands that was
actually meant to help a builder erect a structure is a small plaster plaque found
in the ruins of Takht-i Sulayman, the late thirteenth-century Mongol summer
capital in Iran. The plaque is inscribed with lines that may have told the work-

FIG. 78. *Right-hand frontispiece to the sixth section of a thirty-part Koran manuscript copied at the Rab'-i rashidi in Hamadan for the Ilkhanid sultan Uljaytu. National Library, Cairo [MS 72]*

ers how to assemble a *muqarnas* (stalactite) vault from prefabricated plaster elements (fig. 79). The vault at Takht-i Sulayman has long since collapsed, but at
least one other contemporary muqarnas vault—that over the tomb of Abd al-
Samad at Natanz—survives to give a good idea of how the pieces would have
been put together (fig. 80). The inscribed plaque differs from an architectural
plan in that it seems to have functioned merely as a memory aid for artisans
who already knew the general principles of constructing such a vault; it was not
a complete set of instructions from the planner to the builder. If the excava-
tor's reconstruction based on the diagram is correct, this vault would have been
the most complex example of the type in Ilkhanid architecture. Such graphic
representations would have been increasingly used in building, and this is
confirmed by contemporary texts.

FIG. 79. *Plaster plaque bearing
the design for a* muqarnas *vault,
found in the ruins of the Ilkhanid
palace at Takht–i Sulayman*

FIG. 80. *Shrine of Abd al-
Samad,* muqarnas *vault over
tomb. Natanz, Iran, 1307*

By the second quarter of the fourteenth century, plans, presumably drawn on paper, were drawn up in Tabriz and sent to Yazd for the construction of Rukn al-Din's funerary complex, which included a madrasa, a hostel for descendants of the Prophet, a hospice for Sufis, a bazaar, and a bath. Because drawing and reading plans is a learned skill, designers in Tabriz must have known that builders in Yazd would know how to decode their renderings on paper and transform them into brick, plaster, and tile. Nevertheless, there is no reason to believe that all builders immediately gave up their traditional practices to erect buildings using paper plans, and this supposition is confirmed by the wide variation in buildings erected during the fourteenth century in Iran.

By the fifteenth century plans and other graphic representations had become more important in architectural practice, although wide differences in the metrology of extant buildings—in their dimensions and proportions—suggest that much construction remained largely empirical. Still, references to paper plans proliferate in this period, and the noted Timurid architect Qivam al-Din Shirazi was reportedly skilled in "engineering, building, and drawing." The oldest architectural drawings on paper to survive can be dated as early as the fifteenth century and include the Topkapi Scroll, a paper roll of drawings for architectural decoration probably compiled in the late fifteenth century in northwestern Iran and preserved in the Topkapi Palace Library. The Topkapi Scroll, however, shows no signs of ever having been used by an actual artisan.

If, as the increasing use of plans suggests, architects and builders developed a language of architectural representation beginning in the fourteenth century, builders, more often than not, must have been able to figure out what the designers intended. Because no elevation drawings for buildings have survived, we do not know whether they would have been used, for builders could have been trained to recognize elevations, or perhaps the essential "skeletal" elements of a building, from plans alone.

With the increased use of plans came a growing uniformity of architecture in the Islamic lands in the fifteenth century and later. Some of this uniformity cannot be ascribed to the increased use of paper plans, it is true. If Mamluk architecture exhibits a certain sameness over the course of the fifteenth century, we can look to the itinerant builders of Cairo, Damascus, and Jerusalem, who were constantly exposed to the buildings that existed as well as those being constructed. The builders and decorators were, in this case, easily able to transmit ideas using the traditional means of memory and gesture. It is much more surprising that contemporary Timurid and Ottoman architecture, which is spread over a much larger geographical area, exhibits stylistic homogeneity. Although teams of builders and decorators did travel from one city to another in search of work, the impressive uniformity of buildings in both realms in the fifteenth century is not a function of their itinerancy but of a fundamentally new approach to design: professional architects in one place prepared designs for realization in another.

Architectural drawings on squared (graph) paper were used in fifteenth-century Iran—to wit, some plans preserved in Tashkent, apparently dating from the sixteenth century but presumed to reflect fifteenth-century originals, and the gridded drawings in the Topkapi scroll. Certainly, the popularity of expanses of tilework executed in the *bannai* technique—glazed bricks set against unglazed ones to form large-scale patterns and spell out pious names in square Kufic script—suggests preliminary planning on squared paper, with the squares of the grid corresponding to the bricks. Such grids might also have helped builders to estimate the requisite quantities of materials.

Like pricked drawing, squared paper was apparently an invention whose time had come. In the Islamic lands both appear at the same time, following the opening of links with China. In Europe, in contrast, there was a time lag. Returning European merchants and missionaries may have led the Italian Cennino Cennini to prick designs by the late fourteenth century, but the first European architects to use squared paper worked a century later, and even then it was not common. Grids of squares were just one of the systems that architects used. Other proportional systems were based on the diagonal of the square, the equilateral triangle, the semisquare, and the golden rectangle (1:1.618). Whatever the system, it involved drawing and manipulating on paper to generate the designs eventually realized by builders.

As paper plans and drawings in all the arts led to a separation between the designer who planned a work of art and the artisan who executed it, they also led to the emergence of a new aesthetic, in which originality of conception and composition was replaced by a unity of expression and the ability to spin elegant variations on well-known themes. This change was part of a larger one in the eastern Islamic lands, where the taste for artistic originality that had existed under Mongol patronage reverted to a more traditional Iranian taste for the familiar, however revamped. Contemporary Persian literature also celebrated, not novelty of expression, but a poet's ability to play on forms and themes already in the canon. Artists and architects came to be judged—as calligraphers long continued to be—on their fidelity to their masters' models, and this fidelity was encouraged by new paper-based techniques of reproduction.

As design became separate from execution, the careers and even personalities of individual architects and artists, consigned formerly to the obscurity of a mythic and anecdotal past, emerged into the bright light of historical fact. For the first time we can delineate careers—of the Timurid architect Qivam al-

Din and the Ottoman master Sinan. Master drafters and painters, such as the incomparable Persian painters Bihzad and Sultan-Muhammad, came into the limelight, too: their works are signed, and their distinct styles are recognized. Conversely, artisans still engaged in such traditional Islamic arts as woodwork, metalwork, and ceramics, who—considering the numerous signatures on their works—had once enjoyed renown, receded into anonymity as their role was reduced; no longer artists in their own right, they merely executed designs prepared by others.

This is not to say that all artists and artisans everywhere in the Islamic lands suddenly began to use paper, for the shift was gradual and affected some regions and some media more than others. Iran remained at the forefront of the arts. In the Maghrib (the Islamic west), an area that had for centuries charted an independent artistic course, the new uses of paper had hardly any effect on the arts. Even within a region, there were differences in the use of paper, for the urban-centered arts of the court were far more likely to involve paper than were the arts of villagers and nomads. Throughout the fifteenth century, Iranian carpet weavers, for example, continued to work by memorizing patterns and counting knots, having no need to use paper cartoons. Although images of carpets and textual references to them indicate that they were highly valued at court, the court did not yet control production, so traditional methods prevailed. Meanwhile, the production of other types of textiles, such as fancy robes embroidered with gold around the collars and cuffs, became dependent on paper patterns, several of which survive from the first half of the fifteenth century.

In the late fifteenth century weavers began to use paper cartoons to produce rugs. For centuries Anatolian weavers had knotted rugs with geometric or geometricized patterns. Some of the earliest to survive are the Konya carpets, now dated to the early fourteenth century, which have a central field with small, angular motifs arranged in staggered rows; the contrasting border is of large pseudo-Kufic designs or stars. Comparable designs produced in the second half of the fifteenth century are known as Holbein carpets; they have a field containing several large octagons inscribed in square frames separated and bordered by bands composed of smaller octagons. The octagons are usually decorated with strapwork patterns, and the several borders of varying width are often decorated with elegant pseudo-Kufic inscriptions with intertwined stems (fig. 81). Despite the apparent complexity of the patterns, which were knotted in brightly colored wool yarns, weavers could produce these carpets from remembered designs or copy them by counting knots.

Ushak medallion carpets, however, another contemporary type of carpet, must have been knotted using paper patterns. Also woven in Anatolia, proba-

FIG. 81. *Large-patterned Holbein carpet. Anatolia, late 15th century. Wool pile, 14 x 6½ feet
(4.29 x 2 m). Staatliche Museen zu Berlin, Preussischer Kulturbesitz, Museum für Islamische Kunst
[I. 5526]*

bly in or near the town of Ushak, these carpets are similar in technique and color to the Holbein group, but have curvilinear symmetrical designs of arabesques and small tendrils enclosed within enormous ogival medallions (fig. 82). It is believed that Holbein carpets were made for export to Europe, but the enormous Ushak medallion carpets were woven expressly for the Ottoman court, and this difference may explain the dissimilarities of design. But a further difference is that the higher-quality Ushak carpet required a paper pattern for its execution, whereas the lower-quality Holbein one did not.

A minute analysis of the design elements used in Ushak medallion carpets reveals several that are characteristic of other media. It is unlikely that the weavers themselves generated these motifs; rather, the designs incorporating them were prepared in the royal design studio in Istanbul for execution by weavers in Ushak. The weavers would have been supplied with paper cartoons, which they would have flipped and rotated as they worked. As elsewhere in the Islamic lands, the introduction of paper designs and cartoons for royal carpets made in Ushak did not immediately spell an end to traditional Anatolian techniques of weaving and design, but it did serve to differentiate the urban arts of the courts, which used paper, from nomadic and village production, which did not.

The same process that had taken place in fifteenth-century Anatolia took place in sixteenth-century Iran, when the geometric patterns that had characterized earlier carpets were replaced by extremely fine carpets with complex floral and pictorial designs. Whereas the patterns on earlier carpets could have been knotted from memory, the intricate symmetrical designs on royal carpets of the Safavid period must have been worked out on paper long before the loom was prepared, and the weavers themselves must have tied their knots following the instructions encoded in paper cartoons. The weavers were mechanics, in other words, not artists, and in some respects, the change in role flattened the aesthetic landscape.

To make the matched pair of enormous carpets (34½ by 17½ feet; 10.5 by 5.35 meters) made for the Safavid shrine in Ardabil in 1539–40 all the weavers must have worked either from two identical paper cartoons or reused the cartoon once the first carpet was finished. Both carpets are signed as the work of "the servant of the court, Maqsud of Kashan," who must have been not the actual weaver, who with his assistants tied several million knots, but the designer or supervisor of the project. Similarly, one Ghiyath al-Din Jami signed the huge Safavid throne carpet in 1542–43, a carpet decorated with lively hunting scenes. The design sources can also be recognized in contemporary manuscript illustration. Although these extraordinarily cerebral carpets are unquestionably among the greatest examples of the art, they carry a distinctly different aesthetic message than do cruder—but perhaps equally beauti-

FIG. 82. *Ushak medallion carpet. Wool pile, length 23 ⅔ feet (7.23 m). The al–Sabah Collection, Dar al–Athar al–Islamiyyah, Kuwait [LNS 26R]*

ful—carpets woven from memory. As in Anatolia, only the finest court-spon-
sored carpets were woven in this way; Iranian nomads and villagers continued to
work in the traditional manner well into the nineteenth and twentieth centuries, when European demand for room-sized rugs in standard and often
complex patterns made paper cartoons a necessity.

Although we know very little about the people who made carpets or textiles or any of the other crafts in premodern times, the difference between
making things from memory and working from drawn patterns may also have
had something to do with gender. Until recently, nomad and village women
were responsible for the production of textiles used in daily life, whereas men
in city factories usually made the higher-status and more expensive textiles.
Because the use of paper patterns before modern times is associated exclusively
with the more expensive and high-status textiles, such as tapestry, embroidered
tiraz, drawloom silks, and fine large carpets with curvilinear designs, visual literacy, much like verbal literacy, was, it seems, predominantly—though not
exclusively—associated with men.

CHAPTER 6

In 1483 the printer Ripoli . . . contracted to print a Latin translation of Plato by Marsilio Ficino, charging 3 florins for printing each of the 30 sections, 90 florins in all. Since the whole work was limited to 1,025 copies, each section comprising 4 sheets, the cost price of the paper must have come to 120–160 florins, dearer than the actual printing costs.
—LUCIEN FEBVRE AND HENRI-JEAN MARTIN, *The Coming of the Book*

The transfer of paper and papermaking technology from the Islamic lands to Christian Europe in the eleventh and twelfth centuries prepared the way for the European print revolution of the fifteenth century. Yet Gutenberg's invention might never have taken off if he and his followers had been limited to printing books on parchment. Gutenberg is thought to have printed 200 copies of his Bible, 35 on parchment and 165 on paper, although only about 40 copies survive altogether. Early printers used movable type to produce editions of one hundred to two hundred, but by 1500 print runs of one thousand or two thousand copies—the print run of modern scholarly titles—were not unusual. Martin Luther's complete German Bible was printed in 1534 in an edition of four thousand copies, and it was reprinted many times. By the seventeenth century most important books had print runs of one thousand to two thousand copies, although editions of popular religious titles regularly surpassed that number. All this printing required enormous quantities of paper, and papermills throughout Europe struggled to meet the demand.

The invention of movable type came almost five centuries after the first use of paper in Europe (sometime before the year 1000). In that time, papermaking spread slowly from the Mediterranean region across the Alps, and written records and other forms of notation came to be used more and more—just as those developments had accompanied the spread of paper in the Muslim world. That Europeans learned about papermaking from the Arabs of Spain, North Africa, and the Levant—and not directly from the Chinese or other East Asians—meant that until the nineteenth century all European paper was made from rags. As paper became an essential commodity in Europe new sources of fiber were sought. Even in the seventeenth century, when Europeans encountered East Asian paper made directly from plant fibers, they did not realize its significance and thought it to be a local variant of the "Western" tradition of papermaking.

The first Christians to encounter paper were probably Nestorians living in Central Asia before the coming of Islam, but their small number made them insignificant so far as any technological breakthrough was concerned. The Christians living under the banner of Islam, however, recognized the advantages of paper as soon as they encountered it. Although Christians, like Muslims and Jews, were initially reluctant to transcribe their scriptures on the new material, the Greek Christian manuscript copied in Damascus in 800 shows that the use of paper was not linked to religious affiliation (see fig. 25). Extensive diplomatic and scholarly contacts in the ninth century between Muslims and Christians—specifically, between the Abbasid capital of Baghdad, where paper quickly became common, and the Byzantine capital of Constantinople—should have made the Byzantines aware of paper at an early date, but they seem to have suffered from a sort of technophobia, so paper was hardly used in Byzantium before the eleventh century and did not become common until the late thirteenth. In contrast to the Byzantine Christians of eastern Europe, the Latin Christians of southern Europe learned about paper from Muslims making it in Spain and Sicily and were actively making it themselves by the twelfth century. From southern Europe papermaking was brought north of the Alps to France and Germany. Western European willingness to embrace and improve on this and other new technologies in the late Middle Ages, as opposed to the conservative Byzantine attitude, would have momentous ramifications in the centuries to come.

BYZANTIUM

There is little, if any, evidence that the Byzantines ever manufactured paper themselves. Until paper began to be used in the eleventh century, Byzantine books were usually copied on parchment codices, and state or legal documents were usually copied on papyrus and, later, parchment scrolls. Most modern scholars believe that Byzantium imported all the paper it used, even after it became popular, first from the Arab lands of West Asia, especially Syria, and then from Christian Spain or Italy. Arab paper was known as *bambúkinon* or *bombúkinon* and *bagdatikón,* names derived from the cities of Mambij and Baghdad, respectively.

As in the Islamic lands, bureaucrats were the first to use paper. The earliest preserved example of a Byzantine document on paper is a decree in roll form of the emperor Constantine IX Monomachos dated 1052, and at least thirteen other documents on paper survive from the eleventh century. Usually measuring something under 6½ feet (2 meters) in length, but occasionally as much as 23 feet (7 meters), these documents were pasted up from sheets measuring 14–16 inches (36–42 centimeters) wide. The format, roughly comparable to that of contemporary Fatimid documents preserved at Mount Sinai, shows that in chancellery practice, as in ceremonial practice, the Fatimids and the Byzantines were unusually close. If we can generalize from the nearly six hundred surviving Byzantine documents that date from the eleventh to the fifteenth century, paper and parchment were used in almost equal proportions. Paper, like papyrus, was a luxury product; the conservative imperial chancellery simply replaced the papyrus roll, a commodity imported from Egypt, with paper, a commodity imported from Syria and other Arab lands.

An inventory of the library of the monastery of Attaleiates in Constantinople, written in 1077, lists eight books on paper and six on parchment, indicating that both were used. Contemporaries may have judged parchment to be more durable, for a document written by the empress Irene Doukaina before 1118 states that the original copy of a certain convent's charter was to be preserved on parchment in the church of Hagia Sophia, and paper copies were to be kept in the convent itself. This evidence is confirmed by a manuscript (Gr. 504) in the Vatican, copied in 1105. It is believed to be the oldest dated Byzantine manuscript on paper, although only parts (folios 5–115 and 157–190) were copied on paper, the rest being copied on parchment. The unusually large size and squarish proportions of the paper sheets (16½ by 21½ inches; 42.2 by 55 centimeters), which are unlike those of contemporary Arab paper, are probably due to the mixture of paper and parchment. The size of the more expensive parchment would have determined the shape of the book. The more rectangular sheets of paper would have been trimmed to match, perhaps wasting as much as a third of each sheet.

From the late twelfth century, manuscripts copied on paper became increasingly common in Byzantium, and by the early thirteenth century, they were largely being written on Spanish and Italian papers, indicating new sources of supply. On the one hand, this change can be understood as a general consequence of the Crusades and the constant insecurity in the region, which undoubtedly interrupted Syrian paper production; on the other hand, it can be understood as a specific consequence of the Fourth Crusade, when the Venetians conquered Constantinople, in 1204. European papers became even more common after the Byzantines reconquered the city in 1261. Already in 1260 a Catalan document from Barcelona notes the export of "French cloth, oil, paper and other kinds of merchandise" to Constantinople.

By the second half of the fourteenth century, paper had become the principal material for writing in the Byzantine empire, but now Italian papers dominated the market. Italian commercial superiority and the declining fortunes and diminishing size of the Byzantine empire in the fourteenth and fifteenth centuries made Constantinople an uneconomical place to set up a papermill. This situation changed after the Ottoman conquest of the city in 1453, when the first papermill known of there was established in the suburb of Kagithane (Papermill), and the city, which came to be known as Istanbul, was finally fully integrated into the world of paper. Although chancellery documents, as well as Greek manuscripts produced at the fifteenth-century court of

Mehmed II, were still copied on European, mostly north Italian, paper, Arabic and Persian texts from Mehmed II's royal library were copied exclusively on paper of West Asian manufacture.

By the time that paper production developed in Ottoman Istanbul, however, papermaking had virtually vanished from its traditional Syrian and Egyptian locales. Although the Ottomans may have already established paper-mills in such Anatolian cities as Amasya, the closest and most likely places from which Istanbul papermakers could have learned their craft were the Turkmen-held cities of Shiraz, Isfahan, and Tabriz in Iran, which had been centers of papermaking and the arts of the book at least since the late thirteenth century and which flourished under the patronage of the Aqqoyunlu Turkmens in the fifteenth century. From the 1450s, Ottoman calligraphers adopted the Iranian technique of using a harder size (finish) for their paper, rather than the softer size preferred by Arab calligraphers, and Ottoman illuminators adopted the brilliant Iranian style of illumination characterized by a lavish use of gold. It is likely, therefore, that Iranian artisans brought these techniques to the Ottoman court. At exactly this time, scribes from the Aqqoyunlu court came to work for the Ottomans, introducing the distinctive Iranian chancellery script, known as *taliq,* that the Ottomans assimilated and transformed into their characteristic *divani* script.

SPAIN

The Christians of the Iberian Peninsula were far more receptive to paper than the Byzantines were, a testimony to the sharing of material and technical culture under the Umayyad caliphate. Spanish Christians became familiar with paper well before the year 1000, almost as soon as Muslims began to use it, and as Christians became masters of greater areas of the peninsula after 1000 they used it more. That the use of paper had expanded in Spain by the twelfth century can be seen in the comment of Peter the Venerable, abbot of the Benedictine monastery at Cluny, in France, after returning from a pilgrimage to Santiago de Compostela in 1141. Peter, who had commissioned translations of five Arabic books, including the Koran, had a remarkable knowledge of Islam. Having seen that the monks of the Cluniac monasteries in Spain used paper, he hyperbolically expressed his aversion to it: "In Heaven [says the Jew], God reads the Talmud. But what kind of book is this? In appearance it is like those that we read every day, which are made from the skins of rams, he-goats, and calves [that is, parchment], or the bark of rushes [papyrus] plucked in the swamps of the East. These [papers], however, are made from scraps of old rags, or, perhaps, from even viler stuff; and they are inscribed in foul ink by means of the feathers of birds or swamp reeds." Peter's rantings are important early

---

SPANISH PAPER

Several tenth-century manuscripts from the monastery of Santo Domingo de Silos indicate that paper was available at that time in Spain, although it may not have been made there before the early eleventh century. The characteristic features of Spanish-Arab paper, which have been studied in detail by the Catalan scholar Oriol Valls y Subirà, are long fibers, sizing with starch paste made from wheat or rice, glazing, and zigzag marks. The chain lines, left by the paper molds, are irregularly spaced wavy lines of varying thicknesses, suggesting that the molds lacked ribs to give them dimensional stability. When the unsupported mold mesh sagged with use, it produced sheets appreciably thicker in the middle than at the edges. The laid lines, also left by the molds, are always taut and parallel, however. Apparently, they were produced by hempen threads previously boiled in oil to ensure stiffness; vegetable fibers and horsehair were also used to make the mold mesh. There are normally ten to fifteen laid lines per inch (four to six per centimeter).

The manufacture of paper in Valencia became so important that in 1274, the king, Jaume I, prohibited the sale of rags at fairs to Perpignan merchants, and in 1306, after a disagreement with the king of France, Jaume II placed an embargo on paper,

. . . continued

evidence for the use of paper, but Diderot, in the eighteenth century, considered his comments suspect and erroneously concluded that true paper was unknown in Europe before the thirteenth century.

Fortunately, Peter's rodomontade had little effect on the use of paper, and in the following centuries it became the material of choice in Spain and elsewhere in Europe, particularly for documents and records, if not for books. The Valencian paper industry, centered at Játiva, flourished until it was overshadowed by Italian production in the fourteenth century. Sheets of Játiva paper typically measured 11½ by 16–19 inches (29 by 40–47 centimeters). Size varied wildly, though; before printed books, there was simply no need to make paper in absolutely standard sizes, so even the "standard" sizes discussed in the classical Arabic sources were only approximations. Certainly every sheet produced from a particular mold would have been the same size, but a variation between individual molds of even as much as several inches appears to have been quite acceptable, and such variations were easily accommodated by scribes and bookbinders. The standardization of paper sizes, which, in turn, standardized the size of the codex and accompanied the development of printed books, lay well in the future.

Spanish paper was sold in sheets, quires, and even bound books and was exported to the whole Mediterranean region, including Majorca, Italy, Morocco, Tlemcen (Algeria), Tunis, Athens, Byzantium, Sicily, and Egypt. The rapid acceptance of paper in the Christian regions of Spain itself is attested by the large number of paper documents preserved in the crown archives of Aragon, one of the largest repositories of medieval European (and North African or West Asian) paper. The earliest datable sheet of paper there is a piece of linen rag paper on which is copied a parchment document dated 1178; hundreds of paper documents survive from after that date.

Why did paper and papermaking spread so rapidly in the regions of Iberia then coming under Christian control? As Christian rule expanded over the peninsula, the Muslims now living under Christian rule, who were known as Mudejars, certainly must have practiced their traditional crafts, including papermaking. But this does not explain why papermaking moved into new areas. One scholar, Oriol Valls y Subirà, theorizes that the Almoravids (1056–1147) and Almohads (1130–1269), fundamentalist Muslim dynasties that ruled in the south, persecuted dissident Muslims, including papermakers, and this drove them to settle in the Christian kingdoms of the north. If this argument is correct, the refugees would have established new papermills in such regions as Catalonia and Bilbao as early as the twelfth century. The argument rests on the identification of the many fulling mills—water-driven mills in which woolen cloth was beaten to felt it slightly—mentioned in the sources

among other exports. Several late thirteenth-century documents show that paper was exported from Játiva to Sicily, Byzantium, and other destinations, and a thirteenth-century Constantinopolitan manuscript copied on paper marked with the distinctive Spanish zigzag proves that Spanish paper made its way as far as the Byzantine capital.

Toward the end of the thirteenth century there were several changes in Spanish paper: the chain lines became parallel and more regular, indicating that the molds were of better manufacture, and the fibers—basically linen with a small admixture of hemp—became much shorter and better pulverized, indicating that the stampers for beating the pulp were becoming more efficient. The first Catalan watermarks appeared in the late thirteenth century, too, at the same date as the Italian Fabriano watermarks.

as actually being mills for beating pulp, or at any rate mills that were easily convertible for that purpose. But this was not necessarily the case.

Another theory suggests that when King Jaume (James) II of Aragon conquered the province of Valencia and the city of Játiva in the mid-thirteenth century, the expanded bureaucracy in the regions now opened for Christian settlement demanded documentation, meaning a sharp increase in forms and records, presumably on paper, as officials, settlers, and carpetbaggers made their positions and holdings secure. The Muslims of Játiva had run the paper industry as a cottage craft when they were under Muslim rule, but after the Christian conquest the industry progressively fell under direct crown control, or so the theory goes. Under the benevolent patronage of the Christian king, Muslim and then Christian papermakers would have applied new technologies, whether the improved water-driven hammermill to mass-produce more finely macerated pulp or the improved paper mold woven from brass wire to make better and more consistent sheets. The consequent flood of inexpensive paper allowed by the new technologies would have revolutionized crown recordkeeping, for it would have encouraged bureaucrats to file cheap paper copies of the charters that they sent out as more durable parchments.

Unfortunately, neither theory entirely fits the facts. Although King Jaume's archive undoubtedly reflects the first important government use of paper in Christian Europe, his contemporary King Alfonso the Wise of Castile also used paper, but limited its use to lesser categories of documents, such as commercial permits, routine financial records, broadcast mailings, and passports. Nor can we say for sure that the paper made in Christian Játiva was superior to what Muslims earlier made elsewhere. Most reports and examples over the centuries indicate that Spanish Islamic paper was of consistently high quality (much higher in fact than the problematic treatise of the North African Ibn Badis might suggest; see Chapter 3). Furthermore, water-driven trip-hammer mills were not an invention of Christian Spaniards. Such mills had been known for centuries in the Islamic lands and were probably introduced to the Iberian Peninsula by the eleventh century along with the cultivation of rice, for they were essential to husking the rice without crushing the grain.

Without doubt, however, Europeans—not only Valencians but also Italians and later Germans—harnessed waterpower more efficiently than West Asians and North Africans had, primarily because they used the overshot waterwheel to power their mills. In addition, Europe had a wetter climate and more rugged terrain than most of the Islamic lands, so more water was generally available, and the streams tended to be faster, providing more potential energy to power the mills. Europeans also improved the design of stampers by putting studded iron coverings over the heads of the wooden mallets. Finally,

WIRE DRAWING

In addition to ample supplies of clean water and rags to make the paper pulp and waterpower to run the mill, successful papermaking also required strong molds. At first the strainers, or mold covers, were made from organic materials—hemp threads, for example, or bamboo—but European papermakers switched to thin, flexible iron or copper-alloy wire. Iron, which rusted in the presence of water, was soon abandoned. The first wires for mold covers were probably cut from sheet metal and then hammered round, but eventually the wire was formed by drawing the thin strip through a series of hard metal dies with holes of decreasing size. Each pass through a hole resulted in a thinner and longer wire.

One of the oldest treatises to mention the technique of wire drawing is *De diversis artibus* by Theophilus Presbyter, a monk who wrote in northwest Germany around 1100. From the early Middle Ages, the city of Nuremberg, located on the Pegnitz River close to the regions where metal ores were mined, was a German center for the manufacture of metalwork, and its products were distributed throughout Europe. Brass was made there by 1373. In the fifteenth century Nuremberg became the principal center of copper and brass production in Europe.

A manuscript from Nurem-

. . . continued

the marked improvement of the quality of Játiva paper in the thirteenth century was not an isolated phenomenon, but was part of a much broader trend, for the improvement is also apparent at the opposite end of the Mediterranean, where in thirteenth-century Iran, Iraq, and Egypt paper became whiter, finer, and more evenly beaten. That King Jaume of Aragon negotiated an alliance with the Mongols while Genghis Khan was contemplating invading Europe indicates that such far-flung connections are not improbable.

The earliest Italian paper to appear in the Aragon archives dates from 1291, only a short time after Italian production began in earnest, and the tremendous flowering of the Italian paper industry rapidly brought about the decline of both Iberian and North African production. By the mid-fourteenth century, complaints surfaced about the precipitous decline in the quality and the size of Játiva paper in comparison with the Italian product, but by this time it was too late to improve the situation, and the brief heyday of the Spanish paper industry was over. The word *ream,* which derives from the Arabic word for "bundle" and which entered European languages via the Spanish *resma,* remains a legacy of the important role that Spain played in the history of papermaking.

ITALY

Paper was introduced in Sicily by the late eleventh century, but the major centers of Italian papermaking developed elsewhere in the following centuries. Sicily had shared a cultural heritage and government with North Africa from 827, when the Arabs conquered the island, until 1061, when the Norman conquest was complete. Even after the Normans had established themselves, many Sicilians still regarded the Arab-Islamic culture of North Africa as worthy of emulation. Although North Africans were slow to accept paper, by the late eleventh century they had brought paper to Sicily. The first extant paper document is an order of Adelaide, the widow of the Norman king Roger I, which is dated 1109 and written in Greek and in Arabic. The document shares the format of contemporary Arab paper, indicating that the paper was probably imported from North Africa.

Adelaide's order cannot have been the first use of paper in Sicily, however, because slightly earlier and contemporary documents—dated 1097, 1102, and 1112—were written originally on paper, although they were transcribed onto parchment for safekeeping in 1145 on the orders of Roger II. Nearly eighty years later, in 1222, King William II also had paper documents dated 1168, 1170, and 1187 copied onto parchment, again for safekeeping. In 1231, Frederick II, king of Naples and Sicily, went so far as to prohibit the use of paper for public documents in Naples, Sorrento, and Amalfi because of its perishable nature. Like the Byzantines, the Sicilians did not make paper, but imported it

berg dated around 1390, when Ulman Stromer established his papermill there, contains an illustration of wire drawing. A few years later, at the beginning of the fifteenth century, Nuremberg metalworkers invented a way to draw wire by means of water-power, rather than brute human force. The new technique gave a boost to papermaking there by making strong molds easier—and cheaper—to make.

from North Africa, Islamic Spain, or Valencia. In fact, paper was initially known in Latin as *carta cuttunea,* "cotton papyrus," probably a mistranslation of the Byzantine Greek *charta bombycina,* for Norman Sicilian culture was also heavily dependent on Byzantium. From the second half of the eleventh century Iberian paper, distinguished by its format and by the presence of zigzags, was used in Sicily and southern Italy for copying manuscripts written in Greek.

As far as we can tell, the inhabitants of central and northern Italy did not use paper before the mid-twelfth century, when Genoese notaries started to record their official acts in registers made from paper. With the commercial and legal renewal of the region, the institution of the notary, which had disappeared from northern Italy and southern France since Roman times, was revived, along with the principles of Roman law. Oaths, wills, judicial procedures, and commercial, financial, and marriage contracts were increasingly "notarized." For notaries, paper was a relatively permanent material on which to write; it was also cheaper than parchment and easier to file for reference, presumably because the sheets lay flatter and more compactly. A new system of registering notarial records that developed in twelfth-century Italy contributed to the increased use of paper there. The gradual replacement of parchment by paper, which was more fragile, also caused the disappearance of the lead or wax seals that had been affixed to documents by cords or ribbons threaded through pierced holes. Instead, all but the most important state documents came to be sealed with affixed lumps of wax impressed with a signet.

The most famous register to survive from this period is that of the notary Giovanni Scriba, which, with some gaps, covers the decade from December 1154 to August 1164. The paper he used was probably imported from Spain or possibly North Africa. Paper was cheaper than parchment, but it still was not cheap, for the last folios of Giovanni's register are the remains of an Arabic roll with Latin translations that had already been cut into sheets and reused by a contemporary notary. Although the format is similar to that of sheets used earlier, certain technical characteristics have led scholars to suggest that these somewhat finer sheets were made either in the eastern Mediterranean or in the region corresponding to modern Tunisia.

Other notarial registers from the late twelfth century are on sheets of slightly larger format, and the presence of zigzags suggests that the paper was made somewhere in Spain. This hypothesis is supported by numerous medieval documents mentioning shipments of paper from Barcelona and Valencia. Although the Genoese probably imported their paper from some western Mediterranean port, their strong diplomatic and commercial ties with Byzantium, where paper had been used in the chancellery since the mid-eleventh century, may also have contributed to the increased use of paper in

LAID AND CHAIN LINES

Whatever the material of the sieve or screen in a traditional mold, whether strips of bamboo or metal, paper made with the mold generally displays a distinctive pattern of faint parallel lines, called laid lines, when held up to the light. These are caused by minute differences in the amount of pulp deposited on the sieve. Depending on the thickness of the material used to tie the parallel screen fibers together, "chain lines" perpendicular to the laid lines are more or less visible.

Laid paper

The spacing of laid lines and the spacing and arrangement of chain lines—singly or in groups of two or more—are important aids in the study of old papers, for two sheets made from the same mold will have exactly the same marks. Experience has shown that papermakers in a particular mill or region tended to use similar, if not identical, molds, which produce similar patterns of laid and

. . . continued

Genoa over the course of the twelfth century. Genoa entered into commercial relations with Byzantium in 1142, and in 1155 a formal alliance was concluded between the city-state and the empire.

A decline in the quality of paper used in the Genoese archives suggests that paper was first made in northern Italy in the early thirteenth century. The paper used from around 1215 was like Spanish predecessors in many ways, but the pulp is less well beaten, the laid lines are thicker and unevenly spaced, and the sheet is rougher. By the middle of the century, the sheets had become larger, whiter, and somewhat finer, so whoever was making it was improving rapidly in technique. The only region in northern Italy where paper is known to have been made before 1250 is the Ligurian coast near Genoa. In a contract dated 24 June 1235, a certain Gautier "the Englishman" agreed to make paper with one Mensis of Lucques and promised to teach no one else the technique. Twenty years later, on 18 May 1255, Michele Traverso of Milan and Giovanni of Sant' Olcese (a village near Genoa) also began a paper business.

Ligurian production was short-lived, however, for by the mid-thirteenth century the town of Fabriano, in the Marche of Ancona, in central Italy, was successfully making paper: paper is still being made there more than seven centuries later. A document of 1264 discovered in the archives of the nearby town of Matelica confirms that paper was made and sold there by that date. The first attempts at making paper in Fabriano were probably inspired by Ligurian production, but the Fabriano papermakers appear to have used a somewhat different technique. Fabriano paper is closer to that made by Arab papermakers in the eastern Mediterranean, and production was probably developed through direct contact with that region during the Crusades.

Following the success at Fabriano, papermaking centers developed in such other regions as the Veneto. The eastern Mediterranean origin of the paper-making technique—as opposed to an Iberian origin—is confirmed by the words used for paper in Latin or in the dialects of the Veneto and central Italy, which follow Byzantine Greek usage. In Padua paper was called *carta bambacina*, in Modena *cartas bambaxii*, in Bologna *charta de bambaxe*, in Pistoia *carta de bambacia*, and in San Gimignano *carte bambagie*. Nowhere was it known as *shabti*, the common term used in Spain.

By the end of the thirteenth century, paper made in the Fabriano region was used in Naples, Sicily, and the Balkans, across the Adriatic Sea. Fabriano paper soon dominated the Mediterranean market. By the mid-fourteenth century it competed with Spanish paper even in Spain, causing the decline of the industry there. The instant success of Italian papermakers at making and exporting their product is evident from the fourteenth century. Not only did they take advantage of technological know-how to make large quantities of diff-

chain lines. In addition, if a mold had supplementary ribs, the ribs occasionally interfered with the depositing of fiber when the mold was pulled from the vat. This slight unevenness, known as rib shadow, can sometimes be seen against the light. To localize and date paper made before the invention of watermarks or where watermarks were not adopted, scholars must rely on such features as the size of the sheet, the distinctive arrangement and spacing of laid and chain lines in the paper, and the presence or absence of rib shadows.

All European paper until the eighteenth century displayed a laid pattern of faint parallel lines left from the wires of the mold. In 1756 the English papermaker James Whatman was the first European to produce a perfectly even "wove" paper using a mold of woven wire, and the Birmingham printer John Baskerville used Whatman's paper the following year to print an edition of Virgil. Because of the even surface that readily accepted the impression of type, wove paper quickly became popular among printers and has remained so ever since.

ITALIAN PAPERMAKING

Italian papermakers improved their product and created a huge export market for it beginning in the thirteenth century. Around 1280, Italians around Fabriano invented watermarks to identify their paper and signify its quality. Other Italian inventions were gelatin sizing and a better pulping method.

Paper is sized, or impregnated with starch or some other substance, to keep it from absorbing too much ink when it is written on. Wheat starch, a standard size, was difficult to extract and had a disagreeable odor. Rice starch, which was used in many of the Islamic lands and parts of Spain, was not readily available in much of Europe. In the presence of sufficient humidity, starches could support the growth of molds and other microorganisms, which would eventually destroy the paper itself; this was not normally a problem in the arid lands of West Asia, but the European climate was wetter. Italian papermakers soon, therefore, replaced starch with gelatin, made from the hoofs, hides, and horns of animals. Using gelatin rendered the sheets of paper more resistant to the quill pen, which European writers had grown accustomed to using on parchment; it was a hard, pointed instrument that could puncture or tear the softer paper of the Islamic lands, typically inscribed with reeds.

. . . continued

erent qualities of paper suitable for many uses, but they also understood how to market their product at home and abroad. In Egypt, they sold Italian paper cheaply at first—perhaps even below the cost of production—to increase market share and destroy the local competition. In addition to al-Qalqashandi's disparaging remarks about Italian paper in Egypt (see Chapter 2) and certain North African letters in Spain, we have as evidence a single-volume manuscript of the Koran in the Khalili Collection (see fig. 24). It was transcribed, probably in Baghdad, on Italian paper datable to the 1340s. The paper, heavily watermarked with a double-key design surmounted by a cross, is almost identical to examples made in Arezzo and Torcello, near Venice, which suggests that Genoese and Venetian merchants carried paper on their trading missions to buy textiles and spices in Iraq and Iran. The trade is confirmed by the appearance of Italian, particularly Venetian, papers in Arabic, Persian, and Armenian manuscripts of the fourteenth century copied in Georgia and the Crimea.

EUROPE NORTH OF THE ALPS

Papermaking was significantly slower to take hold north of the Alps than in Italy. The oldest documented use of paper in Germany is dated 1246–47: the dean's register from the cathedral of Passau, which was written on Italian paper. Over the course of the thirteenth century, paper became commoner, particularly in the Tyrol, the Alpine region closest to Italy, which was crossed by important trade routes. Ulman Stromer (or Stromair), a merchant trading in Italy, established the first documented papermill north of the Alps at Gleismühle, near Nuremberg, in 1390. Stromer had apparently seen the craft practiced in Italy and hired Lombard artisans to work at his mill, which was represented several decades later in Hartmann Schedel's woodcut view of the city (see fig. 1).

Stromer's enterprise was followed by others at Ravensburg (1393–94), Chemnitz (1408–25), Strasbourg (1445), and Basel (mid-fifteenth century). The first papermill in Austria was established in 1498. Papermills had already been established in Brabant and Flanders by the late fourteenth century and were established in the Netherlands in the sixteenth century.

Before Johann Gutenberg invented printing with movable type and produced the Bible at Nuremberg in the 1450s, the expansion of paper was generally slower in Europe than in the Muslim world. Although paper was cheaper than parchment—at Bologna in 1280, sheets of paper were six times cheaper than equal-sized sheets of parchment—parchment was still moderately priced and relatively abundant in some regions. Paper was sold by mercers in the fourteenth century and by apothecaries in the fifteenth.

Naturally enough, paper spread more quickly in some regions than in others. In Catalonia, Tuscany, and the south of France it spread rapidly. Italian merchants used paper registers at the Champagne fairs between 1277 and 1282. In France, as in Genoa, the use of paper went hand in hand with new notarial practices and brought notaries a new clientele of more modest means. One clerk from Ghent bought "writing paper" when he passed through Montpellier in the 1270s. In Castile, a region known for its many sheep, paper came into use at a later date than in other regions of Spain. The adoption of paper in England may have been retarded for similar reasons. The oldest paper fragment found in the Public Record Office in London dates from around 1220, but papermaking did not begin in Britain until the very end of the fifteenth century, and even then it was a hit-and-miss operation.

Other arts developed in northern Europe with the increasing use of paper, paralleling the course of their development in the Islamic lands, although paper itself was not widely available north of the Alps until the fourteenth century. Throughout the Romanesque and early Gothic periods, builders normally erected churches without using preliminary drawings. A few architectural drawings on parchment survive from the mid-thirteenth century, but more are associated with the masons' lodges of northern Europe in the late Middle Ages. The most profound changes occurred in the second half of the fifteenth century, however, when increased production of paper, undoubtedly a by-product of the print revolution, encouraged greater freedom in design and drawing methods, with communication between architect and builder coming gradually to depend less on verbal instructions and more on notation.

The triumph of paper over papyrus and parchment in Europe was due not only to the relative cheapness of the final product but also to the availability, as well as the low cost, of the raw materials from which it was made. In other words, enough paper could be made to meet the demand. That demand grew dramatically in the wake of Gutenberg's invention. But if the papermaking industry had not been poised to meet the demand for printed books, Gutenberg's invention would have failed in its effect. Thus, the availability of paper allowed the production of books on a previously unknown scale. It is for this reason that we can talk of a paper revolution following the invention of printing with movable type.

Gelatin, unlike starch, also inhibited the growth of microorganisms on the paper. The first dated paper sized with gelatin is a document of 1264, although many papermills continued to size with starch after 1300.

Italians also mechanized the pulping process. As in Spain, the papermakers harnessed the power of the faster and more abundant local streams to power their stampers, an advantage they had over papermakers in the Islamic lands, who usually had to make do with sluggish rivers. Italian papermakers also innovated by arranging their stampers in batteries, so that the rags, passing successively from one stamper to another, were pounded into a finely and evenly beaten pulp. As a result, paper of high quality could be produced cheaply and quickly.

CHAPTER 7

Goethe, the greatest writer of the generation in which the [Great Western] Transmutation culminated, has suitably been called the "last of the universal men"; yet even he cannot have hoped to follow minutely all the technical processes in which the tools were cast which made the machines to service his theatrical innovations. [Yet] either Ibn Khaldun or Leonardo could still have done the equivalent in their time.

—MARSHALL G. S. HODGSON, *The Venture of Islam*

Over the course of the seven centuries between 800 and 1500, inhabitants of the Islamic lands—who were largely but not exclusively Muslims—carried their knowledge of paper and papermaking across a vast swath of Eurasia and North Africa. Had they not mediated between the cultures of the Far East and the Far West, Europeans would probably have remained ignorant of paper—as well as such other Chinese inventions as gunpowder and the compass—until the first European mariners reached Far Eastern ports in the sixteenth century. Had they not brought paper to Europe, Gutenberg's invention of printing with movable type in the mid-fifteenth century, dependent as it would have been on expensive parchment, probably would not have expanded the reading public in such a revolutionary fashion.

But, as many historians have already remarked, the Muslim lands *did* serve as the entrepôt for the transmission of new ideas from China across the continent to Europe. No firm boundaries divided the Eurasian and African landmass in the way that the Atlantic and Pacific oceans separated the Old World from the New, or the narrow Isthmus of Panama separated North America from South America. Over the millennia, virtually any new development or invention, whether the domestication of plants and animals, papermaking, the water-driven hammermill, the spinning wheel, or the stirrup, was gradually adopted everywhere in Eurasia within the space of four or five centuries—even more rapidly sometimes, as in the case of gunpowder weapons. Following a well-established pattern, then, paper and papermaking, both of Chinese origin, were diffused across Eurasia with the spread of Islam.

What most people have not recognized is that paper, long associated with and overshadowed by printing, was itself an engine of social, intellectual, and artistic change between the eighth century and the sixteenth. Introduced in the Islamic lands to meet the demands of a huge bureaucracy attempting to govern the largest empire the world had ever seen, paper was quickly seized on by writers on all subjects as an ideal medium—strong, flexible, light, and cheap—on which to record and transmit their thoughts. This process was encouraged not only by a societal reverence for the written word but also by ingenious and efficient methods of duplicating and disseminating manuscripts. Writing on an enormous variety of subjects proliferated. Writers also discovered that paper could be used for recording notations other than words, which ranged—in these centuries of intellectual curiosity—from mathematical calculations to genealogical charts to battle plans.

Although much of the appeal of paper arises from its being less costly than parchment and more readily available than papyrus, the two most common writing materials of antiquity, paper was always much more expensive in medieval times than it is today. The invention of papermaking machines and the discovery of virtually infinite sources of fiber have made paper cheaper today than ever before. But even in the medieval Islamic lands paper eventually became cheap enough that ordinary people used it for purposes other than transcribing the written word. Once artisans began to use paper, it had a decisive impact on the ways in which the arts developed after around 1200. Many typical Islamic arts—Persian miniatures, Oriental carpets, the Taj Mahal—are inconceivable without the direct or indirect use of paper for preliminary sketches, encoded instructions, or measured drawings.

Muslims introduced papermaking in southern Europe in the eleventh century, and by about 1500 virtually all of Europe was making paper. The introduction of papermaking in Europe coincided with such European developments as the expanded use of documents, the acceptance of Hindu-Arabic numerals, the refinement of double-entry bookkeeping, and a certain freedom in design and drawing—all paralleling earlier developments in the Islamic lands that came with the use of paper—but the degree to which the European developments were due specifically to the introduction of paper remains to be explored.

Despite the demonstrable importance of paper, its history and role in the Islamic lands has been underappreciated for two reasons. First, papermaking had largely ceased in some of the Islamic lands by the time Europeans began writing its history in the eighteenth century. Syria, Egypt, and North Africa—those Islamic regions closest to Europe and most susceptible to European economic competition—had effectively stopped making paper and instead imported their supplies from Europe. Spain, which had been an important center of Muslim papermaking since the eleventh century, still made paper, although now the papermakers were Christians rather than Muslims, and the mills were located in Catalonia rather than Valencia.

At the other end of the Mediterranean, the Byzantines of Constantinople did not make paper, although they used it by the eleventh century. Once the city became the Ottoman capital in the fifteenth century, paper began to be made there to meet the needs of the burgeoning bureaucratic and intellectual establishments. In spite of the Ottomans' close ties to Europe, their paper-makers followed Eastern, rather than European, papermaking techniques and traditions. European paper was still imported into the Ottoman lands; it was not, however, normally used for those books that followed Islamic, and particularly Iranian, traditions. Iranians, the first in the Muslim lands to make paper, still made it—and made it beautifully—in 1500, but within a few centuries even they succumbed to European, especially Russian, imports. India, which must have been exposed to paper in the first centuries of the Common Era, when Buddhist monks returned from China with knowledge of this material, did not make paper until the fifteenth century, when Muslim rule was established there. The Indian book industry—at least the production of books on paper—was only in its infancy in 1500, but by the end of the century, thanks to the Mughal rulers' taste for all things Persian, Indian paper—and the associated arts of the book—was the equal of that made anywhere.

The enormous success of European, particularly Italian, papermakers in the late Middle Ages was due partly to their technical improvements in the papermaking process and partly to their aggressive marketing techniques. Compared to their West Asian and North African colleagues, Italian paper-makers were able to harness waterpower more efficiently to run more efficient stampers; the resulting pulp was formed on molds made from brass wire and emblazoned with watermarks to guarantee the quality of every sheet. Neverthe-less, until the invention of the Hollander beater in the late seventeenth century, techniques of papermaking remained essentially similar across Eurasia. The best Italian paper of the fifteenth century is not, for example, better than the best Iranian paper of the same period; rather, the two kinds of paper had markedly different qualities because their makers intended them to be used in different ways. The Italians' technical prowess notwithstanding, parity reigned among the agrarian societies of Eurasia. In 1500 the Ottomans were on essentially the same cultural level as the Spanish, the Indians, and the Chinese.

The second reason that Europeans have largely ignored the history of paper in the Islamic lands is because paper has been so closely identified with printing in both China and Europe. Islam's "failure" to accept printing has often been seen as the key moment when the rough parity that had existed among all these cultures began to dissolve and the once-great Islamic civiliza-tion began to "decline." The reluctance of Islamic societies to adopt printing has been explained in several ways.

One explanation is practical. Arabic script was used to write not only Ara-bic but also Persian and Turkish, the three languages spoken (and written) over most of the vast area that comprises the traditional Islamic lands, and Arabic writing is unique in always being cursive: letters within a word have to be joined

HOLLANDER BEATER
The Hollander beater, or Hollander, is a Dutch invention that mechanized and sped up the transformation of rags into paper pulp. By the seventeenth century Germany, Switzerland, and France dominated the paper industry, for their fast-flowing streams and rivers powered the trip-hammer mills used to beat rags into pulp. Holland, although it was a center of printing from the sixteenth century, did not begin to produce high-quality paper until the last quarter of the seventeenth century. Holland had no lack of water or linen rags—it was famed for its linens—but it did not have the fast-flowing streams of other papermaking centers. The Dutch did use wind-mills to grind grain and pump water, but using windmills to power stampers to pound rags into pulp may have seemed impractical.

Some enterprising individual, however, conceived a new way of reducing rags to fibers by beating them in water between a ridged cylinder and a bedplate. The original "Hollander" consisted of an oval wooden tub with a free-standing vertical partition stretch-ing down the middle of the tub to create a continuous channel. Suspended between the partition and the wall of the tub was a solid wooden roller fitted with iron knives that revolved over a metal or stone bedplate. The height of the

. . . continued

ARABE DE LA COLLECTION 24 POINTS.   ARABE DE LA COLLECTION 24 POINTS.

FIG. 83. *The twenty-four-point Arabic font from the Imprimerie Nationale, Paris*

roller over the plate could be adjusted, and the pulp circulated constantly around the channel to be beaten as it passed between the roller and the bedplate. Powered by a windmill, a single Hollander could prepare in one hour the same quantity of pulp it took a stamper twenty-four hours to produce.

A Hollander beater

Johann Joachim Becher, a German writer on mechanics, saw this new type of pulpmill in Serndamm, Holland, on his way to England; he was the first to describe it, in a book published in 1682. By the early eighteenth century, the use of the Hollander, now powered by water, had spread to Bavaria, but it did not universally replace the old stampers. In some cases Hollanders operated along-side stampers, which were used for the initial beating of the rags.

With few modifications, Hollanders are still used, processing anywhere from a few to 3,000 pounds (1,350 kilograms) of pulp at a time, although modern mills have replaced Hollanders with huge continuous refiners based

. . . continued

wherever possible. The script is characterized, therefore, by joins between most letters in a word, as well as by different initial, medial, final, and free-standing forms for many letters. A disconnected way to write Arabic, comparable to the individual characters in Hebrew, Greek, and Latin, never evolved. The Arabic script therefore presents typographical problems quite unlike those presented by other alphabets, or even by Chinese, with its thousands of discrete characters. Arabic type requires an extremely high level of skill in punch cutting to imitate calligraphic norms, and the compositor must also know which form of a particular letter to use when. A complete font of Arabic type, including the vowel marks required for Koranic and other vocalized texts, can easily run to more than six hundred sorts, or individual characters, plus huge quantities of leads and quadrats to be placed between vowel marks and lines. The twenty-four-point Arabic font developed for the French Imprimerie Nationale in the nineteenth century filled four cases and contained 710 different sorts (fig. 83).

In spite of the inherent difficulties, Arabic writing was printed from an early date. Some form of xylography, or block printing, was practiced as early as the tenth century, as several amulets discovered in Egypt show. Most of the known examples were block-printed on paper (fig. 84), but one example was printed on papyrus, and two were printed on parchment. Although these examples are undated, the use of papyrus and parchment suggests an early date, confirmed by the style of script and by another bit of evidence: scholars have interpreted occur-rences of the obscure Arabic term *tarsh* in poems of the tenth and fourteenth centuries as references to printing amulets and charms with engraved tin plates. The headpieces on some of the surviving block-printed amulets have designs incorporating bold lettering and ornamental motifs, sometimes in reserve, which may have been printed with separate woodblocks. Early in the twentieth century the scholar B. Moritz noted the existence of six printing plates in the ancient Khedival Library in Cairo, which he dated to the Fatimid period (tenth–twelfth centuries), but their present location is unknown.

Block printing was also used in Iran in 1294, when the Ilkhanid ruler Gaykhatu briefly but unsuccessfully tried to introduce block-printed paper money, which had been used in China as early as the ninth century. And some Egyptian bookbinders used block printing in the fifteenth century to decorate inexpensive leather doublures (endpapers). Contemporary Iranian leather bindings were pressure-molded using delicately carved metal stamps, so many aspects of printing technology were already available in the Islamic lands before Gutenberg's time.

Much the way European papermakers exported their product to West Asia and North Africa almost as soon as they began making it, European printers quickly realized that printed books in Arabic could be commercial commodities, despite the difficulties of designing and producing the fonts. The earliest Arabic printed text that has survived is the *Kitab salat al-sawai,* a book of hours produced in Fano by the master Venetian printer Gregorio de' Gregori in 1514. It was intended for Melkite Christians in Lebanon and Syria, but the type design is inelegant, and it was set in a clumsy, disjointed manner. Two years later, in Genoa, the typographer Pier Paolo Porro printed a trilingual Psalter in Greek, Hebrew, and Arabic with an Arabic preface.

on a prototype designed a century ago by the American Joseph Jordan and comparable to a leviathan food-processor.

FIG. 84. *Block-printed amulet on paper excavated at Fustat, Egypt, 950–1050*

Perhaps the most important—and most elusive—printed book in Arabic is the edition of the Koran produced by the Venetian printer Paganino de' Paganini in 1537–38. All copies were thought to have perished in a fire until one remaining example was discovered in the 1980s in the library of the Frati Minori di San Michele ad Isola in Venice (fig. 85). The edition was probably intended as a commercial venture, but its odd typeface was quite unacceptable by Muslim calligraphic norms, and the numerous errors in the Koranic text were even more objectionable to Muslim sensibilities. As a commercial—or even an evangelical—venture, it was not a success.

Within a century of Gutenberg's invention the first truly elegant Arabic typefaces were cut in Rome by the French type-designer and bookseller Robert Granjon, who derived his letter forms from the best scribal models and made liberal use of ligatures (joined letters). Italy remained the center of Arabic book production, particularly after Pope Gregory XIII advised Cardinal Ferdinando de' Medici to establish the Typographia Medicea linguarum externarum—a foreign-languages press. Under the supervision of the Orientalist Giovan Battista Raimondi, the press produced a series of Arabic works, including a translation of the Bible and the Four Gospels, Avicenna's medical canon, and the text of al-Idrisi's geographical work *Pleasant Journeys,* written at the Norman court in Sicily almost five centuries earlier. In later years, other leading European typographers, such as the Englishman William Caslon and the Italian Giambattista Bodoni, were also involved in the design of Arabic fonts.

F I G . 85. *Opening pages of the Koran printed by Paganino de' Paganini in Venice, 1537–38. Library of Frati Minori di San Michele ad Isola, Venice*

A second explanation for how long printing took to be established in the Islamic lands is social. Considering the extraordinarily broad interests of the Renaissance prince and Ottoman sultan Mehmed II, which included the commissioning of Greek manuscripts, the hiring of European artists, and the use of European technology, it comes as somewhat of a surprise that the sultan did not introduce printing to the Ottoman empire during his reign in the mid-fifteenth century. But resistance to printing was strong. The Ottomans did not adopt it, and the Ottoman sultans Bayezid II and Selim I even issued edicts in 1485 and 1515 specifically forbidding Muslims to print texts in Arabic characters, although Jews and eventually other minorities were permitted to print texts in Hebrew and other languages. For the next three centuries, such printing as there was in the Islamic lands was deeply dependent on European models.

The first press in Istanbul was established by Jewish immigrants following their expulsion from Spain in 1492. They may have produced their first publication by late 1493; their second book, an edition of the Torah, was printed in April 1505. A Judeo-Persian edition of the Torah, in Persian written in Hebrew characters, was published in Istanbul in 1594. Armenians began printing in Istanbul in 1567. Their press, established by two Armenians who had learned printing in Venice, was also patronized by the Latin Dominican friars; it produced six books over the next two years using fonts brought from Venice.

The story of printing in Safavid Iran followed the same course. Printing was introduced (or, technically, reintroduced) in Iran in 1629, when Carmelite friars in Isfahan received a printing press from Rome. Included were 349 Arabic letter sorts as well as two instruments to set up the type, but it is not known whether the press printed any books before 1642, when it was handed over to the Carmelites' vicar general. The Dutch East Indies Company kept the press in storage in Isfahan until 1669, when they handed it back to the Carmelites. Meanwhile, an Armenian press was established in New Julfa, a suburb of Isfahan, in 1637, and after seventeen months of trial and error Bishop Khac'atur Kesarac'i succeeded in printing the Psalms in 1638. Although he used wooden, iron, and copper type rather than the standard lead type, his main problem, it appears, was securing good-quality paper and ink, for the finish on Iranian book paper was unsuitable for receiving impressions. He managed to print two more religious books in 1641 and 1642, but he then sent one of his pupils, Hovhannes, to Europe to learn printing. After printing a book in Armenian in Livorno in 1644, Hovhannes returned to Persia with lead type and a printing press. His intention to print the Bible was stymied by a lack of good ink, however, and the press was apparently not used until 1687, when nine books were printed.

Ottoman—and more broadly Islamic—resistance to printing can also be explained in part by the reverence that Muslims, particularly those in the ulema, or religious establishment, accord the (hand)written word. As we have seen, scribes and calligraphers enjoyed a special position in Islamic societies, and they monopolized the transmission and reproduction of texts until the eighteenth century, when Muslims began to print books. Although some members of the ulema were opposed to printing, the major obstacle appears to have been opposition from copyists. In the Ottoman capital, copyists exercised considerable economic and political power. The Bolognese scholar Luigi Ferdinando Marsigli, who had been captured by the Ottomans, sold to a pasha, and redeemed in 1682, estimated that eighty thousand copyists were working in Istanbul. The adopting of printing would have put them—and their colleagues elsewhere—out of work.

Despite this resistance, already in the 1640s the Ottoman diplomat and historian Ibrahim Pechewi, whose family had served the Ottoman sultans for generations, argued in his *History* that the printing press was no longer an alien thing in Turkish society and that society should accept it because of the speed with which it could produce a large number of books once the tedious work of typesetting had been done. Curiously, it was nearly eighty years after Pechewi's death before Ibrahim Müteferrika opened the first Muslim-owned press in the Ottoman empire.

Ibrahim Müteferrika was born of Christian parents between 1670 and 1674 in Ottoman-controlled Transylvania. Educated as a Unitarian in a Hungarian theological college, he fled from Hungary when it came under Catholic Hapsburg rule and joined forces with the Hungarian resistance, which was allied to the Ottomans. Eventually Ibrahim joined the Ottoman bureaucracy and converted to Islam, becoming a member of the sultan's Müteferrika corps, a mounted guard used for important public or political missions. Ibrahim took part in several diplomatic missions to Austria and Russia.

After visiting France as the ambassador plenipotentiary of Ahmed III to the court of Louis XV in 1720–21, Mehmed Yirmisekiz Chelebi Efendi became convinced of the necessity and permissibility of establishing a printing press in Istanbul. Joined in this endeavor by his son Said Efendi and the grand vizier Damad Ibrahim Pasha, as well as by the Shaykh al-Islam, the most important religious figure in Ottoman society, Mehmed Yirmisekiz encouraged and supported Ibrahim Müteferrika in establishing a press in Istanbul. Ibrahim made a plea for the enterprise in an essay entitled *Wasilat al-tibaa* (The Device of Printing), addressed to the grand vizier. He wrote a brilliant exposition of the losses incurred by Islamic learning because the art of printing was absent among Muslims and of the benefits that the establishment of the press would bring both to Muslims and to the Ottoman state. He cited benefits for the masses needing instruction and for the ruling classes and the benefit of perpetuating books by printing them when manuscripts could be or had been destroyed by war (as in the Christian conquest of Spain and in the Mongol invasion). Ibrahim evinced no interest in printing theologically controversial writings and therefore met no opposition from the ulema. Indeed, he got a fatwa, or legal decision, from the Shaykh al-Islam on the licitness of printing. As might have been expected, the major opposition seems to have come from copyists and calligraphers, who saw their livelihood vanishing before their eyes. Sultan Ahmad III nevertheless issued a firman authorizing the opening of a printing works to specialize in such practical subjects as medicine, crafts, and geography, but not traditional theological sciences.

Ibrahim Müteferrika was therefore the first Muslim to establish a press at Istanbul, but his Unitarian upbringing and European education undoubtedly contributed to his interest in printing. In 1731, Ibrahim wrote a book explaining the decline of the Ottoman empire vis-à-vis the European Christian states and emphasized the Ottomans' need to take advantage of modern sciences, particularly geography and military science. Accordingly, his first attempt at printing, in 1719–20, probably done with plates and a press brought from Vienna, was a map of the Sea of Marmara, which he dedicated to the vizier; in the following years he printed two more maps, one showing the Black Sea (1724–25) and the other showing Iran (1729–30). Before the press closed in 1742, he had printed seventeen works, including dictionaries and other secular books (fig. 86). The printing of the Koran and other religious texts

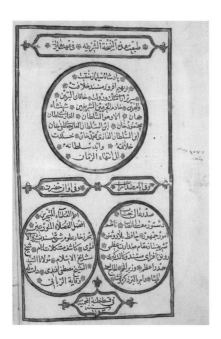

FIG. 86. *Opening page of the* Tarikh-i rashid afandi, *a history of the Ottoman dynasty from 1660, printed by Ibrahim Müteferrika in Qustantiniya (Istanbul), 1741*

remained forbidden. After his death, his foreman and son-in-law Kadi Ibrahim Efendi continued his work, publishing another seven titles between 1755–56 and 1794–95. By the end of the eighteenth century Russian Muslims had even printed the Koran.

Many of the practical and social objections to printing Arabic-script languages disappeared after the Bohemian J. N. F. Alois Senefelder invented lithography in Munich between 1796 and 1799. Unlike cold type, which required each letter to be set individually, lithography allowed the virtually flawless reproduction of entire handwritten pages. In a variation of the process, invented by Senefelder himself, a calligrapher wrote with a special liquid on specially prepared paper. The resulting text was transferred to the printing stone, from which a practically unlimited number of copies could be pulled. Unlike movable type, which took centuries to be adopted in the Islamic lands, lithography appeared there within a few decades.

Although European printers preferred to set Arabic-script languages in cold type, many readers preferred reading lithographed pages, because the results were so similar to reading a manuscript hand. Muslims produced increasing numbers of typeset and lithographed texts in the nineteenth century. Numerous illustrated editions of Persian classics, popular fiction, and translations from European languages were produced by lithography in Tehran and Tabriz from the 1840s. The introduction of Linotype in the early twentieth century and the invention of computer typesetting in the late twentieth century resolved any remaining difficulties in printing Arabic type.

In the longer view of history, therefore, the tardiness of the Muslim world to adopt printing was just a brief pause in a continuous diffusion of inventions across Eurasia. Seen in this light, the history of printing is not so dissimilar from the history of papermaking: both processes were invented in China and spread westward, all the way to the Atlantic. For paper, the route is clear: Europe adopted it from the Islamic lands. For printing, any relation between Gutenberg's invention to earlier uses of movable type in China remains to be established. In any case, printing diffused from Europe to the Islamic lands. The hiatus between Gutenberg's invention in the 1450s and the beginning of printing in West Asia some three centuries later was not crucial, primarily because Islamic society had already developed practical and effective means of reproducing and disseminating large numbers of texts. The invention of printing, therefore, did not have a decisive effect on the history of paper in the Islamic lands.

Far more important in distinguishing the histories of these two regions and establishing why the Islamic paper industry withered was the European development of a "technicalistic" attitude in the late Middle Ages. The historian Marshall G. S. Hodgson, who coined the term, defined technicalism as the expectation of impersonal efficiency through technical precision, and from the sixteenth century the development of a technicalistic approach to problems and problem solving in Europe increasingly differentiated Islamic and European societies.

If later Islamic societies were less receptive to innovation than European ones were, this attitude had not always prevailed. In late eighth-century Baghdad, Muslim bureaucrats had dealt with insufficient quantities of writing material by adopting and producing paper. The early Abbasid period was one of extraordinary cultural curiosity and intellectual ferment, comparable to the European Renaissance. Abbasid scholars were wide open to ideas from all around the world: paper and Hindu-Arabic numerals were among the results. By the late Middle Ages, however, the situation had changed entirely, for Islamic societies had become far less enthusiastic about reinvesting capital in technical improvements. It is at this point that Europe took the lead.

From the late Middle Ages to modern times, European societies have evinced an unprecedented technological inventiveness and an unrivaled capacity to generate economic wealth and project military power. Whereas the major Eurasian societies had enjoyed relative parity around 1500, three centuries later European culture and military might shaped the globe. The origins of this extraordinary development lie in a set of intertwined socioeconomic and cultural conditions: European societies were profoundly different from the Islamic societies of the Middle East in many ways, including family structure and the nature of government, including its connection to religion. They had also long harbored, alongside the Christian church, a belief in independent secular sources of civic and cultural values. All these factors enhanced an inherent pluralism in the European nations and generated a separation of state and church. In the late Middle Ages the initial manifestations were commercial growth, social differentiation, and the stimulation of corporate groups, especially guilds, to advance the interests of their members.

The developing sense of European pluralism, which resulted in an increasing awareness of the individual and the individual's intrinsic worth, can be contrasted to the holistic commitment of Muslim societies to the rule of law, based in the Koran and the example of the prophet Muhammad, and to the community, known in Arabic as the *umma*. An individual's obligations were defined in terms of a religiously commanded participation in the community, which was itself religiously defined.

As early as the thirteenth and fourteenth centuries in Italy, in Flanders, and along the Baltic Sea coast this new orientation was applied to technical invention, such as papermaking, and to the pursuit of material well-being, resulting in new techniques for investment, banking, and insurance. The pluralistic tendencies were exaggerated by the Renaissance and especially by the Reformation, which drove individuals to seek worldly signs of their salvation through methodical and devoted labor. With this transmutation, people systematically subordinated all extraneous personal, emotional, aesthetic, and even ethical considerations to the demand for a patterned way of life. These beliefs resulted in a capacity for making an impersonal and unemotional commitment to the inherent norms of an enterprise and for pursuing specialized goals to their ultimate conclusion. Europeans thereby came to possess a unique form of social and institutional pluralism as well as a mentality that stressed innovation, individual worldly activity, aggressive dominance, and technical experimentation. It was these attitudes that generated the advances that gave them worldwide military and commercial supremacy in the modern era.

The origins of the print revolution in Europe lie, therefore, not simply in Gutenberg's invention of movable type but in a much larger nexus of invention and economic expansion, including the growth of German economic power, the opening of new mines in the Hartz Mountains (in Bohemia, Hungary, and Styria), the development of new metallurgical techniques, the spread of papermaking, the invention of new oil-based inks, new forms of capitalism, and an intellectual revival that made people eager to have books. A similar technicalistic attitude transformed European papermaking beginning in the late seventeenth century and differentiated its products from handmade paper produced elsewhere. The invention of the Hollander beater, which could do in one hour what it took an old hammermill a day to do, was followed at the end of the eighteenth century by the Fourdrinier papermaking machine, which, given sufficient quantities of pulp, could make an endless strip of paper of virtually any width. Meanwhile, European engineers and savants were searching for new raw materials from which to make paper and new ways to exploit them. Their efforts gave us chemical bleaches, which made previously available stocks of fiber now usable for papermaking, and methods to extract virtually limitless quantities of cellulose from trees.

The importance of printing in the great transformation of European civilization is undeniable, but paper, the material that Islamic civilization carried from China to Europe, was an even greater invention in the history of humankind. Cheaper writing materials not only made old learning more accessible but also encouraged new learning and initiated new ways of thinking and representing thought. As Alfred von Kremer realized more than a century ago and as we are only now coming to understand, the "blossoming of mental activity" made possible by paper "started a new era of civilization."

·BIBLIOGRAPHICAL ESSAY·

Full citations of the sources mentioned here are given in the list of works cited. These essays contain personal suggestions for further reading, not complete scholarly bibliographies. For that, ably accomplished, along with a trilingual lexicon of papermaking terms, see Le Léannec-Bavavéas 1998. Abbreviations for frequently cited works are:

DMA	*Dictionary of the Middle Ages*
DoA	*The Dictionary of Art*
EI/2	*The Encyclopaedia of Islam, 2d ed.*

Introduction

Paper sidebar. In addition to such encylopedias and standard works as Hunter 1978 and Tsien 1985, a convenient introduction to the technology of paper-making is Dempsey n.d. For a useful overview of contemporary fine papers, including photographs and samples, see Turner 1998.

There has been no new general history of paper in English since Hunter 1978, which was written in 1947 and is outdated; it barely mentions paper in the Islamic lands. Polastron 1999 is far more global, balanced, and attractive, although it lacks detail. Turner 1998 is a brief introduction to the history of paper and a fine guide to contemporary papers, both handmade and machine-made; it includes samples of many specialty papers. Many of the sources for my research are obscure, but I am delighted to direct the reader to a group of splendid old-fashioned printed reference works including, but not limited to, *The Dictionary of Art (DoA), The Dictionary of the Middle Ages (DMA), The Encyclopaedia Britannica,* 11th ed., *The Encyclopaedia of Islam,* 2d ed. *(EI/2), The Encyclopaedia Iranica,* and *The New Grove Dictionary of Music and Musicians,* as well as several newfangled on-line (nonprint) sources, including: http://www.paperhistory.org (International Association of Paper Historians) and http://www.ipst.edu/amp/museum_dhunter.htm (Institute of Paper Science and Technology in Atlanta, Ga.).

Lalande's plates on papermaking—one is illustrated in Hunter 1978, fig. 138, and another in Polastron 1999, 120—were actually taken from Simonneau 1698. Lalande's entire text (1761) was reproduced in facsimile with other eighteenth-century works in *Les arts du papier* (1984) and has been translated into English (Atkinson 1975). On the identification of the element chlorine and its bleaching properties, see Hunter 1978, 318; *Encyclopaedia Britannica,* s.v. "Chlorine." The history of the papermaking machine and of making paper from woodpulp is discussed by Hunter (1978, chaps. 12–13). Serious study of European watermarks began with Briquet (1907). Diderot's comments can be found in Diderot and d'Alembert 1966, s.v. "Papetterie." Denton's remarks on the poor quality of Chinese paper and Olearius's remarks on goose quills and reed pens are quoted from Bosch, Carswell and Petherbridge 1981, no. 32. The idea of making paper from jute, Réamur's treatise, and Schäffer's experiments are all discussed in Hunter 1978, 313–330. A convenient introduction to Dunhuang is in *DoA.* For the mailbag of Soghdian letters, see *Encyclopaedia Iranica,* 1985–, s.v. "Ancient Letters." The quotation from Thaalibi is taken from Bosworth 1968, 140. For the slow introduction of printing in the Islamic lands, see *DoA,* s.v. "Islamic art §III.8(ii). Arabic Printing in Europe." For Roberts 1997 on the impact of Islamic civilization on Europe, see the review (Kagan 1997). For the first technical analyses of Islamic paper see Wiesner 1986. For the transition from traditional methods of mental recordkeeping to account books, deeds, and charters, see Clanchy 1993; Febvre and Martin 1990.

CHAPTER 1
THE INVENTION OF PAPER

Papyrus sidebar. For the manufacture of papyrus in antiquity, see Parkinson and Quirke 1995; *DoA,* s.v. "Papyrus." For the technical characteristics of Islamic papyri, see Khan 1992 and 1993.

Parchment sidebar. For the manufacture of parchment, see *DoA,* s.v. "Parchment." For the conservation of the Declaration of Independence, see Leary 1999.

Felt sidebar. For the technical differences between papermaking and feltmaking, see Tsien 1985, 36; *DoA,* s.v. "Felt." Papermakers interleave felts between newly formed sheets in a "post," or stack, before pressing.

Japanese Paper sidebar. For Japanese paper, see *DoA,* s.v. "Japan §XVI, 18, Paper," and especially Barrett 1992. For Rembrandt's use of Japanese paper, see Sayre and Stampfle 1969, 178–80. For the European discovery of Japanese goods, including paper, in the nineteenth century, see *DoA,* s.v. "Japonism."

For how the invention of writing transformed human society, see Havelock 1986 and Diamond 1997, chap. 12. The earliest known writing system was invented in Mesopotamia; for the writing system and for many of the ideas about writing in this and the following chapters, see Martin 1994. For possible connections between Mesopotamia and China in the prehistoric period, see Barber 1999. The evolution of cuneiform script on soft clay is discussed in Daniels and Bright 1996, 33 ff.

For a good introduction to the subject of papyrus, see Parkinson and Quirke 1995. The terms *hieroglyphic* and *hieratic* received their names from Clement of Alexandria (late 2d–early 3d century C.E.); see Daniels et al. 1996, 73 ff. The recent discovery near Luxor of what appears to be alphabetic writing inscribed on limestone suggests that the Egyptians may have used an alphabet somewhat earlier than previously thought, perhaps as early as the middle of the second millennium B.C.E.; see Wilford 1999. The stiffer Greek pen was more liable to puncture the fragile writing surface according to *DoA* (s.v. "Papyrus").

The transition from roll to codex format and the concurrent introduction of parchment is discussed by several authors, most notably Roberts and Skeat (1983), who suggest that early Christians recorded the Gospels following the Jewish tradition for writing oral law. The various arguments are summarized in Clement 1996 and in *DoA,* s.v. "Book, §1," where it is argued that Christians adopted the codex to differentiate their writings from the roll-based writings of their contemporaries, including not only the Jews (who wrote their law on leather scrolls) but also the Romans, who wrote their literary works on papyrus scrolls. For the observation that the codex page lent itself to admirably new, nonlinear methods of reading and reference, see O'Donnell 1998 and Pang 1999. The codex in the Chester Beatty Library inscribed with a Greek grammar is discussed in Wouters 1990–91.

The Codex Sinaiticus was discovered in the monastery of St. Catherine on Mount Sinai by Constantine von Tischendorf in the mid-nineteenth century. It was presented in 1855 to Alexander II and remained in St. Petersburg until 1933, when 346 leaves were purchased by the British Museum for £100,000, raised largely by public appeal in Britain and America. Another 43 leaves are in the University Library, Leipzig. Three leaves remain in St. Petersburg, and a few other leaves are still in St. Catherine's Monastery. The Codex Alexandrinus, now in the British Library (Royal MS 1.D.V–VIII), was sent as a gift by the Patriarch of Constantinople to James I of England in the seventeenth century; see *DoA,* s.v. "Book, §1: Origins." For the number of animals slaughtered to make the parchment used in a manuscript, see Hills (1992), who estimates, for example, that each parchment copy of Gutenberg's Bible, consisting of more than 641 leaves, needed the skins of more than 300 sheep.

CLAY TABLETS AND
PAPYRUS ROLLS

WOODEN TABLETS AND
PARCHMENT CODICES

For Arabic papyri in general, see Khan 1993. The two Arabic papyrus codices are mentioned in Bosch et al. 1981, 24. For the use of old papyri to make pasteboard book covers, see also Karabacek 1991, 100–101. M. Lesley Wilkins is currently completing a doctoral dissertation, "From Papyrus to Paper: Technological Change in Medieval Egypt, 868–969," at Harvard University. Her preliminary findings suggest that Muslims were quicker to adopt paper than Christians were, although Assyrian Christians, who had close ties with Iraq, were quicker than the indigenous Coptic Christians. I am grateful for her generosity in sharing this unpublished information with me.

BAMBOO STRIPS
AND SILK CLOTH

The spread of sheep raising from Mesopotamia across Central Asia in prehistoric times (Barber 1999) suggests that writing might have followed a similar path. The origins of writing in China are imaginatively presented by Wheatley (1971) and less idiosyncratically by Tsien (1962). A convenient and balanced introduction is *DoA,* s.v. "China §XIII, 3(i) Manuscripts."

THE INVENTION
OF PAPER

For the invention of paper and printing in China, see, above all, Tsien 1985. Other convenient introductions are *DoA,* s.v. "China §XIII, 3 Books" and "18 Paper"; Le Léannec-Bavavéas 1998. A recent story in the *China Daily* (1 June 1999) shows that the invention of paper still stimulates the imagination. In this fanciful version, told by a peasant from the region near Xi'an, river floods washed over the region, tearing everything to pieces, including flax and hemp plants. Fallen trees created fermenting pools for the fibers of hemp and bark; then the fibers were caught on house curtains, which also got caught in the flood. When the flood receded, the natural pulp caught on the curtains dried in the sun, forming sheets of primitive paper.

The painter Mi Fu's soft and misty effects are briefly discussed in *DoA,* s.v. "Mi (1). Mi Fu," which has a bibliography. For a brief history of the kite in China, see *DoA,* s.v. "China §XIII, 17 Kites." The Greeks also claim the credit for inventing kites, which they attribute to the scientist Archytas of Tarentum, of the fifth century B.C.E. The quotation about the Chinese use of toilet paper is from Tsien 1985, 48. For the miniature charm scroll, see also *DoA,* s.v. "Korea §VIII, 2 (ii) Woodblock printing," where it is described as Korean printing.

THE DIFFUSION
OF PAPER

In addition to Tsien 1985, see Clapperton 1934 for the analysis of fifteen documents dated 406–991 in the British Museum, primarily made of paper mulberry; thirty-two specimens dated 259–960 in the Beijing collection are mostly of hemp. For the use of paper by Silk Road merchants, see *Encyclopaedia Iranica,* 1985–, s.v. "Ancient Letters"; Ierusalimskaja and Borkopp 1997, 101–2. For the origins of writing in India, see Daniels et al. 1996, 165; Losty

1982. I thank my friend Robert Hillenbrand for drawing my attention to the delightful anecdote about the King of the Cockroaches, recounted in Gaček 1986. See also Steingass 1972, 1013b, where the author defines *kabikāj* as "a kind of wild parsley, and a deadly poison; the patron angel of reptiles; king of the cockroaches (in India frequently inscribed on the first page of a book, under the superstitious belief that, out of respect for the name of their king, the cockroaches will spare it)." For the introduction of papermaking to Kashmir, see Humbert 1998, 98; Porter 1994, 17–19; Premchand 1995.

The purported capture of Chinese papermakers by Muslim soldiers is reported recently, for example, in Diamond 1997, 256. Al-Biruni tells a similar story a millennium earlier in his *Kitab al-Hind* (Book of India), as quoted in Porter 1994, 16. Thaalibi's account is accessible in Bosworth 1968. For information about Chinese forces involved in the battle of Talas, see Barthold 1977, 196–97. Du Huan is discussed in Tsien 1985, 297. Al-Nadim's statement about Chinese craftsmen making paper in Khurasan is in al-Nadim 1970, 39–40. For the transition from bast fibers to rags, see Karabacek 1892, xx; Hoernle 1903, 672.

THE INTRODUCTION OF PAPER IN THE ISLAMIC LANDS

CHAPTER 2
THE SPREAD OF PAPERMAKING ACROSS THE ISLAMIC LANDS

Mills and Milling sidebars. For the cultivation of rice in the Islamic lands, see *EI/2*, s.v. "Ruzz," and Wright 1999, 587ff. Al-Biruni's text is quoted in al-Hassan and Hill 1992, 243. There is still no specialized study devoted to the development of mills in the Islamic lands; a general introduction is provided in Hill 1993.

Molds sidebar. For the development of different types of papermaking screens in China, see Tsien 1985, 64–68.

Body Linen sidebar. For the history of the flax breaker and the development of body linen, see *DMA,* s.v. "Linen." On the spinning wheel, see White 1967.

Zigzags sidebar. For a discussion, with an extensive bibliography, of the zigzag marks seen on some early Spanish papers, see Le Léannec-Bavavéas 1998, 68–71.

Watermarks sidebar. European watermarked paper, where the mark is really a form of trademark, should be distinguished from Chinese watermarked paper, decoratively striped with water during the forming of the sheet. Such paper—also known as "overflowing wave paper"—first appeared in the second half of the first millennium. The oldest surviving Chinese watermarked paper therefore predates European watermarked paper by several centuries, but the techniques have very different purposes. On Chinese watermarks, see *DoA,* s.v. "China §XIII,18(iii): Paper: treatment and decoration." On European ones, see Briquet 1907.

IRAQ Paper was entirely unknown to the Sasanian and early Byzantine empires, but Watson (1983, 552 n. *c*) states that under the Sasanians paper was "rare and reserved for official use." I have found no corroboration for this assertion. For copying the *Avesta* on skins, see Porter 1994, 13. The rather confused account of the introduction of papermaking (Bosch et al. 1981, 26) in which it is stated that the Arabs first encountered paper in 650 C.E. is not to be trusted. For the derivation of the word *kaghaz* from the Chinese word *guzhi,* see von Gabain 1983, 622.

For the Barmakids, see *EI/2,* s.v. "Baramika." Franz Rosenthal, the translator of Ibn Khaldun into English, was cautious about ascribing the official introduction of paper in the government offices to the Barmakids, for he considered it to be part of the legend woven around the family by later historians. Nevertheless, this may be one of the cases where the legend is true. See Ibn Khaldûn 1967, 2:392. For the many types and sizes of Arab paper that can only rarely be identified or localized, see *EI/2,* s.v. "Kaghad." For the encyclopedist al-Nadim, see Pedersen 1984, 67, in addition to al-Nadim 1970.

The ninth-century letter from the members of the Babylonian Jewish academy to their colleagues in Fustat, Egypt, is Taylor-Schecter Collection 12.851 in the Cambridge University Library; see Reif 1988; Gil 1997, 2:61–62. I thank Stefan Reif for these references. For Ibn Hanbal's writing preferences, see *EI/2,* s.v. "Raqq"; for those of the Copts, see Wilkins 2001. For the use of paper by Armenians and Georgians, see Le Léannec-Bavavéas 1998, 80, 97. For Hilal al-Sabi, see Hilāl al-Ṣābi' 1977, 103; Sanders 1994, 24. For manuscripts of the *Maqamat,* including Paris, Bibliothèque Nationale, MS arabe 5847, and St. Petersburg, Academy of Sciences, S23, see Grabar 1984, nos. 3 and 4. Al-Qalqashandi is quoted in Quatremère 1968, n. 214.

I was able to examine the magnificent Ahmad al-Suhrawardi page in the collection of the Metropolitan Museum of Art with the gracious help of Marjorie Shelley and Sarah Bertalan of the paper conservation laboratory. For a technical analysis of the contemporary Rashid al-Din manuscript, see Baker 1991. For the sizes of the sheets, see Karabacek 1991, 55; Bosch et al. 1981, 31; James 1988, 235. no. 40. Tsien (1985) does not specifically mention paper formats, although some appear to be large. The counterbalance mechanism is illustrated in Polastron 1999, 45. Yaqut's manuscript is illustrated in *Gulchīnī,* 1375, 50. The movement of artisans from Baghdad to Damascus and Cairo is discussed in James 1988, cat. nos. 28–34. In addition to the manuscript in the

Nour Collection, for which see James 1992, several manuscripts on Italian paper in the Bibliothèque Nationale in Paris are mentioned in Humbert 1998, 2; these are MS arabe 2291, dated 1356; Suppl. Persan 113, copied in 1352 in the Crimea, then a Genoese colony; and Armenian 121, copied in 1386, also in the Crimea.

For papermaking in Raqqa and Manbij, see *EI/2*. For the Byzantine sources of Arab paper, see Atsalos 1977, 85. Wiesner's analyses have been translated and republished in Wiesner 1986. For the absence of papermills in Aleppo, see Elisséeff 1967, 260, 868–89. For the export of Syrian paper to Egypt and Ibn al-Imam's trademark, see Goitein, 1967–94, 1:81 and 410 n. 2; Goitein, 1973, 90 n. 5. For the protocollon, see Khan 1993, 17.

SYRIA

For the earliest Greek manuscript on "Arab" paper, Vatican Gr. 2200, see Perria 1983–84. The *Thousand Nights* fragment was first published in Abbott 1949; see also Bosch et al. 1981, no. 97. For the discovery of the earliest Arabic paper manuscript, see Beit-Arié 1996. The manuscript of Abu Ubayd's work is dated by the colophon on folio 241b to Dhu al-Qada 252 /November–December 866. Voorhoeve (1980, before p. 1), however, is very cautious: "Apparently the earliest dated paper codex in Europe." See also Felix 1952; *Levinus Warner,* 1970, 75–76. The script of the colophon is not representative of the script in the whole codex, about two-fifths of which is lost. A more representative text page is reproduced as the last illustration in the *Levinus Warner* exhibition catalogue. I am most grateful to J. J. Witkam for supplying information about the condition of this manuscript and its paper. For other cases of delamination of paper, see Don Baker in Karabacek 1991, 89 (note to p. 53).

Bird paper is described in Karabacek 1991, 65, 69; al-Qalqashandī n.d., 6:192. For the postal service, see al-Maqrīzī 1853, 2:211. For not recycling paper inscribed with sacred texts or names, see Le Léannec-Bavavéas 1998, 75.

For textual sources relating to Iranian paper, including the quotations from Manuchiri, Mafarrukhi, and Jamal-i Yazdi, see Afshar 1995; Porter 1994, 14–28. For the oldest known paper manuscript in the Persian language, see Duda 1983, 51–52 and ills. 1 and 2. The Chinese wrote on only one side of the paper, according to Rashīd al-Dīn Faḍlallah Hamadānī 1368/1989, 37, 87).

IRAN AND CENTRAL ASIA

For the Arabic copy of the *Compendium of Chronicles,* see Blair 1995; Baker 1991. The pages of the two Persian versions of the *Compendium* in Topkapi Palace Library (Hazine 1653 and 1654) measure 542 by 377 millimeters and 557 by 388 millimeters, respectively. The copy of Rashid al-Din's theological works is in Paris (Bibliothèque Nationale, MS arabe 2324). The anthology of poetry associated with the Rashidiyya scriptorium is in the India Office Library, London (Ethé 903, 911, 913, and 1028); see Robinson 1976, nos. 1–53; Blair 1996. The pages now measure 385 by 275 millimeters, so they were probably trimmed. The written area is the same size (365 by 255 millimeters) as that in the Arabic and first Persian copies of the *Compendium* (Hazine 1653). The autograph copy of Rashid al-Din's endowment deed now measures 340 by 270 millimeters, with a written surface of 290 by 230 millimeters, but the original sheets must have been somewhat larger, according to Afshar and Minovi (1350/1972), who published the facsimile edition.

For the Great Mongol *Shahnama,* see Grabar and Blair 1980. Illustrated manuscripts made in Shiraz are discussed by Wright (1997, 163). I am most grateful to her for sharing this unpublished information with me. For metalworkers and potters brought to Samarqand by Timur, see Komaroff 1992; Golombek, Mason, and Bailey 1996. The sheet of Chinese paper some 17 meters long is mentioned in Tsien 1985, 48.

The translation of Qadi Ahmad's anecdote about Umar-i Aqta is adapted from Soudavar 1992, 59. Simi Nishapuri's remarks are translated in Thackston 1990. For the classical moment in the Persian arts of the book, see Lentz and Lowry 1989. For papers of varying thickness in a single volume, see Wright 1997, 168–70. Sultan-Ali Mashhadi's poem is translated in Minorsky 1959, 114. For the use of Chinese paper, see Minorsky 1959, 113, and especially Blair 2000. For the document bearing the name of Husayn Mirza see Soucek and Çağman 1995, 200–201. For Shahrukh's manuscript of Attar on Chinese paper, see Lentz et al. 1989, cats. 39, 40. For the copy of Mir-Haydar Khwarazmi's *Makhzan al-asrar,* see Soucek 1988. For gold sprinkling, see Porter 1994, 49–51; for Chinese marbling, see Tsien 1985, 94; and for Iranian marbling, see Porter 1994, 45–49. For the spread of the technique to Europe, see Wolfe 1991. The Safavid work on administration is mentioned in Porter 1994, 17; for paper in India, see Premchand 1995. For a technical examination of the paper from Persian manuscripts, see Snyder 1988.

EGYPT   For the travelers to Egypt see al-Muqaddaī 1967, 32 ff., 193 ff., 202 ff.; Pedersen 1984, 62. The paper and textile finds during the 1980 season in Fustat were published in Kubiak and Scanlon 1989. For the papyrus and parchment documents found in the Fayyum in 1877–78, see Karabacek 1892. For early fragments brought from Syria to Egypt, see—in addition to Abbott 1949—Hoernle 1903. For the nature and discovery of the Geniza fragments, see Goitein, 1967–94, 1:1–28. For the Freer Geniza collection, see Gottheil and Worrell 1927. The Taylor-Schechter collection is immense; convenient access to a selection of the material is provided in Cambridge University Library 1900.

Minute fragments of woven cloth are visible to the naked eye in the sheet

TS 16.203 in the Cambridge University Library. Papermills were confined to Fustat according to al-Maqrīzī 1853, 1:366; note that Goitein (1967–94, 1:81 and n. 2) refers to him as Abu Said. For the decline of grain exports and the rise of flax as the primary Egyptian export, see Mayerson 1997. Abd al-Latif's story about graverobbers is told in Lombard 1978, 205. The Maine paper-maker who used mummy wrappings to make coarse brown paper is mentioned in Hunter 1978, 382. For the use and reuse of small pieces of paper, see Goitein, 1967–94, 1:241. An example of a page made up of the full width of the original sheet is Cambridge University Library, TS 32.2; examples pasted up from smaller pieces of paper are TS 28.14, 28.15, and 28.2. For poor-quality paper and for writing a word across a join, see Goitein, 1967–94, 2:232–33; the comparable use of a seal on a document of the Mongol ruler Gayhatu is illustrated in Soudavar 1992. The effects of gall-based (as opposed to carbon) ink can be seen on Cambridge University Library, TS 16–37, a document of 995. For the Geniza correspondence of Ben Yiju, see Goitein, 1973, 186 ff.); and especially Ghosh 1993, an utterly magical book.

Surviving decrees of the Fatimid period were published in Stern 1964. The six Egyptian letters in the Aragonese archives are mentioned in Valls i Subirà 1970, 11. Writing materials remained relatively precious, according to Le Léannec-Bavavéas 1998, 133.

For the price of paper and the purchasing power of the dinar, see *EI/2*, s.v. "Kaghad"; Goitein, 1967–94, 1:7, 344. The anecdote about the use of paper in the Yemen is quoted in Abbott 1939, 14. I thank Robert Hillenbrand for bringing this amusing anecdote to my attention. Ibn Baṭṭūṭa (1993, 36) mentions the use of stamps. For documents written on parchment, see Goitein, 1967–94, 1:112; for one on silk, see Ragib 1980. For Mamluk Koran manuscripts, see James 1988. For information about the seven-volume manuscript commissioned by Baybars al-Jashangir, see Blair and Bloom 1994, 100.

For European paper sent to Tripoli and other Syrian cities, see Ashtor 1977, 270. The almost-complete pack of hand-painted cards was published in Mayer 1971. For Cairo as a redistribution point for the export of European paper and the decline of bookselling, see Raymond 1973–74, 130, 343.

The oldest surviving Maghribi Koran manuscript on paper was sold at Christie's in London, on 9 October 1990 (pl. 46 in the sales catalogue). It is illustrated in Khemir 1992, 117. For Ibn Badis's account, see Levy 1962. For Fez paper shipped to Majorca and Aragon, see Burns 1985, 174–76; for Italian paper exported to Tunis, as well as for the sheet bearing both the watermark and a zigzag, see Valls i Subirà 1970, 11–12. For Fibonacci in Tunis, see

THE MAGHRIB (NORTH AFRICA AND SPAIN)

Abulafia 1994, 16. The decision recorded by the Fez jurist al-Wansharisi is summarized in Lagardière 1995, 42. I am most grateful to David S. Powers of Cornell University for bringing this reference to my attention.

Pedersen (1984, 62) quotes Ibn Abd al-Rabbih on the different kinds of reed pens most suitable for writing on parchment, papyrus, and paper. For the only manuscript to survive from al-Hakam's library, see Lévi-Provençal 1934. For the Mozarabic Breviary and Missal in Silos, as well as for the papermill in Ruzafa, see Valls i Subirà 1970, 5, 9. Idrīsī (1968, 233) praised Shatiba for its paper. For the market inspector and papermakers, see Lévi-Provençal, 1947, 107 (Arabic text, 150). For sheets of Andalusian or Toledan paper sent to Egypt, see Goitein, 1967–94, 5:288 n. 72, 5:457; Constable 1994, 195–96. Colored nasri papers are discussed in Valls i Subirà 1970, 12. The only surviving Spanish-Arabic manuscripts are discussed in James 1992, 212. For the romance of *Bayad and Riyad* (Vatican Ar. 368.), see Dodds 1992, 312–13; Nykl 1941.

CHAPTER 3
PAPER AND BOOKS

The Islamic Book sidebar. On the format of books in the Islamic lands, see Bosch, Carswell, and Petherbridge 1981; Orsatti 1993; *DoA*, s.v. "Islamic art III: Arts of the Book." The technical aspects of the Islamic book, ranging from supports and inks to binding and collecting, are fully treated in Déroche 2000.

For yet another negative assessment of Islamic civilization's failure to adopt printing, see Landes 1998, 401–2. For the size of Chinese editions, see Tsien 1985, 369 ff. The estimate of extant Arabic manuscripts was made by Gaček (1983, 175). For the diversity of early Islamic society, see Daftary 1998, 21–22. For discussion of the transition from a culture based on memory and gesture to one grounded in the written record, see Havelock 1986 and Clanchy 1993.

THE KORAN AND ORAL CULTURE

A convenient introduction to the early history of Arabic is Beeston et al. 1983, 1–22. Graham 1993 is an eloquent discussion of orality and scripture in the Islamic world. The reliance of the Egyptian standard edition of the Koranic text on oral transmission is discussed in *EI/2*, s.v. "Kur'an." For the opposition to writing down Koranic cantillation, see Sadie 1980, s.v. "Islamic religious music." The anecdote about the young caliph al-Mamun is reported in Pedersen 1984, 28.

As we can judge from the contracts from medieval Egypt, even oral Arabic had to be "explained" to the parties, indicating a lack of arabization after more than three hundred years of Arabic linguistic dominance. The contracts also confirm the lack of arabization and conversion in Egypt suggested by both contemporaries and modern researchers. See, for example, Ibn Hawqāl 1967, 161; Frantz-Murphy 1985, 37.

For Fatima Mernissi's account of learning to read in a traditional Moroccan household, see Mernissi 1995, 96.

For memorization of the Koran as a prerequisite for further study, see Graham 1993, 105–6. For information about learning the hadith, see Beeston et al. 1983, chap. 10, and especially Makdisi 1981, 99–105, where the amusing anecdotes about al-Ghazali and Ibn Durayd are reported. On the complex question of when the hadith were written down, see "The Writing Down of the Hadith" in Goldziher 1971, 2:181–88. On the continued primacy of oral learning, see Bulliet 1994, 15. The quotation is from Rosenthal's translation of Ibn Khaldûn 1967, 2:393–94. On the manipulation of the written word in Islamic law, see Powers 1993, 390. On the role of written documents in Islamic law, see Tyan 1959; Wakin 1972; Cook 1997. For the indispensability of written documents, see Schacht 1966, 82, 193.

WRITTEN ARABIC

For the Koran as a written document, see Pedersen 1984, 57. For the role of documents in replacing rather than supporting memory, see Graham 1993, 15. For the various views on the early history of the written text of the Koran, see *EI/2*, s.v. "Kur'an." For the dating of the earliest manuscripts of the Koran, see, among others, Whelan 1990; Déroche 1983, 1992. Arabic scripts on private and commercial documents are analyzed in Khan 1993.

Some scholars believe that vertical-format ("portrait") Koran manuscripts copied in a distinctive script that slopes to the right can be dated to the early eighth century because they have identified the script as the *hijazi* script mentioned in texts. Nevertheless, this identification is based on several false assumptions. See Déroche (1987–89; 1983, 14) and especially Whelan (in press) for a convincing reappraisal of these manuscripts. Only one "secular" manuscript—an as-yet-unidentified genealogical work—is known to have been copied in Kufic script; see Whelan 1990, 122 and n. 94.

The late Estelle Whelan, who was working on early Arabic calligraphy at her untimely death in 1997, proposed calling the new script *warraq* script, in homage to the stationers and copyists who promoted its use. She had not fully developed her elegant hypothesis about the relation of secretaries and copyists to the emergence of new calligraphic styles, but see Whelan, in press. For a related approach, we await the next publication of Blair (2002), who calls it "broken cursive." On the responsibilities of the secretary, see *EI/2*, s.v. "Katib."

For the portion of the manuscript by Ali ibn Shadan al-Razi in Istanbul

University Library, A. 6778, see *Catalogue of the 1931 Exhibition*, 1931, 70, no. 126D. For the portion in the Chester Beatty library, see Arberry 1967, 13, no. 35; James 1980, 27, no. 13. Most of the four-volume anonymous manuscript copied in Isfahan in 993 is in the Museum of Turkish and Islamic Art, Istanbul, although leaves have been sold at auction, and one leaf is in the Nour Collection, London—for which see Déroche 1992, 154. Another is in the Metropolitan Museum of Art. For the 897 Gospel manuscript at Mount Sinai, which was copied on parchment in the new script, see Atiya 1955, 4, no. 72, and pl. VI. For an explanation of the different types of ink, see *DoA*, s.v. "Ink." Recipes are given in Levy 1962. Two late and particularly fancy examples of broken cursive are the dispersed "Qarmathian" Koran (James 1980, no. 15) and the *Kitab al-Diryaq* (Book of the Theriac) dated 1198—99 (Paris, Bibliothèque Nationale, MS arabe 2964), for which see Farès 1953. Broken cursive continued to be used for headings in manuscripts into the fourteenth and fifteenth centuries.

AN EXPLOSION OF BOOKS

For books in general, see *EI/2*, s.v. "Kitab." For the process of conversion, see Bulliet 1979; these dates mark the beginning of Bulliet's "late majority" phase. For Islamic law, see Schacht 1966, 44. For the rise of historical writing, see Duri 1983, 22; Cahen 1990, 207. For new types of secular literature, see Irwin 1994, 78; Wright 1999. For cookbooks, see Rodinson 1949—50, 97; al-Nadim 1970, 742—43. About the authors of cookbooks, see Mez 1937, 394. The recipe for apricot stew was first translated in Arberry, 1939, 40, and also appears in Bloom and Blair 2000. For a fuller discussion of the composition and transmission of Arabic books, see Pedersen 1984, chap. 3. For the translation of Greek materials into Arabic, see Cahen 1990, 483, and the more recent Gutas 1998. Rashid al-Din's instructions to his copyists are translated in Thackston 1995, 114. The interpretation of the Dioscorides frontispiece was proposed by Ettinghausen (1962, 67—70). The small but lavish copy of the Koran made for the Zangid ruler of Mosul was published in James 1992, no. 7, and the Artuqid school of painting was delineated in Ward 1985.

COLLECTIONS AND
LIBRARIES

For estimates of the size of the library in Alexandria, see Wasserstein 1990—91. According to Martin (1994, 56), the Ptolemaic library in Alexandria contained 490,000 scrolls and the library of the Serapeum 42,800. For the size of medieval libraries, see *DMA*, 1982—89, s.v. "Libraries," 7:562; Manguel 1997, 189. The library in Paris is discussed in Martin 1994, 154. For al-Nadim and the *Fihrist*, see Dodge's introduction to al-Nadim 1970. For libraries in the Arab lands, see Eche 1967. At this time the dirham, or silver coin, was nominally worth about one-thirteenth of a dinar, or gold coin.

The seventh-century Umayyad prince Khalid ibn Yazid is sometimes said to have devoted his life to the study of Greek sciences, particularly alchemy and medicine, but this is legend based on a mistranslation of the sources. See *EI/2*, s.v. "Khalid b. Yazid b. Mu'awiya." For the caliphal library in Baghdad, see Young, Latham, and Serjeant 1990, chap. 28; *EI/2*, s.vv. "Bayt al-Hikma," "Dar al-'Ilm," and "Maktaba." For the anecdote about Ibn al-Bawwab and Adud al-Dawla's library in Shiraz, see Pedersen 1984, 86, 123; as well as Rice 1955. For al-Hakam's library in Córdoba, see Wasserstein 1990–91. The only surviving manuscript known to come from the library, written in broken cursive script, is the *Mukhtasar* of Abu Musab ibn Abi Bakr al-Zurhi, made by Husayn ibn Yusuf for al-Hakam in 970; see Lévi-Provençal 1934.

For the Fatimid libraries, see Walker 1997; *EI/2*, s.v. "Dar al-'Ilm." The basic source is al-Maqrīzī 1853, 1:409. The two manuscripts to survive from the Fatimid library are (1) a unique copy of Abu Ali al-Hajari's *al-Taliqat wa'l-nawadir,* which is divided between the National Library in Cairo and the library of the Asiatic Society of Bengal in Calcutta, and (2) an autograph copy by the noted grammarian Ishaq al-Najayrami of his genealogical work, *Kitab hadhf min nasab Quraysh an Muarrij b. Amr al-Sadusi* (Abridgement of the Genealogy of the Quraysh by Muarraj b. Amr al-Sadusi). The first manuscript was written for al-Afdal's library in the mid-twelfth century, but a few years later the book was incorporated into the library of the caliph al-Faiz. The second manuscript, now in the Public Library of Rabat, Morocco, was copied before 966 in Baghdad, so it is therefore not technically a Fatimid manuscript. It bears an inscription stating that it was *li'l-hizana al-saida al-Zafiriyya,* that is, belonging to the library of the Fatimid caliph al-Zafir, father of al-Faiz. For both these manuscripts, see Fu'ad Sayyid 1998, 82–83.

For the transformation from oral to scribal culture, see Graham 1993, 15–17; Clanchy 1993. For a provocative discussion of the changing relationships between religious authority and society in this period, see Bulliet 1994, 21–22. For a description of Islamic education as it evolved under the Mamluks of Egypt, see Berkey 1992.

A CULTURE OF WRITING

CHAPTER 4
PAPER AND SYSTEMS OF NOTATION

For an introduction to the concept of notation, see *The New Grove Dictionary of Music and Musicians,* 1980, s.v. "Notation" 13:334. For a brief introduction to the history of numerical notation, see J. S. Pettersson's essay in Daniels and Bright 1996, 795–806.

MATHEMATICS

A convenient introduction to Arab mathematics and other subjects discussed in this chapter is Hill 1993. For the different systems of counting used in the Islamic lands, see *EI/2*, s.vv. "Abdjad," "Hisab al-Djummal," and "Ta'rikh III"; see also MacDonald 1992. For the history of Greek and Roman numerals see Daniels et al. 1996, 804. For an extraordinarily clear explanation of how the abacus was used to multiply and divide Roman numerals, see *DMA*, 1982–89, s.v. "Mathematics." For dactylonomy in the Muslim world, see *EI/2*, s.v. "Hisab al-'akd." Much of my discussion of arithmetic in the Muslim world is based on the illuminating article by A. I. Sabra (*EI/2*, s.v. "Ilm al-Hisab"). For the origins of Hindu-Arabic numerals, see Saidan 1996, 333–34. For the origins of the word *algorithm,* see *EI/2*, s.v. "Algorithmus." For al-Nadim and al-Khwarizmi, see *DMA*, 1982–89, s.v. "Arabic Numerals." For the history of the pencil, see Petroski 1992. On the introduction of Arabic numerals to Byzantium, see *DMA*, 1982–89, s.v. "Arabic Numerals." On the use of Arabic numerals on casting counters, see *EI/2*, s.v. "Hisab al-Ghubar." On Italian merchants and Arabic numerals see Crosby 1997. On paper and ink replacing casting counters in Italian banks, see Rowland 1994; Barnard 1916; Crosby 1997.

COMMERCE

For the reconstruction of medieval Jewish (and Islamic) economic life on the basis of paper documents, see Goitein 1967–94. The Khurasani tax collector is quoted in Mez 1937, 109. On the role of textiles in medieval Islamic societies, see Lombard 1978. For sealed purses, see Goitein 1967–94, 1:230. On money and the monetization of Islamic society, see Bates 1978. For the use of credit, see Goitein 1967–94, 1:240–50. For al-Sarakhsi and the absence of banks, see *DMA*, 1982–89, s.v. "Banking, Islamic." The anecdote about the disappointed poet is quoted in Mez 1937, 476. For cash discounts and the *suftaja,* see Goitein 1967–94, 1:199, 245–46. For paper money in China, see Tsien 1985, 96–102; for the introduction of paper money into Iran, Boyle 1968, 374–75. For the daftar and medieval Islamic accounting, see Goitein 1967–94, 1:204–9. For the origins of double-entry bookkeeping in Italy, see *DMA*, 1982–89, s.v. "Accounting."

CARTOGRAPHY

Much of the information in this section is based on the excellent articles in Harley and Woodward 1992, as well as the introduction by Karamustafa (1992). See King and Lorch 1992 on qibla mapping and Savage-Smith 1992 on celestial mapping. The Zodiac of Qusayr Amra is discussed in Saxl 1969; Beer 1969. The Bodleian al-Sufi manuscript was published in Wellesz 1959. Al-Biruni's account about al-Sufi tracing a globe is recounted in Savage-Smith 1992, 55. The earliest Islamic maps are discussed in Tibbetts 1992. For Masudi's account of al-Mamun's globe, see Mas'udi 1964, 33; the text is translated in Tibbetts 1992, 95. For the orientation of Islamic maps, see Tibbetts 1992, 105. The Fatimid world map is described in al-Maqrīzī 1853, I:417, lines 12 ff.; cf. also Combe, Sauvaget, and Wiet 1931–, 4:186, no. 1654. For the "routes and kingdoms" school of mapmakers, see Tibbetts 1992, 105; Mas'udi 1964. For European mappae mundi, see *DoA*, s.v. "Map 2. Western world maps." Idrisi's maps are discussed in Ahmad 1992; the earliest to survive is Paris, Bibliothèque Nationale, MS arabe 2221, fols. 3v–4r. For Chinese maps, see Steinhardt, 1997, 1998.

Much of the information in my discussion of notation of Arab music is based on several articles in *The New Grove Dictionary of Music and Musicians,* 1980, including, "Arab music §I,2," "al-Kindi," "Notation," and "Safi al-Din," as well as articles in *EI/2,* including "Ghina," "Kutb al-Din Shirazi," and "Musiki." I am most grateful to Owen Wright for answering my questions about al-Kindi's system of notation.

MUSIC, GENEALOGY, AND BATTLE PLANS

For genealogies and family trees, see *EI/2,* s.vv. "Hamdani" and "Nasab." For the manuscript of Rashid al-Din, see Richard 1997, 44. The genealogical chart covers folios 265b to 277a. For other charts illustrated with schematic portraits, see Blair 1995, 110 n. 45. For diagrams in Furusiyya manuscripts, see *EI/2,* s.v. "Furusiyya"; Hillenbrand 1999, 518–21. For the al-Aqsarai manuscript in the Chester Beatty Library, Dublin, Add. MS. 1, see Atil 1981, 262.

CHAPTER 5
PAPER AND THE VISUAL ARTS

Some of the material in this chapter has already appeared in a different form in Bloom 1993 and Bloom 2000. The literature on the subject of Islamic aniconism, or avoidance of images, is vast. For a summary, see Allen 1988, chap. 2. A relatively small number of images with ostensibly "religious" subjects, such as Muhammad's mystical night journey, were produced at various times and places, but most, if not all, of these should be understood as illustrations to historical and poetic works, not as works of devotional art. For illustrated Islamic manuscripts before 1350, see Holter 1937, and the supplement, Buchthal, Kurz, and Ettinghausen 1940. For the Dioscorides manuscript, see Weitzmann 1971, 252, and pl. xxxiv, figs. 8 and 11; Grube 1959, 169, 175, fig. 5.

BEFORE THE THIRTEENTH CENTURY

The interpretation of the Fustat fragments is fraught with difficulties. On the oldest illustrated Arabic manuscript, see Rice 1959. Dealers have been known not only to forge but also to "embellish" or "improve" genuine medieval pages and drawings to increase their worth on the art market by providing them with identifying texts or illustrations. It is extremely risky to use such examples as the Kab al-Ahbar leaf illustrated with a lion as conclusive evidence for early book illustration, as does Hoffman (2000). For a more balanced assessment, see Stefano Carboni in *Trésors fatimides du Caire,* 1998, 99. The purported frontispiece to the volume of Umayyad poems was published in Wiet 1944; Grube 1976, 33. Another well-known drawing of two warriors, most recently published in *Trésors fatimides du Caire* (1998, no. 22), is equally suspicious, particularly since some authors describe it as an ink drawing, whereas others claim it to be a block print. As far as I can determine, these works all appeared on the Cairo art market in the 1930s and 1940s, at the same time as a group of Persian silks purporting to date from the "Buyid" period (Wiet 1948). The textiles, which have been shown to be modern forgeries, were initially authenticated by using the securely dated texts and poetry inscribed on them; see Blair, Bloom, and Wardwell 1993. Although I do not believe in guilt by association, the Fustat paper fragments have been inscribed with texts in much the same way, and it remains hazardous to base much on them until they have been scientifically examined.

The passage from Masudi is quoted in Rice 1959, as is the passage from al-Nadim (al-Nadim 1970, 832). For Mansur al-Suri, see Hillenbrand 1991, 161 n. 48, with reference to Mohiuddin 1981. For illustrated *Kalila and Dimna* manuscripts, see Grube 1990–91. Ibn al-Muqaffa's introduction has been quoted many times, including in Rice 1959, 209. For the Central Asian sources of the earliest *Kalila and Dimna* illustrations, see Raby 1987–88.

The purported function of the Fustat fragments is stated in Grube 1976, 26–27. For the early inscribed pottery of Khurasan and Transoxiana, see Volov (Golombek) 1966; Wilkinson 1973. For examples of textiles woven to the identical pattern on different looms, see Blair, Bloom, and Wardwell 1993.

The use of architectural plans in early Islamic architecture, and specifically at the Dome of the Rock, is discussed in Creswell 1969, 101 ff., 109–11, and specifically in Bloom 1993, which takes quite a different approach. For plans of the Zaytuna mosque in Tunis, see Creswell 1989, 386–87; Golvin 1970–, 3:156–60. For additional references to architectural "plans," see Necipoğlu 1995, 3–4. The passage from al-Masudi was quoted recently in Matthews and Daskalakis Matthews 1997. For the Great Mosque of Taza, see Terrasse 1943. The illogical extension of the practice of relying more on what plans show than on the three-dimensional experience of a building can be seen in Ewert and Wisshak 1981, 127. The authors believe that the concentric octagons in the plan of the Dome of the Rock were repeated consciously in the columnation of the Great Mosque of Kairouan, although these "octagons" are apparent only in highly schematized plans of the mosque's columns. For contemporary manuals of calligraphy, see Blair 2002. For differences between theory and practice, see Rogers 1973–74.

Arabic copies of al-Buzajani's text include one made in the fifteenth century for the library of Ulugh Beg in Samarqand (Istanbul, Süleymaniye Library, MS Ayasofya 2753) and one in Milan (Ambrosiana, Ar. 68). Later Persian translations made from the Arabic manuscripts include Paris, Bibliothèque Nationale, MS persane 169, and Tehran, University Library, MS 2876; see Sezgin 1974, 324. For an entirely different interpretation of Abu'l-Wafa's role, see Necipoğlu 1995, which is to be used with caution, according to Saliba 1999. On different types or degrees of literacy, see Ettinghausen 1974. For the role of belles lettres in Arabic culture, see, for example, *EI/2,* s.v. "Adab."

The literature on the development of Islamic painting, particularly illustrated manuscripts, is also vast. For a summary, see, for example, Raby 1987–88. For the view that illustrated manuscripts were produced in early times but have not survived, see Ettinghausen 1942; Grube 1976; and, most recently, Hoffman 2000, which, like Weitzmann 1971, approaches the Islamic book as an outgrowth of late antiquity. For the illustrated book as a product of the emergence of an urban bourgeoisie, see Grabar 1970. In the absence of a general history of the illustrated book in this period, see, for example, Blair and Bloom 1994, passim, and *DoA,* s.v. "Islamic art, §III, 4(v) Painted book illustration c. 1250–c. 1500."

FROM THE THIRTEENTH CENTURY

For the romance of *Bayad and Riyad,* see Dodds 1992, no. 82; see the full publication in Nykl 1941. Ravandi's account is discussed in Blair 1995, 55–56. Porter (1994) has gathered some other references to illustrated books in contemporary texts. Literary evidence for illustrated *Shahnama* manuscripts produced for the Qarakhanid court in the twelfth century is found in Melikian-Chirvani 1988, 43–45. For the romance of *Warqa and Gulshah,* see Melikian-Chirvani 1970. Illustrated copies of the *Maqamat* are discussed in Grabar 1984.

For the origins and development of the illustrated book in fourteenth-century Iran, see Blair 1993. For the "Small" *Shahnama* manuscripts, see Simpson 1979. For an attempt to unravel the sizes of paper used in Persian (unillustrated) manuscripts, see Humbert 1998. The dimensions given for the textblock of the *Warqa and Gulshah* manuscript in Ateş 1961 are inaccurate; see Melikian-Chirvani 1970; Çağman and Tanındı 1986, nos. 21–24. For the Great Mongol *Shahnama,* see Grabar and Blair 1980. The Istanbul albums are incompletely published. For two of the albums with some fourteenth-century paintings, see Roxburgh 1996. Illustrations from a dismembered fourteenth-century *Kalila and Dimna* manuscript have been published by Cowen (1989), although her conclusions are not universally accepted. For the Berlin albums, see Ipşiroğlu 1964. For thirteenth- and fourteenth-century Koran manuscripts, see James 1988.

For the classic formulation of the three styles of Kashan luster pottery, see Watson 1985. The Kashan style is exhaustively discussed in Guest and Ettinghausen 1961. A somewhat different explanation of the relations between ceramics and book painting in this period is offered in Hillenbrand 1994. For Abu'l-Qasim, see, in addition to Watson 1985, Blair 1986b; Allan 1973. Dust Muhammad's preface is translated in Thackston 1989, 345. On the repetition of figures and compositions, see Titley 1979; Adamova 1992. For the Iskandar Sultan anthology, see Gray 1979, 134. A brief history of pricked drawings is in *DoA,* s.v. "Pouncing." Iznik vessels and tiles, as well as a pricked drawing, are published in Atasoy and Raby 1989, 56–57. For the use of paper patterns in the late sixteenth century, see Necipoğlu 1990, 155. For metalwork designs and manuscripts in fourteenth-century Iran, see Komaroff 1994. For decorators and illuminators working from common sources, see Sims 1988.

For a judicious selection of fifteenth-century drawings on paper, see Lentz and Lowry 1989, chap. 3. Baysunghur's work order to Jafar b. Ali Tabrizi is translated in Thackston 1989, 323–27. Several examples showing the transfer of motifs from one medium to another are exhibited in Rogers 1983. The unfinished inscription at the Blue Mosque in Tabriz is discussed in Rogers 1989. The small plaster plaque discovered in Takht-i Sulayman is published in Harb 1978. For Rukn al-Din's funerary complex in Yazd, see Jafari 1338/1960, 88–89; Blair 1986a, 33, 92 n. 10; Afshar 1979. For Iranian architecture of the fourteenth century, see Wilber 1969; for that of the fifteenth century, see Golombek and Wilber 1988. For the oldest surviving architectural drawings as well as the Topkapi Scroll, see Necipoğlu 1995. For itinerant artisans, see Meinecke 1992, 130–52; 1996. For the new "professional" approach to design in Timurid architecture, see Golombek and Wilber 1988, chap. 7.

Several drawings by the Italian architect Baldassare Peruzzi are on squared paper, but most fifteenth-century Italian architectural drawings are not. I thank Myra Nan Rosenfeld, senior research curator at the Centre Canadien d'Architecture, for this information. For Italian architectural drawings, see Frommel 1997. For the proportional systems used in Timurid architecture, see Golombek and Wilber 1988, chap. 7. For an example of a designer's ink drawings and an artisan's dependent realizations, see the stamped bookbindings of the mid-fifteenth century discussed in Raby and Tanındı 1993, 15–17. For a brilliant and concise assessment of Timurid literature, see Wheeler M. Thackston's entry in *EI/2* (s.v. "Timurids 2. Literature"). The work of Qivam al-Din is discussed in Golombek and Wilber 1988, 189–93; Wilber 1987.

Sinan is the subject of many studies, including Kuran 1987. For Bihzad, see Priscilla P. Soucek in *DoA* (s.v. "Bihzad"); see also the illustrations in Bahari 1996. For Sultan-Muhammad, see Soucek 1990.

For examples of Timurid metalwork and woodwork based on paper designs, see, for example, Lentz and Lowry 1989, 206–9; Grube 1974. For an overview of the arts in this period, see Blair and Bloom 1994, passim. For the use of paper patterns for fifteenth-century embroideries, see Lentz and Lowry 1989, cat. nos. 95–98. The evolution of carpet design is discussed in Blair and Bloom 1994, chaps. 10 and 16. For Ushak medallion carpets, see Raby 1986. The Ardabil carpets are discussed in Stead 1974; *Encyclopaedia Iranica*, 1985–, s.v. "Ardabil Carpets."

CHAPTER 6

THE TRANSFER OF PAPER AND PAPERMAKING
TO CHRISTIAN EUROPE

Spanish Paper sidebar. On Spanish paper in general, see Valls i Subirà 1970 and 1978. For the thirteenth-century Constantinople manuscript, see Le Léannec-Bavavéas 1998, 71; Canart 1982.

Wire Drawing sidebar. On Theophilus, see *DoA,* s.v. "Theophilus." For mechanization of wire drawing in Nuremberg, see Le Léannec-Bavavéas 1998, 59.

Laid and Chain Lines sidebar. The technical characteristics of a sheet of paper, including laid and chain lines, are clearly discussed by Turner (1998, 26 ff.). A useful glossary of papermaking terms was prepared by Garlock (1983).

Italian Papermaking sidebar. For the history of early Italian paper, see Hills 1992.

For the spread of papermaking in Europe after the invention of printing with movable type, see Febvre et al. 1990, 112–113, 216–22.

The early history of paper in Byzantium has been studied by Irigoin (1953). Nicholas Oikonomidès (1977) has argued that papermakers are mentioned in two medieval Byzantine texts. The Catechism of Theodore the Studiite enumerates the professions practiced in his monastery in the ninth century. That of the *kartopoio,* those who make kartes, is distinguished from that of the *membranopoio,* who make parchment. The emperor Constantine Porphyrigenito's tenth-century treatise on statecraft, *On the Administration of the Empire,* also mentions a group of kartopoio. Oikonomidès assumed that these kartopoio were papermakers, but because papyrus was known in Greek as kartes and because Egypt continued to produce and export papyrus until the tenth century, these

BYZANTIUM

individuals undoubtedly worked with papyrus. Once papyrus was no longer available, scribes had to seek a substitute.

For a comparison between Byzantine and Fatimid ceremonial practices, see Canard 1951. For the increasing popularity of European paper in Byzantium after the Fourth Crusade, see Irigoin 1977. For the export of paper from Barcelona to Constantinople, see Burns 1985, 174. For the early history of papermaking under the Ottomans, see Kağîtçi 1963, 37. Babinger (1931) argued the mill in Kagithane did not begin working until the eighteenth century, although the name is attested at least two centuries earlier. Something is clearly wrong here. For the types of paper used at the Ottoman court, see Raby et al. 1993, 69, 215. For the movement of calligraphers from the Turkmen court to the Ottoman court, see Blair 2002.

SPAIN

For the shared material culture of medieval Spain, see Mann, Glick, and Dodds 1992. The history of Spanish—and particularly Catalan—paper has been the special passion of the Catalan scholar Oriol Valls i Subirà (1978). Le Léannec-Bavavéas (1998, 87–95, 132) has presented the state of current knowledge about the pre-watermarked papers of Spain. The quotation from Peter the Venerable is taken from Valls i Subirà 1970, 5–6. Burns (1980; 1985, 180) considers that the standardization of paper size helped prepare the way for printing. On the technology of the mill in Spain, see Glick 1979, 230–34. The contents of the Aragonese archives have been studied by Valls i Subirà (1970). On the introduction of Italian papers to Spain, see Irigoin 1977, 48; 1960.

ITALY

The origins of Italian papermaking and the notarial registers have been studied by Irigoin (1963) and Le Léannec-Bavavéas (1998, 107–10). The technological component has been studied by Hills (1992). For the importation of Spanish papers to Italy, see Constable 1994, 196.

EUROPE NORTH OF THE ALPS

For the establishment of papermills north of the Alps, see Martin 1994, 209. For a comparison of the cost of paper to parchment, see Irigoin 1950. Dates for the introduction of paper in northern Europe can be found in Le Léannec-Bavavéas 1998, 80, 129–30, 134. For the impact of paper on methods of design and drawing, see *DoA,* s.v. "Architectural Drawing."

CHAPTER 7
PAPER AFTER PRINT

Hollander Beater sidebar. The invention and development of the Hollander beater is discussed in Hunter 1978, 162 ff.

On the effects of the print revolution, see Martin 1994 and Febvre et al. 1990. On the general advantages of the Eurasian landmass, see Diamond 1997. For the spread of sheep raising from Mesopotamia to Central Asia, see Barber 1999. For the stirrup and mills, see White 1967. For the transmission of ideas and techniques in the Islamic period, see Hodgson 1974, 3:200. Apart from Burns 1980, the role of paper in the transformation of premodern Europe seems not to have been explored.

For printing in the Islamic lands, see *DoA,* s.v. "Islamic Art, §III.8(i) Block-printing"; and *EI/2,* s.v. "Matba'a." For block-printed amulets, see Bulliet 1987; Kubiak et al. 1989, 69–70. For block-printed doublures, see Bosch et al. 1981; Haldane 1983. Pressure-molded bookbindings are discussed in Raby et al. 1993, 13. For the first printed Koran, see Nuovo 1987, 1990. The book was exhibited in Venice in 1993; see Curatola 1993, no. 298. For many other examples of early printed books, see [Kreiser] 2001.

On Mehmed's Greek library, see Raby 1987. On the question of printing in the Ottoman empire, see Faroqhi 1995, 111–13. On the development of printing in the Ottoman empire and Safavid Iran, see *EI/2,* s.v. "Matba`a." On Pechewi, see *EI/2,* s.v. "Pečewi." For his assessment of printing, see *EI/2,* s.v. "Matba'a." For the Imprimerie Nationale font of Arabic type, see Atanasiu 1999, 47–48. On Ibrahim Müteferrika, see *EI/2,* s.v. "Ibrahim Muteferrika"; *DoA,* s.v. "Islamic art, §III, 8 Printing." For the technique of lithography, see *DoA,* s.vv. "Lithography" and "Islamic art §III,4(vi)(b): Painted book illustration: Iran, c. 1750–c. 1900."

For the changing receptivity of Islamic culture to new ideas, see Hodgson 1974, 3:179 ff. For the new European ideas, see Lapidus 1988, 268–75, 553. The quotation at the end is from Alfred von Kremer's *Culturgeschichte des Orients* (1875–77) as quoted in Karabacek 1991, 72; the longer passage from which the quotation is taken was my choice for the epigraph of this book.

·WORKS CITED·

Abbott, Nabia. 1939. *The Rise of the North Arabic Script and Its Kur'ānic Development, with a Full Description of the Kur'ān Manuscripts in the Oriental Institute*. Chicago: Oriental Institute, University of Chicago Press.

———. 1949. "A Ninth-Century Fragment of the 'Thousand Nights': New Light on the Early History of the *Arabian Nights*." *Journal of Near Eastern Studies* 8, no. 3: 129–64.

Abulafia, David. 1994 "The Role of Trade in Muslim-Christian Contact During the Middle Ages." In *The Arab Influence in Medieval Europe*, ed. Dionisius A. Agius and Richard Hitchcock. Folio Scholastica Mediterranea, 1–24. Reading, U.K.: Ithaca Press.

Adamova, A. 1992. "Repetition of Compositions in Manuscripts: The *Khamsa* of Nizami in Leningrad." In *Timurid Art and Culture: Iran and Central Asia in the Fifteenth Century*, ed. Lisa Golombek and Maria Subtelny. Supplements to Muqarnas, 67–75. Leiden: E. J. Brill.

Afshar, Iraj. 1979. "Architectural Informations Through the Persian Classical Texts." In *Akten des VII. Internationalen Kongresses für Iranische Kunst und Archäologie. Munchen 7.–10. September 1976*, 612–16. Berlin.

———. 1995. "The Use of Paper in Islamic Manuscripts as Documented in Classical Persian Texts." In *The Codicology of Islamic Manuscripts, Proceedings of the Second Conference of al-Furqān Islamic Heritage Foundation, 4–5 December 1993*, ed. Yasin Dutton, 77–91. London: Al-Furqān Islamic Heritage Foundation.

Afshar, Iraj, and M. Minovi, eds. 1340/1972. *Vaqfnama-yi Rab'-i Rashidi*. Tehran.

Ahmad, S. Maqbul. 1992. "Cartography of al-Sharif al-Idrisi." In *The History of Cartography*, vol. 2: *Cartography in the Traditional Islamic and South Asian Societies*, ed. J. B. Harley and David Woodward, 156–74. Chicago: University of Chicago Press.

Allan, J. W. 1973. "Abu'l-Qasim's Treatise on Ceramics." *Iran* 11:111–20.

Allen, Terry. 1988. *Five Essays on Islamic Art*. [Sebastapol, Calif.]: Solipsist Press.

Arberry, Arthur J. 1939. "A Baghdad Cookery-Book." *Islamic Culture* 13:21–47, 189–214.

———. 1967. *The Koran Illuminated: A Handlist of Korans in the Chester Beatty Library*. Dublin: Hodges, Figgis.

Les arts du papier. 1984. Geneva: Slatkine Reprints.

Ashtor, E. 1977. "Levantine Sugar Industry in the Later Middle Ages—An Example of Technological Decline." *Israel Oriental Studies, Tel Aviv University* 7:226–80.

Atanasiu, Vlad. 1999. *De la fréquence des lettres et de son influence en calligraphie arabe*. Paris: L'Harmattan.

Atasoy, Nurhan, and Julian Raby. 1989. *Iznik: The Pottery of Ottoman Turkey*. London: Alexandria Press.

Ateş, Ahmed. 1961. "Un vieux poème romanesque persan: Récit de Warqah et Gulshah." *Ars Orientalis* 4:143–52.

Atil, Esin. 1981. *Renaissance of Islam: Art of the Mamluks*. Washington, D.C.: Smithsonian Institution, Freer Gallery of Art.

Atiya, A. S. 1955. *The Arabic Manuscripts of Mount Sinai*. Baltimore, Md.: Johns Hopkins University Press.

Atkinson, Richard M. 1975. *Joseph de Lalande: The Art of Papermaking*. Sixmilebridge, Ireland.

Atsalos, Basile. 1977. "Terminologie médiévale et description codicologique." In *La Paléographie grecque et byzantine*, ed. Jacques Bompaire and Jean Irigoin, 83–91. Paris: Editions du CNRS.

Babinger, Franz. 1931. "Papierhandel und Papierbereitung in der Levante." *Wochenblatt für Papierfabrikation* 62:1215–19.

Bahari, Ebadollah. 1996. *Bihzad, Master of Persian Painting*. London: I. B. Taurus.

Baker, Don. 1991. "The Conservation of *Jami' al-Tawarikh* by Rashid al-Din (1313)." *Arts and the Islamic World* 20 (Spring): 32–33.

Barber, Elizabeth Wayland. 1999. *The Mummies of Ürümchi*. New York: W. W. Norton.

Barnard, Francis Pierrepont. 1916. *The Casting-Counter and the Counting-Board: A Chapter in the History of Numismatics and Early Arithmetic*. Oxford: Clarendon Press.

Barrett, Timothy. 1992. *Japanese Papermaking: Traditions, Tools, and Techniques*. 1983. New York: Weatherhill.

Barthold, W. 1977. *Turkestan Down to the Mongol Invasion*. 4th ed. E. J. W. Gibb Memorial. Philadelphia: Porcupine Press.

Bates, Michael L. 1978. "Islamic Numismatics." *Middle East Association Bulletin* 12, no. 2:1–16; no. 3: 2–18.

Beer, Arthur. 1969. "The Astronomical Significance of the Zodiac of Qusayr 'Amra." In *Early Muslim Architecture*, vol. 1, by K. A. C. Creswell, 432–40. Oxford: Clarenden Press.

Beeston, A. F. L., T. M. Johnstone, R. B. Serjeant, and G. R. Smith. 1983. *Arabic Literature to the End of the Umayyad Period*. Cambridge History of Arabic Literature. Cambridge: Cambridge University Press.

Beit-Arié, Malachi. 1996. "The Oriental Arabic Paper." *Gazette du livre médiéval* 28 (Spring): 9–12.

Berkey, Jonathan. 1992. *The Transmission of Knowledge in Medieval Cairo: A Social History of Islamic Education*. Princeton: Princeton University Press.

Blair, Sheila S. 1986a. *The Ilkhanid Shrine Complex at Natanz, Iran*. Cambridge: Harvard University Center for Middle Eastern Studies.

——. 1986b. "A Medieval Persian Builder." *Journal of the Society of Architectural Historians* 45:389–95.

——. 1993. "The Development of the Illustrated Book in Iran." *Muqarnas* 10:266–74.

——. 1995. *"A Compendium of Chronicles": Rashid al-Din's Illustrated History of the World*. London: Nour Foundation in association with Azimuth Editions and Oxford University Press.

——. 1996. "Patterns of Patronage and Production in Ilkhanid Iran: The Case of Rashid al-Din." In *The Court of the Il-Khans, 1290–1340*, ed. Julian Raby and Teresa Fitzherbert, 39–62. Proceedings of the Barakat Trust Conference on Islamic Art and History, St. John's College, Oxford, 28 May 1994. Oxford Studies in Islamic Art, vol. 12. Oxford: Oxford University Press for the Board of the Faculty of Oriental Studies, University of Oxford.

——. 2000. "Color and Gold: The Decorated Papers Used in Manuscripts in Later Islamic Times." *Muqarnas* 17:24–36.

——. 2002. *Islamic Calligraphy*. Edinburgh: Edinburgh University Press. Forthcoming.

Blair, Sheila S., and Jonathan M. Bloom. 1994. *The Art and Architecture of Islam, 1250–1800*. Pelican History of Art. London: Yale University Press.

Blair, Sheila S., Jonathan M. Bloom, and Anne E. Wardwell. 1993. "Reevaluating the Date of the 'Buyid' Silks by Epigraphic and Radiocarbon Analysis." *Ars Orientalis* 23:1–42.

Bloom, Jonathan M. 1993. "On the Transmission of Designs in Early Islamic Architecture." *Muqarnas* 10:21–18.

——. 1999. "Revolution by the Ream." *Aramco World Magazine* 50, no. 3: 26–39.

——. 2000. "The Introduction of Paper to the Islamic Lands and the Development of the Illustrated Manuscript." *Muqarnas* 17:17–23.

Bloom, Jonathan, and Sheila Blair. 2000. *Islam: One Thousand Years of Faith and Power*. New York: TV Books.

Bosch, Gulnar, John Carswell, and Guy Petherbridge. 1981. *Islamic Bindings and Bookmaking*. Exh. cat. Chicago: Oriental Institute, University of Chicago.

Bosworth, C. E., trans. 1968. *The Laṭā'if al-Ma'ārif of Tha'ālibī / The Book of Curious and Entertaining Information*. Edinburgh: Edinburgh University Press.

Boyle, J. A. 1968. "Dynastic and Political History of the Il-Khans." In *The Cambridge History of Iran*, vol. 5: *The Saljuq and Mongol Periods*, ed. J. A. Boyle, 303–421. Cambridge: Cambridge University Press.

Briquet, Charles-Moïse. [1907] 1968. *Les filigranes, dictionnaire historique des marques du papier dès leur apparition vers 1282 jusqu'en 1600*. Amsterdam: Paper Publications Society (Lebarre Foundation).

Buchthal, Hugo, Otto Kurz, and Richard Ettinghausen. 1940. "Supplementary Notes to K. Holter's Check List of Illuminated Islamic Manuscripts Before A.D. 1350." *Ars Islamica* 7:147–64.

Bulliet, Richard W. 1979. *Conversion to Islam in the Medieval Period: An Essay in Quantitative History*. Cambridge: Harvard University Press.

———. 1987. "Medieval Arabic *Tarsh*: A Forgotten Chapter in the History of Printing." *Journal of the American Oriental Society* 107, no. 3: 427–38.

———. 1994. *Islam: The View from the Edge*. New York: Columbia University Press.

Burns, Robert I. 1980. "The Paper Revolution in Europe: Crusader Valencia's Paper Industry—a Technological and Behavioral Breakthrough." *Pacific Historical Review* 50:1–30.

———. 1985. *Society and Documentation in Crusader Valencia: Diplomatarium of the Crusader Kingdom of Valencia—The Registered Charters of Its Conqueror Jaume I, 1257–1276*. Princeton: Princeton University Press.

Çağman, Filiz, and Zeren Tanındı. 1986. *The Topkapi Saray Museum: The Albums and Illustrated Manuscripts*. Ed. and trans. J. M. Rogers. Boston: Little, Brown.

Cahen, Claude. 1990. "History and Historians." In *The Cambridge History of Arabic Literature*, vol. 2: *Religion, Learning and Science in the 'Abbasid Period*, ed. M. J. L. Young, J. D. Latham, and R. B. Serjeant, 188–233. Cambridge: Cambridge University Press.

Cambridge University Library. 1900. "University Library, Cambridge, TS Class List (Glass) Taylor Schechter Collection List (Glass Catalogue) of Fragments (Formerly) in Glass." Unpublished manuscript.

Canard, Marius. 1951. "Le cérémonial fatimide et le cérémonial byzantin: Essai de comparaison." *Byzantion* 21:355–420.

Canart, Paul. 1982. "A propos du Vaticanus graecus 207: Le recueil scientifique d'un érudit constantinopolitain du XIIIe siècle et l'emploi du papier à zig-zag dans la capitale." *Illinois Classical Studies* 7:271–98.

Catalogue of the International Exhibition of Persian Art at the Royal Academy of Arts, London, 7th January to 28th February 1931. 1931. London: Office of the Exhibition.

Clanchy, M. T. 1993. *From Memory to Written Record: England, 1066–1307*. Oxford: Blackwell.

Clapperton, R. H. 1934. *Paper: An Historical Account of Its Making by Hand from Its Earliest Times Down to the Present Day*. Oxford: Shakespeare Head Press.

Clement, Richard W. 1996. "Medieval and Renaissance Book Production—Manuscript Books." In *ORB Online Encyclopedia*. http://orb.rhodes.edu.

Combe, Etienne, Jean Sauvaget, and Gaston Wiet. 1931–. *Répertoire chronologique d'épigraphie arabe*. Cairo: Institut Français d'Archéologie Orientale.

Constable, Olivia Remie. 1994. *Trade and Traders in Muslim Spain: The Commercial Realignment of the Iberian Peninsula, 900–1500*. Cambridge: Cambridge University Press.

Cook, Michael A. 1997. "The Opponents of the Writing of Tradition in Early Islam." *Arabica* 44:43–53.

Cowen, Jill Sanchia. 1989. *Kalila wa Dimna: An Animal Allegory of the Mongol Court*. New York: Oxford University Press.

Creswell, K. A. C. 1969. *Early Muslim Architecture*. Vol. I. 2d ed. Oxford: Clarendon Press.

———. 1989. *A Short Account of Early Muslim Architecture*. Revised and enlarged by James W. Allan. Aldershot, U.K.: Scolar.

Crosby, Alfred W. 1997. *The Measure of Reality: Quantification and Western Society, 1250–1600*. Cambridge: Cambridge University Press.

Curatola, Giovanni 1993. *Eredità dell'Islam*. [Venice]: Silvana Editoriale.

Daftary, Farhad. 1998. *A Short History of the Ismailis: Traditions of a Muslim Community*. Islamic Surveys. Edinburgh: Edinburgh University Press.

Daniels, Peter T., and William Bright. 1996. *The World's Writing Systems*. New York: Oxford University Press.

Dempsey, David. n.d. *The History and Technology of Papermaking*. Northampton, Mass.: Smith College Museum of Art.

Déroche, François. 1983. *Les manuscrits du coran, aux origines de la calligraphie coranique*. Paris: Bibliothèque Nationale, Département des Manuscrits, Catalogue des Manuscrits Arabes.

———. 1987–89. "Les manuscrits arabes datés du IIIe/IXe siècle." *Revue des études islamiques* 55–57:343–79.

———. 1992. *The Abbasid Tradition: Qur'ans of the Eighth to the Tenth Centuries AD*. Ed. Julian Raby. Nasser D. Khalili Collection of Islamic Art. London: Nour Foundation in association with Azimuth Editions and Oxford University Press.

Déroche, François, et al. 2000. *Manuel de codicologie des manuscrits en écriture arabe*. Paris: Bibliothèque Nationale de France.

Diamond, Jared. 1997. *Guns, Germs and Steel: The Fate of Human Societies*. New York: W. W. Norton.

The Dictionary of Art. 1996. Ed. Jane Turner. London: Macmillan.

Dictionary of the Middle Ages. 1982–89. Ed. Joseph R. Strayer. New York: Charles Scribner's Sons.

[Diderot, Denis, and Jean Le Rond d'Alembert]. 1966. *Encyclopédie, ou Dictionnaire raisonné des sciences, des arts et des métiers, par une société de gens de lettres, mis en ordre et publié par Mr. ****. Stuttgart: Friedrich Fromann Verlag, 1966.

Dodds, Jerrilynn D., ed. 1992. *Al-Andalus: The Art of Islamic Spain*. New York: Metropolitan Museum of Art.

Duda, Dorothea. 1983. *Islamische Handschriften*. Vol. I, *Persische Handschriften*. Die Illuminierten Handschriften und Inkunabeln der Österreichischen Nationalbibliothek. Vienna: Verlag der Österreichischen Akademie der Wissenschaften.

Duri, A. A. 1983. *The Rise of Historical Writing Among the Arabs*. Ed. and trans. Lawrence I. Conrad. Princeton: Princeton University Press.

Eche, Youssel. 1967. *Les bibliothèques arabes publiques et semi-publiques en Mésopotamie, en Syrie et en Egypte au moyen age*. Damascus: Institut Français de Damas.

Elisséeff, Nikita. *Nur ad-Din, un grand prince musulman de Syrie au temps des croisades (511–569 H./1118–1174)*. Damascus: Institut Français de Damas, 1967.

The Encyclopaedia Britannica. 1910. 11th ed. New York: Encyclopaedia Britannica Company.

Encyclopaedia Iranica. 1985–. Ed. Ehsan Yarshater. London: Routledge.

The Encyclopaedia of Islam. 1960–. New ed. Ed. H. A. R. Gibb and others. Leiden: E. J. Brill.

Ettinghausen, Richard. 1942. "Painting in the Fatimid Period: A Reconstruction." *Ars Islamica* 9:112–24.

———. 1962. *Arab Painting*. Geneva: Skira.

———. 1974. "Arabic Epigraphy: Communication or Symbolic Affirmation?" In *Near Eastern Numismatics, Iconography, Epigraphy and History: Studies in Honor of George C. Miles,* ed. Dikran Kouymjian, 297–317. Beirut.

Ewert, Christian, and Jens-Peter Wisshak. 1981. *Forschungen zur almohadischen Moschee*. Vol. I, *Vorstufen. Hierarchische Gliederungen westislamischer Betsäle des 8. bis 11. Jahrhunderts: Die Hauptmoscheen von Qairawān und Córdoba und Ihr Bannkreis*. Madrider Beiträge. Mainz: Philipp von Zabern.

Farès, Bishr. 1953. *Le livre de la thériaque: Manuscrit arabe à peintures de la fin du XIIe siècle conservé a la Bibliothèque Nationale de Paris*. Art Islamique. Cairo: Institut Français d'Archéologie Orientale.

Faroqhi, Suraiya. 1995. *Kultur und Alltag im osmanischen Reich: Vom Mittelalter bis zum Anfang des 20. Jahrhunderts*. Die Welt des Islam. Munich: C. H. Beck.

Febvre, Lucien, and Henri-Jean Martin. 1990. *The Coming of the Book: The Impact of Printing, 1450–1800*. Trans. David Gerard. London: Verso.

Felix, D. A. 1952. "What Is the Oldest Dated Paper in Europe?" *Papiergeschichte* 2, no. 6 (December): 73–75.

Frantz-Murphy, Gladys. 1985. "Arabic Papyrology and Middle Eastern Studies." *Middle East Studies Association Bulletin* 19, no. 1 (July): 34–48.

Frommel, Christoph Liutpold. 1997. "Reflections on the Early Architectural Drawings." In *The Renaissance from Brunelleschi to Michelangelo: The Representation of Architecture*, ed. Henry A. Millon and Vittorio Magnago Lampugnani, 101–22. New York: Rizzoli.

Fu'ad Sayyid, Ayman. 1998. "L'art du livre." *Dossiers d'archéologie*, no. 233 (May): 80–83.

Gaček, Adam. 1983. "Some Remarks on the Cataloguing of Arabic Manuscripts." *Bulletin of the British Society for Middle Eastern Studies* 10.

———. 1986. "The Use of Kabikaj in Arabic Manuscripts." *Manuscripts of the Middle East* 1:49–53.

Garlock, Trisha. *Glossary of Papermaking Terms: A Selection of Terms Prepared on the Occasion of the International Paper Conference, 1983, Japan*. San Francisco: World Print Council, 1983.

Ghosh, Amitav. 1993. *In an Antique Land*. New York: Alfred A. Knopf.

Gil, Moshe. 1997. *Be-Malkhut Yishmael Bi-Tekufat Ha-Geonim. Pirsume Ha-Makhon le-Heker Ha-Tefutsot; Sefer 117–120*. Tel Aviv: Tel Aviv University.

Glick, Thomas F. 1979. *Islamic and Christian Spain in the Early Middle Ages: Comparative Perspectives on Social and Cultural Formation*. Princeton: Princeton University Press.

Goitein, S. D. 1967–94. *A Mediterranean Society*. Berkeley: University of California Press.

———. 1973. *Letters of Medieval Jewish Traders*. Princeton: Princeton University Press.

Goldziher, Ignaz. 1971. *Muslim Studies (Muhammedanische Studien)*. Ed. S. M. Stern. Trans. C. R. Barber and S. M. Stern. Chicago: Aldine.

Golombek, Lisa, and Donald Wilber. 1988. *The Timurid Architecture of Iran and Turan*. Princeton: Princeton University Press.

Golombek, Lisa, Robert B. Mason, and Gauvin A. Bailey. 1996. *Tamerlane's Tableware: A New Approach to the Chinoiserie Ceramics of Fifteenth- and Sixteenth-Century Iran*. Costa Mesa, Calif.: Mazda in association with the Royal Ontario Museum.

Golvin, Lucien. 1970. *Essai sur l'architecture religieuse musulmane*. Paris: Klincksieck.

Gottheil, R., and W. H. Worrell. 1927. *Fragments from the Cairo Genizah in the Freer Collection*. New York.

Grabar, Oleg. 1970. "The Illustrated Maqamat of the Thirteenth Century: The Bourgeoisie and the Arts." In *The Islamic City*, ed. A. H. Hourani and S. M. Stern, 207–22. Oxford: Bruno Cassirer.

———. 1984. *The Illustrations of the Maqamat*. Chicago: University of Chicago Press.

Grabar, Oleg, and Sheila Blair. 1980. *Epic Images and Contemporary History: The Illustrations of the Great Mongol Shah-Nama*. Chicago: University of Chicago Press.

Graham, William A. 1993. *Beyond the Written Word: Oral Aspects of Scripture in the History of Religion*. New York: Cambridge University Press.

Gray, Basil, ed. 1979. *The Arts of the Book in Central Asia: Fourteenth–Sixteenth Centuries*. Boulder, Colo.: Shambhala/UNESCO.

Grube, Ernst J. 1959. "Materialien zum Dioskorides Arabicus." In *Aus der Welt der Islamischen Kunst: Festschrift für Ernst Kühnel*, 163–94. Berlin: Mann.

———. 1974. "Notes on the Decorative Arts of the Timurid Period." In *Gururājamañjarikā: Studi in onore di Giuseppe Tucci*, vol. 1, pp. 233–79. Naples.

———. 1976. "Fustat Fragments." In *Islamic Painting and the Arts of the Book*, ed. B. W. Robinson, 23–66. Keir Collection. London: Faber and Faber.

———. 1990–91. "Prologomena for a Corpus Publication of Illustrated *Kalila wa Dimna* Manuscripts." *Islamic Art* 4:301–482.

Guest, Grace D., and Richard Ettinghausen. 1961. "The Iconography of a Kashan Luster Plate." *Ars Orientalis* 4:25–64.

Gulchīnī az qur'ānhāyi khattī mūza-yi dawrān-i islāmī (A Selection of Koran Manuscripts in the Museum of the Islamic Eras) (in Persian). 1375/1997. Tehran: Muze-yi dawrān-i islāmī.

Gutas, Dimitri. 1998. *Greek Thought: Arabic Culture*. London: Routledge.

Haldane, Duncan. 1983. *Islamic Bookbindings in the Victoria and Albert Museum*. London: World of Islam Festival Trust in association with the Victoria and Albert Museum.

Harb, Ulrich. 1978. *Ilkhanidische Stalaktitengewölbe: Beiträge zu Entwurf und Bautechnik*. Berlin, 1978.

Harley, J. B., and David Woodward, eds. 1992. *Cartography in the Traditional Islamic and South Asian Societies*. Vol. 2 of *The History of Cartography*. Chicago: University of Chicago Press.

al-Hassan, Ahmad Y., and Donald R. Hill. 1992. *Islamic Technology, an Illustrated History*. Cambridge: Cambridge University Press.

Havelock, Eric A. 1986. *The Muse Learns to Write*. New Haven: Yale University Press.

Hilāl al-Ṣābi'. 1977. *Rusūm dār al-khilāfah (The Rules and Regulations of the 'Abbāsid Court)*. Trans. Elie A. Salem. Beirut: American University.

Hill, Donald R. 1993. *Islamic Science and Engineering*. Islamic Surveys. Edinburgh: Edinburgh University Press.

Hillenbrand, Carole. 1999. *The Crusades: Islamic Perspectives*. Edinburgh: Edinburgh University Press.

Hillenbrand, Robert. 1991. "Mamluk and Ilkhanid Bestiaries." *Ars Orientalis* 20:149–87.

———. 1994. "The Relationship Between Book Painting and Luxury Ceramics in Thirteenth-Century Iran." In *The Art of the Saeljuqs in Iran and Anatolia: Proceedings of a Symposium Held in Edinburgh in 1982*, ed. Robert Hillenbrand, 134–45. Costa Mesa, Calif.: Mazda.

Hills, Richard L. 1992. "Early Italian Papermaking, a Crucial Technological Revolution." In *Produzione e commercio della carta e del libro secc. xiii–xvii. Atti della "Venitreesima Settimana di Studi," 15–20-aprile*, ed. Simonette Cavaciocchi, 73–97. Florence: Le Monnier.

Hodgson, Marshall G. S. 1974. *The Venture of Islam*. Chicago: University of Chicago Press.

Hoernle, A. F. Rudolf. 1903. "Who Was the Inventor of Rag-Paper?" *Journal of the Royal Asiatic Society* 43:663–84.

Hoffman, Eva R. 2000. "The Beginnings of the Illustrated Arabic Book: An Intersection Between Art and Scholarship." *Muqarnas* 17:37–52.

Holter, Kurt. 1937. "Die Islamischen Miniaturhandschriften vor 1350." *Zentralblatt für Bibliothekwesen* 54:1–34.

Humbert, Geneviève. "Papiers non filigranés utilisés au proche-orient jusqu'en 1450, essai de typologie." *Journal Asiatique* 286, no. 1: 1–54.

Hunter, Dard. [1947] 1978. *Papermaking: The History and Technique of an Ancient Craft*. New York: Dover.

Ibn Baṭṭūṭa. 1958–94. *The Travels of Ibn Baṭṭūṭa*. Ed. and trans. H. A. R. Gibb. London: Hakluyt Society.

Ibn Hawqāl, Abū'l-Qāsim. [1938] 1967. *Kitāb ṣūrat al-arḍ*. Ed. J. H. Kramers. Bibliotheca Geographorum Arabicorum. Leiden: E. J. Brill.

Ibn Khaldûn. [1958] 1967. *The Muqaddimah: An Introduction to History*. Trans. Franz Rosenthal. New York: Bollingen Foundation.

Idrīsī. [1866] 1968. *Description de l'Afrique et de l'Espagne par Edrîsî*. Eds. R. Dozy and M. J. De Goeje. Leiden: E. J. Brill.

Ierusalimskaja, Anna A., and Birgitt Borkopp. 1997. *Von China nach Byzanz: Frühmittelalterliche Seiden aus der Staatlichen Ermitage St. Petersburg*. Exh. cat. Munich: Bayerische Nationalmuseum.

Ipşiroğlu, M. 1964. *Saray-Alben: Diez'sche Klebebände aus den Berliner Sammlungen*. Wiesbaden.

Irigoin, Jean. 1950. "Les premiers manuscrits grecs écrits sur papier et le problème du bombycin." *Scriptorium* 4:194–204.

———. 1953. "Les débuts de l'emploi du papier à Byzance." *Byzantinische Zeitschrift* 43:314–19.

———. 1960. "L'introduction du papier italien en Espagne." *Papiergeschichte* 10, no. 3 (July): 29–32.

———. 1963. "Les origines de la fabrication du papier en Italie." *Papiergeschichte* 13, nos. 5–6 (December): 62–67.

———. 1977. "Papiers orientaux et papiers occidentaux." In *La paléographie grecque et byzantine*, ed. Jacques Bompaire and Jean Irigoin, 45–54. Paris: Editions du CNRS.

Irwin, Robert. 1994. *The Arabian Nights, a Companion*. London: Allen Lane/Penguin Press.

Ja'fari, Ja'far ibn Muhammad ibn Hasan. 1338/1960. *Tarikh-i Yazd*. Tehran.

James, David. 1980. *Qur'ans and Bindings from the Chester Beatty Library: A Facsimile Exhibition*. Exh. cat. N.p.: World of Islam Festival Trust.

———. 1988. *Qur'ans of the Mamluks*. London: Alexandria Press, and Thames and Hudson.

———. 1992. *The Master Scribes: Qur'āns of the Tenth to the Fourteenth Centuries A.D.* Ed. Julian Raby. Nasser D. Khalili Collection of Islamic Art. London: Nour Foundation in association with Azimuth Editions and Oxford University Press.

Kagan, Donald. 1997. "Continent No. 1: Review of J. H. Roberts, *A History of Europe*." *New York Times Book Review*, 28 December, p. 8.

Kağîtçi, Mehmed Ali. 1963. "Beitrag zur türkischen Papiergeschichte." *Papiergeschichte* 13, no. 4: 37–44.

Karabacek, Joseph von. 1892. *Führer durch die Ausstellung Papyrus Erzherzog Rainer*. Vienna: Selbstverlag der Sammlung.

———. 1991. *Arab Paper, 1887*. Trans. Don Baker and Suzy Dittmar. London: Islington Books.

Karamustafa, Ahmet T. 1992. "Introduction to Islamic Maps." In *The History of Cartography*, vol. 2: *Cartography in the Traditional Islamic and South Asian Societies*, ed. J. B. Harley and David Woodward, 1–11. Chicago: University of Chicago Press.

Khan, Geoffrey. 1992. *Arabic Papyri: Selected Material from the Khalili Collection*. London: Nour Foundation in association with Azimuth Editions and Oxford University Press.

———. 1993. *Bills, Letters and Deeds: Arabic Papyri of the Seventh to Eleventh Centuries*. Ed. Julian Raby. Nasser D. Khalili Collection of Islamic Art. London: Nour Foundation in association with Azimuth Editions and Oxford University Press.

Khemir, Sabiha. 1992. "The Arts of the Book." In *Al-Andalus: The Art of Islamic Spain*, ed. Jerrilynn D. Dodds, 115–25. New York: Metropolitan Museum of Art and Harry N. Abrams.

King, David A., and Richard P. Lorch. 1992. "Qibla Charts, Qibla Maps." In *The History of Cartography*, vol. 2: *Cartography in the Traditional Islamic and South Asian Societies*, ed. J. B. Harley and David Woodward, 189–205. Chicago: University of Chicago Press.

Komaroff, Linda. 1992. *The Golden Disk of Heaven: Metalwork of Timurid Iran*. Persian Art Series. Costa Mesa, Calif.: Mazda.

———. 1994. "Paintings in Silver and Gold: The Decoration of Persian Metalwork and Its Relationship to Manuscript Illustration." *Studies in the Decorative Arts* 2, no. 1 (Fall): 2–34.

[Kreiser, Klaus, ed.] 2001. *The Beginnings of Printing in the Near and Middle East: Jews, Christians and Muslims*. Wiesbaden: Harrassowitz.

Kubiak, Władysław, and George T. Scanlon. 1989. *Fustat C*. Vol. 2 of *Fustat Expedition Final Report*. Winona Lake, Ind.: Eisenbrauns for the American Research Center in Egypt.

Kuran, Aptullah. 1987. *Sinan: The Grand Old Master of Ottoman Architecture*. Photographs by Ara Güler and Mustafa Niksarli. Washington, D.C.: Institute of Turkish Studies; Istanbul: Ada Press.

Lagardière, Vincent. 1995. *Histoire et société en occident musulmane au moyen-age: Analyse du Mi'yar d'al-Wanšarisi*. Collection de la Casa de Velázquez. Madrid: Casa de Velázquez.

Lalande, Joseph Jérôme le Français de. 1761. *Art de faire le papier: Descriptions des arts et métiers faites our approuvées par Messieurs de l'Académie Royale des Sciences, avec figures en taille-douce*. Paris.

Landes, David S. 1998. *The Wealth and Poverty of Nations: Why Some Are So Rich and Some So Poor*. New York: W. W. Norton.

Lapidus, Ira M. 1988. *A History of Islamic Societies*. Cambridge: Cambridge University Press.

Leary, Warren E. 1999. "New Framers of the Declaration of Independence Act to Save It in Parchment." *New York Times*, 7 February.

Le Léannec-Bavavéas, Marie-Thérèse. 1998. *Les papiers non filigranés médiévaux de la Perse à l'Espagne: Bibliographie, 1950–1995*. Paris: Editions du CNRS.

Lentz, Thomas W., and Glenn D. Lowry. 1989. *Timur and the Princely Vision*. Los Angeles: Los Angeles County Museum of Art.

Levinus Warner and His Legacy: Three Centuries Legatum Warnerianum in the Leiden University Library. 1970. Exh. cat. Leiden: E. J. Brill.

Levy, M. 1962. "Medieval Arabic Bookmaking and Its Relation to Early Chemistry and Pharmacology." *Transactions of the American Philosophical Society* 40:3–79.

Lombard, Maurice. 1978. *Les textiles dans le monde musulman VIIe–XIIe siècle*. Civilisations et Sociétés 61. Paris: Mouton.

Losty, Jeremiah P. 1982. *The Art of the Book in India*. London: British Library.

Lévi-Provençal, E. 1934. "Un manuscrit de la bibliothèque du calife al-Ḥakam II." *Hespéris* 18:198–200.

———, trans. and ed. 1947. *Séville musulmane au début du XIIe siècle: Le traité d'Ibn 'Abdun*. Paris: G. P. Maisonneuve.

Lockwood-Post's Directory of Products of Pulp, Paper Mills, Converters, and Merchants. 1996. San Francisco: Miller-Freeman.

Lockwood's Directory of the Paper and Stationery Trades. 1908. New York: Lockwood.

Loveday, Helen. 2001. *Islamic Paper: A Study of the Ancient Craft*. [London:] Don Baker Memorial Fund.

MacDonald, M. C. 1992. "On the Placing of S in the Maghribi Abjad and the Khirbet al-Samra' ABC." *Journal of Semitic Studies* 37:155–66.

Makdisi, George. 1981. *The Rise of Colleges: Institutions of Learning in Islam and the West*. Edinburgh: Edinburgh University Press.

Manguel, Alberto. 1997. *A History of Reading*. New York: Penguin.

Mann, Vivian B., Thomas F. Glick, and Jerrilynn D. Dodds. 1992. *Convivencia: Jews, Muslims, and Christians in Medieval Spain*. New York: George Braziller in association with the Jewish Museum.

al-Maqrīzī, Taqī al-Dīn Aḥmad. 1853. *al-Mawā'iẓ wa'l-i'tibār bi-dhikr al-khiṭaṭ wa'l-athār* (Exhortations and Instructions on the Districts and Antiquities). Cairo.

Martin, Henri-Jean. 1994. *The History and Power of Writing*. Trans. Lydia G. Cochrane. Chicago: University of Chicago Press.

Mas'udi. 1964. *Kitāb al-tanbih wa'l-ishrāf*. Ed. M. J. de Goeje. Bibliotheca Geographorum Arabicorum. Leiden: E. J. Brill.

Matthews, Thomas F., and Annie-Christine Daskalakis Matthews. 1997. "Islamic-Style Mansions in Byzantine Cappadocia and the Development of the Inverted T-Plan." *Journal of the Society of Architectural Historians* 56, no. 3 (September): 294–315.

Mayer, L. A. 1971. *Mamluk Playing Cards*. Ed. R. Ettinghausen and O. Kurz. L. A. Mayer Memorial Studies in Islamic Art and Archaeology. Leiden: E. J. Brill.

Mayerson, Philip. 1997. "The Role of Flax in Roman and Fatimid Egypt." *Journal of Near Eastern Studies* 56, no. 3 (July): 201–7.

Meinecke, Michael. 1992. *Die Mamlukische Architektur in Ägypten und Syrien*. Abhandlungen des deutschen Archäologischen Instituts Kairo, Islamische Reihe. Glückstadt: J. J. Augustin.

———. 1996. *Patterns of Stylistic Change in Islamic Architecture: Local Traditions Versus Migrating Artists*. New York: New York University Press.

Melikian-Chirvani, A. S. 1970. "Le Roman de Varqe et Golšâh." *Arts Asiatiques* 22.

———. 1988. "Le livre des rois, miroir du destin, I." *Studia Iranica* 17, no. i: 7–46.

Mernissi, Fatima. 1995. *Dreams of Trespass: Tales of a Harem Girlhood*. Photographs by Ruth V. Ward. Reading, Mass.: Addison-Wesley.

Mez, Adam. 1937. *The Renaissance of Islam*. Trans. Salahuddin Khuda Bakhsh and D. S. Margoliouth. Patna: Jubilee.

Minorsky, V., trans. 1959. *Calligraphers and Painters: A Treatise by Qāḍī Aḥmad, Son of Mīr-Munshī (Circa A.H. 1015/A.D. 1606)*. Occasional Papers. Washington, D.C.: Smithsonian Institution, Freer Gallery of Art.

Mohiuddin, A. 1981. "Muslim Contribution to Biology." In *Proceedings of the International Symposium on Islam and Science*, 81. Islamabad.

al-Muqaddasī [1906] 1967. *Aḥsan al-taqāsīm fī ma'rifat al-alaqālīm*. Ed. M. J. de Goeje. Bibliotheca Geographorum Arabicorum. Leiden: E. J. Brill.

al-Nadim. 1970. *The Fihrist of al-Nadim: A Tenth-Century Survey of Muslim Culture*. Ed. and trans. Bayard Dodge. New York: Columbia University Press.

Necipoğlu, Gülru. 1990. "From International Timurid to Ottoman: A Change of Taste in Sixteenth-Century Ceramic Tiles." *Muqarnas* 7:136–70.

———. 1995. *The Topkapi Scroll — Geometry and Ornament in Islamic Architecture*. Getty Center in the History of Art and Humanities. Santa Monica, Calif.: Getty Center and Oxford University Press.

New Grove Dictionary of Music and Musicians. 1980. Ed. Stanley Sadie. London: Macmillan.

Nuovo, A. 1987. "Il Corano arabo ritrovato (Venezia, P. e. A. Paganini, tra l'agosto 1537 e l'agosto 1538)." *La Bibliofilia* 89:237–71.

———. 1990. "A Lost Arabic Koran Rediscovered." *Library,* 6th ser. 12:273–92.

Nykl, A. R. 1941. *Historia de los Amores de Bayāḍ y Riyāḍ, una Chantefable Oriental en Estilo Persa (Vat. Ar. 368)*. New York: Hispanic Society of America.

O'Donnell, James. 1998. *Avatars of the Word: From Papyrus to Cyberspace*. Cambridge: Harvard University Press.

Oikonomidès, Nicolas. 1977. "Le support matériel des documents Byzantins." In *La paléographie grecque et byzantine,* ed. Jacques Bompaire and Jean Irigoin, 385–416. Paris: Editions du CNRS.

Orsatti, Paola. 1993. "Le manuscrit islamique: Caractéristiques matérielles et typologie." In *Ancient and Medieval Book Materials and Techniques,* ed. Marilena Maniaci and Paola F. Munafò, 269–332. Studi e Testi, vols. 57–58. Vatican City: Biblioteca Apostolica Vaticana.

Pang, Alex Soojung-Kim. 1999. "The Book Is Here to Stay." *American Scholar* 68, no. 1 (Winter): 136–39.

Parkinson, Richard, and Stephen Quirke. 1995. *Papyrus*. Egyptian Bookshelf. Austin: University of Texas Press.

Pedersen, Johannes. [1946] 1984. *The Arabic Book*. Trans. Geoffrey French. Princeton: Princeton University Press.

Perria, L. 1983–84. "Il *Vat. Gr.* 2200. Note codicologiche e paleografiche." *Revista di Studi Byzantini e neoellenici,* n.s. 20–21:25–68.

Petroski, Henry. 1992. *The Pencil: A History of Design and Circumstance*. New York: Alfred A. Knopf.

Polastron, Lucien X. 1992. *Le papier: 2000 ans d'histoire et de savoir-faire*. Paris: Imprimerie Nationale.

Porter, Yves. 1994. *Painters, Paintings and Books: An Essay on Indo-Persian Technical Literature, Twelfth–Nineteenth Centuries*. Trans. Mrs. S. Butani. New Delhi: Manohar, Centre for Human Sciences.

Powers, David S. 1993. "The Maliki Family Endowment: Legal Norms and Social Practices." *International Journal of Middle East Studies* 25, no. 3: 379–406.

Premchand, Neeta. 1995. *Off the Deckle Edge: A Paper-Making Journey Through India*. Bombay: Ankur Project.

al-Qalqashandī, Abī al-'Abbās Aḥmad ibn 'Alī. n.d. *Subḥ al-a'shā fī sin'at al-inshā*. Cairo.

Quatremère, Etienne. [1836] 1968. *Raschid-Eldin: Histoire des mongols de la perse — texte persan, publié, traduit en français accompagnée de notes et d'un mémoire sur la vie et les ouvrages de l'auteur*. Amsterdam: Oriental Press.

Raby, Julian. 1986. "Court and Export. Part 2: The Ušak Carpets." In *Oriental Carpet and Textile Studies*, vol. 2: *Carpets of the Mediterranean Countries, 1400–1600*, ed. Robert Pinner and Walter B. Denny, 177–88. London.

———. 1987. "East and West in Mehmed the Conqueror's Library." *Bulletin du Bibliophile* 3:297–321.

———. 1987–88. "Between Sogdia and the Mamluks: A Note on the Earliest Illustrations to Kalila wa Dimna." *Oriental Art* 33, no. 4 (Winter): 381–98.

Raby, Julian, and Zeren Tanindı. 1993. *Turkish Bookbinding of the Fifteenth Century: The Foundations of an Ottoman Court Style*. Ed. T. Stanley. London: Azimuth Editions on behalf of l'Association internationale de bibliophilie.

Ragib, Yusuf. 1980. "Un contrat de mariage sur soie d'Egypte fatimide." *Annales islamologiques* 16:31–37.

Rashīd al-Dīn Faḍlallah Ḥamadānī. 1368/1989. *Āthār va aḥyā (A Fourteenth Century Persian Text on Agriculture)*. Ed. Manoochehr Sotoodeh and Iraj Afshar. History of Science in Islam. Tehran: McGill University Institute of Islamic Studies, Tehran Branch, in collaboration with Tehran University.

Raymond, André. 1973–74. *Artisans et commerçants au Caire au XVIIIe siècle*. Damascus: Institut Français de Damas.

Reif, Stefan. 1988. *Published Material from the Cambridge Genizah Collections: A Bibliography, 1896–1980*. Genizah Series. Cambridge: Cambridge University Press.

Rice, D. S. 1955. *The Unique Ibn al-Bawwāb Manuscript in the Chester Beatty Library*. Dublin: Chester Beatty Library.

———. 1959. "The Oldest Illustrated Arabic Manuscript." *Bulletin of the School of Oriental and African Studies* 22:207–20.

Richard, Francis. 1997. *Splendeurs persanes: Manuscrits du XIIe au XVIIe siècle*. Paris: Bibliothèque Nationale de France.

Roberts, Colin H., and T. C. Skeat. 1983. *The Birth of the Codex*. London: Oxford University Press for the British Academy.

Roberts, J. H. 1997. *A History of Europe*. New York: Allen Lane.

Robinson, B. W. 1976. *Persian Paintings in the India Office Library, a Descriptive Catalogue*. London.

Rodinson, Maxime. 1949–50. "Recherches sur les documents arabes relatifs à la cuisine." *Revue des études islamiques* 17–18:95–165.

Rogers, J. M. 1973–74. Review of *The Formation of Islamic Art*, by Oleg Grabar. *Kunst des Orients* 9:152–66.

———. 1983. *Islamic Art and Design: 1500–1700*. London: British Museum.

———. 1989. Review of *Timurid Architecture in Khurasan*, by Bernard O'Kane. *Bulletin of the Asia Institute* 3:129–38.

Rowland, Ingrid D. 1994. "Character Witness." *New York Review of Books*, 1 December, p. 30.

Roxburgh, David J. 1996. "'Our Works Point to Us': Album Making, Collecting, and Art (1427–1565) Under the Timurids and Safavids." Ph.D. diss. University of Pennsylvania.

Saidan, Ahmad. 1996. "Numeration and Arithmetic." In *Encyclopedia of the History of Arabic Science*, ed. Roshdi Rashed, 331–48. London: Routledge.

Saliba, George. 1999. "Artisans and Mathematicians in Medieval Islam." *Journal of the American Oriental Society* 119, no. 4: 637–45.

Sanders, Paula. 1994. *Ritual, Politics, and the City in Fatimid Cairo*. Albany: State University of New York Press.

Savage-Smith, Emilie. 1992. "Celestial Mapping." In *The History of Cartography*, vol. 2: *Cartography in the Traditional Islamic and South Asian Societies*, ed. J. B. Harley and David Woodward, 12–70. Chicago: University of Chicago Press.

Saxl, Fritz. 1969. "The Zodiac of Qusayr 'Amra." In *Early Muslim Architecture*, vol. I, by K. A. C. Creswell, 424–31. Oxford: Clarendon Press.

Sayre, Eleanor A., and Felice Stampfle. 1969. *Rembrandt: Experimental Etcher*. Exh. cat.

Museum of Fine Arts, Boston; Pierpont Morgan Library, New York. Greenwich, Conn.: New York Graphic Society.

Schacht, Joseph. 1966. *An Introduction to Islamic Law.* 1964. Oxford: Clarendon Press.

Sezgin, Fuat. 1974. *Mathematik bis ca. 430 H.* Geschichte des arabischen Schrifttums. Leiden: E. J. Brill.

Simonneau, Louis. 1698. *Description de l'art du papier.* Desbillettes.

Simpson, Marianna Shreve. 1979. *The Illustration of an Epic: The Earliest Shahnama Manuscripts.* New York: Garland.

Sims, Eleanor. 1988. "The 'Iconography' of the Internal Decoration in the Mausoleum of Uljaytu at Sultaniyya." In *Content and Context of Visual Arts in the Islamic World,* ed. P. P. Soucek, 139–76. University Park: Pennsylvania State University Press for the College Art Association of America.

Snyder, Janet G. 1988. "Appendix 10: Study of the Paper of Selected Paintings from the Vever Collection." In *An Annotated and Illustrated Checklist of the Vever Collection,* ed. Glenn D. Lowry and Milo Cleveland Beach, 433–40. Washington, D.C.: Smithsonian Institution, Arthur M. Sackler Gallery.

Soucek, Priscilla P. 1988. "The New York Public Library *Makhzan al-Asrār* and Its Importance." *Ars Orientalis* 18:1–38.

———. 1990. "Sultan Muhammad Tabrizi: Painter at the Safavid Court." In *Persian Masters: Five Centuries of Painting,* ed. Sheila R. Canby, 55–70. Bombay: Marg.

Soucek, Priscilla P., and Filiz Çağman. 1995. "A Royal Manuscript and Its Transformation: The Life History of a Book." In *The Book in the Islamic World: The Written Word and Communication in the Middle East,* ed. George N. Atiyeh, 179–208. Albany: State University of New York Press.

Soudavar, Abolala. 1992. *Art of the Persian Courts: Selections from the Art and History Trust Collection.* New York: Rizzoli.

Stead, Rexford. 1974. *The Ardabil Carpets.* Malibu, Calif.

Steingass, F. [1892] 1972. *A Comprehensive Persian-English Dictionary Including the Arabic Words and Phrases to Be Met With in Persian Literature.* Beirut: Librairie du Liban.

Steinhardt, Nancy Shatzman. 1997. "Chinese Cartography and Calligraphy." *Oriental Art* 43, no. 1: 10–20.

———. 1998. "Mapping the Chinese City: The Image and the Reality." In *Envisioning the City: Six Studies in Urban Cartography,* ed. David Buisseret, 1–33. Chicago: University of Chicago Press.

Stern, S. M. 1964. *Fatimid Decrees: Original Documents from the Fatimid Chancery.* All Souls Studies. London: Faber and Faber.

Terrasse, Henri. 1943. *La grande mosquée de Taza.* Paris: Editions d'Art et d'Histoire.

Thackston, Wheeler M. 1989. *A Century of Princes: Sources on Timurid History and Art.* Cambridge, Mass.: Aga Khan Program for Islamic Architecture.

———. 1990. "Treatise on Calligraphic Arts: A Disquisition on Paper, Colors, Inks and Pens by Simi of Nishapur." In *Intellectual Studies on Islam: Essays Written in Honor of Martin B. Dickson, Professor of Persian Studies, Princeton University,* ed. Michel M. Mazzaoui and Vera B. Moreen, 219–28. Salt Lake City: University of Utah Press.

———. 1995. "Articles of Endowment of the Rab'i-Rashidi, by Rashiddudin Fazulluh." In *A Compendium of Chronicles: Rashid al-Din's Illustrated History of the World,* by Sheila S. Blair, 114–15. London: Nour Foundation in association with Azimuth Editions and Oxford University Press.

Tibbetts, Gerald R. 1992. "The Beginnings of a Cartographic Tradition." In *The History of Cartography,* vol. 2: *Cartography in the Traditional Islamic and South Asian Societies,* ed. J. B. Harley and David Woodward, 90–107. Chicago: University of Chicago Press.

Titley, Norah M. 1979. "Persian Miniature Painting: The Repetition of Compositions During the Fifteenth Century." In *Akten des VII. International Kongresse Iranische Kunst und Archäologie, 1976,* 471–91. Berlin: D. Reimer.

Trésors fatimides du Caire. 1998. Exh. cat. Paris: Institut du Monde Arabe.

Tsien, Tsuen-Hsuin. 1962. *Written on Bamboo and Silk: The Beginnings of Chinese Books and Inscriptions*. Chicago: University of Chicago Press.

———. 1985. *Paper and Printing*. Vol. V:1 of *Science and Civilisation in China*, ed. Joseph Needham. Cambridge: Cambridge University Press.

Turner, Sylvie. 1998. *The Book of Fine Paper*. New York: Thames and Hudson.

Tyan, Emile. 1959. *Le notariat et le régime de la preuve par écrit dans la pratique du droit musulman*. Beirut.

Valls i Subirà, Oriol. 1970. *Paper and Watermarks in Catalonia*. Monumenta Chartae Papyracea Historiam Illustrantia. Amsterdam: Paper Publications Society (Labarre Foundation).

———. 1978. *The History of Paper in Spain (X–XIV Centuries)*. Madrid: Empresa Nacional de Celulosa.

Volov (Golombek), Lisa. 1966. "Plaited Kufic on Samanid Epigraphic Pottery." *Ars Orientalis* 6:107–34.

von Gabain, A. 1983. "Irano-Turkish Relations in the Late Sasanian Period." In *The Cambridge History of Iran*, vol. 3: *The Seleucid, Parthian and Sasanian Periods*, ed. Ehsan Yarshater, 613–24. Cambridge: Cambridge University Press.

Voorhoeve, P. M. 1980. *Handlist of Arabic Manuscripts*. Codices Manuscripti. The Hague.

Wakin, Jeanette A. 1972. *The Function of Documents in Islamic Law*. Albany: State University of New York Press.

Walker, Paul E. 1997. "Fatimid Institutions of Learning." *Journal of the American Research Center in Egypt* 34:179–200.

Ward, Rachel. 1985. "Evidence for a School of Painting at the Artuqid Court." In *The Art of Syria and the Jazīra, 1100–1250*, ed. Julian Raby, 69–84. Oxford Studies in Islamic Art. Oxford: Oxford University Press for the Board of the Faculty of Oriental Studies.

Wasserstein, David. 1990–91. "The Library of al-Hakam II al-Mustanṣir and the Culture of Islamic Spain." *Manuscripts of the Middle East* 5:99–105.

Watson, Oliver. 1985. *Persian Lustre Ware*. London.

Watson, William. 1983. "Iran and China." In *The Cambridge History of Iran*, vol. 3: *The Seleucid, Parthian and Sasanian Periods*, ed. Ehsan Yarshater, 537–58. Cambridge: Cambridge University Press.

Weitzmann, Kurt. 1971. "The Greek Sources of Islamic Scientific Illustrations." In *Studies in Classical and Byzantine Manuscript Illumination*, ed. Herbert L. Kessler, 20–44. Chicago: University of Chicago Press.

Wellesz, Emmy. 1959. "An Early al-Sufi Manuscript in the Bodleian Library in Oxford: A Study in Islamic Constellation Images." *Ars Orientalis* 3:1–27.

Wheatley, Paul. 1971. *The Pivot of the Four Quarters: A Preliminary Enquiry into the Origins and Character of the Ancient Chinese City*. Chicago: Aldine.

Whelan, Estelle. 1990. "Writing the Word of God: Some Early Qur'ān Manuscripts and Their Milieux, Part I." *Ars Orientalis* 20:113–48.

———. In press. "The Phantom of *Hijāzī* Script: A Note on Paleographic Method." *Manuscripts of the Middle East* 8.

White, Lynn, Jr. 1967. *Medieval Technology and Social Change*. Oxford: Oxford University Press.

Wiesner, Julius. 1986. *Mikroskopische Untersuchung der Papiere von El-Faijûm (Microscopic Examination of the Faijûm Papers)*. 3d ed. Ed. Jack C. Thompson. Trans. Gudrun Aurand. Portland, Ore.: Caber Press.

Wiet, Gaston. 1944. "Une peinture du XIIe siècle." *Bulletin de l'Institut d'Egypte* 26:109–18.

———. 1948. *Soieries persanes*. Cairo.

Wilber, Donald N. 1969. *The Architecture of Islamic Iran: The Il Khânid Period*. New York: Greenwood.

———. 1987. "Qavam al-Din ibn Zayn al-Din Shirazi: A Fifteenth-Century Timurid Architect." *Architectural History* 30:31–44.

Wilford, John Noble. 1999. "Finds in Egypt Date Alphabet in Earlier Era." *New York Times*, November 14, p. 1.

Wilkins, M. Lesley. 2001. "From Papyrus to Paper: Technological Change in Medieval Egypt, 868–969." Ph.D. diss. Harvard University.

Wilkinson, Charles K. 1973. *Nishapur: Pottery of the Early Islamic Period*. New York.

Wolfe, Richard J. 1991. *Marbled Paper: Its History, Techniques, and Patterns*. Philadelphia: University of Pennsylvania Press.

Wouters, A. 1990–91. "From Papyrus Roll to Papyrus Codex: Some Technical Aspects of the Ancient Book Fabrication." *Manuscripts of the Middle East* 5:9–19.

Wright, Clifford A. 1999. *A Mediterranean Feast: The Story of the Birth of the Celebrated Cuisine of the Mediterranean, from the Merchants of Venice to the Barbary Corsairs, with More Than Five Hundred Recipes*. New York: William Morrow.

Wright, Elaine Julia. 1997. "The Look of the Book: Manuscript Production in the Southern Iranian City of Shiraz from the Early Fourteenth Century to 1452." Ph.D. diss. Faculty of Oriental Studies, Oxford University.

Young, M. J. L., J. D. Latham, and R. B. Serjeant. 1990. *Religion, Learning and Science in the 'Abbasid Period*. The Cambridge History of Arabic Literature. Cambridge: Cambridge University Press.

·INDEX·

· PHOTO CREDITS ·